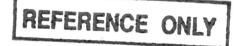

IRISH TOWNS:
A GUIDE TO SOURCES

Edited by
William Nolan and Anngret Simms

The editors and publisher are grateful to
Bord Fáilte for its generous subvention
towards the cost of publication.

Published in Ireland by
Geography Publications,
Kennington Road,
Templeogue, Dublin 6W

© The authors 1998

ISBN 0 906602 26 2

Designed and typeset by Phototype-Set Ltd., Lee Road, Dublin Industrial Estate, Dublin 11.
Printed by Betaprint, Dublin

IRISH TOWNS: *A Guide to Sources*

Compiled by

Ríonach Ní Néill assisted by Yvonne Whelan

Edited by

William Nolan and Anngret Simms

Table of Contents

LIST OF FIGURES

LIST OF CONTRIBUTORS

J. H. Andrews, retired Associate Professor of Geography. Trinity College Dublin.

Philomena Connolly, Archivist, National Archives, Dublin.

Raymond Gillespie, Lecturer in History, National University of Ireland, Maynooth.

Arnold Horner, Lecturer in Geography, University College Dublin.

Desmond McCabe, Research Fellow, Eurocit Project, Leicester.

F. X. McCorry, Vice-Principal, St. Paul's Junior High School, Lurgan.

Ríonach Ní Néill, Research Fellow, Eurocit Project, Dublin and Leicester.

William Nolan, Lecturer in Geography, University College Dublin.

Jacinta Prunty, Lecturer in Geography, University College Dublin.

Raymond Refaussé, Archivist, Representative Church Body Library, Dublin.

Anngret Simms, Associate Professor of Geography, University College Dublin.

Yvonne Whelan, Research Assistant, Department of Geography, University College Dublin.

Patrick Wallace, Director, National Museum of Ireland, Dublin.

Foreword

This guidebook is dedicated to all men and women, young and old, who have committed themselves to research the rich heritage of Irish towns. It is intended to be their companion on an exciting but often difficult journey of discovery.

The idea of compiling such a guidebook on urban sources was born out of the wish to show gratitude to the Heritage Towns Programme launched by Bord Fáilte in 1989 under the direction of Noel Kavanagh. The means of extending this project into its present form came with a grant from the European Commission to the EUROCIT project, an international research project on European urbanisation in the modern and contemporary period, which was carried out in a number of European countries under the direction of Professor Peter Clark, Centre for Urban History, University of Leicester. The Irish co-ordinators were Drs Joe Brady and Anngret Simms.

I would like to express my gratitude to the chief compiler of this book, Dr Ríonach Ní Néill and to those who helped her: Aideen Ireland and Frances McGee (National Archives, Dublin), Dr A.P.W. Malcolmson (Public Record Office of Northern Ireland, Belfast), Dr Noel Kissane (National Library, Dublin), Dr Bill Crawford (Federation of Ulster Local Studies), Edmund Bourke (Office of Public Works), Yvonne Whelan (Department of Geography, University College Dublin) and Mary Davies (Irish Historic Towns Atlas, Royal Irish Academy). We are grateful to those scholars, who have contributed chapters on the study of urban history in Ireland from their specialised perspectives. We are pleased to reproduce Dr Desmond McCabe's bibliography of Irish towns, which he compiled under the auspices of the EUROCIT project and published in 1996 in the *Studia Historica Gandensia*, Gent, Belgium. I would like to thank Bord Fáilte for sponsoring this volume and the Department of Geography in University College Dublin, in particular Professor Anne Buttimer, Head of the Department and Stephen Hannon, Cartographer, and Drs Edel Sheridan and Jacinta Prunty who began the project. I wish also to thank the archives and institutions which have facilitated us by providing illustrations. Dr William Nolan in agreeing to be joint editor and publisher gave us the benefit of his wide experience with sources.

This book is designed as a reference work. It begins with a short overview of the evolution of towns in Ireland and ends with personal reports on research into two specific towns, one of medieval origin and the other a plantation town. The bulk of the book provides an introduction to the major sources for each period of Irish urban history, a short description of the purpose for which particular sources were created, the type of information which they contain as well as the time period which they cover and where located. The extensive bibliography on Irish towns can be used under general headings as well as in relation to specific places.

Anngret Simms,
February 1998

CHAPTER ONE

Introduction

1. The Early History of Irish Towns (Anngret Simms)

In the past Irish towns have contributed very little towards symbolising our identity. The political leaders of the first generation after independence evoked an image of Irish society which was almost exclusively rural. And indeed even today most postcards sent from Ireland show landscapes of wild cliffs along the coast, thatched cottages in green fields, empty roads and herds of cattle and sheep, Victorian pubs or perhaps an architectural landmark – seldom any urban landscape. It is hard to understand why this should be so, because towns are an important component in the history of a country. They are important pointers in the search for identity. We can discover the story of our towns from the physical signs of their origin and development. The imprint of the past is particularly strong in the historic cores of our towns. The layout of the streets, the very street-names and public buildings, hold memories which are important for the inhabitants of that particular town, but they are also part of the story of the country as a whole. Each of these towns represents a tangle of private and public passions and the desire of institutions, for example the churches, to assist people in their private lives but also to dominate them. Add to this the story of economic achievements and failures, as well as the spiritual paths of many individuals over the centuries, and you begin to realise the complexity of urban life. If we approach any of our towns with a questioning mind, then its fabric will turn into a living document in front of our eyes, recalling important chapters in the long history of the people of Ireland. Such stories are of great human interest, not only for those who live there but also for visitors.

Could it be that the reluctance to accept towns as part of the Irish heritage is related to the difficulty of defining our cultural identity? This is not a matter which we can brush aside as of no consequence because it affects our practical politics. Is it possible that the long neglect of Irish towns is related to the colonial history of our country? There is no doubt that, to a large extent, the formation of the urban network in Ireland was accelerated under the influence of repeated colonisation movements. Ireland is not alone in this. There were other countries in Europe that were subject to colonisation during the middle ages, when a transition towards urbanisation was taking place. Medieval colonisation movements helped to spread cultural innovations and foremost among those was the idea of the chartered town, that is, a settlement with a specific town law. For a long time it was not appreciated in these (colonised) countries that many of the present-day towns have roots that are firmly embedded in the pre-colonial past. This is true of Wales and Ireland, for example, where Anglo-Norman settlement was superimposed on Celtic settlement. The same is true of the area east of the River Elbe in former East Germany and Poland, where medieval German settlements were superimposed on West Slavic stronghold settlements. The reason why the formation of towns in countries which experienced colonisation movements was for so long solely associated with the newly planted colonial towns can partially be found in our understanding of the nature of towns. Until the middle of the twentieth century the study of urban origins was predominantly an aspect of legal and constitutional history. This approach produced a narrow definition of a town based on a specific town law and the formation of a municipal authority. The simple evaluation was that a settlement without a charter could not be considered a town. This very legalistic concept disregarded the importance of earlier periods for the formation of towns.

This at last brings us to the important question: which were the most significant periods of town formation in Ireland? As we have already hinted, on the basis of archaeological and documentary evidence, we now know that nucleated settlements regarded by scholars as incipient towns or proto-towns existed in Ireland before the coming of the Anglo-Normans. The oldest towns in Ireland, dating to the later tenth and the eleventh centuries, are associated with either Gaelic ecclesiastical sites or Viking sea-ports which date to the period between the ninth and the twelfth centuries; then follow the towns with a specific town law, which the Anglo-Normans introduced to Ireland. In fact, their colonisation, which began towards the end of the twelfth century, led directly to a century of new town building. The second important phase of new town building came after the re-conquest of Ireland by the English with the plantations of the sixteenth and seventeenth centuries. These towns were primarily intended to be centres of anglicisation and to act as military strongpoints. In the eighteenth century, landlords initiated the building of estate towns; and during the nineteenth century we find a number of new towns developing as resorts or railway centres followed by a number of satellite towns which were established around the major urban centres of Dublin and Belfast in the twentieth century (fig. 1.1).

Towns no doubt were an instrument of colonisation through which the colonisers hoped to pacify and develop their newly conquered territories in military and economic as well as cultural terms. In those circumstances it is not surprising that in the past the relationship between towns and their hinterlands was more often than not antagonistic. This would have been equally true for other parts of Europe where towns were developed by a colonising people, as for example medieval Danzig (present-day Gdansk in Poland), where the town was predominantly German in population while the hinterland was Polish.

One of the important features of Irish history is that the country was never part of the Roman Empire. Like Scandinavia, Scotland and the regions east of the River Elbe in Germany, Ireland was never directly influenced by Roman urban culture. The Celtic scholar D.A. Binchy described this situation very forcefully in a Thomas Davis lecture in 1953:

> The example of Wales and Ireland shows that the urban civilisation that was transmitted to northern and western Europe through Graeco-Roman influence remained foreign to the Celtic-speaking peoples of these islands until it was more or less imposed on them by foreign conquerors.
>
> (D.A. Binchy, 'Secular institutions' in M. Dillon (ed.), *Early Irish society* (Cork, 1954).

But in the light of more recent research it would appear that the early introduction of Christianity transmitted many ideas from the Roman world to Ireland as the early medieval Latin texts written here would suggest, and that the large Early Christian monasteries performed the functions of incipient towns. After all, the concept of a town as a cult or ceremonial site as well as a market place became one of the most powerful ideas which the medieval period inherited from the Roman world.

The Early Christian monasteries in Ireland played an important role as central places with far-reaching territorial connections. They fulfilled a variety of important functions. For example, the Columban monastery of Kells fulfilled educational functions. The religious houses taught the young in special schools. They were also patrons of the arts, as the beautiful high crosses at Kells show, and keepers of treasures, which at times of danger were hidden in round towers, and

Fig 1.1: The origin of Irish towns from *The atlas of Ireland* (Edinburgh, 1979), compiled by A. Simms and K. Simms.

granted sanctuary to those under persecution at a time when no government provided individuals with protection. They encouraged the development of a market place and they functioned as political centres. Kildare, for example, was described by the seventh-century writer Cogitosus as the treasury of kings, while in the twelfth century Kells was the centre of the Gaelic kingdom of Breifne.

Traces of these incipient towns are preserved in the alignment of the modern street pattern which, as for example in Kells, follows the curve of the outer and inner monastic enclosures containing the round tower, the stone crosses and the site of the medieval church and churchyard. The more secular part of the monastery was developed south-eastwards where the market was held just outside the eastern gate. Kells is typical of other monastic sites like Armagh and Kildare which appear to have been designed in conformity with a planned arrangement. The round tower usually stands to the west of the church, where in times of danger it could be reached quickly from the exit of the church. The entrance to the enclosure was generally located to the east and was marked by a special cross, a boundary cross, around which market functions developed. It has been suggested that the concept of the market was brought into Ireland by the Vikings. Already before the Viking invasion an opportunity for the exchange of goods had developed in the form of the tribal *oenach*, or assembly, held on the borders of tribal territories. From the ninth century onwards, probably as the result of internal trade with the Vikings, some of the bigger monasteries took over the function of market places. The Irish word *margadh* is a Scandinavian loan-word meaning market. By the eleventh century the major monasteries not only held markets but they also had paved streets, rows of houses and quarters for craftsmen.

The late monastic towns constituted the cultural and economic power centres of early-medieval Ireland when the Viking invasions began to disrupt the country. From the ninth century onwards the Vikings began to establish coastal trading places and these developed into important ports in the Hiberno-Norse period because of their long-distance trade, extending from Dublin in the west to Novgorod in the east. These towns also greatly benefited from their rich hinterlands. They included Dublin, Waterford, Cork and Limerick, with a few smaller ports like the walled Hiberno-Norse town of Wexford. These settlements became so important that the focus of economic life shifted from inland locations to the coast and in particular to the east coast. No amount of regional planning in our time has so far been able to reverse this pattern.

Both the monastic towns and the Hiberno-Norse towns lacked a specific town law with an urban constitution. These attributes were to come with the institution of the town charter, which granted burgesses the privilege of self-government. The concept of a chartered town was borrowed from formerly romanised Europe. The oldest known surviving town charter north of the Alps was issued in 1066, to Huy in present-day Belgium. The constitutional ideas of the town charter, which established autonomous government for the burgesses, were reflected in the town plan. The town walls dramatically expressed the need for communal protection and also symbolised the fact that there was a legal difference between town and country people. There is no doubt that the Anglo-Norman colonisation linked Ireland culturally and economically to contemporary developments in the rest of Europe.

Dublin is the prime example in Ireland of a Viking stronghold which developed into a fully-fledged Anglo-Norman borough. There is an excellent scale model of the late-medieval town on display in *Dublinia*, at Christ Church, which gives us an idea of what a walled town looked like. The historical events happened like this. After the Anglo-Normans invaded Ireland the English king Henry II promoted the former Hiberno-Norse towns. Dublin was the first one to be granted a charter, modelled on the law of Bristol. In 1171 and 1172 it was granted to the men of Bristol; in 1192 the first full charter of urban liberties was issued for Dublin and this one set the stage for the development of an urban network in Ireland. Although there were approximately 270 places in medieval Ireland for which we have some kind of evidence for the existence of burgesses, only about fifty-six of those are known to have been genuine towns from the functional point of view in contrast to the purely legal one. Most of the towns in Ireland have their origin in this period. The greatest density of these newly-established medieval towns is in the east and the south-east, while the north-west which was largely outside Anglo-Norman influence was left out and had to wait until the Ulster plantation in the seventeenth century for the development of its urban network.

A large number of Anglo-Norman towns were newly built. Some of those were established in the context of a 'feudal' castle as Carrickfergus and Athlone illustrate very well. In both places the castle still dominates the present-day streetscape. Both towns once had enclosing walls and they have a linear street-pattern typical of many of the planned Anglo-Norman towns. Sligo and Dungarvan are good examples of medieval towns without the presence of an imposing castle. Their main medieval streets were wide enough to accommodate the market. Typically there was only one medieval parish church. But just outside the medieval walls stood the Dominican and Franciscan religious houses, symbolising the importance of the monastic orders. The Augustinian canons are the only large order whose houses occur more frequently within the medieval town walls. The existence of friaries on the peripheries of medieval towns is probably related to their attempt to be independent of the jurisdiction of the town, to the likelihood that by the time of their foundation land within the walls had become scarce, and finally to the fact that many of them served as hospitals for the sick.

In the political uncertainty of the post-medieval period towns in Ireland stagnated, but in the sixteenth century this situation changed when the English government decided to reconquer Ireland by means of plantation. The Munster plantation in the late sixteenth century led to far-reaching settlements in the province and to the foundation of new towns by a few private individuals, for example Sir Richard Boyle who founded Bandon. Bandon became a Protestant stronghold with neatly laid out streets and Protestant churches in prominent positions. Enniscorthy is a good example of a plantation town in Leinster and further north the town of Lurgan illustrates the impact of the Ulster plantation.

Characteristic of towns in eighteenth century Ireland is the landlord intervention either by improving existing towns or creating entirely new ones. A recent survey suggests that over 750 provincial towns and villages of all sizes throughout Ireland display some evidence of landlord impact. A good example of a regularly planned estate town is Maynooth, built by the earls of Kildare. The Irish landlords did no more than follow their English and continental counterparts when they introduced the concept of formalism into their settlements. But the fact that generally, although not in the case of Maynooth, they were the descendants of a colonial elite belonging to the established Protestant church rather than to the Catholic faith of the majority brought latent cultural and political tensions.

New towns were built in Ireland in the nineteenth century as railway towns or resort towns, as for example Bray, which happily combined both functions, being on the railway line from Dublin to the south and a gateway to Wicklow. One of the striking features of nineteenth century Irish towns is the re-emergence of Catholicism as a formal institutional force. Contrary to the perceived image, institutional Catholicism was strongest in the richer areas of Ireland in the south-east among the upper classes and in the towns. The building of neo-Gothic Catholic cathedrals in dominant positions and the religious houses and schools of the teaching orders of the Presentation and Mercy nuns and the Christian Brothers, together with diocesan boarding colleges, created the new Catholic institutional sector of the existing towns, as the example of Thurles demonstrates so clearly.

The topographical history of our towns as expressed in their streets and buildings can no more be separated from the history of urban society than one can separate the physical appearance of a human being from his or her personality. We have seen that our towns reflect the culture of the coloniser and the colonised, but they also represent a unity which is the result of their own lived experience, embracing cultural continuity, cultural adaptations and innovations. It is in the concept of continuity within discontinuity, a pattern created by repeated colonisation movements, that the complexities of Irish cultural identity are best explained.

(This is a slightly shortened version of a chapter which was published by Mercier Press in
Irish country towns edited by A. Simms and J.H. Andrews (Cork, 1994), pp 11-20.)

2. Short Guide to State Repositories (Ríonach Ní Néill)

The single most comprehensive pre-1980s guide to source materials are R.J. Hayes (ed.), *Manuscript sources for the history of Irish civilisation*, 11 vols (Boston, 1965), 3 vols supplement ed. D. Ó Luanaigh (Dublin, 1979) and R.J. Hayes (ed.), *Guide to the periodical sources for the history of Irish civilisation*, 9 vols (Boston, 1970), henceforth referred to as Hayes *Manuscript* and *Periodical* sources respectively. Hayes is a union catalogue and indexes the holdings of manuscripts of Irish interest in libraries and archives in Ireland and abroad. Sources are indexed by place, name and subject, and the *Manuscript sources* are also indexed by date. The *Periodical sources* lists articles of Irish interest. Also essential for locating sources is S. Helferty and R. Refaussé (eds), *Directory of Irish archives* (Dublin, 1988, 2nd edn. 1993), which gives the address, telephone number and opening hours for 224 repositories in Ireland with a summary description of their holdings; a new edition is expected soon.

National Library of Ireland, Kildare Street, Dublin

The National Library is a reference-only public institution. The National Library is the principal repository of private records and printed material (books, newspapers, periodicals and official publications). It also contains copies (on microfilm) of much material in overseas institutions. To read in the National Library one should apply for a reader's ticket. To read manuscripts, an additional manuscripts reader's ticket is required. Copies of records may be ordered. There are a number of finding aids to the library's records, including the Hayes *Manuscript and Periodical* guides. The subject index is the main finding aid. The Printed Books Catalogue (pre 1968 after which there is a card catalogue and computer catalogue) lists books and pamphlets. The librarian on duty can help with specific queries. Two useful publications are the *Sources for local studies in the National Library of Ireland* leaflet, and T.P. O'Neill, *Sources of Irish local history* (Dublin, 1958). The National Library also publishes a number of folders of historical documents relating to particular aspects of Irish history, culture or urban historical geography. They have been compiled by the National Library's Education Officer, Dr Noel Kissane, and are listed in the bibliography at the end of this chapter. The trustees publish an annual report which lists accessions through purchase and gift and the Library is entitled to a copy of every new work published in the state.

The National Archives, Bishop Street, Dublin

Formerly known as the Public Record Office and the State Paper Office, this is a reference-only public archive. The National Archives is the national public records repository. It holds material from the medieval period to the late twentieth century. Government records (of departments and state bodies) are transferred here after thirty years. It contains the records among others of the Office of Public Works. The National Archives holds non-governmental papers also – such as census returns, estate papers, business records, trade union records and records of charitable and religious organisations. A reader's ticket is issued on the first visit. Copies of material may be ordered.

Public Record Office of Northern Ireland (PRONI), Balmoral Avenue, Belfast

PRONI was established in 1923, providing a state archive for Northern Ireland and also a repository for records of private provenance. Many of the public records dealing specifically with the six counties were transferred from the Public Record Office of Ireland to PRONI. These included testamentary collections.

PRONI has an extensive collection of estate records from all Ireland, details of which are available on its web-site. Also available on the internet are a publications list, detailing books and articles published by PRONI, including the *Reports of the deputy keeper of the records* (those for 1954-9 and 1960-5 contain indexes of townlands, subjects and personal names); information leaflets on *Local History*, *Family History* and *Emigration* as well as details of its published guides to documents series which include *Guide to sources in county Armagh*, *Guide to church records* and *Guide to cabinet conclusions*, as well as a wealth of other information. *Reports of the deputy keeper* have now been replaced by *Annual reports*.

For personal callers, the interactive touch-screen videos provide a useful explanation of the finding aids and guides to PRONI and its records, while touch-screen computerised geographical and subject indexes allow easy access to literally tens of thousands of reference numbers.

3. Territorial Divisions-based on *Census of Ireland* (Dublin, 1991)

Before one begins detailed research it is imperative to be familiar with the territorial administrative framework within which your town is located because sources are generally organised according to this network. There are many different territorial divisions of the country of which the most important, from the point of view of the urban researcher, are defined here. All the areas are as defined at the date of the 1991 census and any subsequent revisions have not been taken into account. A number of changes in legally defined boundaries were made by government orders in the period since 1986. The following text is based mainly on *Census of Ireland* (Dublin, 1991), i, 'Areas'.

Townlands

The enumeration of the census is carried out, in the first instance, by townlands in rural areas and by streets in urban areas. The townland is the smallest territorial division used for administrative purposes. Population figures in respect of townlands, of which there are about 51,000, have not been published since the census of 1911. Townlands are not used as administrative areas within the boundaries of legally defined urban areas – county boroughs, urban districts and towns, under the Towns Improvement (Ireland) Act, 1854. For most other urban areas, without legal boundaries, it is not possible to compile townland population figures, as building development has completely obliterated the physical features by which townland boundaries were originally defined on Ordnance Survey maps. Since most towns have outgrown their nineteenth century frames and 'captured' contiguous townlands it is important to know the earlier make-up of places. The townland index maps are the key source for locating townlands.

District Electoral Divisions/Wards

The smallest administrative area for which population statistics are published is the district electoral division or, in the county borough, the ward (fig. 1.2). In rural areas each district electoral division consists of an aggregation of entire townlands. There are 3,440 district electoral divisions and wards in the state. Wards by definition are also the electoral divisions of the county boroughs of cities; city constituencies are based on them. Because of urban growth they have been much subdivided in recent years. Today many nameplates remain in cities identifying wards. The Ordnance Survey has published a map of dispensary districts and district electoral divisions in county boroughs, boroughs, municipal boroughs and urban districts.

Urban and Rural Districts

District electoral divisions are aggregated to give urban districts (or boroughs where appropriate) and (former) rural districts which, in turn, build up to counties. The rural districts, which numbered 160, were abolished as administrative areas in 1925 (in the case of rural districts in county Dublin, in 1930) but have been retained for census purposes as convenient units of area, intermediate in size between district electoral divisions and counties. The records of rural district councils are valuable sources for the development of local government and services. A.A. Horner, J.A. Walsh and J.A. Harrington analysed the 1981 Census on a rural district basis in *Population in Ireland, a census atlas* (Dublin, 1984).

CITY OF DUBLIN.

SOUTH DUBLIN UNION.

TRINITY WARD.

No. of reference to Map.	Local Numbers	Names.		Description of Tenement.	Area.			Rateable Annual Valuation.		Total Annual Valuation of Rateable Property.
		Streets, &c., and Occupiers.	Immediate Lessors.		A.	R.	P.	Land. £ s. d.	Buildings. £ s. d.	£ s. d.
		BAMFIELD-LANE. (Ord. S. 15.) PARISH OF ST. MARK.								
1	1	Vacant, . . .	Austin Ward, .	House (dilapidated), .	—			—	0 10 0	0 10 0
2	2	Vacant, . . .	Same, .	Office (dilapidated), .	—			—	1 0 0	1 0 0
3	3	Austin Ward (lodgers),	Same, .	House, . . .	—			—	2 10 0	2 10 0
3½		John Tyrrell, .	Same, .	Sheds and dairy-yard,	—			—	2 0 0	2 0 0
4	4	Joseph Mahon (lodgers),	Joseph Mahon, .	House, . . .	—			—	2 0 0	2 0 0
		Here Gloucester-street, South, intersects.								
5	5	Michael Mullen, .	Catherine Murphy, .	House (dilapidated), .	—			—	4 10 0	4 10 0
6	6	Joseph Berry (lodgers),	Joseph Berry, .	House (dilapidated), .	—			—	5 0 0	5 0 0
7	7	Edward Moore, .	John Maher, .	Forge, . . .	—			—	2 10 0	2 10 0
		BASS-PLACE. (Ord. S. 22.) PARISH OF ST. MARK.								
1	1	Jason Sherwood (lodgers),	Jason Sherwood, .	House and small yard,	—			—	3 10 0	3 10 0
2	2	Jason Sherwood (lodgers)	Same, .	House and small yard,	—			—	3 10 0	3 10 0
3	3	Jason Sherwood (lodgers)	Same, .	House and small yard,	—			—	3 10 0	3 10 0
4	4	Geo. F. Mowles (lodgers),	George F. Mowles, .	House, . . .	—			—	3 10 0	3 10 0
5	5	Geo. F. Mowles (lodgers),	Same, .	House, . . .	—			—	3 10 0	3 10 0
6	6	Geo. F. Mowles (lodgers),	Same, .	House and small yard,	—			—	3 10 0	3 10 0
7	7	Geo. F. Mowles (lodgers),	Same, .	House and small yard,	—			—	3 10 0	3 10 0
8	8	Geo. F. Mowles (lodgers),	Same, .	House and small yard,	—			—	3 10 0	3 10 0
9	9	Joseph A. Duncan (lodgs.)	Joseph A. Duncan, .	House and small yard,	—			—	5 0 0	5 0 0
10	10	Jason Sherwood (lodgers)	Jason Sherwood, .	House and small yard,	—			—	5 0 0	5 0 0
11	11	Ralph W. Champion (lodgers), . . .	Ralph W. Champion, .	House and yard, .	—			—	5 10 0	5 10 0
		Here Boyne-street intersects.								
12	12	Ralph W. Champion (lodgers), .	Same, .	House and small yard,	—			—	9 0 0	9 0 0
13	13	Jason Sherwood (lodgers)	Jason Sherwood, .	House, . . .	—			—	8 0 0	8 0 0
14	14	Mary Lampston, .	Same, .	Offices and dairy-yard,	—			—	6 0 0	6 0 0
1	STABLE-LANE.	John M'Guinness, .	Patrick K. Gibbon, .	Stable, . . .	—			—	2 10 0	2 10 0
2		John Vallely, . .	Same, .	Stable, . . .	—			—	2 0 0	2 0 0
3		Bryan Dunne, . .	Same, .	Stable, . . .	—			—	1 10 0	1 10 0

Fig 1.2: *Primary valuation of tenements, South Dublin Union* (Dublin, 1854).

Counties and County Boroughs

In the census reports the country is divided into 29 counties and 5 county boroughs. Outside Dublin there are 26 administrative counties (Tipperary North Riding and Tipperary South Riding each ranks as a separate county for administrative purposes) and 4 county boroughs, i.e. Cork, Limerick, Waterford and Galway. In Dublin four areas are identified separately, i.e. Dublin County Borough and the three electoral counties of Dublin: Belgard (South Dublin), Fingal, and Dún Laoghaire-Rathdown.

The boundaries of the county boroughs are subject to periodic extensions to keep pace with building developments and it is not possible, therefore, to show comparable retrospective population figures over an extended period. Counties, on the other hand, have only been affected to a very minor extent by boundary changes and it is possible to compare county populations (including the appropriate county boroughs) over a long period of time.

County and Borough Electoral Areas

For the purpose of county council elections each county is divided into electoral areas which are constituted on the basis of orders made under the Local Government Act, 1941. These areas are, in general, formed by aggregating district electoral divisions; in a number of cases, however, district electoral divisions are divided between county electoral areas to facilitate electors. In the case of the county boroughs the corporation elections are based on borough electoral areas.

Civil Parishes

Originally an ecclesiastical division and later used for civil purposes, the civil parish has for many years been obsolete as an administrative unit of area, and populations relating to civil parishes for the country as a whole have not been published since the 1911 census. Because the civil parish network is defined by map it has been used extensively by researchers for comparative purposes.

Towns

For census purposes towns fall into two types, namely those with and those without legally defined boundaries. The first type comprises:
- five county boroughs and the Borough of Dún Laoghaire
- five municipal boroughs
- forty-nine urban districts
- thirty-two towns under the Towns Improvement (Ireland) Act, 1854.

A list of all towns with legally defined boundaries is given on pages 19-20. The second category is comprised of 'census towns', whose boundaries are determined, for census purposes only, by the Central Statistics Office. They numbered 542 in 1991.

(a) Towns with legally defined Boundaries

Many towns have expanded beyond their legally defined boundaries. As a result, large numbers of persons in the communities for which these towns are the nuclei would be excluded if the coverage were confined strictly to legally defined boundaries. This problem tends to become more pronounced from one census to the next as urban areas extend further into the surrounding countryside. Revisions of the legally defined boundaries tend to lag behind these developments as they are dependent on other factors besides the necessity of defining urban areas for Census of Population purposes.

Much of the census analysis is concerned with the overall size of population clusters and not simply with legally defined boundaries. Consequently, where urban areas have extended beyond the legally defined town boundary, the Central Statistics Office draws up new boundaries defining the *suburban* areas of county boroughs/boroughs and the *environs* of other legal towns for census purposes.

Suburbs/environs are defined, in conformity with United Nations recommendations, as the continuation of a distinct population cluster outside its legally defined boundary in which no occupied dwelling is more than 200 metres distant from the nearest occupied dwelling outside the legal boundary within the new limit. In applying the 200 metre criterion, industrial, commercial and recreational buildings and facilities are not regarded as breaking the continuity of a built-up area.

Suburban areas for Dublin County Borough, Cork County Borough and the Borough of Dún Laoghaire were defined for the first time at the 1951 census. For the 1956 census all towns with legally defined boundaries were examined in co-operation with the local authorities concerned and, where necessary, suburban areas or environs were defined for them for census purposes. The suburban boundaries were reviewed for each subsequent census. A comprehensive review was carried out as part of the processing phase of the 1991 census.

(b) Census Towns

As in censuses since 1971 a census town is defined as a cluster of fifty or more occupied dwellings, not having a legally defined boundary, in which within a distance of 800 metres there is a nucleus of either thirty occupied houses on both sides of the road or twenty occupied houses on one side of the road. A complete review was carried out of the boundaries of the existing and potential census towns as part of the processing phase of the 1991 census. In this review the limits to existing census towns were extended where appropriate, using the 200-metre criterion as described for suburban areas above. Fifteen new census towns were created for the 1991 census.

For the censuses of 1926 to 1951 a census town was defined simply as a cluster of twenty or more houses and the precise delimitation of the town was left to the discretion of the individual enumerator concerned. As part of the general review of towns for the 1956 census, the boundaries for the census towns were drawn up in consultation with the various local authorities applying uniform principles in all areas of the country. The definition of a census town was changed at the 1956 census from twenty houses to twenty occupied houses; this definition was also applied at the 1961 and 1966 censuses.

Dublin Area

The description *Greater Dublin Area* was introduced for the 1981 census to denote Dublin County Borough, Dún Laoghaire Borough and their suburbs (i.e. Greater Dublin Suburbs). These suburbs include six population centres which had previously been separately distinguished as towns.

Suburbs of Cork County Borough

Because of continued suburban expansion around Cork County Borough, Leemount, which was separately identified as a census town at the 1986 census, has been subsumed into the suburbs of Cork County Borough.

Aggregate Town and Aggregate Rural Areas

In continuation of the definition used in reports of censuses since 1966, the population in the aggregate town area is defined as those persons living in population clusters of 1,500 or more inhabitants. If a town with a legally defined boundary has a suburban area or environs outside this boundary and if the total population made up of the population inside the legally defined boundary plus that in the suburbs or environs amounts to 1,500 persons or over, this town (including its suburbs or environs) is classified as belonging to the aggregate town area. Similarly, a census town with 1,500 inhabitants or over is classified as belonging to the aggregate town area. The population residing in all areas outside clusters of 1,500 or more inhabitants is classified as belonging to the aggregate rural area. It should be particularly noted that the term 'aggregate rural area' is not connected with that of rural districts as described earlier. Whereas the 'aggregate rural area' is a statistical concept, the rural district is an (former) administrative unit of area. The aggregate town area population was 2,010,700 persons in 1991. Of this 1,279,377 resided within legally defined boundaries of towns while 731,323 resided in the suburbs or environs of these towns or in census towns.

Planning Regions

The census also has returns for the geographical sub-division of planning regions. These regions, which do not have a statutory basis, are used as a convenient statistical classification of counties/county boroughs at an intermediate level between that of counties/county boroughs and the state as a whole. Their composition is as follows:

Region	Composition
East	Counties of Dublin, Kildare, Meath and Wicklow, Dublin County Borough
South West	Counties of Cork and Kerry, Cork County Borough
South East	Counties of Carlow, Kilkenny, Tipperary South Riding, Waterford and Wexford, Waterford County Borough
North East	Counties of Cavan, Louth and Monaghan
Mid West	Counties of Clare, Limerick and Tipperary North Riding, Limerick County Borough
Donegal	County Donegal
Midlands	Counties of Laois, Longford, Offaly, Roscommon and Westmeath
West	Counties of Galway and Mayo, Galway County Borough
North West	Counties of Leitrim and Sligo

Towns with legally defined boundaries, 1991

County Boroughs	County
Cork	Cork
Dublin	Dublin
Galway	Galway
Limerick	Limerick
Waterford	Waterford

Borough	County
Dún Laoghaire	Dublin

Municipal Boroughs	County
Clonmel	Tipperary South Riding
Drogheda	Louth
Kilkenny	Kilkenny
Sligo	Sligo
Wexford	Wexford

Urban Districts	County
Arklow	Wicklow
Athlone	Westmeath
Athy	Kildare
Ballina	Mayo

Urban Districts	County	Urban Districts	County
Ballinasloe	Galway	Kinsale	Cork
Birr	Offaly	Letterkenny	Donegal
Bray	Wicklow	Listowel	Kerry
Buncrana	Donegal	Longford	Longford
Bundoran	Donegal	Macroom	Cork
Carlow	Carlow	Mallow	Cork
Carrickmacross	Monaghan	Middleton	Cork
Carrick-on-Suir	Tipperary, S.R.	Monaghan	Monaghan
Cashel	Tipperary, N.R	Naas	Kildare
Castlebar	Mayo	Navan (An Uaimh)	Meath
Castleblayney	Monaghan	Nenagh	Tipperary, N.R.
Cavan	Cavan	New Ross	Wexford
Ceannanus Mór	Meath	Skibbereen	Cork
Clonakilty	Cork	Templemore	Tipperary, N.R.
Clones	Monaghan	Thurles	Tipperary, N.R.
Cobh	Cork	Tipperary	Tipperary, S.R.
Dundalk	Louth	Tralee	Kerry
Dungarvan	Waterford	Trim	Meath
Ennis	Clare	Tullamore	Offaly
Enniscorthy	Wexford	Westport	Mayo
Fermoy	Cork	Wicklow	Wicklow
Killarney	Kerry	Youghal	Cork
Kilrush	Clare		

Towns under the Towns Improvement (Ireland) Act, 1854

Urban Districts	County	Urban Districts	County
Ardee	Louth	Kilkee	Clare
Balbriggan	Dublin	Leixlip	Kildare
Ballybay	Monaghan	Lismore	Waterford
Bandon	Cork	Loughrea	Galway
Bantry	Cork	Mountmellick	Laois
Belturbet	Cavan	Muinebeg (Bagenalstown)	Carlow
Boyle	Roscommon	Mullingar	Westmeath
Callan	Kilkenny	Newcastle	Limerick
Cootehill	Cavan	Passage West	Cork
Droichead Nua (Newbridge)	Kildare	Portlaoighise (Maryborough)	Laois
		Rathkeale	Limerick
Edenderry	Offaly	Roscommon	Roscommon
Fethard	Tipperary, S.R.	Shannon	Clare
Gorey	Wexford	Tramore	Waterford
Granard	Longford	Tuam	Galway
Greystones	Wicklow	Tullow	Carlow.

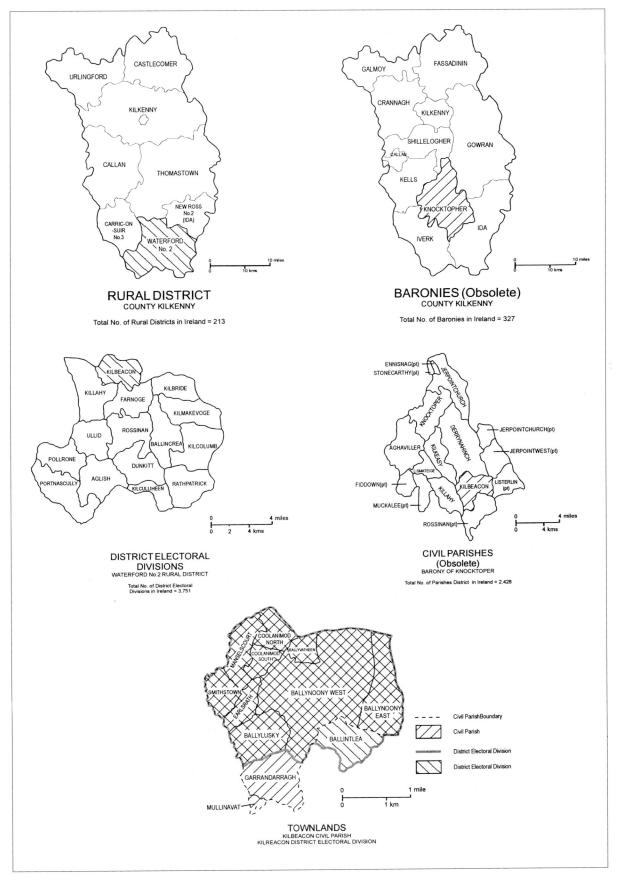

Fig 1.3: Territorial divisions from *The atlas of Ireland* (Edinburgh, 1979).

CENSUS OF IRELAND FOR THE YEAR 1851.

No. of Sheet of the Ordnance Survey Maps.	Townlands and Towns.	Area in Statute Acres. A.	R.	P.	County.	Barony.	Parish.	Poor Law Union in 1857.	Townland Census of 1851, Part I. Vol.	Page
18, 23	Keenogduff	172	3	31a	Monaghan	Cremorne	Aghnamullen	Cootehill	III.	258
27	Keenoge	185	1	2	Meath	Upper Duleek	Duleek	Drogheda	I.	197
28	Keenoge	134	2	15	Meath	Upper Duleek	Moorechurch	Drogheda	I.	198
29	Keenoge	295	1	30	Monaghan	Farney	Inishkeen	Dundalk	III.	271
17	Keenoge	89	1	38	Westmeath	Rathconrath	Killare	Ballymahon	I.	283
49, 56	Keenogue	268	0	33	Tyrone	Omagh East	Kilskeery	Lowtherstown	III.	313
93, 107	Keenrath	424	3	31	Cork, W.R.	East Carbery (W.D.)	Fanlobbus	Dunmanway	II.	132
32	Keentagh	138	1	32	Down	Ards Upper	Witter	Downpatrick	III.	161
15	Keeny	220	2	20	Cavan	Lower Loughtee	Annagh	Cavan	III.	79
6, 11	Keeran	418	2	24	Fermanagh	Lurg	Derryvullan	Lowtherstown	III.	204
6	Keeran	71	3	9	Fermanagh	Lurg	Drumkeeran	Lowtherstown	III.	206
7	Keeran	106	3	3	Meath	Lower Slane	Siddan	Ardee	I.	224
20, 21	Keeranbane	479	0	38b	Donegal	Inishowen East	Moville Upper	Inishowen	III.	119
35	Keeran Beg	81	3	11	Fermanagh	Clankelly	Galloon	Lisnaskea	III.	198
35	Keeran More	160	1	21	Fermanagh	Clankelly	Galloon	Lisnaskea	III.	198
81, 93	Keeraun	134	0	34c	Galway	Galway	Rahoon	Galway	IV.	37
90	Keeraunbeg	708	1	5d	Galway	Moycullen	Killannin	Oughterard	IV.	69
79	Keeraunnagark North	918	2	7e	Galway	Moycullen	Killannin	Galway	IV.	69
90, 91	Keeraunnagark South	702	2	4f	Galway	Moycullen	Killannin	Galway	IV.	69
29, 30	Keereen Lower	170	2	2	Waterford	Decies within Drum	Kilmolash	Dungarvan	II.	351
30	Keereen Upper	261	3	26	Waterford	Decies within Drum	Kilmolash	Dungarvan	II.	351
13, 14, 20	Keerglen	1,768	1	16	Mayo	Tirawley	Kilfian	Killala	IV.	169
23	Keerhan	114	3	38	Louth	Ferrard	Tullyallen	Drogheda	I.	183
48	Keerhaunmore	163	3	25	Galway	Ballynahinch	Ballindoon	Clifden	IV.	10
35	Keerhaun North	100	0	3	Galway	Ballynahinch	Ballindoon	Clifden	IV.	10
48, 49	Keerhaun South	185	3	22g	Galway	Ballynahinch	Ballindoon	Clifden	IV.	10
19, 20	Keerin	430	0	30	Tyrone	Strabane Upper	Bodoney Lower	Gortin	III.	323
56	Keernaun	486	3	13	Galway	Clare	Killeany	Tuam	IV.	20
34	Keevagh	218	0	21	Clare	Bunratty Upper	Quin	Ennis	II.	10
18, 21	Keeverstown	223	1	8	Louth	Ferrard	Mullary	Drogheda	I.	182
26	Keggall	478	3	0h	Armagh	Orior Upper	Killevy	Newry	III.	58
14, 19	Keilagh	171	0	5	Cavan	Tullyhunco	Kildallan	Bawnboy	III.	97
118	Keilnascarta	317	0	4	Cork, W.R.	West Carbery (W.D.)	Kilmocomoge	Bantry	II.	144
18	Keiloge	555	0	19	Waterford	Gaultiere	Kilmacleague	Waterford	II.	364
8, 13	Kellistown East	868	3	9	Carlow	Carlow	Kellistown	Carlow	I.	2
7, 8, 12, 13	Kellistown West	983	0	22	Carlow	Carlow	Kellistown	Carlow	I.	2
38, 44	Kells	463	3	16	Antrim	Lower Antrim	Connor	Ballymena	III.	3
17	Kells	745	0	28i	Clare	Inchiquin	Kilkeedy	Corrofin	II.	25
62, 70	Kells	864	3	1j	Kerry	Iveragh	Killinane	Cahersiveen	II.	197
27	Kells	629	3	16	Kilkenny	Kells	Kells	Callan	I.	108
54	Kells	372	2	36	Limerick	Connello Upper	Dromcolliher	Newcastle	II.	232
27	Kellsborough	62	0	37	Kilkenny	Kells	Kells	Callan	I.	108
23, 27	Kellsgrange	478	2	3	Kilkenny	Kells	Kells	Callan	I.	108
38	KELLS T.	—			Antrim	Lower Antrim	Connor	Ballymena	III.	4
27	KELLS T.	—			Kilkenny	Kells	Kells	Callan	I.	108
17	KELLS T.	—			Meath	Upper Kells	Kells	Kells	I.	206
42, 45	Kellybrook	422	2	32	Roscommon	Athlone	Killinvoy	Roscommon	IV.	182
42, 45	Kellybrook	51	1	7	Roscommon	Athlone	St. Johns	Roscommon	IV.	183
24	Kellybrook	111	3	38	Westmeath	Rathconrath	Conry	Mullingar	I.	282
15,16,20,21	Kellymount	1,094	3	31	Kilkenny	Gowran	Shankill	Kilkenny	I.	99
87, 88	Kellysgrove	1,753	0	33k	Galway	Clonmacnowen	Clontuskert	Ballinasloe	IV.	24
40	Kelly's Island	2	0	17	Galway	Ross	Cong	Oughterard	IV.	73
79	Kellysmeadow	3	1	19	Donegal	Raphoe	Urney	Strabane	III.	144
13, 17	Kellystown	174	0	32	Dublin	Castleknock	Clonsilla	Celbridge	I.	24
6	Kellystown	212	3	31	Kildare	North Salt	Laraghbryan	Celbridge	I.	75
21	Kellystown	124	0	12	Louth	Ferrard	Drumshallon	Drogheda	I.	180
26	Kellystown	119	1	30	Meath	Lower Duleek	Duleek	Drogheda	I.	195
3	Kellystown	340	2	23	Meath	Lower Slane	Drumcondra	Ardee	I.	222
13, 19	Kellystown	531	0	0	Meath	Upper Slane	Monknewtown	Drogheda	I.	224
25	Kellystown	194	0	35	Queen's Co.	Ballyadams	Rathaspick	Athy	I.	232
31	Kellystown	917	3	16	Wexford	Bantry	Adamstown	New Ross	I.	299
42	Kellystown	92	2	38	Wexford	Forth	Drinagh	Wexford	I.	309
42	Kellystown	93	3	14	Wexford	Forth	Rathaspick	Wexford	I.	312
19	Kellystown	128	1	5	Wicklow	Newcastle	Killiskey	Rathdrum	I.	352
19	Kellyville	409	1	10l	Queen's Co.	Ballyadams	Ballyadams	Athy	I.	231
27	Kelsha	279	1	12	Wicklow	Upper Talbotstown	Kiltegan	Baltinglass	I.	365
27	Kelshabeg	245	2	18	Wicklow	Upper Talbotstown	Kiltegan	Baltinglass	I.	365
21	Kelshamore	330	0	9	Wicklow	Upper Talbotstown	Donaghmore	Baltinglass	I.	363
49	Kemmins Mill	81	2	34	Meath	Upper Deece	Kilclone	Dunshaughlin	I.	193
93	Kenmare	268	1	2	Kerry	Glanarought	Kenmare	Kenmare	II.	186
93	Kenmare Old	253	2	35	Kerry	Glanarought	Kenmare	Kenmare	II.	186
93	KENMARE T.	—			Kerry	Glanarought	Kenmare	Kenmare	II.	186
53	Kennaghstown	79	2	19	Meath	Dunboyne	Dunboyne	Dunshaughlin	I.	199

(a) Including 39A. 2R. 22P. water.
(b) Including 16A. 1R. 8P. water.
(c) Including 4A. 3R. 30P. water.
(d) Including 26A. 1R. 25P. water.
(e) Including 11A. 1R. 30P. water.
(f) Including 32A. 2R. 21P. water.
(g) Including 5A. 3R. 35P. water.
(h) Including 39A. 1R. 16P. water.
(i) Including 173A. 2R. 8P. water.
(j) Including 11A. 0R. 11P. water.
(k) Including 9A. 3R. 12P. water.
(l) Including 14A. 3R. 26P. water.

Fig 1.4: Map reference to territorial divisions from the townland to the county from the *General alphabetical index to the townlands and towns, parishes and baronies of Ireland* (Dublin, 1861, reprint Baltimore, 1992).

Fig. 1.3 shows the major territorial subdivisions based on examples from county Kilkenny. Genealogists have always used these divisions in their work. Brian Mitchell and his team from Derry, for example, have produced three important reference books primarily for genealogists but also of use to the student of urban history. The first publication, *A new genealogical atlas of Ireland* (Baltimore, 1986), shows the location of baronies, poor law unions and civil parishes on a county basis, thereby facilitating a range of distributional maps which can highlight the impact of towns within regions. The second book, *The guide to Irish parish registers* (Baltimore, 1988), is an invaluable reference listing the earliest date of surviving parish registers for the major religious denominations. The third book, *A guide to Irish churches and graveyards* (Baltimore, 1990), locates churches and graveyards with reference to their location on the genealogical map.

An essential aid is the *General alphabetical index to the townlands and towns, parishes and baronies of Ireland* (Dublin, 1861, reprint Baltimore, 1992) (fig. 1.4) which is available for consultation in the main repositories. This is an alphabetical index of towns and it gives the district electoral division, townland and civil parish in which a town (or part thereof) is situated – essential information for locating sources. The surnames index to the Tithe Composition Applotment Books and Primary Valuation contains a map of the Catholic parishes in each county and a guide to their corresponding Church of Ireland parish. There are many regional archives and historical organisations, such as the various county historical and archaeological societies and heritage centres. One should check with these and county town libraries for information held locally before consulting the central record archives.

SELECT BIBLIOGRAPHY

1. The History of Irish Towns
J. Bradley, 'Planned Anglo-Norman towns in Ireland' in H.B. Clarke and A. Simms (eds), *The comparative history of urban origins in non-Roman Europe* (Oxford, 1985), pt ii, pp 411-67
J. Bradley, *Walled towns in Ireland* (Dublin, 1995)
R.A. Butlin (ed.), *The development of the Irish town* (London, 1977)
G. Camblin, *The town in Ulster* (Belfast, 1951)
H.B. Clarke (ed.), *Irish cities* (Dublin, 1995)
H.B. Clarke, 'Decolonization and the dynamics of urban decline in Ireland, 1300-1550' in T.R. Slater (ed.), *Towns in decline* (Leicester and London, forthcoming 1998)
L.M. Cullen, *Irish towns and villages* (Dublin, 1979)
M. Daly, 'Irish urban history: a survey' in *Urban History Yearbook* (Cambridge, 1986), pp 61-72
C. Doherty, 'The monastic town in early medieval Ireland' in H.B. Clarke and A. Simms (eds), *The comparative history of urban origins in non-Roman Europe* (Oxford, 1985) pt i, pp 45-76
B.J. Graham and L.J. Proudfoot (eds), *Urban improvement in provincial Ireland, 1700-1840* (Athlone, 1994)
G.H. Martin and S.C. McIntyre, *Bibliography of British and Irish municipal history* (Leicester, 1972)
L. Proudfoot, *Property ownership and urban and village improvement in provincial Ireland, ca. 1700-1845* (London, 1997)
A. Simms, 'The origins of towns in medieval Ireland. The European context' in J.M. Duvosquel and E. Thoen (eds), *Peasants and townsmen in medieval Europe* (Gent, 1995), pp 93-116
A. Simms and J.H. Andrews (eds), *Irish country towns* (Cork, 1994)
A. Simms and J.H. Andrews (eds), *More Irish country towns* (Cork, 1995)
P. Wallace, 'The archaeological identity of the Hiberno-Norse town' in *Journal of the Royal Society of Antiquaries of Ireland*, cxxii (1992), pp 35-64

Maynooth Local History Studies
D. Broderick, *The Dublin-Dunleer turnpike, 1731-1855* (Dublin, 1996)
J. Byrne, *War and peace: the survival of the Talbots of Malahide, 1641-71* (Dublin, 1997)
P. Connell, *Parson, priest and master: national education in county Meath, 1821-41* (Dublin, 1995)

J. Crawford, *St Catherine's parish, Dublin, 1840-1900: portrait of a Church of Ireland community* (Dublin, 1996)

D. Cronin, *A Galway gentleman in the age of improvement: Robert French of Monivea, 1716-79* (Dublin, 1995)

B. Cullen, *Thomas L. Synott: the career of a Dublin Catholic, 1830-70* (Dublin, 1997)

W. Gacquin, *Roscommon before the famine, 1749-1845* (Dublin, 1996)

F. Kelly, *Window on a catholic parish: St. Mary's Granard, 1933-68* (Dublin, 1996)

B.T. King, *Carlow: manor and town, 1674-1721* (Dublin, 1997)

B. Ó Dálaigh, *Ennis in the eighteenth century* (Dublin, 1995)

D. O'Dowd, *Changing times: the story of religion in nineteenth century Celbridge* (Dublin, 1997)

P. Ó Duigneáin, *The priest and the protestant woman: the trial of Rev Thomas Maguire, 1827* (Dublin, 1997)

S. Ó Maitiu, *The humours of Donnybrook: Dublin's famous fair and its suppression* (Dublin, 1995)

C. Smith, *Dalkey: society and economy in a small medieval Irish town* (Dublin, 1996)

Fascicles of the *Irish Historic Towns Atlas.*, Series editors: A. Simms, H.B. Clarke, R. Gillespie; consultant editor: J.H. Andrews; cartographic editor: K.M. Davies
No. 1 J.H. Andrews, *Kildare* (Dublin, 1986)
No. 2 P. Robinson, *Carrickfergus* (Dublin, 1986)
No. 3 P. O'Flanagan, *Bandon* (Dublin, 1988)
No. 4 A. Simms with K. Simms, *Kells* (Dublin, 1990)
No. 5 J.H. Andrews with K.M. Davies, *Mullingar* (Dublin, 1992)
No. 6 H. Murtagh, *Athlone* (Dublin, 1993)
No. 7 A.A. Horner, *Maynooth* (Dublin, 1995)
No. 8 R.H. Buchanan and A. Wilson, *Downpatrick* (Dublin, 1997)
No. 9 K.M. Davies, *Bray* (Dublin, 1988)

Volumes of the *Irish County History Series*
W. Nolan and T. McGrath (eds), *Tippperary* (Dublin, 1985)
W. Nolan and K. Whelan (eds), *Wexford* (Dublin, 1987)
W. Nolan and K. Whelan (eds), *Kilkenny* (Dublin, 1990)
F.H. Aalen and K. Whelan (eds), *Dublin* (Dublin, 1992)
W. Nolan, T. Power and D. Cowman (eds), *Waterford* (Dublin, 1992)
P. O'Flanagan and C. Buttimer (eds), *Cork* (Dublin, 1993)
K. Hannigan and W. Nolan (eds), *Wicklow* (Dublin 1994)
W. Nolan, L. Ronayne and M. Dunlevy (eds), *Donegal* (Dublin, 1995)
G. Moran and R. Gillespie (eds), *Galway* (Dublin, 1996)
L. Proudfoot (ed.), *Down* (Dublin, 1997)

2. Short Guide to Major Repositories in Ireland
S.J. Connolly, *The public record: sources for local studies in the Public Record Office of Ireland* (Dublin, 1982)

R.J. Hayes (ed.), *Manuscript sources for the history of Irish civilisation*, 11 vols (Boston, 1965), 3 vols supplement (1979)

R.J. Hayes (ed.), *Guide to the periodical sources for the history of Irish civilisation*, 9 vols (Boston, 1970)

N. Kissane, *Treasures from the National Library of Ireland* (Dublin, 1994)

S. Helferty and R. Refaussé (eds), *Directory of Irish archives* (Dublin, 1988, reprinted, 1993)

R. Lohan, *Guide to the archives of the Office of Public Works* (Dublin, 1994)

T.P. O'Neill, *Sources of Irish local history* (Dublin, 1958)

H. Wood, *Guide to the records deposited in the Public Record Office of Ireland* (Dublin, 1919)

Relevant educational facsimiles produced by the National Library of Ireland
The past from the press (Dublin, 1984)
Ireland from maps (Dublin, 1980)
Historic Dublin maps (Dublin, 1988)

Guides to the holdings of the Public Record Office of Northern Ireland (PRONI)
Guide to cabinet committees
Guide to cabinet conclusions, 1921-43

Guide to sources for women's history
Guide to educational records
Guide to county sources: Fermanagh
Guide to tithe records
Guide to landed estates (2 vols)
Guide to church records (Published by Ulster Historical Foundation on behalf of PRONI)
Guide to county sources: Armagh
Guide to London Companies
Guide to Probate Records

Publications by the Public Record Office of Northern Ireland (PRONI)
A.P.W. Malcolmson (compiler), *Eighteenth century Irish official papers in Great Britain*, i (Belfast, 1973), ii (Belfast, 1990)
S.T. Carleton, *Heads and hearths: the hearth money rolls and poll tax returns for county Antrim, 1660-69* (Belfast, 1991)
R.G. Gillespie, *Settlement and survival on an Ulster estate: the Brownlow leasebook 1667-1711* (Belfast, 1988)
P.E. Greer, *Road versus rail* (Belfast, 1982)
G. Hamilton, *Northern Ireland town plans* (Belfast, 1981)
PRONI, *Problems of a growing city: Belfast, 1780-1870* (Belfast, 1973)
PRONI, *Ballymoney: sources for local history* (Belfast, n.d.)

3. Territorial Divisions
B. Mitchell, *A new genealogical atlas of Ireland* (Baltimore, 1986)
B. Mitchell, *A guide to Irish parish registers* (Baltimore, 1988)
B. Mitchell, *A guide to Irish churches and graveyards* (Baltimore, 1990)
General alphabetical index to the townlands and towns, parishes and baronies of Ireland (Dublin, 1861, reprint Baltimore, 1992)

CHAPTER TWO

Maps, Prints and Drawings

1. Maps and Map-related Sources (J.H. Andrews)

Maps in libraries are usually segregated from other kinds of source material, and it is easy to forget that many of them were originally supplemented by non-cartographic data in the form of words and numbers. Others were accompanied by letters or memoranda explaining when, why and how they came to be made. Printed maps were often preceded by publishers' announcements, not all of which can be rejected as untruthful. In some cases, notably that of the Ordnance Survey, we have the raw materials – field books, sketches, name-lists, mathematical computations – from which the maps were composed. Where they survive these ancillary documents should be regarded as part of a single basically cartographic source-type. What the librarian has divided, the researcher should seek to re-unite.

However, the map itself must still retain several kinds of uniqueness – that is why the librarians were able to recognise it in the first place – which it derives from the infinite divisibility of terrestrial space and from the great extension of that space compared with the modest resources of time, money and energy available to most of history's mapmakers. And from the map's uniqueness we can deduce a number of interpretative principles, obvious enough to the ordinary modern reader but for some reason easily forgotten when the reader chooses to become a historian. First, a map is more selective than a picture: absence from its surface does not imply non-existence on the ground. At the same time the map is less selective than a passage of prose. If it shows two places, it must also show all the space that lies between them. There is no obligation to draw or write anything in this space, but cartographers are often tempted to do so, partly for aesthetic reasons and partly for fear of admitting ignorance. Thus although map-students are rightly urged to note the motivation behind any given cartographic endeavour, the finished product will almost always show some detail not essential to its purpose and not necessarily as authoritative as other parts of the same map. The moral is inescapable but sometimes hard to accept: if you are interested in one type of map you must be interested in all types.

Another difference between map and picture is that to save time, a cartographer will often classify and conventionalise phenomena without attempting to express their individuality. The line he fixes between realism and convention varies from one period to another and one culture to another, which makes it all too easy for the present-day historian to interpret past conventions over-literally. Finally, the drawing and reproduction of maps is a rare skill, especially as they have so often been regarded as works of art and not just repositories of knowledge. As a result, the cartographic draughtsman often has no first-hand knowledge of the area he is mapping. His work is therefore peculiarly vulnerable to errors of transcription and comprehension, and if possible it should always be supplemented by other kinds of evidence.

Maps of Ireland

Now to practical matters. Do you know the whereabouts of all the maps that show your town or any part of it? At first sight this may seem to be asking too much. Surely we can safely ignore those maps that do no more than represent each town by a single schematic dot-symbol, such as maps of the world, of Europe, and even of the British Isles? After all, their authors are unlikely to have anything new to tell us about a country as small and little-known as Ireland. Yet in practice the separating of cartographic sheep from goats may be more difficult than we might expect. Thus a historian of Bangor, Co. Down, would surely wish to know that this was one of only four Irish settlements to appear on the thirteenth century Hereford map of the world. On the other hand, what looks like a reasoned assessment of contemporary importance in such a map may have been no more than an ignorant copyist's arbitrary choice from a larger total that is no longer available to us. (On the earliest maps the 'towns' thus selected may turn out not to have been towns or even settlements.) But if nothing else, old maps can tell us how the names were spelt.

The foregoing argument applies to medieval *mappaemundi* and, in the case of ports and harbours, to the portolan charts of the fourteenth and fifteenth centuries, a good source of information for both these categories being the first volume of Harley and Woodward. It is also true of early published maps like Gerard Mercator's Europe (1554), which finds room for Mullingar and even Leixlip as well as a number of more important Irish towns. It is in the sixteenth century, however, that emphasis shifts decisively from international to national maps, which if they got into print will be found listed by Bonar Law. From Tudor times onwards a map can be expected to classify its towns, however rudimentarily, and not just to record their bare existence (Andrews, 1997). Some categories, like boroughs or bishop's seats, may be more easily found in documentary sources. For other concomitants of urban activity, such as markets, barracks, post offices and bridges, the map may prove to be the only available source. For instance, there can be few if any non-cartographic authorities that anticipate Henry Pratt's *Tabula Hiberniae* in recording a bridge across the Liffey at Newbridge, Co. Kildare, as early as 1708. Admittedly Newbridge was not yet a town, but by this time, when maps of Ireland were beginning to show roads as a matter of course, the importance of a settlement may be roughly estimated from the number of routes converging on it.

Regional Maps

Regional maps in the present context are those that show less than the whole of Ireland but more than the built-up area of a single town. The earliest examples, dating mainly from the late sixteenth and early seventeenth centuries, may broadly be described as political or governmental and are unlikely to have been considered worth printing. Surviving specimens are divided among a relatively small number of repositories, for which the best guide is Hayes-McCoy. At scales usually ranging between five and ten miles to the inch, they include coasts, rivers, lakes, hills, large tracts of forest, and important settlements, as well as major territorial divisions and their dominant families. The series culminates in the provincial maps of John Speed (1610), which most contemporaries accepted as definitive. These in turn were eventually replaced in public favour by William Petty's county atlas, *Hiberniae delineatio* (1685), which may be seen as representing a transition from political to topographical cartography. Early regional maps mark bridges, though seldom roads. They distinguish towns by conventional or semi-conventional symbols which often embody a girdle of fortifications. Petty shows town walls at Ardee, Callan, Dingle, Enniscorthy, Naas and elsewhere, but not at Dungarvan, Loughrea, Sligo, Tralee or Wicklow: presumably his town symbols were not meant to be altogether arbitrary. In unwalled towns the *Delineatio* often attempts a diagrammatic rendering of the location and alignment of the principal street.

The mid-eighteenth century brought a different kind of regional map to Ireland, designed as much for the ordinary traveller as for military commanders or administrators. Usually at a scale of between half an inch and two inches to a mile, it was dominated by relief features and roads, with

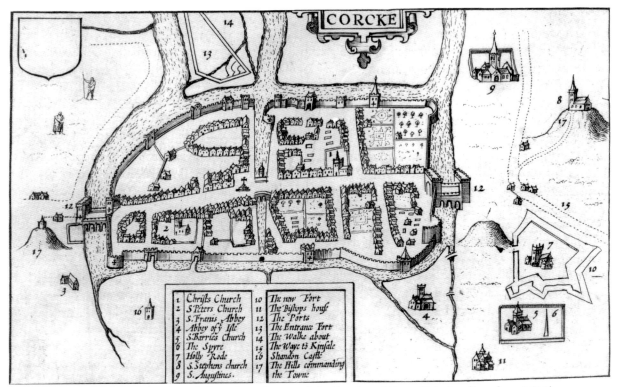

Fig. 2.1: John Speed's map of Cork from his *Theatre of the Empire of Great Britaine* (London, 1611).

as much coverage of settlement as the scale allowed, even a considerable town perhaps occupying less than one square centimetre on the paper. Examples are the published grand jury maps of Irish counties, the road maps of George Taylor and Andrew Skinner (1778), the military sketches of Charles Vallancey (1776-96), and the surveys of the government-appointed Irish bogs commission (1810-14). County maps are listed by Andrews (1985). For other kinds of topographical map the search should begin with Ferguson (1983), which its author is now in the process of up-dating. Coeval with the topographical surveys and in many ways comparable with them is the kind of engineer's map devoted to a single turnpike road, mailcoach road, river, canal or harbour. Many of these are listed by Hayes. Although they may be drawn on larger scales, their representation of urban detail is often similarly incomplete. On a regional topographical map we can expect to see the course of main roads through the built-up area of each town, with ribbon suburbs extending plausibly enough into the adjacent countryside, a number of filled-in street blocks in the town centre, and some attempt at individualising peripheral churches, castles and mansions. This gives at least a general impression of overall size, and the morphological distinctiveness of places like Armagh, Castledermot, Cookstown and Strokestown is often just about recognisable. Not much reward for the researcher's efforts, perhaps, but for a town of less than 5000 people these may be the earliest maps to convey any impression of urban form.

Plans of Individual Towns

We now come to maps in which a single town is the principal *raison d'être*. Despite their importance, these have never been comprehensively listed: the best starting points are Ferguson (1983) and Hayes. In Ireland, as in most cultures, towns have long been an attractive subject for cartographic portraiture. Concentrating a variety of notable features into a small space, they yield an unusually large extent of ink-covered paper per unit of surveyor's travel-time. This makes them more likely than most places to be mapped simply for the fun of it – in defiance of historiographical dogma, it must be said, and perhaps without offering interpretative clues to the modern researcher. Ideologically the town plan is often an expression of civic or colonial pride, celebrating the subjugation of nature or, more specifically, the conquest of a pre-existing rural population. Such purposes can be achieved without perfect accuracy, and many early town plans are a good deal more schematic than they look: it has even been known for full-page maps of supposedly different towns to be printed from the same block.

Another important motive for urban mapping has been military defence. Castles and curtain walls could apparently be built and maintained without the aid of maps, but the advent of artillery gave fortifications a more complicated outline, harder for builders, soldiers or paymasters to keep in their heads, so that in many early town plans the emphasis is on bastions, gates, ramparts, ditches and batteries, shown in sufficient detail to explain why they were costing so much. Information outside and inside the defence-lines on the same map may remain misleadingly diagrammatic, and extra-mural suburbs may sometimes have been omitted altogether.

Early Irish town plans are unevenly distributed in both space and time. Strategic importance depended on position as well as size, and the places most likely to be mapped were either on the coast, provided that their harbours were accessible to warships, or in areas where rebellion had been threatened or recently suppressed. Towns in peaceable inland situations naturally attracted less notice – Clonmel and Kilkenny lagged well behind Carrickfergus and Kinsale as subjects for the cartographer – but in Ireland such areas were comparatively small.

Extant town maps from the period between the 1560s and the 1620s are surprisingly numerous. Later, when warfare became more organised, the military surveyors began to concentrate on the sites of sieges, notably at Limerick, Athlone and Londonderry, which often generated news-maps and history-maps for public consumption as well as confidential reports. (The manoeuvre map was a peacetime descendant of this genre.) But the most influential Irish military surveys were made in a year of peace, 1685, when most of the country's important towns were mapped by Captain Thomas Phillips. Many subsequent maps, both manuscript and printed, were derived from Phillips's work, sometimes with emendations and additions apparently supplied by surveyors of a later generation.

In the eighteenth century, town plans like regional maps began to change considerably in both style and substance, partly in step with European cartography as a whole and partly as a reflection of more peaceful conditions in Ireland. Most of these later plans were probably intended for publication, though they did not always achieve it: only a large and wealthy or well-frequented town could justify the cost of engraving and presswork. But some maps were carried into print on the back of a larger project: perhaps as an inset to a regional map, like John Speed's plans of Cork (fig. 2.1), Dublin, Galway and Limerick (1610) and John Rocque's of Armagh and Newry (1760); perhaps as a book illustration like James Ferrar's plan of Limerick (1787); perhaps as an element in a towns atlas. Publication of free-standing plans begins precociously with the so-called pictorial map of Galway in c.1660. Later examples were John Carty's Cork (1726), Charles Brooking's Dublin (1728) and Joseph Ravell's Drogheda (1749).

Apart from the defensive features already mentioned, the earliest Irish town plans show water-courses, streets and built-up street frontages, bridges, market crosses, quays, abbeys (even if ruined) and Church of Ireland churches (though not parish boundaries), together with both water mills and wind mills. Most cartographers found names for streets and other urban features, useful not only in themselves but as a way of stressing the author's preference for realism over convention. In Georgian Ireland the range of subjects widened to match the growing diversification of urban life. A typical eighteenth century plan might show a market house, town hall, custom house, prison, barracks, infirmary, school and fair green, as well as one or more Catholic chapels and non-conformist meeting houses.

Stylistically the main development of the post-Phillips era was a change from profile or bird's-eye view to planiformity in the mapping of houses, churches, castles, walls and bridges. A profile can give interesting architectural information, at any rate for one side of a building, but it may also force a cartographer to be misleadingly precise, both as to the number of houses in a street and their appearance. In practice, and for fairly obvious reasons, the quantity of housing seems to have been under-stated, the quality over-stated. Can we believe a map of Galway that furnishes the whole length of St Augustine Street with three-storey courtyard houses in the middle of the seventeenth century? But even the most schematised representation may contain some small nugget of realism. In the earliest surviving plan of Dublin Castle (1609), for instance, nearby dwelling-houses appear collectively as one zig-zag line with not a single wall, window or door. But this line tells us that it was then considered normal for gable ends to face the street.

By contrast, planiform buildings have little to say about architecture. But they were easier to fit into an otherwise accurate large-scale map (scales were getting larger in the eighteenth century) and they also saved trouble for the draughtsman as well as facilitating the process of generalisation. In manuscript, built-up spaces could be distinctively coloured; in print they were usually indicated by diagonal ruling, either in strips of more or less uniform width along the streets, or else as infills for an entire street-block, thus differentiating two levels of building density. Before the mid eighteenth century, the strips are seldom divided by transverse lines to simulate individual dwellings; nor are they generally given realistic-looking rearward projections. Where such features do appear, we may infer a genuine effort to distinguish individual structures. Such efforts were certainly made (fig. 2.2) by Ireland's revolutionary Anglo-Irish cartographer John Rocque (1754-60). In the best of his town plans party walls and return projections go hand in hand with the accurate surveying of street widths and the seemingly veridical representation of outbuildings.

Planiform buildings can also be differentiated into classes by varying their colour or tone, but in Irish maps this practice seems to have been disappointingly rare. The most we can expect from the average town plan is for public buildings to be shown in black. Rocque pioneered a more interesting distinction in both manuscript and print, with carmine set against grey or stipple against ruling, the first apparently for residential, the second for non-residential use. A little-known variant of this principle in the 1830s was the use of black for low value housing in the government's maps of parliamentary and municipal boundaries.

The ground immediately behind a row of houses was often a town cartographer's *terra incognita*, not easily accessible to strangers and probably of no particular interest to the general public. In an early plan such spaces often look somewhat improbable, being either left blank or occupied by squarish garden plots where one would expect strips. Not that a credible appearance need be any guarantee of accuracy. In one block of central Dublin Rocque (1756) showed a plausible network of walls and buildings parallel with the adjoining streets, ignoring the diagonal line of medieval city wall recorded shortly afterwards by a local property surveyor.

Estate Maps

This brings us to the cartography of landed estates. Here the main object was to delimit the interests of one or more proprietors or tenants and usually also to calculate the acreage or footage involved. In Ireland the precursor of the estate map is the sixteenth- or seventeenth century plantation survey, of which the proprietor was a victim rather than a beneficiary. On the whole, the Irish plantations involved comparatively large tracts of land, for which the most convenient cartographic scale (typically 40 perches to an inch) was too small to do justice to a single urban property. Nevertheless, as with every other kind of map, it is risky for the urban historian to ignore the plantation surveys altogether. A very few of them are genuinely urban, naming the occupants of individual houses. Others are more rarely and more capriciously informative. The most famous plantation admeasurement was the Down Survey, organised by Dr William Petty in 1655-9 (fig. 2.3). Petty hoped incidentally to provide the basis for a national topographical map; in practice few of his surveyors gave much attention to the visible landscape, though there are a few striking exceptions such as Adare in county Limerick.

As the landlords of the post-plantation era began to consolidate their position, the private mapping of estates, tenements, messuages and individual buildings became increasingly common.

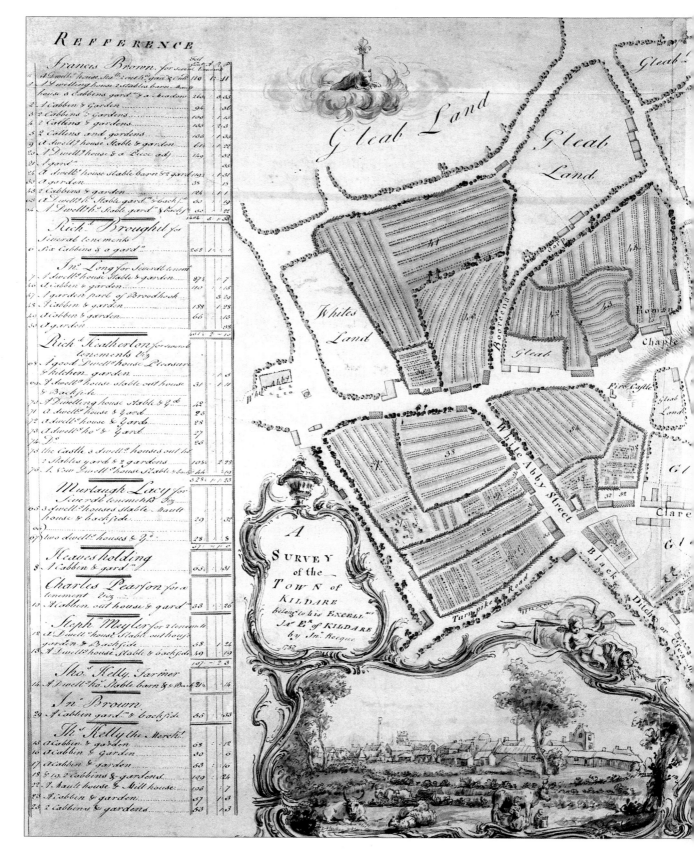

Fig. 2.2: John Rocque's estate map of Kildare town, 1757 (National Library of Ireland).

32

REFERENCE

26	A cabbin & garden	73	35		Elizabeth Kenigen	
27	a good dwelling house Stable Barn garden	63	31	58	A Cabbin	13
28	The Kildare Arms a good dwell house out house Stable garden & yard				Wm Kenigen	
			15	59	A Cabbin & gardn	
31	A cabbin gardn & forge	22	17		Edwd Meddlicot 2 tent	
32	2 Cabbins Stable garde				Calld ye Boys Hold Ec	
33	A forge Cabbin & gardn	16	21	61	A Dwell house Stable out house gard & Backside	
35	A Cabbin & garden	82	137			
40	2 Cabbins & garden	100	216	62	A Cabbin & gardn	29
					Jno McLoughlen	
	Christopher Garden for several tenements Viz			51	A Cabbin & gardnl	
34	2 Cabbins Stables & Gr	331	32			
38	2 Cabbins & gardns	331	13		Jno Hand 2 tenements	
39	2 Cabbins & gardens	70	21	52	A Cabbin & gardn	
41	A Little Croft	9	40	53	A Cabbin & gardn	
42	A Cabbin & gardn	65	17			
44	A Cabbin Gard & ye Roman Chaple	98	323	54	James Belwood	
45	A Cabbin & garden	163	11		A Cabbin in Ruins & garn	
					Wm Farrell for a Tenmt	
	Richd Dun for several tenements			55	A Cabbin & gardn & Bricks	
36	2 Cabbins & gardens	63	11		Richd Beaghan	
37	2 Cabbins & gardn	68	12	56	a Cabbin & gardn	37
37	A Cabbn & gardn	168	21			
					Darby Kinchella	
	Usher Belwood			57	A Cabbin & gardn	
60	A Cabbin & garden	80	22			

NB. Lord Kildare's Land 730

Total 21:1:

Gleab Land

Gleab

Newgent Street

Gleab

Gleab

The Church

Corporation

The Markett house

The Well

Street

Corporation

Gleab

Gleab

Dublin Street

Boreena Cloh Bo Lane

Tully

The Pound

A Scale of 500 Feet

Four Perch's to an Inch

Fig. 2.3: Extract from Down Survey map of Adare, county Limerick by Francis Cooper, 1657 (National Library of Ireland).

A striking feature of many estate maps is the irregularity of their shape: no landowner wishes to pay for measuring his neighbours' property. But an estate surveyor might at least show an occasional street or landmark in the gaps of a fragmented property, while his client's holdings were not necessarily mapped in as much topographical detail as the scale would allow: at worst a complete tenement map may consist of four lines bounding a small and apparently empty rectangle. However, the distinctiveness of estate surveys makes them complementary to other kinds of town plan in two important respects: the smaller the town, the more likely it was to be fully mapped; and when it did get mapped, the features most carefully recorded were those of least interest to the general public. To the historian, of course, these features are the very opposite of uninteresting: not only did property boundaries help to channel the course of future urban development, they are also thought to reflect the pattern of earlier occupation, perhaps as far back as the twelfth and thirteenth centuries. The most problematic aspect of estate maps is the difficulty of finding them. The most accessible, in theory, should be surveys of land which belonged to the crown or to municipal corporations, or which came within the ambit of statutory bodies like the wide streets commissioners of Dublin and Cork. Many private estate maps are now in the National Library and other public repositories, but some remain in the possession of former landowning families or firms of solicitors. One check on their existence or former existence is the memorials in the Registry of Deeds, Dublin, where maps are often cited in delimitations of property boundaries. For example we know from this source that an estate plan of Ballymote in Co. Sligo was available in 1759.

The Nineteenth and Twentieth Centuries

The distinction between topographical maps and property maps was eventually narrowed, and at times obliterated, by the activities of the government's Ordnance Survey department, though several decades went by before the Survey took full effect. The first published Ordnance maps of Ireland (1833-46) showed the layout of every town (slightly widening the streets to accommodate their names) and broke new ground by delimiting urban as well as rural townlands and parishes, though at six inches to a mile they were too small to do the same for individual properties (fig. 2.4). However, the primary purpose of the Survey was to facilitate a nation-wide government valuation of land and buildings, and it soon became clear that larger-scale town plans would be needed for this purpose. During the 1830s and 1840s these were accordingly drawn in manuscript, most of them at five feet to a mile (fig. 2.5). Matters were complicated by the existence of a separate non-Ordnance valuing department which for some reason decided to produce its own plans (fig. 2.6) (Ferguson, 1977). Both sets have survived (each with its own distinctive weaknesses), without ever being brought into harmony until the Royal Irish Academy began the publication of its *Irish historic towns atlas* in 1986. This period of inter-departmental misunderstanding was ended when the Ordnance Survey began to publish completely new and fully accurate plans at either 1:1056 or 1:500, showing the true ground plan of every building (sometimes even inserting the interior walls), together with all fences, trees and watercourses as well as up-to-date administrative boundaries. Names and descriptive captions were given for churches, public buildings, major industrial premises and large dwelling houses; also for sites of archaeological interest, though inevitably some of the Survey's historical judgements have been overruled by more recent scholars. The new generation of printed plans was duly adopted by the Valuation Office, with the result that from the mid nineteenth century onwards the size and shape of every urban tenement in Ireland can be read from a plan that is part printed, part manuscript. Though policy has changed in detail from time to time, the Ordnance Surveys of Ireland and Northern Ireland have never abandoned the principle of publishing towns on larger scales than rural areas. Revisions and replacements may be followed in the Surveys' published catalogues; the nineteenth century story is reviewed in Andrews (1993).

Town plans have also remained a feature of private publishing throughout the Ordnance Survey era, and not all of them are entirely based on Ordnance Survey information. Some have sought a popular market with marginal views and other eye-catching embellishments, others are thematic maps intended for specialists. The latter may embody considerable inputs of labour: this is certainly true of the fire insurance maps produced by Charles E. Goad between the 1880s and the 1960s, which give details of use, ownership and physical structure for individual buildings in Belfast, Cork, Dublin, Limerick and Londonderry.

Maps: General Conclusion

All in all, surviving early maps of Irish towns form an impressive historical record that stands comparison with those of most other European countries. Perhaps the two biggest gaps in the case of small and medium-sized towns are (1) economic activities (other than those self-evidently manifested in a ground-plan) and in particular the difference between commercial and residential functions; (2) in the majority of post-seventeenth century towns, the third dimension as represented by the number of storeys in a building, the materials of its construction, and the design of its facade. For these subjects our only evidence comes in surveys of recent origin not yet fully accepted by librarians as historical sources, including projects by students of geography or architecture in universities or learned societies. Such studies may be expected to continue: those who undertake them may feel pride in supplying historical evidence for generations of scholars yet unborn.

Fig. 2.4: Six inch Ordnance Survey maps showing Gilford, County Down, in 1831 (top) and in 1861 (bottom) from M. Cohen, 'Rural paths of capitalist development' in L. Proudfoot (ed.), *Down history and society* (Dublin, 1997).

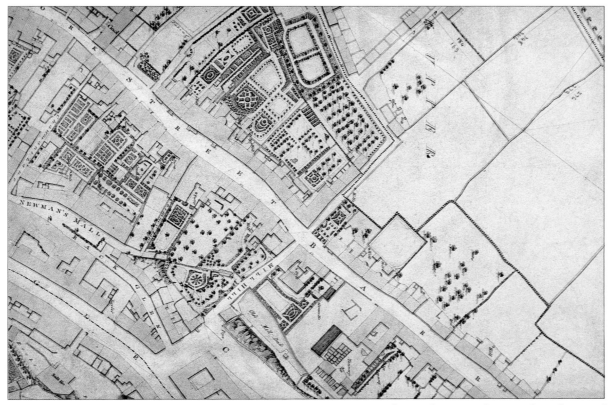

Fig. 2.5: Five feet to one mile manuscript Ordnance Survey map of Kinsale, 1842 (National Archives of Ireland).

2. Ancillary Documents

Several kinds of document can be described as subsidiary to map-making. A cartographer's private diaries, letters and expense accounts may throw light on his methods of work and therefore on the reliability and comprehensiveness of his maps. The same may be true, reading between the lines, of the advertisements, prospectuses and catalogues that he produces for public consumption. At the other extreme there is contemporary criticism of published maps, whether by reviewers, rival map-makers or ordinary users. More revealing, if we had access to them, would be the raw materials of the maps themselves: books of measurements, sketches, diagrams, lists of names, annotated copies of previous maps. What these source-types have in common is their rarity: if they are not reported in the secondary literature of cartographic history they are probably best forgotten.

A major exception to the foregoing statement is the Ordnance Survey of Ireland, many of whose early records survive in the custody of the National Archives. Early Ordnance Survey maps were produced by triangulation. The largest triangles were part of a network that extended over the whole country; their angles were observed with a theodolite and the lengths of their sides deduced from a base-line laid out on the shores of Lough Foyle. Large triangles were subdivided into smaller triangles whose sides were measured with a surveyor's chain. The details of the landscape – house corners, fence-junctions, banks of streams etc. – were then fixed by taking perpendicular offset measurements from the sides of the triangles. The field books recording these measurements can be expected to give the dimensions of each building in numerical terms, but naturally the surveyors generally ignored any information that they did not intend to be plotted, drawn and published. Only in cases of exceptional importance would it be worth checking whether the field book includes any detail absent from the map. This comment also applies to the registers and remark books in which the Survey gave detailed verbal expression to the townland boundaries defined by the government's official boundary department.

Fig. 2.6: Manuscript town plan, Kells, County Meath, ca. 1837 (General Valuation Office).

Not everything on an Ordnance map had previously been entered in a field book. Facts other than measurements – the function of a building, for instance, or the use and appearance of an individual plot of land – were recorded on drafts of the map known as examination traces. Some sites presented problems of description or classification: the resulting correspondence between field officers and the Survey headquarters in Dublin is often of considerable interest, and many of these letters were later arranged by counties in a set of volumes known as 'memorandums' (sic).

The most contentious features of the early Ordnance map were its placenames. For these a separate set of field books listed variant spellings and their authorities, together with 'descriptive remarks' about each named feature, sometimes including dates and statistics. The first-edition six-inch name books are available on microfilm in the National Library of Ireland. There are also name books for the town surveys of the mid and late nineteenthcentury. The name books were made out by the field surveyors; in the original survey of the 1830s and 1840s additional staff-members familiar with the Irish language were employed in an attempt to authenticate the names. The best-known records of this research are the letters written from various field stations by John O'Donovan, but most of these relate to rural areas.

Finally we must consider documents that were addressed to a surveyor's clientele and intended to accompany and explain his map. A military engineer might report on the state of a fortification and the cost of repairing or improving it. Plantation maps were accompanied by 'terriers' naming the owner of each parcel together with its acreage of profitable and unprofitable land. Continuing the tradition of the terrier, estate surveyors often listed tenants and rents together with the use and condition of the land and its buildings. Several examples of urban terriers have been published in the *Irish historic towns atlas*: a typical extract is printed below. In this respect the six-inch Ordnance Survey may be seen as a national estate map, for it was complemented by Richard Griffith's official valuation of land and buildings in every tenement of Ireland, urban and rural, which gives the names of individual lessors and lessees as well as noting the functions of many buildings. Much of the Griffith valuation remains in manuscript, but one edition covering the whole country was published between 1849 and 1865.

Extract from sales particulars of the town and manor of Mullingar, 1858, based on a survey by Brassington and Gale, Dublin

No.	Tenants' names	Premises	Yearly rent £ s d	Lease
66	Thomas Tuite	3 cabins, tan yard, office & garden	36 15 0	2.4.1828
67	Thomas Tuite	5 dwelling houses & offices	6 12 4	27.7.1833
68	The Right Rev. John Cantwell, Richard Connolly Esq, Revd John Nicholls & Thomas Tuite Jnr Esq	Slated dwelling house, offices, yard & garden; chapel, field containing 4A 2R 24P Irish plantation measure	22 7 9	1.3.1858
69	Mary Gannon	9 cabins & gardens	9 0 0	Yearly
70	Margaret Hafford	cabin & garden	1 18 9	Yearly
71	Catherine Kearney	cabin & garden	1 18 9	Yearly
72	Richard Gorman	dwelling house, yard, office etc.	3 15 9	Yearly
73	Catherine Murtagh	5 cabins & gardens	5 5 0	Yearly
74	William Murtagh	cabin & garden	1 18 9	Yearly
75	Bridget Moran	cabin, garden & workshop	3 16 2	Yearly

From J.H. Andrews with K.M. Davies, *Mullingar, Irish historic towns atlas*, no. 5 (Dublin, 1992), appendix c, p. 2.

Outside the special categories of survey reviewed above, many cartographers have sought to accompany their published maps with written descriptions of physical and human geography.

Such combinations of graphic and non-graphic media are difficult to achieve: usually one of the two components has been markedly inferior to the other. Thus Charles Smith's mid-eighteenth century books on county history were better than his county maps, and Daniel Beaufort's map of Ireland (1792) was better than the *Memoir* that accompanied it. Once again the Ordnance Survey provides the best-documented example of a general theme. In 1832 its directors devised an elaborate scheme for compiling descriptive memoirs of every parish in Ireland, but eight years later this ambitious project was discontinued on the orders of the government. By that time one parish (Templemore, including the city of Londonderry) had been printed and there were manuscript memoirs covering most other parts of Ulster, the best of which have been recently published by the Institute of Irish Studies, Belfast, in conjunction with the Royal Irish Academy. Unlike the six-inch maps, the memoirs are often better for towns than for rural areas. Among the subjects covered are local government, proprietorship, public buildings, bridges, roads and waterways, churches, schools, factories (with special reference to energy sources and machinery), wholesale and retail trade, libraries, book clubs and other recreational activities, dispensaries, charitable institutions, postal services, communications, various aspects of demography (for instance longevity, common surnames, pauperism, 'habits of the people') and antiquities. A few extracts from Enniskillen, county Fermanagh, in 1834 will illustrate the scope of this work:

> There are 2 Methodist meeting houses, one of which is situated nearly opposite the Presbyterian meeting house, the other near the west end of the town in a place called Preaching or Meeting House Lane. The latter is a small plain building rebuilt in 1827 (on the site of an old one erected in the year 1792), has no gallery nor enclosed pews, is capable of accommodating about 250 persons, cost 400 pounds. The former was built in the year 1818 on the occasion of the division which took place in the congregation relative to discipline. It is a small plain building, with a gallery having enclosed pews, but moveable unenclosed seats on the ground floor; is capable of accommodating about 400 persons, cost nearly 500 pounds.
>
> There is a discount office lately established (1833) in connection with the Belfast Bank. A branch of the Provincial Bank is held in a 3-storey house, a respectable private residence nearly opposite the church. There has been a new room lately established on a small scale, [which] takes in upwards of 50 pounds worth of newspapers and magazines annually. Terms 1 guinea per year to each subscriber.
>
> The streets are for the most part narrow and irregular, bad pavements and worse flagways, and as they are only swept once a week (Saturday) they are often almost intolerable to pedestrians. The principal street, both winding and hilly, extends from bridge to bridge, having a number of minor streets and lanes branching off on both sides. At the market house the main street opens into what is called the Diamond, though not so in figure but oblong, in area about 4 perches by 6. It is generally acknowledged that the town has made a rapid improvement during these last 10 or 12 years (and is evidently continuing to improve), during which period most of the good or tolerable buildings have been raised. Several improvements, both building and rebuilding, are at present in execution. In fact there is scarce a spot on the whole island that offers anything like an eligible situation that has not already been built upon. Several comfortable dwellings at each end of the town have lately been erected and others [are] at present in progress, yet throughout the whole there is no display of architectural taste or elegance of structure.
>
> The inhabitants of this town and neighbourhood have long borne the name of a peaceable, high-spirited and hospitable people, yet amongst themselves there is great dissension and jealousy with regard to their religious and political views. Their general amusements are horse-racing, boat-racing, hunting, fishing, shooting, sailing and cock-fighting. The latter has of late years become disreputable and is consequently followed by none but the lower class.
>
> (Angelique Day and Patrick McWilliams (eds), *Ordnance Survey memoirs of Ireland, iv, parishes of Fermanagh, 1, 1834-5* (Belfast and Dublin, 1990), pp 54, 55-6, 63)

3. Paintings, Prints, Drawings and Photographs (Ríonach Ní Néill)

Illustrations help us to imagine the experience of urban life at different stages in history. From the fifteenth century onwards (although most records date from after the seventeenth century) Irish towns are pictorially recorded, in drawings, etchings, paintings and prints. These are very useful sources for social and cultural history as they depict phenomena that may have been too ephemeral to record in other documentation, such as the appearance of people of different classes, what they wore to church or to market, street-life, and forms of entertainment. One should be aware that illustrations are subjective, recording a certain point of view, and certain elements – unsightly buildings, beggars, refuse – may be omitted or highlighted depending on the desired impact. Care should be taken in evaluating the detail of all prints and drawings. Artistic licence is very much a reality as is illustrated in Conleth Manning's study 'Delusions of grandeur: the pictorial forgeries of Sheffield Grace' in J. Kirwan (ed.), *Kilkenny. Studies in honour of Margaret M. Phelan* (Kilkenny, 1997), pp 112-29. Scale is often inaccurate: the relative size of a subject may be due more to its importance than to its actual size, as for example the emphasis on castles and churches in early drawings. Fig. 2.7 is an early eighteenth century illustration of 'The city of Kilkenny' from the margin of Henry Pratt's 1708 map of Ireland. It has a key to the principal buildings of the city, allowing us to identify them and their relative location. The approximate architectural styles of buildings are indicated, so that one can compare them to their present aspect. Note the small cabins on the outskirts of the town and the increase in height and size of buildings in the centre. The beginning of urban expansion to the east of the river can be seen on the left-hand side.

The comprehensive *Catalogue of Irish topographical prints and original drawings* (Dublin, 1975), in the National Library of Ireland is a practical starting point for the assembly of illustrations, especially as it is indexed by place. The National Gallery collection also contains topographical illustrations of Irish towns which are indexed by place and artist in the published catalogues of prints and drawings, water-colours and paintings. Of note are the Brocas, Petrie, Du Noyer and Malton (fig. 2.8) collections which contain illustrations of important urban buildings and streetscapes. Other source materials, such as books and pamphlets, also contain illustrations. Many tourists' accounts and guides of the eighteenth and particularly the nineteenth century contain contemporary illustrations of the places described or visited, although frequently these are restricted to the best known or most popular views of picturesque towns and natural landscapes. The dramatic setting of Ballina, for example, made it an ideal subject for the romantic prints of Bartlett's *Guide to the antiquities of Ireland* (fig. 2.9). Petrie's engravings give a more detailed impression of early nineteenth century towns (fig. 2.10).

Bird's-eye views and three-dimensional depictions were used sometimes in place of town plans to show the layout and appearance of a town as the example in fig. 2.11 illustrates. The 1846 *View of Dublin* is a snapshot of the capital city. The west of the city is on the left of the picture. Just south of the river are the rectilinear blocks of Kilmainham Hospital and Kilmainham Gaol. Collins Barracks (then called the Royal Barracks) is on the north bank. The easternmost bridge is the original Sackville Bridge designed by James Gandon. It was later replaced by the present O'Connell Bridge. The Custom House and its basins are at the hub of shipping activity. Little of the reclaimed land to the north and east of it has been developed. The railways were a recent development and we can see that the Loopline Bridge linking Pearse Street Station on the southside to Connolly Station on the north had yet to be built. Other landmarks include Trinity College, the large complex of buildings and open space to the south of Sackville Bridge; Merrion Square and Leinster House, immediately south-east of the college; and to the west, on Dame Street, which runs parallel to the river, Dublin Castle with its towers and chapel royal is clearly seen.

From the 1860s onwards photographs record Irish towns. These are more objective and accurate. The Lawrence Collection for the period 1870-1914, the Eason Collection for the period

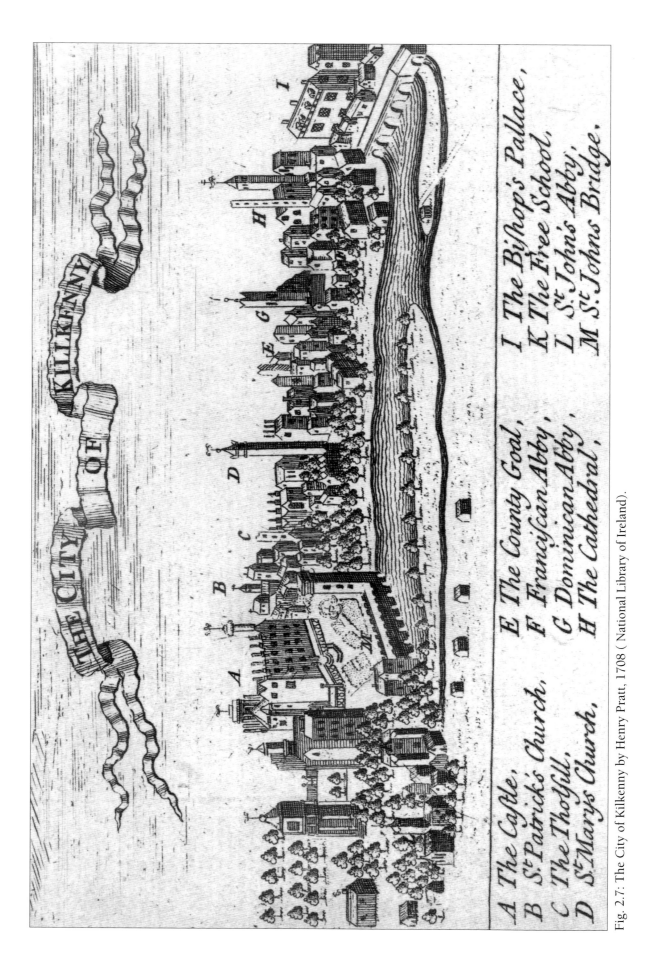

THE CITY OF KILKENNY

A The Castle,
B St Patrick's Church,
C The Tholsell,
D St Marys Church,

E The County Goal,
F Francifcan Abby,
G Dominican Abby,
H The Cathedral,

I The Bifhop's Pallace,
K The Free School,
L St John's Abby,
M St Johns Bridge.

Fig. 2.7: The City of Kilkenny by Henry Pratt, 1708 (National Library of Ireland).

Fig. 2.8: St. Stephen's Green Dublin from Malton's *A picturesque and descriptive view of the city of Dublin, 1792-1799* (Dublin, 1799, reproduced with an introduction by the Knight of Glin, Dublin, 1978).

Fig. 2.9: Ballina from Bartlett's *Guide to the antiquities of Ireland,* ca. 1840.

43

1900-1914 and the Valentine Collection for the period 1900-1960, all of which are in the National Library of Ireland, are comprehensive photographic records of the townscape of this period. The Lawrence Collection is arranged alphabetically by place, and the Eason and Valentine Collections are arranged by county. The subjects of the Lawrence photographs belied their commercial purpose. The largest number are of places which appealed to the Victorian tourist — picturesque tourist towns, seaside resorts, the cities, and of course dramatic rural landscapes. The Killarney area was particularly popular. Urban photographs include street scenes, photos of the exteriors and interiors of public buildings, churches and hotels (fig. 2.12). In 1990-1991 the Lawrence Project, a collaboration between the National Library and local history societies, was undertaken, in which 1,000 of Lawrence's landscape and urban views were rephotographed, showing how much or how little they had changed. These photographs are held in the National Library. The Poole Collection comprises 60,000 glass plates taken in Waterford city and county between 1884 and 1954. Poole's was a photographic business which also undertook press photography work and the collection records important events in the county as well as the everyday social and economic life of the area. The collection is housed in the National Library, which also has a collection of 3,050 stereoscopic views from the period 1860-1880.

The photographs in the Father Browne Collection document many facets of Irish life in the 1930s to 1960s and many have been published. The originals are held by a Dublin commercial photography firm, Davison Associates, and commercial rates are charged for copies. The Irish Architectural Archive has a collection of photographs indexed by place, which includes historical photographs and postcards. It also carries out its own photographic surveys of buildings and streets, and holds An Foras Forbartha's collection of photographs, taken during its operation up to 1985, which covers architecture in every county in the republic. The Royal Society of Antiquaries of Ireland started a photographic survey of Irish monuments upon its establishment in 1849. It also organised a photographic survey of slums in Dublin in 1913. Both sets are in the Society's office in Merrion Square, Dublin.

The National Archives has a miscellaneous collection of photographs. It holds the Purser Griffith collection of glass plates of Dublin's Port and Docks and early twentieth century engineering works throughout Ireland. National School records sometimes contain photographs; these were mostly of students and teachers, but occasionally of the locality. The Archives's prison records also include photographs of convicted criminals which obliquely contain useful information. From the 1860s the government undertook a concerted policy of photographing every Fenian prisoner in the country. This was the first time that official photographs were taken of prisoners, and these could be useful for the demographic or political history of a town. The collection is card indexed. The National Library also has an album of prison photographs of Fenians taken between 1865 and 1871. Since the beginning of the twentieth century the records of every circuit criminal court have included photographic files of crime cases — scenes of murders, victims and neighbourhoods. These can be excellent socio-economic sources, revealing how people lived, what their houses looked like, both inside and outside, what they wore, their means of transport and much more.

The National Gallery of Ireland (Merrion Square, Dublin 2) has published three catalogues of works housed in the Gallery, *National Gallery of Ireland illustrated summary catalogue of paintings* (Dublin, 1981); *National Gallery of Ireland illustrated summary catalogue of drawings, water-colours and miniatures* (Dublin, 1983); *National Gallery of Ireland illustrated summary catalogue of sculpture and prints* (Dublin, 1985). All are indexed by place and artist. Copies of works may be ordered for a fee.

The Cambridge University Collection of air photographs has a substantial Irish component mainly of oblique photographs taken in all parts of the Republic and Northern Ireland (fig. 2.13). The oblique photographs include panoramic views of landscape and scenery, but also record individual elements in the landscapes. Although the emphasis was primarily on archaeological sites, the photographs taken in Ireland in the 1960s and 1970s have coverage of many towns and

Fig. 2.10: George Petrie's view of Kells from the south, 1820, from Thomas Cromwell's *Excursions through Ireland* (London, 1820).

Fig. 2.11: Aerial view of the city of Dublin from the south east, Irish School 1846 (National Gallery of Ireland). For discussion on this see p. 41.

46

Fig. 2.12: Davis Street, Mallow from the Lawrence Collection (National Library of Ireland).

Fig. 2.13: Galway (eastern part) from the Cambridge University Collection of Air Photographs, 1970.

villages. They are particularly relevant to urban studies because they often incorporate town hinterlands, thus affording clues to origins and site selection which may not be apparent either on the ground or from maps. There is a detailed index of the Irish collection by county and subject matter in the National Museum of Ireland. Researchers can access this index through contacting the Museum's Education Officer and photographs can then be ordered from the Committee for Aerial Photography, Cambridge. Both commercial companies and individuals have also amassed photographic collections: *Aerofilms*, for example, have a substantial collection of Irish town photographs.

There are important collections of early photographs housaed in archives in Northern Ireland. Both the Green Collection in the Ulster Folk and Transport Museum at Cultra, County Down and the Welch Collection in the Ulster Museum, Belfast (fig. 2.14) have been used extensively by urban researchers. The Ulster Museum operates a picture library service and the Ulster Folk and

Fig. 2.14: King John's Castle, Carlingford (Ulster Folk and Transport Museum).

Fig. 2.15: The Claddagh (Galway city), from the air by H. Braine (Department of Irish Folklore, UCD).

Transport Museum has a special photographic unit. Early photographs of towns and villages were often taken by visiting scholars and journalists and one of the most comprehensive photographic surveys of an Irish town in the 1930s is that of Rathnew, County Wicklow by Kevin Danagher which is now in the archives of the Department of Irish Folklore, University College Dublin. This archive also has photographs taken in Irish towns by Continental and Scandinavian folklorists such as Von Sydow and Eskersd and Braine (fig. 2.15).

Newspapers are good sources of drawings and photographs as the excerpt from the *United Ireland* Supplement of 1890 reveals (fig. 2.16). This propaganda drawing is a potted social history in itself, indicating the political and social tensions of the 1890s. The Land War was fought in urban as well as rural areas, as depicted here in the clash between the Tenants Defence Association and the Evictors Syndicate. Two opposing views of Tipperary at the turn of the century are shown. A state of military occupation and desolation vies with a utopian vision of a prosperous commercial town centred around the proposed market house. An additional bonus is that the buildings and layout of the town are depicted. A comparison between fig. 2.16 and the almost contemporaneous Lawrence print (fig. 2.17) emphasises the complementarity of sources.

Family and estate papers are also worth checking for photographs and illustrations, which would be noted in their catalogues. One of the more fascinating records of an Irish town is the illustrated valuation book of Arklow produced by W. Townsend-Trench in 1877. This unique volume comprises 215 watercoloured pages and has an index. It is now held by the Arklow Property Company. The valuation was commissioned by Lord Carysfort who had an extensive property in the town and countryside. Local libraries, museums and historical bodies are other possible sources. Another visual source is film. RTÉ has a broadcasting archive, as does the Irish Film Centre, which can provide lists of films by place. Both cater principally for the broadcasting and media sectors and charge fees.

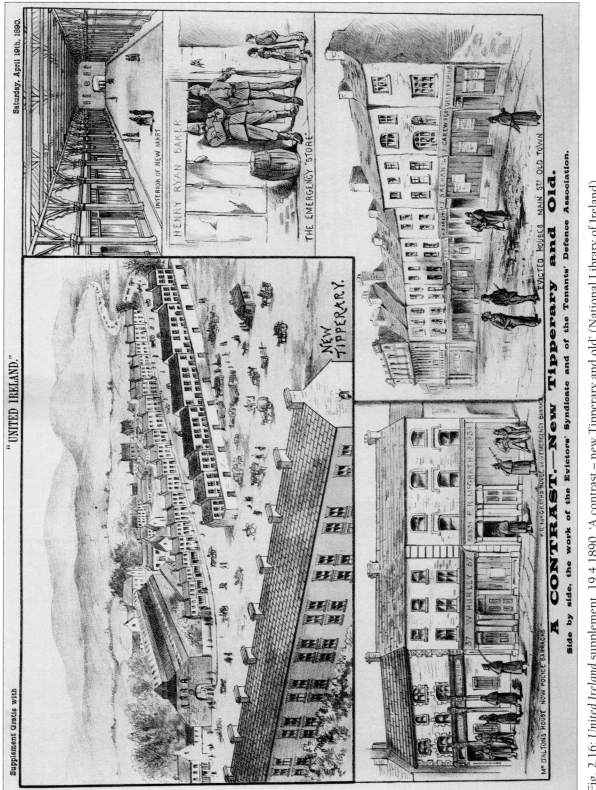

Fig. 2.16: *United Ireland* supplement, 19.4.1890, 'A contrast – new Tipperary and old' (National Library of Ireland).

Fig. 2.17: Dillon Street, Tipperary, from the Lawrence Collection (National Library of Ireland).

SELECT BIBLIOGRAPHY

1. Maps and Related Sources

J.H. Andrews, *Plantation acres: an historical study of the Irish land surveyor and his maps* (Belfast, 1985)

J.H. Andrews, *History in the ordnance map, an introduction for Irish readers* (2nd edn., Kerry, Montgomeryshire, 1993)

J.H. Andrews, *Shapes of Ireland: maps and their makers, 1564-1839* (Dublin, 1997)

M. Clark, *The book of maps of the Dublin city surveyors 1695-1877* (Dublin, 1983)

H.B. Clarke, 'The mapping of medieval Dublin: a case study in thematic cartography' in H.B. Clarke and A. Simms (eds), *The comparative history of urban origins in non-Roman Europe,* part 2 (Oxford, 1985), pp 617-43

P. Ferguson, The maps and records of the Valuation Office, Unpublished B.A. dissertation, Geography Department, University College, Dublin (1977)

P. Ferguson, *Irish map history: a select bibliography of secondary works, 1850-1983, on the history of cartography in Ireland* (Dublin, 1983)

J.B. Harley and D. Woodward (eds), *History of cartography* (Chicago, 1987-)

R.J. Hayes, *Manuscript sources for the history of Irish civilisation* (Boston, 1965 and later supplements)

A. Bonar Law, *The printed maps of Ireland* (Dublin, 1998)

G.A. Hayes-McCoy, *Ulster and other Irish maps c. 1600* (Dublin, 1964)

PRONI, *Northern Ireland town plans 1828-1966* (Belfast, 1977)

2. Paintings, Prints, Drawings and Photographs

W.H. Bartlett, *The scenery and antiquities of Ireland* (London, n.d.)

R.M. Elmes, *Catalogue of Irish topographical prints and original drawings* (revised by M. Hewson, Catalogue of National Library of Ireland holdings (Dublin, 1975)

E.E. Evans and B.S. Turner, *Ireland's eye: the photographs of Robert John Welch* (Belfast, 1977)

N. Kissane, *Ex-Camera 1860-1960. Photographs from the collections of the National Library of Ireland* (Dublin, 1990)

P. Liddy, *Dublin stolen from time: perspectives of Dublin* (Dublin, 1991)

J. Malton, *A picturesque and descriptive view of the city of Dublin* (Dublin, 1799, reproduced with an introduction by the Knight of Glin, Dublin, 1978)

C. Manning, 'Delusions of grandeur: the pictorial forgeries of Sheffield Grace' in J. Kirwan (ed.), *Kilkenny. Studies in honour of Margaret M. Phelan* (Kilkenny, 1997), pp 112-29

National Gallery of Ireland, *Illustrated summary catalogue of paintings* (Dublin, 1981)

National Gallery of Ireland, *Illustrated summary catalogue of drawings, watercolours and miniatures,* compiled by A. Le Harival, introduction by H. Potterton (Dublin, 1983)

National Gallery of Ireland, *Illustrated summary catalogue of Irish watercolours and drawings,* edited by A. Le Harival, photography by J. Kellet and M. Olohan (Dublin, 1991)

National Gallery of Ireland, *Illustrated summary catalogue of sculpture and prints,* edited by A. Le Harival, compiled by S. Dillon *et al.* (Dublin, 1988)

3. Contemporary Illustrations of Irish Towns (major collections)

Beranger's views of Ireland, with text by Peter Harbison (Dublin, 1991). Originals in the Royal Irish Academy (Beranger lived 1729-1817)

The antiquities of Ireland by Francis Grose, 2 vols, Dublin, 1791 (Francis Grose lived 1731-1791)

The antiquities of Ireland a supplement to Francis Grose drawn by Daniel Grose, ed. by R. Stalley (Dublin, 1991)

Hidden landscapes, painted by G.V. du Noyer (Dublin, 1995). (Du Noyer lived 1817-1860)

CHAPTER THREE

The Built Environment

1. Buildings (Ríonach Ní Néill)

The built environment is an important historical source. Churches, courthouses, town gates and walls, market places, cross-roads and fair greens, Georgian terraces and rows of one-storey cottages, are all links with the past. Thorough examination of individual buildings will reveal clues to their origin and history. Without training and expertise, however, trying to date a building by visual survey alone can be a very difficult business. Its appearance can be deceiving. There are many new buildings in a revivalist style and there are others which are an amalgamation of styles. A building may have been drastically altered over time, so that a nineteenth century building might very well have medieval foundations.

There is a good selection of books on the architecture of Irish towns, and on Irish and British architecture in general, which give illustrated descriptions of the major architectural styles and the periods in which they were built. Of particular note are Sean Rothery's A *field-guide to the buildings of Ireland* (Dublin, 1997) with an architectural glossary and Patrick and Maura Shaffrey's *Buildings of Irish towns, treasures of everyday architecture* (Dublin, 1983), which also contains a glossary and typology of Irish building styles (fig. 3.1).

Unfortunately, with the exception of maps, there are few pre-eighteenth century documentary sources for architecture and, in fact, very few records dealing with buildings in themselves. One has to investigate records created for another purpose, such as taxation records or deeds. Many buildings, especially ordinary domestic buildings, simply have not been documented. One must also be aware of the pitfalls of using documentary sources for determining the history of a building on a specific site, as the records may not apply to the existing building, which may have replaced an earlier structure. Documentary evidence needs to be confirmed by a stylistic examination of the building.

Architectural drawings and building plans are the most useful sources. These may include the date of design and the name of the architect, and can be compared with the existing structure to determine whether it has been altered. Pre-eighteenth century plans are rare, and you are more likely to find plans of nineteenth century and later buildings. You should certainly check the catalogue in the Irish Architectural Archives in Dublin for references to your town. A very large number of engravings and drawings are held in the National Library and the *Catalogue of Irish topographical prints and original drawings* provides information on this collection. It is indexed by place. Also in the National Library is a small book with the title *The architecture of Ireland in drawings and paintings*, which contains drawings by great designers from the mid-eighteenth century to modern times and a record of architectural drawings and paintings held in the National Gallery. The Royal Irish Academy holds original prints by nineteenth century antiquarians, for example Beranger, Petrie and du Noyer. Most of these are available in published form (see bibliography). The National Gallery houses a collection of architectural drawings listed in three printed catalogues which are indexed by place and author.

If the building in which you are interested is a public building, such as a school, asylum or courthouse, plans and drawings possibly still exist in the relevant public body records, such as those of the Board of Works, which are held in the National Archives. The Board of Works, later the Office of Public Works, was established in 1831 to carry out public infrastructural works such as the building and maintenance of roads, canals, harbours, piers, bridges, drainage systems and public buildings – including railway stations, post offices, schools, and lunatic asylums – as well as to provide some poor relief assistance. It is therefore worthwhile checking OPW records for nineteenth century public buildings in a town. It should be noted that standard architectural styles were often used, so there might not be building plans for an individual building. Records include minute-books, letter books of correspondence – which could contain references to building work in a town – financial accounts, registers of contracts, and maps and architectural drawings of building schemes. An excellent guide to these records is Rena Lohan, *Guide to the archives of the Office of Public Works* (Dublin, 1994). The National Archives also has the records of the predecessor of the Board of Works, the Civil Building Commissioners, which was instituted in 1802.

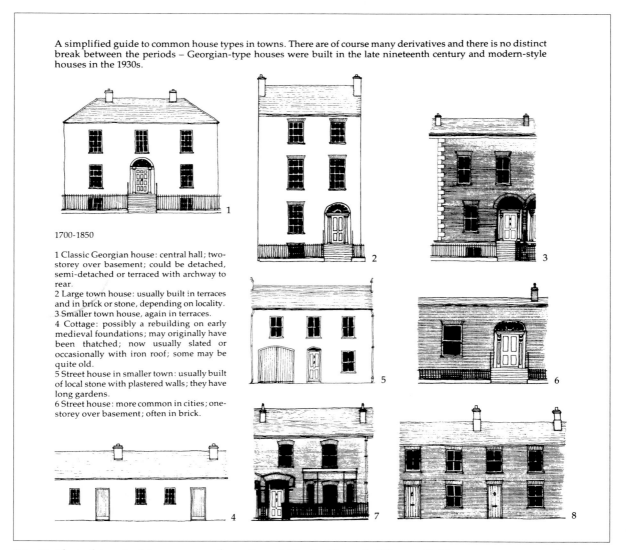

A simplified guide to common house types in towns. There are of course many derivatives and there is no distinct break between the periods – Georgian-type houses were built in the late nineteenth century and modern-style houses in the 1930s.

1700-1850

1 Classic Georgian house: central hall; two-storey over basement; could be detached, semi-detached or terraced with archway to rear.
2 Large town house: usually built in terraces and in brick or stone, depending on locality.
3 Smaller town house, again in terraces.
4 Cottage: possibly a rebuilding on early medieval foundations; may originally have been thatched; now usually slated or occasionally with iron roof; some may be quite old.
5 Street house in smaller town: usually built of local stone with plastered walls; they have long gardens.
6 Street house: more common in cities; one-storey over basement; often in brick.

3.1: Guide to historical house types from P. and M. Shaffrey, *Buildings of Irish towns, treasures of everyday architecture* (Dublin, 1983).

1850-1920

7 Brick-fronted two storey house, often with bay windows and patterned brickwork.

8 Two-storey house: plainer and smaller than 7; typical of industrial and artisan houses; common in Ulster.

9 Single-storey version of 8: brick-fronted; plot size usually quite small; 7, 8, 9 found mostly in cities and large towns.

10 Large house, late nineteenth-century: influenced by Gothic and other styles; built of local stone and often plastered with elaborate details; bay windows: commonly found in resort towns.

11 Tudor revival: timber framing and plaster panels; projecting first floor; usually two-storey; more commonly found in cities.

12 Romantic Gothic style: popular with estates, charitable and commercial organisations; high roofs, projecting porches, leaded windows.

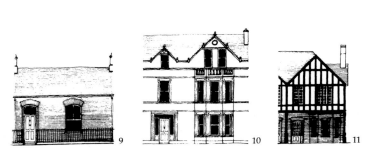

1920-1950

13 Picturesque arts and crafts styles: popular with speculative builders; concrete walls, plastered, tiled roofs; detached and semi-detached.

14 Another variation of 13: essentially a dormer bungalow, built on the then outskirts of towns.

15 Forerunner of the modern bungalow: double fronted bay window; concrete walls, plastered; tiled or slated roof.

16 Early public housing: influenced by Gothic and arts and crafts styles; concrete walls, slated roofs; built in terraces; often with substantial back gardens.

1950 to 1960s

17 Public housing: built in terraces; plastered walls, steel windows, tiled roofs; window sizes becoming larger.

18 Private houses: usually semi-detached with attached garage; half brick front, large horizontal windows, plastered walls, tiled roof.

19 Modern style: dating from the 1930s; flat roof, white walls, steel windows, austere appearance; mostly detached and privately built.

20 Modern bungalow: a mixture of materials; large horizontal windows, tiled roof, attached garage; common all over the country; based on a traditional shape, has evolved into a multitude of designs; usually built on the outskirts of towns.

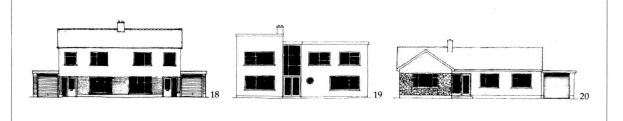

Fig. 3.2: Map and photograph (J. Brady) of Croydon Park Avenue, Marino, Dublin, constructed between 1924 and 1927.

The National Archives has two important private record collections dealing with architecture. These are the papers by Bryan Bolger, who worked for the OPW, and the Sibthorpe papers. The archives of the Department of Finance include papers on 'compensation for damage to property 1916-1923', which give information on the extent of damage caused by the War of Independence and the Civil War. Poor law reports include records, such as plans, elevations and costs, of the workhouses built in each union. Prison records include the annual Report of Inspectors-General of Prisons in Ireland, which has information on the building of prisons. The annual reports of the Congested Districts Board established in 1891 have references to and plans for harbour constructions along the western seaboard. The National Archives holds records of railway companies, harbour authorities and estate papers (see chapter six for estate records).

The *Journals of the House of Commons* are sources of information on the construction and funding of public buildings from the early eighteenth century to 1922. Plans of ecclesiastical buildings may still be in particular church archives. Grand jury presentment books (see pp 112-3) record public works for buildings and engineering works as well as roads. Local authority archives are potential locations for plans of buildings under its control. Planning records are of some use for tracing twentieth-century buildings. It is useful to check the local development plan to see whether a building is listed for conservation, in which case the local authority or local conservation group might already have compiled information on it. Documents may also be held privately by a family or business. For example, the Bank of Ireland holds architectural drawings of many of its nineteenth century bank buildings, including banks which it subsequently took over, such as those of the Hibernian Bank.

Archives may contain quantity surveyors' papers or building accounts relating to a building. These can contain useful information such as when the building was erected, the material from which it was constructed, the builder, architect, and the craftsmen they employed, as well as the cost of development. The study by Jim O'Toole on the construction of the Catholic cathedral in *Thurles: the cathedral town* (Dublin, 1989) is an impressive example of the multi-faceted nature of such a large project. Not only does O'Toole highlight the ways in which Archbishop Leahy, who came from a family of land surveyors, adapted the design of the architect but he also details the origins of the church furnishings.

Maps are a useful source for tracing the history of the built fabric of a town in the absence of other documentary materials. A very approximate date of building can be given by noting when a building or street first appears on a map. Estate-maps and large scale Ordnance Survey maps may include the ground plans of buildings. For example, the five inch to one mile OS town plans may show internal ground floor walls and columns of public buildings. Comparing maps of different periods allows one to trace the development of individual buildings and the town layout (fig. 2.4). Vignettes in maps also offer clues to the earlier appearances of towns and individual buildings. Pre-eighteenth century maps may include more or less realistic profiles or bird's eye views of important buildings and conventionalised views of less important ones.

Valuation records are a good source from the mid nineteenth century onwards. A general idea of the building structure may be deduced from the number of rooms. As rates are partly determined by building condition, valuation records can state whether a building became derelict, was demolished or was refurbished or improved. Thus one can trace the history of buildings on a site by checking through valuation listings over the years – when a building was erected, its dimensions, when extensions were built, or knocked down, and when a new building was erected. The household forms of the manuscript census enumerator's returns should also be consulted for information on the house plan, building materials and building condition. Deeds (see p. 115) and Testamentary Records (pp 144-5) are also potentially valuable sources for details, both external and internal, of buildings.

It is particularly satisfying when the map evidence can be correlated with the photographic evidence as fig. 3.2 demonstrates with the example from the garden suburb of Marino built in the late 1920s.

Trade and street directories may indicate the approximate date of a building by the year of its initial inclusion and they are useful for tracing the function of a building through time. Its function listed in the original entry may indicate whether it was purpose built or not. Such directories also may indicate the physical history of the building as vacant sites, buildings in progress and derelict buildings were sometimes noted, particularly in Thom's Directory. The name of the occupant/rate payer, which might be the nearest clue to ownership in the absence of other sources, is listed.

Newspapers are a useful source of architectural information only from the 1850s. Classified advertisements included contracts for tenders and can indicate the age, owner or architect of a building. Reports in papers of the official opening of new buildings, such as churches, public buildings and places of entertainment, sometimes carry very long and detailed descriptions of the new building, its architect, builders, owners as well as events at its opening. Property supplements are recent additions to newspapers, listing new developments and planning applications.

Professional journals were first published in the 1850s. Initially, Ireland was covered in English periodicals, albeit erratically. These included *The Builder*, which dated from the 1840s; *The Architect* and *The Building News*, which were amalgamated in *The Architect and Building News*; and the *Architectural Review*, which is still in print. Irish journals such as *The Dublin Builder* are invaluable sources. It was first printed in 1859, became *The Irish Builder* in the 1860s and was finally discontinued in the 1950s. Other journals include *The Irish Architect and Craftsman*; *Dublin Penny Journal*; *The Irish Architect*; *Country Life* (which was first published in the 1890s and covers Irish country houses and towns); *Transactions of the Civil Engineers of Ireland*; the *Green Book* of the 1930s and 1940s, and *Plan* which appeared in the 1960s. These journals reported on new, mainly larger, buildings. *The Irish Builder* published a handy list of new and planned developments, their architects and builders. Journals also include interviews with architects, assessments of buildings and discussions of development plans, giving an insight into debates and attitudes concerning architecture. Debates over the rebuilding of Dublin and Cork for example after the War of Independence and the Civil War featured regularly in *The Irish Builder* throughout the 1920s.

There are a number of biographical lists of architects, containing information on the buildings they designed, such as Rolf Loeber's, *A biographical dictionary of architects in Ireland 1600-1720* (London, 1981) and his *Biographical dictionary of engineers in Ireland 1600-1730* (Dublin, 1977). An important unpublished source on architects in Ireland is the Alfred Jones *Index of architects*, which is in the Irish Architectural Archive. Jones compiled files on architects, engineers and some builders and artisans, who worked in Ireland from the seventeenth century to the 1960s. The files are organised alphabetically by name, and consist of transcriptions from source materials such as architects' journals, trade directories and records of architects and engineers associations, creating a biography of architects and their works. The collection has information relating to between 80 to 90 per cent of buildings in Ireland for which there is an identifiable architect. It is being computerised at present by Ann-Martha Rowan of the Irish Architectural Archive. The computer file will also incorporate other collections such as the Irish Architectural Archives files and architectural historians' files. Although the computer file is not available for public access, printouts may be requested.

If the building for which you are seeking information is a significant one, it is likely that some information about it exists in print already. Pre-seventeenth century edifices are automatically classified as national monuments under OPW protection, in which case it should be ascertained whether the OPW has compiled information on them. An Foras Forbartha surveys have been published for a number of towns, which are listed in the bibliography. These books have glossaries and illustrations of buildings which are useful guides to architectural styles. The OPW is engaged in an ongoing survey of the architecture of Irish towns. The Ulster Architectural Heritage Society has produced publications on urban architecture in Ulster. In *The buildings of Ireland* series the regions of North Leinster and North-West Ulster have been covered so far (see bibliography). Almost all libraries now have local history sections.

Guidebooks, either historical or contemporary, can also contain nuggets of information, as for example the *AA road guide to Ireland,* which has brief synopses of buildings of architectural importance. Two topographical books of particular note for architectural information are S. Lewis's *A topographical dictionary of Ireland* (London, 1837, 1846, reprinted Baltimore 1984), and the similar but more detailed *Parliamentary gazetteer.*

Local knowledge is one particular source material which is not stored in any archive. Talking to local residents can be a valuable exercise in any type of historical study, as they may know some useful information in some particular line of inquiry. Locals may remember the name of a half-ruined building, the family previously living there, the name of the local landowner, or if there was a big house which has since been destroyed. You should always cross-check such information against other sources.

Archives specifically concerned with the built environment:

The Irish Architectural Archive, Merrion Square, Dublin 2

This is a reference-only library, open to the public. It contains records of the Royal Institute of Architects of Ireland, and miscellaneous records of architectural significance, including over 300,000 photographs and 50,000 architectural drawings and engravings. The photographic collection of buildings in Ireland is ordered by place. Other material is indexed by place and subject (figs. 3.3 and 3.4). This archive holds a number of collections, which include The Royal

Fig. 3.3: Kells (County Meath) Session House, 1802 (Irish Architectural Archive).

Fig. 3.4: Kells (County Meath) Savings Bank, 1845 (Irish Architectural Archive).

Institute of Architects of Ireland Murray collection, the Ormonde Loan collection and drawings by Francis Johnston and Michael Scott. It also has a library of journals and books related to architecture and the building trade. Copies of some source materials may be ordered. A useful introduction to this archive is a chapter called 'Guide to the collection of the Irish Architectural Archive' in D.J. Griffin and S. Lincoln, *Drawings from the Irish Architectural Archive* (Dublin, 1993).

The Irish Georgian Society, Merrion Square, Dublin 2

Founded in 1958 for the purpose of increasing awareness of Georgian art, architecture and social history, the society funds conservation work throughout Ireland. It publishes extensively on Irish architecture and organises conferences. The *Bulletin of the Irish Georgian Society* is published annually and contains articles on Irish architecture and architects. The proceedings of the Society are also recorded in *The Irish Georgian Society Quarterly Report*. The Society holds the records of the Royal Institute of Architects of Ireland.

Institute of Engineers, Clyde Road, Ballsbridge, Dublin 4

The Institute has an archive of material mainly relating to the Institute itself, and a small library. The Heritage Society of the Institute of Engineers has an ongoing project to record the major engineering works in the country – viaducts, canals, bridges, roads, railway stations. There is a computer index to the survey, and the Irish Architectural Archive has copies.

2. Archaeology (P.F. Wallace)

Thanks to the remarkable quality of organic layers in some of Ireland's early medieval towns (particularly Dublin, Waterford and Wexford) and to their archaeological excavations over the past twenty years, Ireland now is in an excellent position to reconstruct the character of its early medieval urban form, its layout and architectural content. In Ireland we are fortunate to have a more complete evidence for early urban life from artefacts for trade, crafts and daily life than any other country in Western Europe. The Fishamble Street/Wood Quay excavations in Dublin have

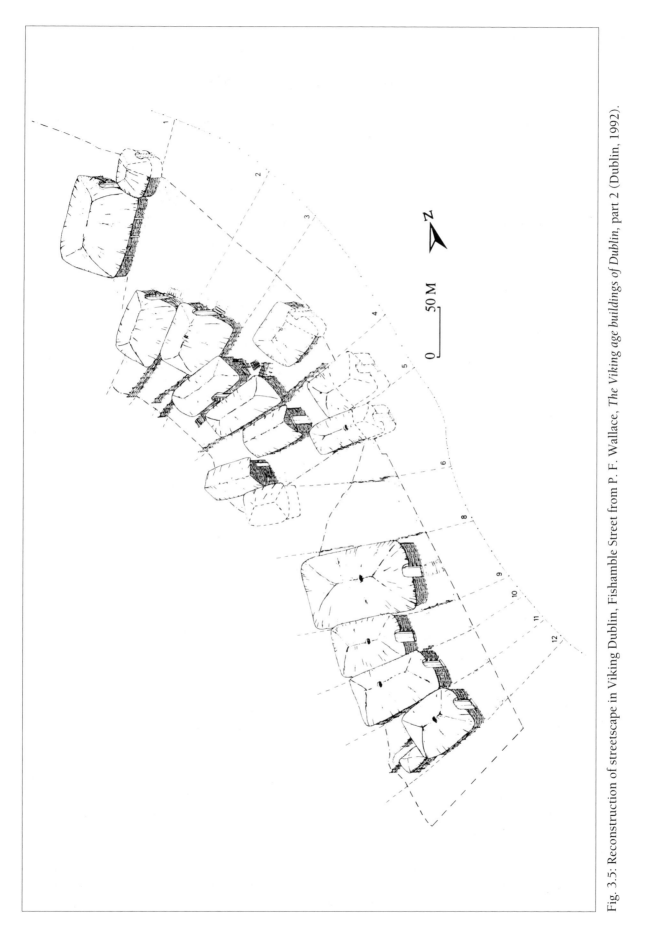

Fig. 3.5: Reconstruction of streetscape in Viking Dublin, Fishamble Street from P. F. Wallace, *The Viking age buildings of Dublin*, part 2 (Dublin, 1992).

provided such information on townscapes from the early tenth to the late eleventh century. The Dublin excavations have also given us information on thirteenth century waterfronts second only to that of London.

The archaeological record comprises drawings, photographs and samples of the physical evidence for urban layout and architecture. As these are of organic building materials, which occur in sequences, they usually have to be dismantled and removed in advance of modern development. The artefacts which are found in these layers and specimens of urban remains are sampled for analysis and study. They include animal bones and soil samples. Soil samples are retained for analysis which is published and artefacts are retained in museums for study and exhibition. From the research point of view the main body of evidence consists of the reconstructed documentary and cartographic evidences for stratigraphy, layout features and buildings. The artefacts provide evidence for industry, personal ornaments, crafts and household utensils. In general the excavations together with the analysis of environmental material provide a picture of the housing (see fig. 3.5), layout, environment, industrial activity, economy and agricultural infrastructure of urban settlements. Archaeological evidence preserved in churches, town defences, buildings, street patterns, property developments, dockside/waterfronts and walls provide evidence for settlement continuity, land holding, religious activity, military activity and the expansion or contraction of urban areas.

The main repository for these artefacts is the National Museum of Ireland, Kildare Street, Dublin 2, although artefacts from some urban centres are often temporarily stored in local museums or by local authorities. Material is often stored by type rather than by site and context and is therefore of less use to the general student of urban history than to the specialist archaeologist. The material can be examined by application to the duty officer, Irish Antiquities Division, National Museum of Ireland. Post-graduates and non-professionals should have a letter of recommendation in support of their application.

The more general results of Irish urban archaeological excavations can be visited at the National Museum's Viking Age Ireland exhibition which is particularly instructive for its display of craft evidence and artefact types as well as for burial evidence of the proto-urban period of the ninth century. A selection of artefacts (on loan from the National Museum) from the thirteenth century waterfront excavations at Wood Quay, Dublin is on show at Dublinia (adjoining Christchurch Cathedral) which also features a large scale model of the medieval town and has a research office (with a growing library) for students of urban medieval research.

The scientific results of the larger urban excavations are unfortunately not published by an individual publisher in a unified format. The large scale excavations carried out by the National Museum in Dublin between 1962 and 1981 are published in a series of monographs by the Royal Irish Academy for the Museum and the Academy. Separate works on the flora and the environment, the Viking Age buildings, the ships timbers, ringed pins, decorated wood and runic inscriptions have already appeared. Others are in preparation and will appear in due course. The Temple Bar Authority is producing a parallel series of reports of excavations in that area of Dublin (notably dealing to date with the results of the Parliament Street and Smock Alley sites). Dublin Corporation has started publishing the results of its excavations with a comprehensive report on the excavations for the pipeline on Winetavern Street. Most of the large-scale excavations carried out in Waterford particularly in the Arundel Square area have recently been published in a gigantic landmark volume by Waterford Corporation (fig. 3.6). This comprehensive compendium will be a reference quarry to which students of urban archaeology and history will refer for a long time to come. Excavation results for Waterford have also been published in the *Journal of the Cork Historical and Archaeological Society* and in *Waterford history and society*, a volume of the Irish County History series.

Many of the smaller scale urban excavations tend to be published in national, regional and local archaeological journals or in the *Proceedings of the Royal Irish Academy*. No substantial results have as yet been published on the important work carried out in Limerick and Galway

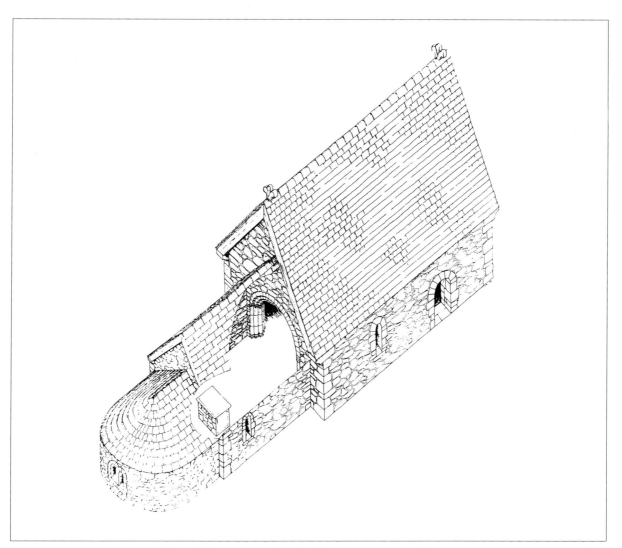

Fig. 3.6: Reconstruction of twelfth-century church, fig. 7.6 in *Late Viking age and medieval Waterford excavations 1986-1992* (Waterford, 1997).

respectively, and only a preliminary report of one of the several excavations in the archaeologically important excavations in Wexford has appeared to date.

The National Monuments and Heritage Branch of the Department of Arts, Heritage, Gaeltacht and the Islands has been conducting a survey since the 1960s of all archaeological monuments and sites and the results are now complete for the Republic of Ireland. These consist of a listing and classification of each monument, the townland name and map references as to its location. These records are available in County Libraries. A series of archaeological inventories for the country is being published, county by county. So far eleven counties have been published in whole or in part and fieldwork is complete in ten others. These inventories consist of a brief description of each archaeological monument together with locational information, maps and some photographs. Full archaeological surveys have been published for Counties Louth and Donegal and full surveys have also been published for the Dingle and Iveragh peninsulas as well as for part of the North Kerry area. Although none of these publications deals specifically with urban archaeology, archaeological monuments in towns are listed and described (fig. 3.7).

The National Monument and Heritage Branch commissioned an urban archaeological survey for each county, which was carried out under the direction of John Bradley mainly in the 1980s. This extensive survey exists in the form of invaluable typescript reports which contain maps,

Fig. 3.7: Cover and extract from M.J. Moore, *Archaeological inventory of county Meath* (Dublin, 1987).

plans and photographs as well as historical and archaeological information which is available in the relevant local government planning offices. Summaries of some of the important towns have been published in various local and national journals but it is regrettable that the overall urban survey has not yet been published.

Excavations of Irish urban sites are often unpublished. However, an annual list of excavations with a short entry briefly describing the material excavated is published in *Excavations Bulletin*, a series produced under the aegis of the Organisation of Irish Archaeologists, as well as short reports in the international journal *Medieval Archaeology*. The copyright for unpublished excavations rests with the excavator and arrangements have to be made with the excavator where it is intended to make use of archival material or unpublished reports. The same system applies to unpublished archaeological theses, lists of which are published annually in *Trowel*, the publication of the Archaeological Society, University College Dublin. The journal *Archaeology Ireland* provides in a readable form both the results of excavations and general discussions concerning urban archaeology.

The welcome economic developments in modern Ireland and particularly the renewal of, and investment in, inner city areas in which urban archaeological deposits are often located has meant that there has been a great demand for excavation in advance of development on many sites. It has been accepted that large-scale, full archaeological excavation is not possible in many cases given the slow pace of archaeological excavation and the conflicting pressure of time within which urban incentive schemes have to be completed. A compromise has been worked out whereby new buildings are allowed to go ahead provided there is minimal intrusion by piles into archaeological layers, to minimise the amount of interference which the piles supporting such buildings cause to archaeologically sensitive, well preserved layers.

Urban archaeologists, in particular town archaeologists, have succeeded in impressing on the minds of planners and developers the need for the maximum spacing of piles as well as for the reduction in the diameters of pile sizes and general piling methods whereby only the minimum of interference is tolerated in the relevant layers. Apart from some useful exercises in public relations and education such as those conducted by Temple Bar in Dublin, the era of large, full scale urban excavations in Dublin and in other towns has passed. The main hope now is that the intrusion of piles into otherwise unexcavated layers will not change the water level or in any other way interfere with and cause damage to unexcavated layers which hopefully will be available for study by future archaeologists.

One of the main challenges facing Irish urban archaeologists is the publication of the information excavated over the past three decades so that it becomes available for comparative studies in a European context. It is also hoped that Irish universities will take more note of the importance of urban archaeology and indeed of medieval archaeology in general and that both curricula and appointments will reflect this in future years. The number of theses now being undertaken on medieval topics (e.g. medieval pottery) is itself indicative of the realisation among students of the growing numbers who will be employed in the contract area, particularly in urban archaeological excavation and rescue.

SELECT BIBLIOGRAPHY

1. Buildings
J. Bradley, *Walled towns in Ireland* (Dublin, 1995)
C.E. Brett, *Court houses and market houses of Ulster* (Belfast, 1973)
C. Casey and A. Rowan, *The buildings of Ireland: north Leinster: the counties of Longford, Meath and Westmeath* (London, 1993)
M. Craig, *The architecture of Ireland* (London and Dublin, 1982)
George Petrie's illustrations in T. Cromwell, *Excursions through Ireland* (London, 1820)
H. Dixon, *An introduction to Ulster architecture* (Belfast, 1975)
P. Harbison, *Guide to national and historic monuments of Ireland* (Dublin, 1992)
P.M. Kerrigan, *Castles and fortifications in Ireland, 1485-1945* (Dublin, 1995)
E. McParland, 'A bibliography of Irish architectural history' in *Irish Historical Studies*, xxvi. no. 102, 1988
National Heritage Inventory, Architectural heritage series; *Cobh* (Dublin, 1979); *Kinsale* (Dublin, 1980); *Tullamore* (Dublin, 1980); *Carlow* (Dublin, 1980); *Bray* (Dublin,1980); *Ennis* (Dublin, 1981), *Galway* (Dublin, 1985), *Drogheda* (Dublin, 1986)
A. Rowan, *The buildings of Ireland: north-west Ulster: the counties of Londonderry, Donegal, Fermanagh and Tyrone* (London, 1979)
S. Rothery, *A field-guide to the buildings of Ireland* (Dublin, 1997)
S. Rothery, *Ireland and the new architecture: 1900-1940* (Dublin, 1991)
P. Shaffrey, *The Irish town; an approach to survival* (Dublin, 1975)
A. Thomas, *The walled towns of Ireland*, 2 vols. (Dublin, 1992)
J. Williams, *A companion guide to architecture in Ireland: 1837-1940* (Dublin, 1994)

2. Inventories
A.L. Brindley, *Archaeological inventory of county Monaghan* (Dublin, 1986)
A. Brindley and A. Kilfeather, *Archaeological inventory of county Carlow* (Dublin, 1993)
V.M. Buckley, *Archaeological inventory of county Louth* (Dublin 1986)
V.M. Buckley and P.D. Sweetman, *Archaeological survey of county Louth* (Dublin, 1991)
P. Gosling, *Archaeological inventory of county Galway*, ii: West Galway (Dublin, 1993)
B. Lacy et al., *Archaeological survey of county Donegal* (Lifford, 1983)
M.J. Moore, *Archaeological inventory of county Meath* (Dublin, 1987)
M.J. Moore, *Archaeological inventory of county Wexford* (Dublin, 1995)

P. O'Donovan, *Archaeological inventory of county Cavan* (Dublin, 1995)

D. Power, *Archaeological inventory of county Cork,* i, West Cork (Dublin,1992)

D. Power et al., *Archaeological inventory of county Cork,* ii, East and South Cork (Dublin, 1994)

G.T. Stout, *Archaeological survey of the barony of Ikerrin* (Dublin, 1984)

P.D. Sweetman, *Archaeological inventory of county Laois* (Dublin, 1995)

C. Toal, *North Kerry archaeological survey* (Dingle, 1995)

3. Urban Archaeology

S. Geraghty, *Viking Dublin: botanical evidence from Fishamble Street. Medieval Dublin excavations 1962-1981,* ii, *series C, environmental evidence* (Dublin, 1996)

H. Murray, *Viking and early medieval buildings in Dublin,* British Archaeological Reports 119 (Oxford, 1983)

G.F. Mitchell, *Archaeology and environment in early Dublin* (Dublin, 1988)

L. Simpson, *Excavations at Isolde's tower, Dublin,* Temple Bar Archaeological Report (Dublin, 1994)

L. Simpson, *Excavations at Essex Street West, Dublin,* Temple Bar Archaeological Report 2 (Dublin, 1995)

P.F. Wallace, 'The archaeology of Viking Dublin' in H.B. Clarke and A. Simms (eds), *The comparative history of urban origins in non-Roman Europe,* British Archaeological Reports, 255, I (Oxford, 1985), pp 103-45

P.F. Wallace, 'The archaeology of Anglo-Norman Dublin' in H. B. Clarke and A. Simms, (eds), *The comparative history of urban origins in non-Roman Europe,* British Archaeological Reports, 255, II (Oxford, 1985), pp 379-410

P.F. Wallace, *The Viking age buildings of Dublin. Medieval Dublin excavations, 1962-1981,* parts 1 and 2, *series A, Buildings and topography* (Dublin, 1992)

P. F. Wallace, 'The archaeological identity of the Hiberno-Norse town' in *Journal of the Royal Society of Antiquaries of Ireland,* 122 (1992), pp 35-64

C. Walsh, *Archaeological excavations at Patrick, Nicholas and Winetavern Streets, Dublin* (Dingle, 1997)

M. Hurley, O. Scully and S. McCutcheon, *Late-Viking age and medieval Waterford excavations 1980-1992* (Waterford, 1997)

CHAPTER FOUR

Medieval and Plantation Records

The further back in time one researches, the more unfamiliar the layout and structure of source materials become. The language and form of record keeping have changed over the centuries, as has the structure and responsibilities of institutions. Medieval source materials are less abundant. Many were written in Latin or Irish, and the English used differs greatly from modern English (although these obstacles have been to a great extent overcome by the translation and publication of many early sources by such bodies as the Irish Manuscripts Commission and the Royal Irish Academy). Inexperienced students may be confused about what sources are available for the study of the medieval history of their town. For these reasons sources for medieval urban history have been treated separately by Philomena Connolly of the National Archives. Irish language sources are discussed in a note by Katharine Simms of Trinity College Dublin. Raymond Gillespie completes this chapter with a note on plantation records.

1. Medieval Records (Philomena Connolly)

Municipal Records

The study of cities and towns in Ireland during the medieval period involves a wide variety of sources, which will vary from locality to locality and from one century to the next. What follows here is intended as an introduction to these sources which the researcher may use as a starting point in tracing the history of a particular place; it is by no means meant to be exhaustive.

Towns and cities in medieval Ireland enjoyed a remarkable degree of self-government, the extent of which varied from place to place, depending on the terms of the original charter and any subsequent extension of the rights granted in it. Urban authorities made regulations relating to local administration, trade and industry, including measures for the improvement of sanitation and the elimination of fire hazards. City and town courts dealt with transgressions of the law committed within the urban boundaries and cases between inhabitants on a wide variety of subjects, including property and trade disputes. The authorities also dealt with financial matters, collecting tolls on goods being imported for sale, rent from burgage tenements and financial penalties imposed by the courts and, in the case of the cities, were responsible for the payment of the annual farm to the exchequer. All of these activities would have produced a wealth of documentary records, but unfortunately few of them have survived to the present time. Reports on the records held by the Corporations of Cork, Dublin, Kilkenny, Limerick and Waterford appeared in *The first report of the royal commission on historical manuscripts* (1870); a report on

(90) RENTALE COMMUNIS REDDITUS UILLE KILKENNIE PER ANNUM
UIDELICET.

Robertus Talbot pro porta del Ireston . . ij*d*.
Johanna Sauage[1]   (xl*d*. ad lumen Ecclesie)
Henricus Mortymer pro porta Fratrum . . ij*d*.
Thomas Woucy . . . iuxta Irestonbarre iiijs.[1] deliberatur
extra manus communitatis
Robertus Folyn pro les schoppes in medio uico   vj*d*.
Thomas Loveday pro una domo in uico Sci. Jacobi iijs.[1]

                          Summa xxix*s*. ij*d*

Johannes Edward pro una domo in qua manet . xl*d*.
Robertus Dullard pro Walkynesbarre (in manu com-
                         munitatis)   xl*d*.
Thomas Exam pro le commone forghe . . ij*s*.
Johannes Croker pro porta Sci. Johannis . . iiij*s*. ij*d*.
Thomas Monester pro porta Sci. Jacobi xijd.[1]   . . .
Nicholaus Kenedy pro domo in qua manet . vj*d*.
Willelmus Payn pro domo in qua Boys manet . vj*d*.
Willelmus Archer carpenter . . . iiij*d*.
Thomas Monyster pro le Castelbarre . . xl*d*.
Nicholaus Kenedy pro uno orto extra portam Castri iiij*d*.
Ric. Brydsall pro uno orto extra eandem portam . vj*d*.
Thomas Chonnyr capellanus pro porta Sci. Patricii vj*d*.
Thomas Graunt pro duobus ortis in uico Sci. Johannis iiij*d*.
Thomas Howlyn pro una domo in eodem uico . xij*d*.
Johannes Croker pro una domo in eodem uico . xij*d*.
Johanes Monan pro una domo in eodem uico . vj*d*.
Willelmus Whyte deyer pro uno orto in eodem uico vj*d*.
Johannes Croker pro le commone . . xij*d*.
Willelmus Whyte deier pro le Portebrygge . viij*d*.
Johannes Marchal pro una *iiijd.*[1] (quia extra manus
                         communitatis)   . . .
Dauid Exam pro . . .. vj*d*.
           Summa xx*s*. v*d*.

[1406, May 28]
(91)
fo. 39
Memorandum quod die Ueneris proximo ante festum Pente-
costes anno regno regis Henrici quarti septimo in quadam con-
gregacione que dicitur sembly in campanile ecclesie Beate Marie

---

[1] These entries were struck out. Summa xxix*s* ij*d* inserted.

Fig. 4.1: An extract from C. McNeill (ed.), *Liber primus Kilkenniensis; the earliest of the books of the corporation of Kilkenny now extant* (Dublin, 1931).

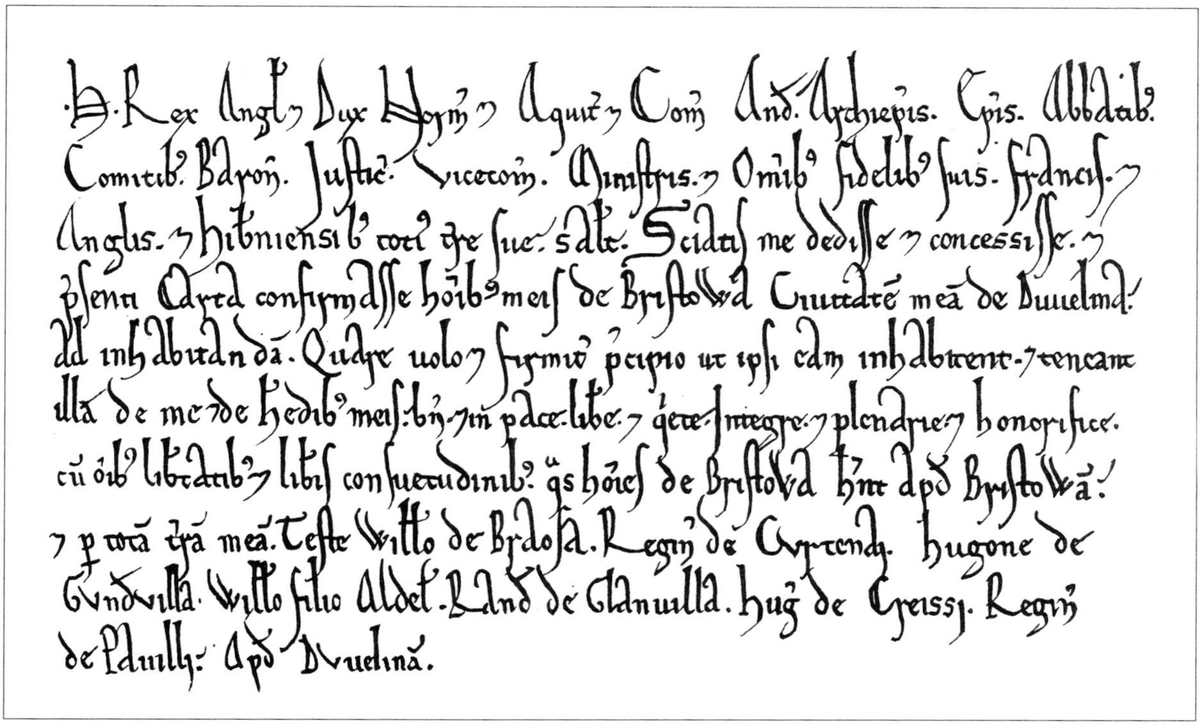

Fig. 4.2: Charter of Dublin, Henry II, 1171 reproduced from *Second report of the Irish Record Commissions printed reports* (Dublin, 1812).

Galway and a further one on Waterford were included in the *tenth report* (1885). Many town and city authorities have unpublished lists of records in their custody.

Dublin is the best documented of the cities and towns which have their origins in the medieval period. The records held in the City Archives include the guild merchant roll, recording the admission of Dubliners and others to the privileges of the guild between 1190 and 1265, the roll of admissions of free citizens to 1249 and the assembly rolls for the period 1447 onwards which provide a record of the decisions and actions of the city assembly. (*The Dublin Guild Merchant Roll, c. 1190-1265* edited by Philomena Connolly and Geoffrey Martin (Dublin, 1992) includes the roll of free citizens. The assembly rolls were printed by J.T. Gilbert in his *Calendar of the ancient records of Dublin,* 18 volumes, 1889-1922). The Chain Book and the White Book are collections of records, including by-laws, kept by the city authorities for future reference, and a similar volume covering the period between 1231 and 1586, the Liber Primus Kilkenniensis, exists for Kilkenny (fig. 4.1). (Calendars of the White and Chain Books were printed by J.T. Gilbert in *Calendar of the ancient records of Dublin*, i. Liber Primus Kilkenniensis, edited by Charles McNeill (1931), gives the Latin text of this manuscript; an English translation by A.J. Otway-Ruthven was published under the same title in 1961.) Cork is the only city to have any surviving financial records for the medieval period, a landgable roll, recording ground rent payments made for house property in the city, dating from the late fourteenth or early fifteenth century. Although there are extracts from municipal court records in other historical sources, no original court rolls are in existence. A town or city would naturally keep its charters as evidence of the type of self-government granted to it by the king or local lord, and sometimes its seals, but not all of these have survived. The Dublin charters go back to the first one granted by Henry II in 1171 and 1172, and Waterford has a late-fourteenth century roll containing copies of charters granted to the city, with portraits of justiciars, mayors and other officials in the margins (figs. 4.2, 4.3, 4.4). See J.C. Walton, *The royal charters of Waterford* (Waterford, 1979). Corporation archives may also contain deeds of properties leased out by the municipality.

Fig. 4.3: John King of England Lord of Ireland AD 1177-1216 from the charter roll of Waterford late fourteenth century, reproduced in J.T. Gilbert (ed.), *Facsimiles of national manuscripts of Ireland* (London, 1884).

Fig. 4.4: Mayors of Dublin, Waterford, Cork and Limerick from J.T. Gilbert (ed.), *Facsimiles of national manuscripts of Ireland* (London, 1884).

Government Sources

Fortunately, towns and cities are mentioned frequently in the records of the central administration, both Irish and English. The chanceries in both countries kept copies of letters issued in the king's name on a variety of subjects, including grants to towns and cities of various privileges and exemptions, licenses to individual merchants to export goods from Ireland, references to military action in the vicinity of towns, and orders for payments for works on castles. None of the Irish chancery rolls survived the Four Courts fire of 1922, but a Latin calendar of these records was published by the Irish Record Commission in 1828: E. Tresham (ed.), *Rotulorum patentium et clausorum cancellariae Hiberniae Calendarium* (Dublin, 1828). A calendar is an abstract of a document which preserves all the essential information contained in the original. The rolls of the English chancery, kept in the Public Record Office in London, are easily accessible through the English calendars published by H.M.S.O. There are three main series of chancery rolls (close rolls, fine rols and patent rolls) and the publication of calendars to them is ongoing. The PRO has also produced calendars of inquisitions taken on the death of a tenant in chief of the crown (inquisitions post mortem), including those who held property in Ireland as well as in England. The class of Ministers' accounts (SC 6) contains a wealth of documentation relating to the Irish estates of the lords of Carlow and Wexford. Other classes of records in the PRO which may prove fruitful are Ancient Correspondence (SC 1), Ancient Petitions (SC 8) and Chancery Miscellanea (C 47). (These have not been published in full, although a large number of items of Irish interest from these classes were printed by G.O. Sayles in *Documents on the affairs of Ireland before the king's council* (Dublin, 1979). A list of the Irish material in C 47 appears in *Analecta Hibernica* 1 (1930), and of that in SC 8 in *Analecta Hibernica* 34 (1987).

Towns and cities feature prominently in the financial records produced by the Dublin exchequer. The pipe rolls, which contain audited accounts of officials accounting at the exchequer, include separate accounts for the cities which paid an annual farm to the king, and for collectors of customs in various ports. There are also some miscellaneous accounts, such as that for the murage of Dunmore,. county Galway in 1279-80, and towns are mentioned in the accounts rendered by the sheriff of each county. No original pipe rolls survive, but the earliest one has been published in full, and calendars of those from 1228 to 1348 were printed as appendices to the Irish deputy keeper's reports (*The Irish pipe roll of 14 John* (1211-1212), ed. Oliver Davies and D.B. Quinn (1941); 35th, 36th, 37th, 38th, 39th, 42nd, 43rd, 44th, 45th, 47th, 53rd and 54th *Reports of the deputy keeper of the public records of Ireland*). Payments made into the treasury by the authorities and inhabitants of cities and towns are recorded on the receipt rolls of the Irish exchequer, and payments made out of the exchequer for military expeditions, gifts and rewards for good service, the garrisoning and provisioning of castles and other purposes were entered on the exchequer's issue rolls. Both of these series of records are held in the Public Record Office, London (class reference E 101), as a result of having been brought to England for the audit of the Irish treasurers' accounts at the English exchequer. Extracts from those for the period up to 1307 are included in Sweetman's *Calendar of documents relating to Ireland* mentioned below, and a full calendar of the issue rolls is currently in preparation for publication by the Irish Manuscripts Commission. The memoranda rolls of the exchequer contain details of exchequer business which were kept for future reference there, and these too should be mentioned as a source, although they are more difficult and troublesome to use. Two original rolls survive (those for 1309-10 and 1319-20) and are held in the National Archives, Dublin, which also holds Latin calendars of other rolls in this series, made by the Irish Record Commission in the early nineteenth century (RC 8). (For a description of the different types of entry to be found on these rolls, see the article by J.F. Lydon in *Analecta Hibernica* 23 (1966))

The records of the court held before the justiciar, or chief governor, of Ireland, provide a great deal of information on social and economic history, including that of the towns and cities. Most of the original rolls were destroyed in 1922, but three volumes of English calendars have been

55

Parliament at Castledermot, Monday after Ash Wednesday, 1378.

PETITION OF THE ABBOT OF TRACTON FOR THE REMISSION OF A
FINE IMPOSED FOR ABSENCE FROM PARLIAMENT.

Memoranda Roll, 3 Richard II, m.35d.[1]

Dominus rex mandauit breue suum de cancellaria sua
Hibernie thesaurario et baronibus huius scaccarii directum, quod
est inter breuia de Anglia de anno primo regis nunc in hec verba :

Ricardus Dei gracia rex Anglie et Francie et dominus
Hibernie thesaurario et baronibus de scaccario suo Hibernie
salutem. Quandam peticionem iusticiario et consilio nostris
in terra nostra Hibernie, in parliamento nostro apud Tristeldermot die lune proxima post festum Cinerum proximo preteri- 8 March
tum summonito et tento, per abbatem domus beate Marie de   1378
Traghton exhibitam et per ipsos ibidem indorsatam vobis
mittimus presentibus interclusam, mandantes quod, visa peticione predicta et indorsamento eiusdem, si per inquisicionem
inde coram vobis capiendam vobis constare poterit contenta
in eadem peticione veritatem continere, tunc ipsum abbatem
de decem libris in dicta peticione specificatis ad idem scaccarium
exonerari et quietum esse faciatis. Et nichilominus deman-
dam, si quam prefato abbati ad respondendum nobis ad idem
scaccarium de decem libris predictis per summoniciones eiusdem
scaccarii feceritis vel facere intenderitis, supersedeatis quousque
de veritate contentorum in peticione predicta per vos inquisitum
fuerit in forma predicta. Teste Iacobo le Botiller, comite
Dormondie, iusticiario nostro Hibernie, apud Tristeldermot,
xxvj. die Marcii anno regni nostri primo.   26 March
Et tenor peticionis, de qua fit mencio superius in breui,   1378
sequitur in hec verba :

A justice et as piers de parlement supplie l'abbé de la meson
de nostre Dame de Traghton qe, come brief le roi Edward,
aiell nostre seigneur le roi q'or'est, lui vint de estre a une parlement tenutz a Dyvelin devaunt monsire William de Wyndesore,
au temps q'il estoit governour et gardeyn de la terre d'Irland,
en le demayn de Typhayn l'an du reign le dit roi aiell xlviij.,[2]

---

[1] Ferguson Coll. II. 69 ; Cal. Mem. Rolls, xxxiii. 66.
[2] There must be a mistake here, for parliament was summoned for the *octave*
of Hilary in 1375 : the parliament summoned for the morrow of Epiphany in
1377 may be intended.

Fig. 4.5: Extract from H.G. Richardson and G.O. Sayles, *Parliaments and councils of medieval Ireland*, i
(Dublin, 1947).

published, covering the period 1295-1314: *Calendar of the justiciar rolls, Ireland, 1295-1303* (Dublin, 1905) and 1305-7 (Dublin, 1914), both edited by James Mills, and that for 1308-14 (Dublin, 1956), edited by Margaret C. Griffith. The National Archives holds further calendars to 1318, and it is hoped to publish these and the two surviving original rolls in the near future. The Irish Record Commission material in the National Archives also includes Latin calendars of justiciary, common bench and other plea rolls (RC 7). Finally, mention should be made of the records of the Irish parliament. The statutes passed in the Irish parliament were published in four volumes extending from the thirteenth century to 1481, and a fifth volume is in preparation, which will bring the series up to 1537. (*Statutes and ordinances and acts of the parliament of Ireland, King John to Henry V*, ed. H.F. Berry (Dublin, 1907); *Statute rolls of the parliament of Ireland, reign of King Henry the sixth*, ed. H.F. Berry (Dublin, 1910); *Statute rolls of the parliament of Ireland, first to the twelfth years of the reign of King Edward the fourth*, ed. H.F. Berry (Dublin, 1914); *Statute rolls of the parliament of Ireland, twelfth and thirteenth to the twenty-first and twenty-second years of the reign of King Edward the fourth*, ed. J.F. Morrissey (Dublin, 1939).) There are numerous mentions of individual towns and cities in the enactments, as well as items relating to municipalities in general. Fig. 4.7 is an extract from H.G. Richardson and G.O. Sayles, *Parliaments and councils of medieval Ireland*, i (Dublin, 1947), relating to a parliament held at Castledermot in 1378.

Ecclesiastical and Private Records

Collections of deeds kept by religious houses are an important source of topographical information. Most of the surviving material relates to Dublin abbeys and monasteries, but since these held lands and property in places outside Dublin, they are worth consulting. The original deeds relating to the property of Christ Church, Dublin, were destroyed in 1922, but fortunately a calendar to the medieval records had been compiled and published by the Public Record Office of Ireland before their destruction (20th, 23rd and 24th *Reports of the deputy keeper of the public records of Ireland*. There is a separate index in the 27th *Report*). The records of other religious houses exist in the form of cartularies, or registers containing copies of grants of lands and rents to the monastery or abbey, and those for St Mary's Abbey, Dublin (including the daughter house at Dunbrody), St Thomas' Abbey, Dublin, the Hospital of St John outside the New Gate of Dublin, All Hallows Priory, Dublin, the monastery of Tristernagh in Westmeath and St Saviour's chantry in Waterford have all been printed, as have calendars of the deeds of various Dublin parishes. (See J.T. Gilbert (ed.), *Cartularies of St Mary's Abbey, Dublin*, 2 vols. (Dublin, 1884); J.T. Gilbert (ed.), *Register of the abbey of St Thomas, Dublin* (Dublin, 1889); E. St J. Brooks (ed.), *Register of the Hospital of St John the Baptist without the New Gate, Dublin* (Dublin, 1936); R. Butler (ed.), *Registrum Prioratus Omnium Sanctorum juxta Dublin* (Dublin, 1845); M.V. Clarke (ed.), *Register of the priory of Tristernagh* (Dublin, 1941); G. Mac Niocaill (ed.), 'Registrum cantariae S. Salvatoris Waterfordensis', in *Analecta Hibernica*, 24 (Dublin, 1967). Deeds relating to the Dublin parishes of St James, St Catherine and St Werburgh are calendared in *Proceedings of the Royal Irish Academy* xxxv (1918-20) C, 265-315).

Secular landholders produced similar sources, for example, the Gormanston register dealing with the property of the Preston family in Meath and Louth, the Dowdall deeds, relating mainly to Louth, and the Ormond deeds (fig. 4.6) relating to that family's property which included lands in Tipperary, Kilkenny, and Dublin. (See *Calendar of the Gormanston register*, ed. J. Mills and M.J. McEnery, 1916; *Dowdall deeds*, ed. C. McNeill and J. Otway-Ruthven, 1960; *Calendar of Ormond deeds*, ed. E. Curtis, (6 vols., 1932-43).) In addition to these, there are collections of deeds not associated with particular families, such as MS 1207 in Trinity College, Dublin, and individual items which have been acquired by purchase or donation by the National Archives, National Library and other institutions. Most archival finding aids have not been published, but are available to readers in the repository or library concerned.

Addressed: To the right honorable and myn Especiall gode lord the Erle of Ormond.
Endorsed: E. goldyng.

(92)

[c.1515]. James Sherlock of Waterford to Earl of Ormond.
P.R.O. *Anc. Corr.* S.C. 1/52/54.

"Moste honorable and my specyale goode lorde in my moste humeliest maner. vnto your lordship I me recomaund. And there as it pleased your lordshup to directe your writtinge vnto your servantes into this land of Irland shewing vnto them by your said writting how that one Jowan Nagle sholde haue send a lettre vnto your lordshup. claymyng a title in your myll called the town myll In kylkeny by a lesse made vnto hir by my lorde John of Ormounde of whos soule Ihesue take mercie and also there as ye comaunded your said servauntes by your writting to take examinacion of hir title and of my title pleased your lordshup. to know such title as she shewed in presence of your said servaunts she shewed a lesse made by my said lord John vnto Thomas sherloke and it is xliij wyntre sithen the said lesse was made. And as touching that lesse I submitte the trialle therof vnto your lordshup whedre my said lord John had power to make a lesse of ony parte of his landes othre where he had lyvery of his landes. Wherby his lesse sholde be a sufficient title for the said Jowan. for here ben dyverse that showed that my said lord John had not his pardon. iiij yers aftre. the lesse was made vnto the said Thomas. Also the said Jowan shewed an acte of parlament laboured **by one** Waltre Archer. confermyng the said lesse and as for that acte. I haue shewed your said seruantes. an acte of parlament of a latre date by x. wint[res] which passed and anulled the oathre acte purchasse by the said Water . Which your said seruantes may [shew] your lordshup all the matier att leynthe . beseching your lordshup to bee my good lorde and gracious. as my[   ] full truste is in your lordshup . and god preserve your lordshup in great felicite. Written In Watirford the [x?   ]

By your servaunt Jeames sherlo[k]
Marchaunt dwelling in watirford."

Addressed: To my Right worshupfull lord Sir Thomas Erl of Ormond with concurance (?) be this gyven.
Endorsed: Jeames Shirlok.

Fig. 4.6: Extract from E. Curtis (ed.), *Ormond deeds*, iv (Dublin, 1937), relating to property in Waterford city.

Chronicles

The nature and extent of narrative sources for the medieval period have been examined by Gearóid Mac Niocaill in *The medieval Irish annals* (Dublin, 1975). Although there are no municipal chronicles in Ireland, two surviving Anglo-Irish narratives should be mentioned in this context. The so-called Pembridge annals, probably written by a Dublin Dominican, provide much information about the capital, while the annals of Friar John Clyn are an important source for the

Kilkenny area. (The Pembridge annals are printed in volume ii of *Cartularies of St Mary's Abbey*, Dublin, ed. J.T. Gilbert, and Clyn's annals in *The annals of Ireland by Friar John Clyn and Thady Dowling* (Dublin, 1845). A new edition of Clyn, with an English translation, is in progress).

Other sources

In addition to the sources described above, there are several compilations of documents from a variety of sources which should be mentioned. *The calendar of documents relating to Ireland, 1171-1307* (5 vols, 1875-86), edited by H.S. Sweetman, contains abstracts of English chancery rolls, letters, Irish receipt rolls and several other classes of records in the Public Record Office, London. John T. Gilbert's *Historic and municipal documents of Ireland, 1172-1320* (Dublin, 1870) deals mainly with Dublin and Drogheda, but contains references to other towns and cities. Gearóid Mac Niocaill's *Na buirgéisí XII-XIV Aois* (2 vols, Dublin, 1964) is a two volume work dealing with Irish boroughs in the medieval period; the first volume is a collection of charters and other documents, while the second contains essays on various aspects of town life and government.

Works on local history written before 1922 such as William Carrigan, *History and antiquities of the diocese of Ossory*, 4 vols (Dublin, 1905 repr. Kilkenny, 1981) and William Burke, *History of Clonmel* (Waterford, 1907 repr. Kilkenny, 1983), sometimes contain transcripts of records which no longer exist. Hayes *Periodicals* is a useful finding aid to articles published in local historical and antiquarian journals. The bibliography in volume two of *A new history of Ireland* includes sections on records relating to local administration, ecclesiastical records, and family and personal records and the journal *Analecta Hibernica*, published by the Irish Manuscripts Commission, contains guides to records of Irish interest in various repositories as well as lists of records in private custody. (The Manuscripts Department of the National Library has further unpublished lists of records in private custody.) The researcher working on the history of a particular town should consult the places volumes of Hayes, *Manuscript sources* which provides references to documentary material in the National Library and elsewhere.

2. Irish Language Sources (Katharine Simms)

Gaelic sources for urban history are few and far between, reflecting the rural base of Gaelic society itself. The Irish annals, most editions of which are conveniently provided with parallel English translations and person and place indices, are an important source for those towns which originated as pre-Norman settlements, monastic or otherwise, and entries for the later period mention Norman and Tudor towns in the context of raids made on them by the Gaelic chiefs. The oldest surviving annals are the Annals of Inisfallen, which end in 1326. Annals recording the sixteenth century are of great importance as records of the Irish viewpoint on Gaelic struggles against Tudor expansion. For example the Annals of the Four Masters, which recorded events from earliest mythological antiquity to 1616, include accounts of Donegal in the early sixteenth century before English invasion, such as this reference to the burning of Killybegs in 1513:

> Owen O'Malley came by night with the crews of three ships into the harbour of Killybegs; and the chieftains of the country being all at that time in O'Donnell's army, they plundered and burned the town, and took many prisoners in it. They were overtaken by a storm, so that they were compelled to remain on the coast of the country; and they lighted fires and torches close to their ships. A youthful stripling of the MacSweeny's, i.e. Brian, and the sons of Brin, son of the Bishop O'Gallagher, and a party of farmers and shepherds overtook them and attacked them courageously, and slew Owen O'Malley and five or six score along with him, and also captured two of their ships, and rescued from them the prisoners they had taken, through the miracles of God and St. Catherine, whose town they had profaned.
> *Source:* J. O'Donovan (ed.), *Annals of the Four Masters*, 7 vols (Dublin, 1851), v, p. 1323.

Similarly bardic poetry makes occasional references, for example to the militia of Dublin fleeing in battle, to a decapitated chieftain's head exhibited on the town gates, and in one amusing passage to the mayoral elections held in Anglo-Irish towns on the Monday after Michaelmas.

There are few legal deeds in Irish with urban relevance, apart from the tenth to twelfth century charters inserted in the blank pages of the Book of Kells, which deal with the pre-Norman monastic settlement there, but an interesting one from a later period is the agreement reached in 539 between the chiefs Maghnus Ó Domhnaill and Tadhg Ó Conchobhair over control of Sligo castle, and the exaction of dues from Sligo burgesses.

In the early modern period *Cin Lae Uí Mhealláin*, a friar's diary of the 1641-47 Ulster campaigns during the wars of the mid seventeenth century, mentions many small urban settlements in Ulster and county Louth. The second part of *Parliment Chlainne Tomáis*, a mid-seventeenth century satire, contains unfriendly social comment on Irish-speaking artisans from the towns of Meath. *Cinn Lae Amhlaoibh Uí Shúileabháin*, the diary of Humphrey O'Sullivan, a schoolmaster and draper from Callan, county Kilkenny, who died in 1837, is one of the very few Irish language sources to describe small-town life in Ireland from the inside. What the early Gaelic sources may lack in quantity and precision, they make up for in human interest.

3. Plantation Records (Raymond Gillespie)

Between 1500 and 1700 Ireland was repeatedly settled by waves of immigrants mainly from England, Scotland and Wales while a smaller number came from continental Europe. Some of this settlement was privately sponsored and managed by individual land owners, but from time to time central government plantations. In particular the settlement of Leix and Offaly in the 1550s, the settlements of Munster in the 1580s and the plantation of Ulster after 1608 were all government schemes. These plantations differed from more informal privately sponsored settlement in that strict rules were laid down, though not always enforced, by central government which delineated the kind of society that was to emerge from the plantation process. The creation of towns, which were considered necessary agents for economic change, security and administration, was a key component of plantation policy.

The towns which emerged varied widely. In some cases, as for example Youghal (fig. 4.7), Enniskillen and Dungannon, older medieval centres were reinvigorated as a result of the plantation process. In other instances at Portlaoise and Coleraine new settlements were created on virtually green-field sites by entrepreneurial landlords. One of the principal sources for the understanding of these towns is the street pattern, whether it be a classically planned, grid iron structure such as at Derry (fig. 4.8) or Coleraine with central squares or more haphazard older settlements which were developed with the arrival of the new settlers. Here the primary tools for study are maps of the settlements. Patrick O'Flanagan's *Bandon*, a fascicle of the *Irish historic towns atlas*, will give some impression of the sort of cartographic evidence available for a planned plantation town. Because they were part of a corporate planned exercise, records have survived for many plantation towns. The records of the London companies who were involved in the settlement of Londonderry contain drawings and plans for the towns to be built on their lands. These records are still held by the companies in London. We can get some idea of the settlements as they actually evolved from subsequent maps. The government was keen to commission maps of their new settlements and many of these are now in the Public Record Office, London and Trinity College, Dublin. Two maps of Maryborough (Portlaoise) from the 1550s survive among this collection (PRO, SP63/2/66 and TCD, MS 1205 no. 10). For the Londonderry settlement there are picture maps made by Thomas Raven in 1622 which clearly show the towns as small affairs, clustered around the houses of landlords. These are all published in D.A. Chart (ed.), *Londonderry and the London Companies* (Belfast, 1928). See also G.A. Hayes McCoy, *Ulster and other Irish maps c. 1600* (Dublin, 1964) and J.T. Gilbert, *Facsimiles of the national manuscripts of Ireland* (London, 1884). Unfortunately few other plantation schemes produced maps depicting

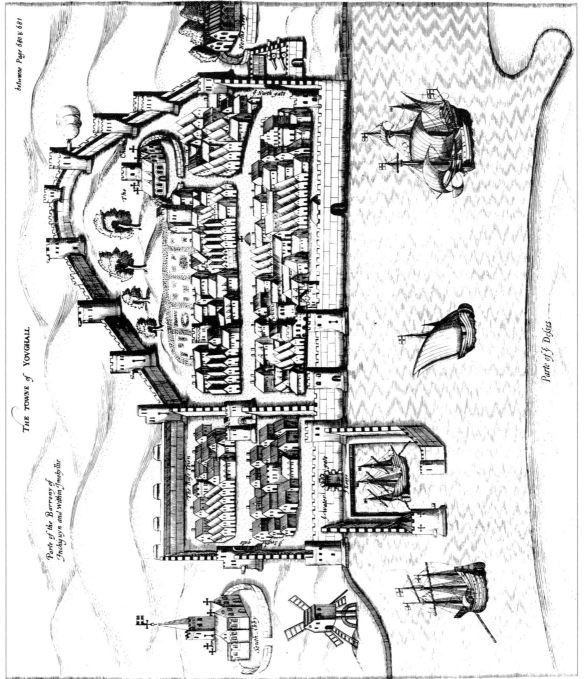

Fig. 4.7: Youghal from *Pacata Hibernia, Ireland appeased and reduced* (London, 1633).

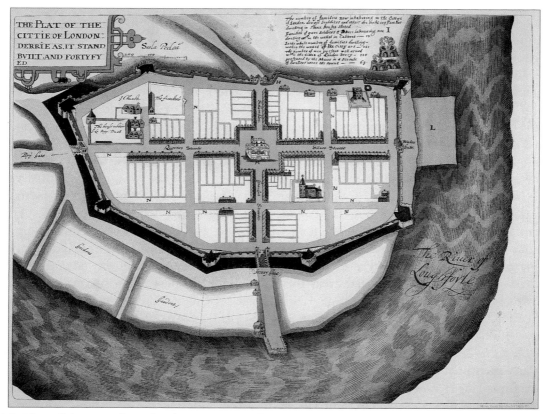

Fig. 4.8: Plan of the city of Londonderry AD 1622 from the Survey of AD 1622, by Sir Thomas Phillips and Ralph Hadsor from J.T. Gilbert, *Facsimiles of the national manuscripts of Ireland* (London, 1884).

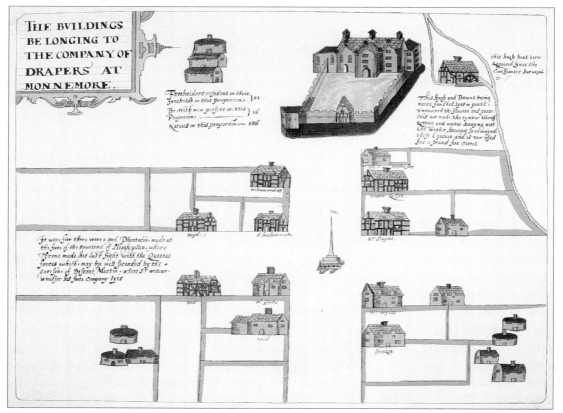

Fig. 4.9: Plan of Moneymore, 1622 from J.T. Gilbert, *Facsimiles of the National Manuscripts of Ireland* (London, 1884).

urban settlements in this detail although there are a number of written descriptions which have been underused. The *Civil Survey* (10 volumes edited by R.C. Simington, Dublin 1931-61) contains a great deal of material about towns in planted areas and records the effects of the wars of the 1640s on those settlements. In most cases we have to rely on estate papers to provide topographical information about towns. Here too the haul is meagre but a truly magnificent lease book for the Brownlow estate in Lurgan, county Armagh edited by Raymond Gillespie, *Settlement and survival on an Ulster estate: the Brownlow leasebook 1667-1711* (Belfast, 1988), makes a detailed reconstruction of the town possible.

Topographical pictures of towns are of limited value unless we can establish some form of ranking and develop a sense of their relative importance. One of the ways of doing this is to use population data. Here there is a significant body of evidence for plantation towns since governments, anxious to know how their plans were progressing, made a number of surveys of the plantations in which material about towns is located. For Ulster there are surveys in 1611, 1613 and 1619 (printed in HMC, *Report on the manuscripts of R.R. Hastings*, iv (London 1974), *Calender of Carew MSS, 1603-25* and George Hill, *A historical account of the plantation of Ulster* (Belfast, 1977).) And for all planted areas the 1622 commissioners made surveys of work done and towns built (British Library, Add MS 4756). These provide not only population estimates but evidence for the physical fabric of the town. The so-called 'Census of 1659', in fact a poll money tax for 1660, provides demographic material for towns after the wars of the 1640s and is accessible in S. Pender (ed.), *A census of Ireland c. 1659* (Dublin, 1939). Small towns are usually not clearly identified here but are normally distinguishable by having a higher population density than neighbouring denominations. We can bring some life to these bare numbers with the names of some urban residents recoverable for Ulster from the undertakers certificates returned to the 1622 commissioners (National Library of Ireland, MS 8012-5), the Muster roll of 1630 (British Library, Add, 4777), and for both Ulster and other planted areas from the hearth money returns of the 1660s which recorded the payment of hearth tax.

These lists of urban residents are important as it is from them that we can obtain some idea of urban economy for the smaller plantation towns. The 1622 undertakers certificates, for example, list tanners, smiths, cloth workers, shoe makers, millers, masons, butchers, carpenters and weavers in the towns as well as people who held farms in the surrounding countryside. Small towns provided services for their hinterlands, the most important being markets and fairs which linked these towns with the wider world. Market crosses and poles are prominent on Raven's Londonderry maps and the planned square, or diamond, in Ulster plantation towns points to the importance of the marketplace. It is possible to trace the creation of markets and fairs through the grants made by central government to landowners to hold these events which are listed in the nineteenth century parliamentary paper *Report of the fairs and markets for Ireland*, 1674 H.C. 1852-3 xli. One needs to be wary of this source for it is as much an expression of wishes as a record of reality. Many landlords took out grants of markets and fairs in the hope of quick profit only to see them fail within a few years. It is necessary to match the awarding of a grant with evidence that a fair was actually held by finding that it was recorded in an almanac such as Richard Bourke's almanac in 1683. Even its non-appearance here is only suggestive that the market or fair was not held since landlords paid to have these events noted in almanacs and some may not have done so.

In the plantation towns that were also ports we have additional evidence for trading activity. The port books for Derry and Coleraine, as well as for some non-plantation towns, have survived for 1612-15 in Leeds City Library as part of the Temple Newsham collection. After 1615, and for other parts of the country, we are dependent for information about trade on the English port books in the Public Record Office, London. In some ways this is unsatisfactory but archaeological evidence in the future may tell us more about non-English trade. The importance of the port books lies in the fact that they give us not only cargoes but also the merchant's name. It therefore becomes possible to match these names with other sources, such as wills and the depositions taken after the outbreak of the rebellion on 1641 in order to build up pictures of urban wealth and trading patterns. In some ways this helps to fill the lacunae created by the lack of freeman's rolls in plantation towns, which would give a more comprehensive picture of the urban occupational and social structure.

One of the most difficult problems in the study of plantation towns is that of urban government. At the top of the urban hierarchy were the corporate towns which were given royal charters in 1612/13. This process can be traced in the Municipal Corporations reports of 1835-6. Each town with a corporation had a sovereign and some were given the right to elect a member to the Irish parliament. However, it is difficult to know how plantation corporations worked. There are no known corporations books for the Ulster plantation towns before that of Derry in the 1670s (now in PRONI) although those for Youghal and Kinsale, towns which grew as part of the Munster Plantation, do survive and were edited by Richard Caulfield in the nineteenth century. In practice most of these corporation towns seem to have been under the control of local landlords who nominated the first members, who were named in the fiants for the creation of the corporation. These fiants can be found in the Bodleian Library, Oxford, Carte MSS, although most are in the *Calendar of state papers Ireland 1611-14*. Moreover, with the exception of Derry and Coleraine, none of the Ulster plantation corporations was given land by their landlord as the plantation scheme required and hence had no income of its own. In many cases towns, both great and small, were governed by landlords using their manor courts for which no records in an urban context survive.

In many cases the sources for the study of plantation towns in Ireland are fragmentary but just as those towns were dominated by their landlords so it is estate papers which hold out the best chance of making interesting finds relevant to their history. Urban rentals, such as that for Derry in 1628 printed in C.S. King (ed.), *A particular of the howses and famylyes in London Derry, May 15 1628* (Derry, 1936) or collections of urban leases, for example, are often part of larger estate collections and need to be studied further in order to reconstruct the lives of those who lived in Irish plantation towns.

SELECT BIBLIOGRAPHY

1. Central Government Records

H.F. Berry (ed.), *Statutes and ordinances and acts of the parliament of Ireland, King John to Henry V* (Dublin, 1907)

H.F. Berry (ed.), *Statute rolls of the parliament of Ireland, reign of King Henry the sixth* (Dublin, 1910)

H.F. Berry (ed.), *Statute rolls of the parliament of Ireland, first to the twelfth years of the reign of King Edward the fourth* (Dublin, 1914)

Calender of the Carew manuscripts preserved in the archiepiscopal library at Lambeth, 1515-74 (etc.), 6 vols (London, 1867-73)

Calendar of documents relating to Ireland, 1171-1251 (etc.) ed. H.S. Sweetman and G.F. Handcock, 5 vols (London, 1875-86)

Calendar of the justiciary rolls of Ireland, ed. J. Mills et al., 3 vols (Dublin, 1905-)

Calendar of entries in the papal registers relating to Great Britain and Ireland: papal letters, 1198-1304 (etc), (London, 1893-)

Calendar of patent and close rolls of chancery in Ireland, Henry VIII to 18th Elizabeth, ed. J. Morrin (Dublin, 1861)

Calendar of patent and close rolls of chancery in Ireland, Elizabeth, 19 years to end of reign, ed. J. Morrin (Dublin, 1862)

Calendar of patent and close rolls of chancery in Ireland, Charles I, years 1 to 8, ed. J. Morrin (Dublin, 1864)

Irish patent rolls of James I: facsimile of the Irish record commissioners' calendar prepared prior to 1830, *with foreword by M.C. Griffith* (Dublin, 1966)

Calendar of state papers relating to Ireland 1509-73 (etc.), 24 vols, London (1860-1911)

Calendar of state papers, domestic series, 1547-80 (etc.), (London, 1856-)

Calendar of pipe rolls 1224-1348, in 35th-54th Reports of the deputy keeper of the public records in Ireland

R. Dunlop, *Ireland under the commonwealth*, 2 vols (Manchester, 1913)

O. Davies and D.B. Quinn, *The Irish pipe roll of 14 John (1211-1212)* in *Ulster Journal of Archaeology*, 3rd series, iv (1941), supplement

J.F. Morrisey (ed.), Statute *rolls of the parliament of Ireland, twelfth and thirteenth to the twenty-first and twenty-second years of the reign of King Edward the fourth* (Dublin, 1939)

H.G. Richardson and G.O. Sayles, *Parliaments and councils of medieval Ireland* (Dublin, 1947)

H.G. Richardson and G.O. Sayles, *The administration of Ireland, 1172-1377* (Dublin, 1963)

Rotulorum patentium et clausorum cancellariae Hiberniae calendarium (Dublin, 1828)

2. Registers and Cartularies

E. St. J. Brooks (ed.), *The Irish cartularies of Llanthony Prima and Secunda* (Dublin, 1953)

E. St. J. Brooks (ed.), *Register of the hospital of St John the Baptist, Dublin* (Dublin, 1936)

M.V. Clarke (ed.), *Register of Tristernagh* (Dublin, 1941)

P. Connolly and G.H. Martin (eds), *The Dublin guild merchant roll, c. 1190-1265* (Dublin, 1992)

J.T. Gilbert (ed.), *Cartularies of St Mary's Abbey, Dublin* (2 vols, London, 1884-6)

J.T. Gilbert (ed.), *Register of the abbey of St Thomas, Dublin* (London, 1889)

J.T. Gilbert (ed.), *Calendar of the ancient records of Dublin* (18 vols, Dublin, 1889-1922)

C. McNeill (ed.), *Registrum de Kilmainham* (Dublin, n.d.)

G. Mac Niocaill (ed.), *The Red Book of the earls of Kildare* (Dublin, 1964)

J. Mills (ed.), *Account roll of the priory of the Holy Trinity, Dublin, 1337-1346* (Dublin, 1891)

J. Mills and M.J. McEnery (eds), *Calendar of the Gormanston register* (Dublin, 1916)

J. McCaffrey (ed.), *The Black Book of Limerick* (Dublin, 1907)

C. McNeill (ed.), *Calendar of Archbishop Alen's register, c. 1172-1534* (Dublin, 1950)

N.B. White (ed.), *Extents of Irish monastic possessions, 1540-1541* (Dublin, 1943)

N.B. White (ed.), *The Red Book of Ormond* (Dublin, 1932)

3. Annals, Chronicles and Narrative Descriptions

R. Butler (ed.), *The annals of Ireland by Friar John Clyn and Thady Dowling* (Dublin, 1849)

A.M. Freeman (ed.), *Annála Connacht: the Annals of Connacht, A.D. 1244-1544* (Dublin, 1944)

W. Hennessy (ed.), *The Annals of Loch Cé: A chronicle of Irish affairs, 1014-1690*, 2 vols (London, 1871)

W. Hennessy and B. MacCarthy (eds), *The Annals of Ulster*, 4 vols (Dublin, 1887-1901)

S. Mac Airt (ed.), *The annals of Inisfallen* (Dublin, 1951)

G. Mac Niocaill, *The medieval Irish annals* (Dublin, 1975)

D. Murphy (ed.), *The annals of Clonmacnoise* (Dublin, 1896)

J. O'Donovan (ed.), *Annála rioghachta Éireann: Annals of the Kingdom of Ireland by the Four Masters from the earliest period to the year 1616*, 7 vols (Dublin, 1851)

J. C. Walton, *The royal charters of Waterford* (Waterford, 1979)

See also the Bibliography by P.W. Asplin in A. Cosgrove (ed.) *A new history of Ireland*, ii, 1169-1534 (Oxford, 1987), pp 827-941

4. Plantation Sources

D.A. Chart (ed.), *Londonderry and the London Companies* (Belfast, 1928)

G.A. Hayes McCoy, *Ulster and other Irish maps c. 1600* (Dublin, 1964)

R. Gillespie, *Settlement and survival* on an Ulster estate: *the Brownlow leasebook 1667-1711* (Belfast, 1988)

G. Hill, *An historical account of the plantation in Ulster at the commencement of the seventeenth century 1608-1620* (first ed Belfast 1877, reprint Dublin, 1970; Belfast 1977)

R.C. Simington, *The transplantation to Connacht* (Dublin 1970)

5. The Civil Survey

The Civil Survey was edited by R.C. Simington and was published by the Irish Manuscript Commission in Dublin

Vol. I, *County Tipperary, east and south* (1931)
Vol. II, *County Tipperary, west and north* (1934)
Vol. III, *County Donegal, Derry and Tyrone* (1938)
Vol. IV, *County Limerick* (1938)
Vol. V, *County Meath* (1940)
Vol. VI, *County Waterford, Muskerry Barony (Co. Cork) and Kilkenny City* (1942)
Vol. VII, *County Dublin* (1945; reprint 1995)
Vol. VIII, *County Kildare* (1952)
Vol. IX, *County Wexford* (1953)
Vol. X, *Miscellanea* (1961)

CHAPTER FIVE

Records of Central and Local Government after 1700 (Ríonach Ní Néill)

1. Official Papers

Central government records cover all areas of government; the day-to-day affairs and correspondence of the administration, parliamentary debates and legislation, minutes of select committees and the records of state bodies. They reveal the decision-making process of government in urban development. There is a paucity of surviving pre-1586 state records. Thereafter there was an increasing volume of documents as English rule was gradually established over every part of Ireland and the sphere of government activity expanded. These documents record the changing preoccupations of government: property confiscation, valuation and reallocation in the sixteenth and seventeenth centuries; surveys, taxation records, trade and commerce, and infrastructural improvements in the eighteenth and nineteenth centuries, the alleviation of poverty and disease and the problems of economic recession which were of great concern in the nineteenth and early twentieth centuries. Many of these records do not deal directly with towns, and references to individual towns may be buried in them, but if one is interested in a particular topic, such as living conditions in a particular period, or social problems such as drunkenness, or the level of political activity in a town, it is worthwhile to trawl through them.

Central government records are in a number of locations. Most papers are in manuscript form in the National Archives, the National Library and for Northern Ireland in the Public Record Office of Northern Ireland, Belfast. The Irish Manuscripts Commission has printed some earlier records, which may otherwise be too fragile for public access. A number of state papers are still in English repositories. Irish State Papers in the Public Record Office in London are the papers sent to the secretary of state (later home office) by the lord lieutenant, chief secretary and under secretaries in Dublin Castle. The records of politicians and departments in Britain with responsibilities for Ireland are also still in England. (A useful guide to government papers for Ireland under the Union is A. Maltby and J. Maltby, *Ireland in the nineteenth century, a breviate of official publications* (Oxford, 1979). For Republic of Ireland papers see A. Maltby and B. McKenna, *Irish official publications; a guide to Republic of Ireland papers with a breviate of reports, 1922-72* (Oxford, 1980). For Northern Ireland papers see *Catalogue and breviate of Northern Ireland government publications 1922-72* (Shannon, 1974). An account of the English government departments and organisations with records covering Ireland is in A. O'Day and J. Stevenson, *Irish history documents since 1800* (Dublin, 1992). The British and Irish Governments' stationary offices also publish annual lists of government publications, including acts of government, departmental reports, minutes of evidence and reports of commissions.

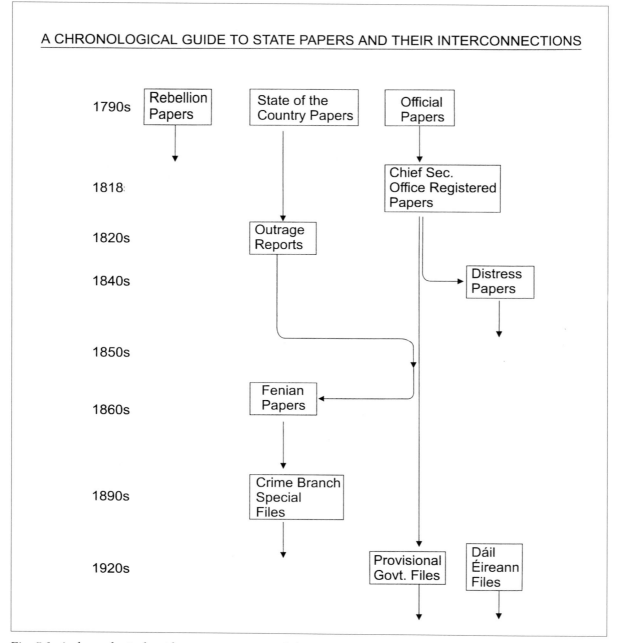

A CHRONOLOGICAL GUIDE TO STATE PAPERS AND THEIR INTERCONNECTIONS

Fig. 5.1: A chronological guide to state papers and their interconnections (National Archives of Ireland).

Records of the State Paper Office

The State Paper Office records are the records of the British administration in Ireland in the period from 1702, when the office was established, to 1922. These are now in the National Archives in Bishop Street, Dublin (fig. 5.1). Fortunately there are finding aids to them, and also the forthcoming *Short guide to the national archives* will list the various state papers in the Archive and how to find them. The records are as varied as the interests of government, although military activities and intelligence reports on suspects and the problems of political unrest feature strongly throughout these records. The following are some of the collections containing records of urban interest.

As heads of state (the lord lieutenant was the monarch's representative in Ireland, and the chief secretary headed the civil service), the lord lieutenant and chief secretary's papers dealt with all aspects of government of Ireland until 1922. Many of these are in the UK, either in public archives or private collections, as it was the usual practice until the late seventeenth century for these officeholders to take their papers back to England after their term of office. (Further description of such papers may be found in A.P.W. Malcolmson, *Eighteenth century Irish official papers in Great Britain* (i, Belfast, 1973, ii, 1990).

After the Irish State Paper Office was established in 1702 some of the papers began to be deposited there. The earliest chief secretary's office records date from 1790.

Official Papers/National Archives

Official papers, which were a class of incoming correspondence to the chief secretary's office, cover the period from 1790 to 1831. They are quite easy to use. From 1790 to 1831 they were classified by date and subject, under 47 headings, such as health, post office, military, public works, many of which deal with towns. Later papers were indexed only and so more persistence is needed to find relevant information. Papers dealing with rebellions and unrest in the country are listed separately in the late eighteenth to early nineteenth centuries. These include the Outrage papers (1832-1852), which were reports to the chief secretary with reference to law and order in the country and are arranged on a county basis by year; Rebellion papers (1790-1807) indexed by person, place and subject and State of the Country papers (1790-1831) calendared by county. An extract from the Outrage papers is included below:

> Robert Little for himself deposith that on the evening of the 18th day of January Inst that he saw a riot in the town of Bantry and that in the midst of said riot he saw Richd Clarke of Bantry with several others yet unknown to said informant – and said informant was struck, kicked and knocked down by some of said rioters – and he also saw the said Richard Clarke, with several others assault the above mentioned William Britt, who was thrown down by some of the Rioters. William Britt for himself deposith that on the 18th day of January Inst he went to the assistance of Patk Sheehan sub constable who was endeavouring to quell said riot, upon which he was assaulted and thrown down by Richd Clarke and others. Informants each bound in the sum of five pounds Sworn before me this 19th day of January 1836, Str to prosecute at the next Bantry Petty Sessions
>
> Richard White, S.O. for further investigation William Britt Robert Little
>
> *Source:* Cork County West Riding, the joint informations of Robert Little and William Britt, National Archives of Ireland, Outrage papers, County Cork 1836; 22.868.

After 1852 these papers on crime and unrest were listed as Chief Secretary's Office registered papers. Other papers dealing with unrest and political dissidence include the Fenian papers (1857-1883), Irish Land League and National League papers (1878-1890), records of the Special Crime Branch (1887-1917), and Intelligence notes (1895-1917).

Registered Papers date from 1818 to 1922. They are records of incoming correspondence which were all listed in registers, hence the title. They have a similar wide-ranging content to Official Papers. The registers, within which correspondence was catalogued alphabetically by subject, person and place, were ordered by year. Between 1835 and 1852 they are also ordered by county.

Parliamentary Papers and Papers of Parliamentary Commissions

Parliamentary records include acts of parliament and reports of parliamentary commissions and committees on the concerns of the day – health, poverty, rebellion, crime, planning (which may contain maps of proposed developments), and education, many of which affected the growth and development of Irish towns. Numerous reports included statistical abstracts, as for example on the state of trade, output and revenues, literacy, and the Irish-speaking population. Some of these give figures for individual towns, making them an easily accessible and valuable source of information.

The best guides to the parliamentary papers are the official *Indexes to parliamentary papers*, published every ten years, with the exception of 1801-1852, for which there are only three indexes, and 1852-1869, for which there is only one. Minutes of the various parliamentary committees can be accessed through the *General index to the reports of select committees 1801-1852*, which is ordered by subject. As the indexes are ordered alphabetically by subject and not by place, material of local relevance can be subsumed under the sheer enormity of information. Unless one has a specific act or commission in mind, then using the papers may seem overwhelmingly difficult. One approach is to choose a subject and date, for example policing in 1804, and search through for local information. A useful introduction to the content of parliamentary papers is A. and J. Maltby's *Ireland in the nineteenth century* (Oxford, 1980), which gives selections of summarised papers under such topics as government, health and living conditions, trade, industry, labour, and civil commotion. Another such book (on which Maltby's was based) is P. and G. Ford, *A breviate of parliamentary papers 1900-1916; the foundation of the welfare state* (Shannon, 1969) which includes a separate section on Irish papers.

Irish Free State and Republic of Ireland (*Éire*) government papers date from 1922. They include the *Acts of the Oireachtas, Dáil Éireann debates* and *Seanad Éireann debates*, all of which are published, as well as departmental papers and reports commissioned by the government. These are held in the National Library of Ireland and are indexed.

Parliamentary records may be divided firstly into those which deal specifically with Ireland, e.g. the records of the Irish Houses of Parliament and post-Independence records, and secondly into those which deal with Ireland in the context of Great Britain and Ireland, e.g. the records of the British Houses of Parliament. (A helpful introduction to the British administrative structure in Ireland from 1800 is in A. Prochaska, *Irish history from 1700: the sources* (London, 1986), pp 8-11).The earliest Irish parliamentary papers date to the first Anglo-Norman king, John, in the late twelfth century. In 1621 all acts from 1310 to 1615 were published, and acts of parliament were published from then on. In addition, the debates and decisions of both the lower and upper Houses of Parliament were published in the *Journals of the house of commons of the kingdom of Ireland* from 1613, and the *Journals of the house of lords of the kingdom of Ireland* from 1634, respectively. These document the daily administration of the country, and contain much of urban interest, touching such matters as state investment in towns, for example in barracks or canals. (H. Wood included a list of parliamentary records dating from 1634 in his *Guide to the records deposited in the Public Record Office of Ireland* (Dublin, 1919). As the English parliament also enacted laws governing Ireland in the pre-1800 period, the corresponding English acts of parliament and journals of the Houses of Commons and Houses of Lords are valuable sources. Hansard, the official record of debates in both houses of Parliament in Great Britain and Ireland, is an important source for contextual information on the great variety of topics within the remit of government. Individual volumes are arranged by parliamentary session and they carry detailed tables of contents. The National Library has a comprehensive collection of English official publications.

From 1800 to 1922, Ireland was governed by the parliament of the United Kingdom of Great Britain and Ireland. British Parliamentary Papers, otherwise known as the Blue Books, record the government of this period, and comprise more than 7,000 published volumes, complete sets of which are held in the major Irish repositories. General reports for the whole country can contain evidence relating to local conditions; select committees interviewed witnesses on a regional basis. The first report of the commissioners appointed to inquire into the municipal corporations in Ireland [23] H.C. 1835, XXXII (fig. 5.2), has been used extensively to detail local government in the early nineteenth century by scholars such as Kenneth Milne. The report of the Fairs and Markets commission has been used by Patrick O'Flanagan to establish a typology of settlement in Munster and Cork, respectively, and Patrick O'Connor has used an impressive range of state papers in his excellent study of nucleated settlement in county Limerick; statistics on all manner of topics were tabulated from a national to parish scale and the replies to questionnaires tabulated and published. The *Commissioners for inquiry into the condition of the poorer classes in Ireland* sent questionnaires on local employment, wages, rents, clothing, housing and emigration to parish priests, Church of Ireland rectors and justices of the peace. They received 1,600 replies which

BOROUGH OF KILDARE.

1. THE Limits of the Borough of Kildare extend considerably beyond the town, and are Limits. stated to include about 3,000 acres of land, known by the name of "the Curragh," and 700 acres of common, lying to the south of the town, called, "the King's Bog or Commons of Kildare."

These appear to be inconvenient limits for municipal jurisdiction, inasmuch as their extent beyond the town, in different directions, is very unequal, and as portions of the district are separated from the rest by the intervention of other lands.

It appears by ancient records that William De Vescy, in the twenty-fifth year of Edward I., 25 Edward I. and in the year of our Lord 1297, surrendered to King Edward "his castle, manor, and county of Kildare, with their appurtenances and liberties;" and that by letters patent, bearing date the 18th of February, in the same year, Edward empowered his chief justice and other persons to take possession of the same, and keep them for his use until further order.

King Edward II., by letters patent bearing date the 2d day of August, in the thirteenth year 13 Edward II. of his reign, and in the year of our Lord 1319, granted to John Fitz-Thomas, and to the 1319. heirs male of his body lawfully begotten, the castle and town of Kildare, with the liberties to the town and castle appertaining, at the service of five knights' fees for ever.

The above documents relate to the town of Kildare, without any allusion to a corporation; and I have not been able to discover in Chancery, or Exchequer, in Ireland, any record of an enrolment of a charter, except one, of the 4 James II., of which mention will be presently made. There was no charter, or copy of a charter, in the possession of any person who attended the Inquiry at Kildare. It was stated by gentlemen, who had been for many years members of the corporation, that Charles II. had granted a charter to this borough; but, although diligent search has been made, no enrolment or trace of any such charter has been found.

An original charter of Kildare has been found in the record office of the Court of Chancery. It is truly described in the book of reference in that office, as "a fragment of an old charter of the town of Kildare." It is so torn and obliterated as to be almost illegible. It is a charter of one of the Henrys; (probably the Eighth;) it is dated "7th October," and contains a schedule of tolls for murage and other public purposes.

I find in the second volume of the "Journals of the House of Commons," of Ireland, p. 539, a report upon a petition of the "burgesses of the corporation of Kildare," under date the 7th of October 1707, in which a witness is reported to have stated before the committee that the charter was lost.

2. A Charter was granted by King James II., dated the 31st of March, in the fourth year of Charters. his reign. It is enrolled in Chancery. (Rot. Pat. 4 Jac. II. p. 2. No. 121.) After reciting that Charter of 4 Jac II. Kildare had been an ancient borough, but that its franchises, liberties, and privileges had been 31st March. seized into the King's hands by a judgment of the Court of Exchequer, this charter declared that Kildare should be a free borough, extending to the same metes and bounds as at any former period, and that its corporation should consist of one sovereign, two provosts, twenty burgesses, and a commonalty; and that all the inhabitants within the borough should be one body politic. It prescribed the mode of electing the officers, contained a grant of a court limited to five marks, granted a free market on every Monday, and confirmed to the corporation all the lands, messuages, curtilages, customs, petty duties, tolls, markets and fairs, franchises and liberties, which they had at any time enjoyed. It reserved to the chief governor of Ireland for the time being, the power of removing all or any of the officers of the corporation, and conferred upon the sovereign, portreeve, and burgesses the right of returning two Members to Parliament. This charter, like the others of James II., was founded on a void judgment, the Exchequer having no jurisdiction to entertain proceedings in *quo warranto*.

3. The Title given to the corporation by this charter, is that of "The Sovereign, Portreeves, Title. Burgesses, and Freemen of the Borough of Kildare."

4. The Officers of the corporation were, Officers.
   One Sovereign,
   Two Portreeves,
   Twenty Burgesses,
   One Recorder,
   One Prothonotary or Town Clerk,
   Two Serjeants at Mace, or Town Bailiffs; and there were also Freemen.

The Sovereign was elected by a majority of the sovereign, portreeves, and burgesses, out of Sovereign, how the body of the burgesses. By the charter of James, he was to be elected for one year, and elected. until a successor to him should be elected.

The day prescribed by the charter of James, for the election of the sovereign, was the 24th of June; but in practice it took place on the 1st of September, to serve for one year, from the 29th of the same month. Three burgesses were proposed, and one of them selected.

Fig. 5.2: Extract from *Municipal corporations in Ireland*, Borough of Kildare, giving four of the fifteen headings reported on in the inquiry.

were printed in three volumes in their 1835 report. (*Report of the commissioners for inquiry into the condition of the poorer classes in Ireland, 1835* (House of Commons, 1836) xxxi-xxxiii. Clare Local Studies Project has published the minutes of the evidence of this commission for the county; see *Poverty before the famine, county Clare 1835* (Ennis, 1996). Records of importance for urban studies include the railway commission report 1837-38 and various reports on markets and fairs, such as the *Report on the fairs and markets for Ireland*, H.C., 1852-3 [1674], xli, an extract from the *Minutes of evidence, 1854-55* [1910] xix which is included below:

Minutes of Evidence
Thomas Rogers, Weighmaster examined.

287. What is your occupation? I am a weighmaster in this town.
288. Under what patent is the market held? I do not know.
289. When was the market established? I believe from time immemorial.
290. How often is it held? Every Saturday
291. Who is the owner of the market? I hold under Lord Headfort, who is the proprietor of the market-place; he built the market house, and leased it to me.
307. What quantity of corn is generally sold during the week in your town? I should say about 300 barrels.
308. What is the largest quantity you ever knew sold in a week? About 1,000 barrels.
309. What is the weight of a barrel of wheat? Twenty stone.
310. What of oats? Fourteen stone.
311. What of barley? Sixteen stone.
312. What of beans, peas and c? Twenty stone.
313. What of potatoes? Twenty stone.
314. Is a hundred weight of weight stone 112 pounds? Yes.
315. What is the weight of a stone of wool? Sixteen pounds.
316. What are the average receipts of your weighing fees? About £50 per annum.
317. Do you think, if a law was passed, providing a public market in every town, with sufficient accommodation to weigh all the produce in the public scales, and obliging all agricultural produce to be sold and weighed there, would it have a good effect? I think it would prevent fraud.
318. Are the weights and measures properly looked after and stamped? I have not known any fraud to arise from want of it.
319. Do you think an assimilation of weights all over Ireland would be desirable? I think it would be of great benefit.

2. Records of Government Commissions and Surveys

It is only possible here to detail some of the more important records for urban history in order to give an idea of the wealth of information in such sources. Records in the National Archives can be accessed via its many finding aids. Manuscript items in the National Library, National Archives of Ireland and elsewhere are accessed via the subject volumes of Hayes' Manuscript sources. Published material may be accessed through the subject volumes of the Printed books catalogue. The more recent papers are good sources for the evolution of government policy concerning urban housing and the provision of employment through industrialisation.

Poor Law Records

The establishment of a nationwide, locally administered, system of social welfare in the nineteenth century resulted in the life of the urban poor being recorded, sometimes in minute detail. Under the 1838 Poor Law Act, local management boards, called boards of guardians, were elected to administer the affairs of poor law unions, each one of which supported a local workhouse. Rate payers within each union's area paid a 'poor rate' to support the boards' activities. There were 163 poor law unions by the early 1920s, when the poor law system began to be dismantled.

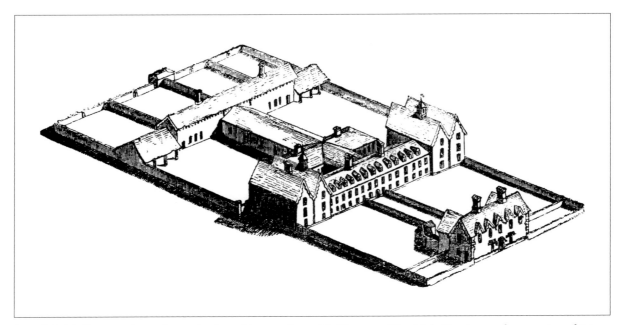

Fig. 5.3: Bird's-eye view of a typical workhouse from N. Kissane, *The Irish Famine: a documentary history* (Dublin, 1995).

The initial responsibility of the poor law unions was to provide poor relief through the establishment of a workhouse system, but they grew to provide local government services (related to public health) such as sanitation (construction of sewers, slaughtering of diseased animals, compulsory vaccination), construction of waterworks and wells, supervisors of graveyards. They had some responsibility for housing through the provision of labourers' cottages, and paid for the services of some public officials, such as doctors and sanitation workers. During the nineteenth and early twentieth centuries, the boards had an important role in alleviating the miserable living conditions in many Irish towns and cities, and in the gradual development of a modern, more healthy urban system. As such, their records are important sources for urban social history.

Workhouses were built mainly in the decade of famine 1841-1851 (fig. 5.3). They were transferred to the local authority in the early 1920s, with the exception of Dublin where the poor law unions continued until the 1940s. Many workhouses were abandoned and are now in ruins; others became county homes under the new dispensation and they continue to function under the regional health boards. The responsibilities of the boards of guardians were transferred to the board of health and public assistance (see records of Republic of Ireland departments in the National Archives) and to the local authority. Outdoor relief became home assistance in the 1920s, administered by the board of health and public assistance. This board was disbanded in 1942 when the county manager system was set up, and its functions were then taken over by county councils until 1978 when the health boards were established.

The boards of guardians for each poor law union generated the following categories of records: minute books of the board of guardians, correspondence, accounts, administration of work-houses, registers of the inmates of workhouses, of workhouse infirmaries and records of out-relief. Of importance are the statistics concerning those being provided for, their names, ages, sex and origin, health and returns of birth and deaths. The indoor register recorded paupers as they arrived into the workhouse. Each workhouse would have produced 30-40 rolls of these registers during its existence, but the survival rate is poor. Eva Ó Cathaoir's work on county Wicklow workhouses and Ann Lanigan's specialised study of the workhouse in Thurles are very fine examples of the use of this material. Most of the plethora of famine books have used this data extensively, for example Christine Kinealy's *The great calamity*. The printed reports of the

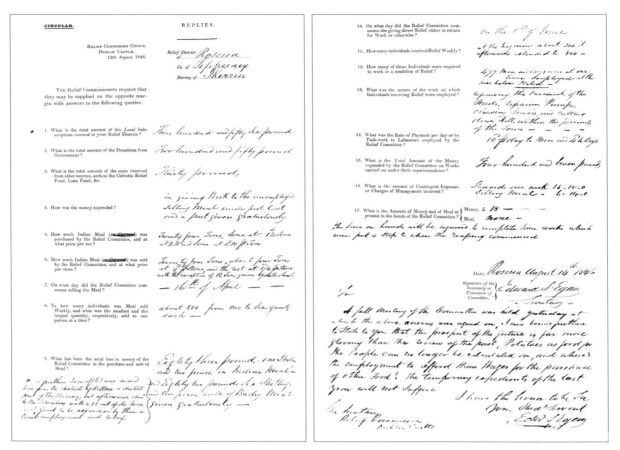

Fig. 5.4: Relief Commission replies to circulars, August 1846, Edward S. Egan of Roscrea (National Archives).

commissioners of the poor law are also of interest, especially with respect to the evidence given on the conditions of persons in the towns.

The bulk of poor law records are held locally, either in county libraries or regional archives. (S.C. O'Mahony, 'The Poor Law records of counties Limerick, Clare and Tipperary', supplement to *North Munster Antiquarian Journal*, 21 (1979), catalogues the extant poor law records of these counties). The National Archives has a substantial collection of board of guardian records. Its Department of Environment archive papers include Dáil Éireann Ministry of Local Government files of poor law union minutes, 1919-1922 and books of transcripts of poor law guardians' minutes, 1916. Board of guardian records for 27 poor law unions in Northern Ireland (which continued until 1948), are held in PRONI.

The Famine Relief Commission was established in 1846 to administer aid to victims of the potato blight. Its records, covering the period 1845-47, are held in the National Archives. They include incoming correspondence from local relief committees and others who applied for assistance and gave accounts of local famine conditions and the administration of relief. The commission sent inspectors to stricken areas to assess the level of distress and make recommendations as to the amount of aid that the commission should extend to them. Their reports, sent back to Dublin, are graphic accounts of the impact of famine in both urban and rural areas (fig. 5.4). The National Archives has two other collections for the famine period – Central Relief Committee of the Society of Friends (Quakers) papers and the Relief of distress papers.

The documentation arising from the solution of the land problem provides information on urban as well as rural Ireland. The Encumbered Estates Court, the Land Commission, and the Congested Districts Board, were all instrumental in transforming the Irish landscape.

In 1849 the Encumbered Estates Court was established to facilitate the sale of debt-ridden estates. (It became the Landed Estate Court in 1858, and the Land Judges Court in 1877.) Town properties, houses, commercial and industrial establishments, were sold through these courts. Between 1849 and 1857 over 3,000 estates were sold through the Court. Its records are useful for tracing now extinct estates, some of which included estate towns or villages. Printed estate rentals are advertisements of the sale of properties sold in the courts. They include the location of the property and its measurements; the contents of the estate (i.e. estate house, farmland, townhouses, industrial premises); the valuation of the properties, owner, and importantly, their title to the property; the names of tenants and their rents and conditions of tenure. All contain maps and many contain lithographs of the advertised properties – including views of town buildings (fig. 5.5). Rentals often had detailed descriptions of the money-making components of a property – such as descriptions of the size of and equipment in a mill, as well as elucidating the locational advantages of an area, i.e. near, or in, a prosperous market town with good transport facilities. Such records facilitate the research of landownership and tenancy patterns in a locality, as well as researching the economy of a town. The National Archives has a set of 75,000 rentals covering the period between 1850 and 1885, and the National Library also has an indexed set of rentals, as has the Registry of Deeds.

The Land Commission was established in 1881. When the Land Commission acquired properties, it also acquired records, such as leases and deeds, relating to their earlier histories. Its records are held by the National Archives but are not accessible to the public. The National Archives also holds the 1922 Dáil Éireann Land Settlement Commission records. The National Library has indexes of the Land Commission deeds, and references to all the estates sold either under the Estate Commissioners or its successor the Irish Land Commission. Because they have both cartographic and descriptive data these sources are invaluable. The index was compiled by the late Ned Keane.

The Congested Districts Board was established in 1891 and it was disbanded in 1923. The annual reports of the Congested District Board, the minutes of the proceedings of the Congested Districts Board and the baseline reports of Congested Districts Board local inspectors document the work of the Board in nurturing economic development along the western seaboard. Much of this material is rural oriented but the Board's infrastructural developments such as harbours, piers and factories relate to towns. The Congested Districts Board and the Irish Industries Association, for example, promoted a hand-weaving industry in Ardara, county Donegal through the establishment of a marketing centre. The National Library has microfilms of the Congested Districts baseline reports, one of the earliest social and economic surveys commissioned by a government agency. Although this report is primarily concerned with conditions of rural life it links country and town through information on employment, migration and markets (fig. 5.6).

3. Census Records

Detailed ten-yearly population censuses were taken for Ireland from 1821 onwards. The earlier censuses are limited and now incomplete, but nevertheless provide some useful information, combined with other population records. (See R. Ffolliott, 'Irish census returns and census substitutes' in D. Begley (ed.), *Irish genealogy: a record finder* (Dublin, 1981), pp 51-74; S.A. Royle, 'Irish manuscript census records: a neglected source of information' in *Irish Geography*, 2, 1978, pp 110-125). The 'Census' of 1659 names 'tituladoes', apparently the persons of highest standing in the local community, and details the numbers of Irish and English. In the northern counties the Scots are classified with the English. This census shows the almost exclusive non-Irish ethnicity of the urban places by this date (fig. 5.7). The Dublin example shown here gives a glimpse of the occupational structure of the city. W.J. Smyth has constructed population distribution maps for the country from the evidence of this census or poll tax.

1868-1878	James Mulcahy, leasing from the Trustees of Lady Margaret Charteris
1878-1880	Charles Wise, of Rochestown, leasing from the Trustees of Lady Margaret Charteris
1880-1891	Susan Wise, leasing from the Trustees of Lady Margaret Charteris
1891-1904	Francis H. Wise, leasing from the Trustees of Lady Margaret Charteris
1904-1916	Lady Margaret Charteris, in fee
1916-1919	The Trustees of Richard B. Charteris, in fee
1919-1922	Jean Wyse, leasing from the Trustees of Richard B. Charteris
1922-1949	Francis Wyse [but Wise, from 1929], leasing first from the Trustees of Richard B. Charteris, and from late in 1922 the Trustees of Lady Margaret Charteris

CAHIR CASTLE
Co. of TIPPERARY
Rae & FitzGerald
Surveyors & Valuers
11 Upper Ormond Quay Dublin

Caher Cottage (The Swiss Cottage), Cahir, Co. Tipperary
Lithograph by Maurice Collis, CE, MRIA
11th of November, 1853
(also superseded by the Rae & Fitzgerald lithograph of 1857, which is utterly charming, and includes the newly constructed rustic bridge.)
NA 1A/3/24:39

Fig. 5.5: Cahir Castle, lithograph reproduced in M. Lyons, *Illustrated incumbered estates, Ireland 1850-1905* (Ballinakella, 1993).

(8.) Markets and fairs for cattle and produce of district; also a statement as to where the people obtain food and other supplies, and the prevailing custom with regard to the disposal of butter, eggs, and poultry; to what extent they are sold in the first instance to local shopmen and dealers, and generally speaking how old the eggs are when sold to the first buyer, and about how old when they reach their ultimate destination in Great Britain.

The principal markets are Kilmacrenan and Letterkenny, the former is attended by those living in Termon Electoral Division. The latter by those in Seacor and Templedouglas Divisions. The principal fairs are in Church-hill and Blownrock, in the district, and in Brockagh, Fintown, Creeslough, Kilmacrenan, and Letterkenny. From Termon Electoral Division some go to Millford Fair. Millford and Creeslough are the most important horse fairs. In Church-hill Electoral Division meal is sometimes obtained from Letterkenny, and sometimes from Millford. It is also obtainable in Church-hill itself. In the upper portions of Glendoan it is obtained at a dealer's at the lower end of the Glen. Tea, sugar, tobacco, &c., are obtained at the small local shops. Butter is sold either by the firkin or in the lump. Those who cannot make up a firkin sell it in pound or two-pound lumps to the local dealers. Eggs are sold once or twice weekly by every one, generally a dozen at a time or two dozen; in exchange for the eggs, tea and sugar are given, but never cash.

Poultry are not much sold throughout the country, though lately a greater quantity was sold owing to the competition between the itinerant vendors who go about from time to time among the houses buying poultry at from 4d. to 1s. and 1s. 3d. a head. Eggs are sold almost invariably to the local shop-keepers and dealers, though a few deal direct with the final markets. The age of an egg varies generally from a day to three days when sold to the first buyer, he may keep it for a week, and then it will probably be another week before it reaches the final market. If eggs are sold to the "tea men" they often keep them for a week or fortnight waiting for a rise in the price. Between a fortnight and eight days was, I should say, the average age of an ordinary egg before reaching the English markets.

(9.) Rail, steamer, sailing boat, road, postal and telegraph facilities.

There is no railway in the district. The nearest railway station is Letterkenny which is ten miles from Church-hill. When the Glenties Railway is completed the station at Fintown will only be five or six miles from the head of Glendoan. A railway was at one time prospected through the district, but the project fell through, owing, I believe, to divisions among the promoters as to which was the preferable route.

The road facilities are, on the whole, fair. A road from the head of Glendoan to meet the Glenties and Letterkenny road a little north-west of Meeniroy Hill would be a most useful link and enable the people to get their produce to the fair at Fintown, which, now the railway passes by, promises to become an important centre. The length of road to be made would be about two miles, and all over a level tract of mountain. The road from the beginning of the glen to the head is rough and badly laid out, but could easily be improved.

The postal facilities might be improved. There is only a postal messenger from Letterkenny to Church-hill and the surrounding country. If a mail car could run through Foxhall, Blownrock, Church-hill, and on to Gweedore or Carrickart, it would be an immense improvement. As it is at present, although the Mail does not leave Letterkenny, ten miles distant, till eight at night, the Post leaves Church-hill at two o'clock, whereas with a through car service it need not leave till five P.M. at least. There are Post Offices at Church-hill, Kilmacrenan, Termon, Swilly Bridge, Glendoan and Rashedoge, at all of which there is a daily delivery. There is no Telegraph Office in the district, the nearest to the district is that in Creeslough, which is about three miles from the nearest point. A line of telegraph through the district is, I think, much needed, either by establishing an office at Kilmacrenan and connecting it with Church-hill, or else connecting Letterkenny and Church-hill. The line might not pay the necessary guarantee at first, but would, I am sure, before very long as people began to appreciate it.

(10.) Employment for labourers in district, whether temporary or constant, and rate of wage.

There is not much employment for labour in the district except in the immediate neighbourhood of Church-hill, where Mr. Hewetson keeps a good many hands working on his estate. Mrs. Adair has at present about fifteen men working at the construction of a new road from Glenveagh Castle to the main road near Gartan Lough. This work will, of course, be only temporary. A soap-stone quarry has been opened in Glendoan, at which about

Fig. 5.6: *Inspector's local reports, Congested Districts Board for Ireland, county of Donegal* – unions of Letterkenny and Millford, report of Mr. Gahan, inspector, district of Gartan.

Parishes	Streets and Lanes &c	Numb's of People	Tituladoes Names	Eng	Irish
	Kysars lane	056	Mchant, Philipp Costleloe Shop Keeper, William Cramby Mct. Regnell Ball gent Ephram Hardy gent	045	011
(folio 16). St Mich- ells Parish.	High Streete	274	Mynard Christian Mctt, William Whitihell Mctt, Doctr Fennell lodgur, William Brooking Mctt, James Wade Apothicary, John Knot clothier, Samuell Chandler Mctt, Capt Robert Locke, Thomas Whitmore gent, Sr Robert Ford Knt, John Smyth Merchant, Thomas Kenedy gent, Joshua Rawlinson Mctt, Mathew French merchant, Stephen Butler Esq, Alderman Marke Quinn, Geo: Fisher Shopkeeper, Francis Har- vy Esq, Alderman Kenedy, Tho- mas Brett gent, Alderman Cooke, Henry Reynolds gent, Rich: Millinton Merchant, Coll Owens, (more tituladoes names), Judge Whaly, Capt Chambers, Capt Chambers, Barnard Wizard, John Foxall Merchant.	220	054
(folio 17).	St Michells lane	120	Thomas Hutchinson gent, Mr Mortomer Esq, Henry Martin Attorny	092	028
	Cork Hill pte	027	— — —	024	003
	Christs Church Lane	047	James Galbelly gent James Jones gent	039	008
	Scoole house lane	021	Thomas Richardson Esq	016	005
	Cooke Street	086	Mr Young gent, William Howard M'chant, Edward Barrytt Grocer, Richard Price gent.	068	018
	Rose Mary lane	018	John Sergent Merchant	012	006
	Merchants Key	049	John Hankshaw Merchant, Mathew Barry Esq, Gerrald Fay gent, Daniell Wybrant Merchant, John Beuchamp Merchant, Maior Brighness gent, Mr Lecch Mer- chant.	043	006
(folio 18).	Skippers Lane	036	Mr Bruister gent, Timothy Miller gent, John Kelly gent, John Bygins Phis'.	026	010

Fig. 5.7: S. Pender (ed.), *A census of Ireland, circa 1659* (Dublin, 1939).

The Religious Census of 1766, carried out with parliamentary sanction, lists the names of heads of households, their religion and the number of their children. However, those not liable for tithe assessment seem to have been omitted. Transcripts of this census made by Tennison Groves are available in the National Archives and in the Library of the Church Representative

Body. Printed returns are in the Genealogical Office. Parish registers recorded baptisms and deaths, and are a useful source on population between census years. After the Compulsory Registration Act of 1863 a civil register of births, marriages and deaths was established (civil registration of non-Roman Catholic marriages having begun earlier in 1845). The records of the Registrar General's Office give a full breakdown of the statistics for births, marriages and deaths in each of the towns of Ireland for the period 1864 onwards.

It is generally accepted that the first reliable population census of Ireland was taken in 1841. The two previous official censuses had serious shortcomings; that of 1821 had grossly underestimated population numbers, while the 1831 census is unreliable. Therefore the 1821 and 1831 censuses must be used with caution. T.W. Freeman used the returns of the 1841 census to produce a comprehensive analysis of population, industry, literacy, agriculture and regions in his pioneering work *Pre-Famine Ireland*.

Census data information is presented in two forms – manuscript census returns, and printed reports. The survival rate of manuscript census material between 1821 and 1851 is patchy. A small amount of manuscript returns survive for 1821, 1831, 1841 and 1851 censuses for parts of counties Antrim, Cavan, Cork, Galway, Dublin, Fermanagh, Offaly, Derry, Meath and Waterford. None survives for the years 1861, 1871, 1881, and 1891. Originals of some of the censuses between 1821 and 1851, are in the National Archives. These census reports, with population figures by townland, and statistical abstracts on topics such as occupations, literacy, housing, were also included in British parliamentary papers between 1821 and 1911, and in Irish and Northern Ireland publications afterwards. Printed census reports are available, in the National Library and the National Archives; there are also microfiche copies. There is a total closure on manuscript census returns after 1926. Only printed reports are available for this period.

The type of information gathered and the manner of its presentation varied from census to census, which one should bear in mind when making comparisons. Census material contains information on population structure, occupations, education, religious denomination and housing quality information which can be used to give a detailed and accurate picture of the general social and economic structure of an urban area. Manuscript census enumerator returns contain the information taken by the enumerator – initially in enumerators' notebooks, and in later years in forms filled in by the household. Returns give information at the level of the individual household and contain the core information upon which the printed reports were based and from which statistical summaries were drawn. There are two forms. Form A (fig. 5.8) recorded the household data, giving details of individual persons, including their names, relationship to the head of the household, place of birth, age, sex, marital status, religious profession, occupation, and education. Form B, the house and building return, recorded the nature and condition of houses, was introduced in 1841 in order to provide information on the conditions of the people and was used to determine the quality of housing. It noted the house number, whether it was built or in the process of building, the type of tenure, building materials (whether perishable or not), the number of rooms and windows, the number of persons in each household and the number of rooms they occupied, and it noted the quality classification of the house.

A classification system was introduced based on quality of house and density of occupation. In practice the census administrators used the following criteria in assessing the value or condition of a house: extent (measured by number of rooms), quality (measured by number of windows), solidity (shown by the material of its walls and roofs). The fourth or lowest class comprised one-roomed, thatched, mud cabins without windows. Slightly better, but still lowly were third class houses, mud cabins with two to four rooms and windows. The typical second class house in an urban context was 'in a small street', having from five to nine rooms and windows, while first class houses were all those of a superior description. The classification system was also based on the density of occupancy of a building so as to give a more realistic picture of standard of living. The following definitions were applied; first class accommodation: first class house, containing one family only (including servants); second class accommodation: second class house,

CENSUS OF IRELAND, 1901.

(Two Examples of the mode of filling up this Table are given on the other side.)

FORM A.

No. on Form B. _____

RETURN of the MEMBERS of this FAMILY and their VISITORS, BOARDERS, SERVANTS, &c., who slept or abode in this House on the night of SUNDAY, the 31st of MARCH, 1901.

No.	NAME and SURNAME. Christian Name / Surname	RELATION to Head of Family.	RELIGIOUS PROFESSION.	EDUCATION.	AGE. Years last Birthday / Months for Infants	SEX.	RANK, PROFESSION, OR OCCUPATION.	MARRIAGE.	WHERE BORN.	IRISH LANGUAGE.	If Deaf and Dumb; Dumb only; Blind; Imbecile or Idiot; or Lunatic.
1	William Ridge	Head of Family	Church of Ireland	Read & Write	61	M	Ironmonger	Married	England		
2	Mary Shannon		Society of Friends	do	44	F	Housekeeper	not married	Kilkenny		
3	Maurice Allen		Church of Ireland	do	17	M	Ironmonger apprentice	not married	Co Tipperary		
4	William Davidson		Society of Friends	do	22	M	Ironmonger	Married	Co Down		
5	Edward Kilroe		Plymouth Brethren	do	22	M	Ironmonger	not married	Roscommon		
6	Samuel Kymer		Society of Friends	do	16	M	Ironmonger apprentice	Married	Dublin		
7	Frederick Matton		Presbyterian	do	24	M	Ironmonger	Married	Co Tyrone		
8	Richd Swaile		Church of Ireland	do	26	M	Clerk	Married	Queens Co	✓	
9	Henry Thompson		Wesleyan	do	17	M	Ironmonger apprentice	not married	Co Dublin		
10	Christopher Williams		Society of Friends	do	19	M	Ironmonger apprentice	Married	Wexford		
11	William Williams		Society of Friends	do	15	M	Ironmonger apprentice	Married	Dublin		
12	Bridget Buggy	Servant	Roman Catholic	do	24	F	Domestic Servant	Married	Kilkenny		
13	Mary O Connor	do	Roman Catholic	do	17	F	Domestic Servant (General)	not married	Dublin		
14	Kate Denney	do	Roman Catholic	do	21	F	Domestic Servant (General)	Married	Mayo		
15											

I hereby certify, as required by the Act 63 Vic., cap. 6, s. 6 (1), that the foregoing Return is correct, according to the best of my knowledge and belief.

William Ridge (Signature of Enumerator.)

I believe the foregoing to be a true Return.

William Ridge (Signature of Head of Family.)

Fig. 5.8: Census of Ireland 1901, form A for 33 Capel Street, Dublin.

containing one family, or first class house containing two or three families; third class accommodation: third class houses containing one family or second class house containing two or three families or first class house containing four or five families; fourth class accommodation: all fourth class houses, all third class houses containing more than one family, all second class houses containing more than three families, all first class houses containing more than five families (fig. 5.9). Brian Murnane's typology of housing in the Mountjoy ward of Dublin is derived from the 1901 manuscript census returns.

Form N, which is the enumerator's abstract for street or townland, is also important. It recorded whether building were inhabited or not, the number of households, of persons per house, the number of males and females per house and their religious affiliations (fig. 5.10).

Printed reports summarised census information at national, provincial, county, barony, civil parish, town and townland levels. Villages of less than twenty houses were not treated individually, but were included in barony-scale summaries. Later printed reports give some excellent details, including essays on particular issues. For example, the 1841 census was the first to include statistics on literacy in the English language. Statistics on the number speaking Irish as well as English were first given in 1851, making it a good source for tracing the survival of the language in the town. Recent research using the manuscript return of the 1911 census for county Down provides a cautionary note concerning the reliability of the census for language statistics. Ó Duibhinn was unable to find any correspondence between the manuscript and published figures, thereby casting doubt on their authenticity. Religious affiliation was also tabulated for the first time in 1861, but on an all-Ireland basis only.

The introduction, the general report, to a census, explains the classification system used in that census and details any changes from the previous census, such as changes in boundary delineations and definitions of towns. The general report often contains some useful tables such as education tables for counties and towns, giving the percentage of the population that could not read or write English, towns arranged by their order of education; or tables of emigration, which gave the birth places of all persons not born within the county/city/town in which they were

100

Four storey over basement first class house, Mountjoy Square.

Three storey over basement first class house, Mountjoy Square.

Two storey terraced second class house.

One storey terraced cottage, Clonliffe Road.

One storey cottage third class, Spring Garden Street.

Fig. 5.9: Brian Murnane's typology of housing in the Mountjoy Ward Dublin derived from the 1901 manuscript census returns. B. Murnane 'The recreation of the urban historical landscape: Mountjoy ward, Dublin, *ca.* 1901' in W.J. Smyth and K. Whelan (eds), *Common ground* (Cork, 1988).

Location	Head of household				Household structure (no. of persons)					
	SURNAME	OCCUPATION	RELIGION	PLACE OF BIRTH	HUSBAND	WIFE	CHILDREN	KIN	SERVANTS	LODGERS
1 Mountjoy Square	Healy	MP-Barrister	RC	Cork	1	1	3		4	
2 Mountjoy Square	Wilkinson	Salesmaster	CI	Meath	1	1	3	1	2	
12 Mountjoy Square	Barry	Cornmerchant, Knights Bachelor	RC	Wexford	1	1	3		2	
29 Mountjoy Square	Hutton	Coachbuilder	CI	Dublin	1	1	1		3	
53 Clonliffe Road	Byrne	Timber merchant	RC	Down	1	1	7		1	1
71 Clonliffe Road	Davies	Accountant	MT	Kildare	1	1	3		1	
43 Charleville Ave	Biggar	Accountant	MT	Scotland	1	1	4			
27 Nottingham Street	Wherry	Chief Steward	CI	England	1	1	3		1	1
4 Emmet Street	Howe	Journalist	CI	Kilkenny	1	1	3		1	
12 O'Sullivan Ave.	Little	Printer	CI	England	1	1	3			
17 Clonliffe Ave.	Boyle	Lithoprinter	RC	Dublin	1	1	9	1		
1 Summerhill Parade	Fitzsimon	Corn, potato factor	RC	Dublin	1	1		1	1	1
23 Upr. Gloucester St	Fitzpatrick	Baker	RC	Dublin	1	1	6			
	Mrs Cooley	Wife	RC	Queens		1	4			
	Bradshaw	Van driver	CI	Wicklow	1	1	3			
	Mrs Fitzpatrick	Wife	RC	Dublin		1	3	1		
	Callan	Labourer	RC	Louth	1	1	2			
	Mrs Kelly	—	RC	West-Meath				3		
	Mrs Doyle	Charwoman	RC	Dublin		1	2			
	Mrs Dalton	Charwoman	RC	Dublin		1				
	Miss Callan	French polisher	RC	Dublin		1				
	Cooke	Labourer	RC	Dublin	1	1				
	Gray	Labourer	RC	Kildare	1	1	1			
24 Lr. Gloucester St	Mrs Griffin	Domestic	RC	Queens		1	2			
	Mrs McHugh	—	RC	Galway		1	2			
	Doyle	Coach builder	RC	Dublin	1	1	6			
	Mrs Shanley	Domestic	RC	Longford		1				1
	O'Connor	Joiner	RC	Galway	1	1	1			
	Boole	Labourer	CI	England	1		1			
14 Middle Gardiner St	Lawes	Labourer	RC	Dublin	1	1	3			
	Murray	Brass moulder	RC	Dublin	1	1	2			
	Mrs Lyons	Scholar	RC	Dublin		1	1	1		
	McKinley	Labourer	RC	Dublin	1	1	3	1		
	Mrs Brennan	Bookfolder	RC	Dublin		1				

Fig. 5.10: Samples of household composition in Mountjoy Ward 1901 showing variations in occupancy density and social class, from Murnane, 'Mountjoy ward' (see fig. 5.9).

dwelling; whether they were born in adjoining counties, in other provinces, in Great Britain, or in foreign countries.

Detailed occupational tables ('division of persons'), from the census of 1851, allows the economic structure of Irish towns to be analysed, and the summary of Ireland tables of occupation allows the local situation to be placed within an all-Ireland context. Changes in individual sectors, e.g. textiles, can be traced for the period 1841-71 but direct comparisons with later census years are more problematic, as the system of occupational classification was altered Problems with respect to the accuracy of census data are addressed in chapter ten below.

CITY OF KILKENNY.

PARISHES.	AREA.			POPULATION IN 1841.			POPULATION IN 1851.			NUMBER OF HOUSES IN 1841.				NUMBER OF HOUSES IN 1851.				POOR LAW VALUATION IN 1851.		
	A.	R.	P.	Males.	Females.	TOTAL.	Males.	Females.	TOTAL.	Inhabited.	Uninhabited.	Building.	TOTAL.	Inhabited.	Uninhabited.	Building.	TOTAL.	£	s.	d.
St. Canices P., pt. of: (q3)	458	1	21	3,245	3,761	7,006	2,763	3,286	6,049	1,243	127	9	1,379	1,089	161	1	1,251	4,248	18	4
St. Johns P., pt. of: (r2)	262	2	31	1,780	2,013	3,793	1,351	1,660	3,011	620	43	1	664	504	35	.	539	3,671	19	0
St. Marys P.,	65	3	24	2,254	2,862	5,116	1,827	2,398	4,225	652	68	3	723	596	147	2	745	8,010	15	0
St. Mauls P., pt. of: (s3)	68	2	15	591	675	1,266	434	535	969	256	22	.	278	203	26	.	229	526	1	6
St. Patricks P., pt.of: (t3)	65	2	30	895	995	1,890	539	645	1,184	286	25	2	313	183	32	.	215	2,192	6	0
	921	1	1	8,765	10,306	19,071	6,914	8,524	15,438	3,057	285	15	3,357	2,575	401	3	2,979	18,649	19	10
Workhouse,	.	.	.	.	.	.	1,735	2,430	4,165	.	.	.	.	7	.	.	7	.	.	.
County Gaol,	.	.	.	.	.	.	207	.	207	.	.	.	.	1	.	.	1	.	.	.
City do.,	.	.	.	.	.	.	39	28	67	.	.	.	.	1	.	.	1	.	.	.
Do. Bridewell,	.	.	.	.	.	.	.	1	1	.	.	.	.	1	.	.	1	.	.	.
Do. House of Correction,	.	.	.	.	.	.	.	57	57	.	.	.	.	1	.	.	1	.	.	.
County Infirmary,	.	.	.	.	.	.	22	16	38	.	.	.	.	1	.	.	1	.	.	.
Total, .	921	1	1	8,765	10,306	19,071	8,917	11,056	19,973	3,057	285	15	3,357	2,587	401	3	2,991	18,649	19	10

(q3) The remainder of the parish of St. Canices is in the baronies of Crannagh and Shillelogher; the entire parish contains 7,686 persons.
(r3) The remainder of the parish of St. Johns is in the baronies of Gowran and Shillelogher; the entire parish contains 8,722 persons.
(s3) The remainder of the parish of St. Mauls is in the barony of Gowran; the entire parish contains 1,128 persons.
(t3) The remainder of the parish of St. Patricks is in the barony of Shillelogher; the entire parish contains 2,419 persons.

N.B.—The Government Valuation of the city of Kilkenny, made in 1850, under the direction of Mr. GRIFFITH, amounted to £20,622 9s. 0d.

Fig. 5.11: *Extract from the Census of Ireland 1881* relating to the city of Kilkenny.

4. Taxation Records

The seventeenth century Hearth money rolls listed the names of all householders with hearths in the country for the purpose of levying a two shilling tax ostensibly for the upkeep of the established church (fig. 5.12). The records are kept in the National Archives. Between 1822 and 1838 a nationwide survey was undertaken in order to calculate a tax – the tithe. The tithe was an agricultural tax, levied on occupiers of land according to the church amount and quality of land they held. The Tithe composition applotment books catalogue these tithes by Church of Ireland parish, and record property sizes and boundaries, head of households, land uses and relative property valuation (fig. 5.13.) (See R.C. Simington, 'The tithe composition applotment books' in *Analecta Hibernica*, 10 (1941), 295-98.) Tithe applotment books do not have a full population count as they only recorded the name of the land-holder. While essentially a record of agricultural land, the applotment books have some information on urban areas, as this example reveals. Tithe records are held in the National Archives. Applotment books for Northern Ireland are held in PRONI. There is also a surnames index for the tithe composition applotment books in the National Library and in the National Archives.

The extension of the British Poor Law of 1834 to Ireland in 1838 required a valuation of property for the entire country, as the new system of state relief was to be financed through the levying of local poor rates. The General valuation of Ireland, popularly called the Primary valuation or Griffith's valuation after its director, Richard Griffith, was a massive countrywide effort at determining the valuation of every single tenement in the country. Records include survey fieldbooks, maps and printed listings. Survey fieldbooks were the notebooks of the district valuers – who assessed the value of properties – and were used in the preparation of the valuation listings. Each tenement was described in them including land, buildings and commercial enterprises (fig. 5.14). The dynamic nature of the townscape is suggested by fig. 5.14, a section of the Valuation manuscript town plan for Kells in approximately 1854 showing part of Headfort Street. The expansion of the Catholic sector which occurred in most towns after Catholic Emancipation

PAROCHIA DE BALLYSTINAN—Continued.

	Hths.	s.
Patrick Hackett, Garran	1	2
William Kelly ″	1	2
Teige Dermody ″	1	2
Thomas Darmody ″	1	2
Conor Meara ″	1	2
Thomas Cowen, Kylballyherbry	1	2
Ullicke Boorke ″	1	2
Roge Ganane ″	1	2
Conor Dwyer ″	1	2
Thos. Rushell ″	1	2
Elizab. Powell, of Ballyherbry	1	2
Donogh McDaniell ″	1	2
John Hall ″	1	2
Richard Blake ″	1	2
William Fahy ″	1	2
Edmond Hackett, Grangeconneta and Grangebegge Vill.	1	2
Thomas Henesy ″	1	2
John McDaniell ″	1	2
Thomas Prutt ″	1	2

	Hths.	s.
George Slaughter, Kyllegh	1	2
Mathew Smith ″	1	2
Donogh Kenedy ″	1	2
Patk. Vyne, Toburdeory	1	2
Roger Higin ″	1	2
Margt. Comerford, Gleanbane	1	2
Edmond Stapleton ″	1	2
William McShauge ″	1	2
Owen McPhippe ″	1	2
Thady McWilliam ″	1	2
John Leamy, Rathclogh	1	2
Conor Headin ″	1	2
John Lahy ″	1	2
Mathew Dwyer ″	1	2
Daniell Glishane ″	1	2
Walter Dougan, Graigenoe	1	2
David Quiddihy ″	1	2
John Meagher ″	1	2
William Donogh ″	1	2

Baronia de Elliogurty and Ikyryn.

PAROCHIA DE THURLESSE.

	Hths.	s.
The Lady Viscountesse de Thurlesse	4	8
Ml. James Buttler ″	3	6
Edmond Buttler ″	1	2
John Dwyer ″	1	2
William Lyons ″	1	2
Patrick Gormuck ″	1	2
Richard Purcell ″	1	2
Edmond Sally ″	1	2
Nicholas Walsh ″	1	2
John Hackett FitzJohn	1	2
Jesper Harford ″	1	2
Donnoge Corkerane ″	1	2
Derby Riane ″	1	2
Giles Pitman ″	2	4
James Maltby ″	1	2
Pierce Power ″	2	4
Daniell Kennedy ″	1	2
William Smallbones ″	1	2
Michell Browne ″	1	2
Ullicke Wall ″	1	2
Thomas FitzGerald ″	1	2
Patrick Hackett ″	3	6
Morgan Pheland ″	1	2
Teige Ryane ″	1	2
Thomas Williams ″	1	2
Edmond Gerraldin ″	1	2
Derby Connell ″	1	2

	Hths.	s.
John Hackett, Codagh	1	2
Derby McOwen ″	1	2
William Hicky ″	1	2
John McMahanny ″	1	2
William Meary ″	1	2
Edward Cormocke ″	1	2
John Meagher ″	1	2
William O'Shea ″	1	2
William Purcell ″	1	2
Thos. Power, junior ″	1	2
Donogh Meagher ″	1	2
Richd. Buttler ″	1	2
Arnold Thomas ″	2	4
John Deane ″	1	2
Laghlin Kenedy ″	1	2
Daniell Smith ″	1	2
James Hicky ″	1	2
Patrick Comack ″	1	2
John Hunt ″	1	2
Teige McWilliam ″	1	2
David Hiffernane ″	1	2
Phillippe Hackett ″	1	2
John Flood ″	1	2
William Cormack, Brogmal	1	2
Pierce Purcell ″	1	2
Mrs. Eliz. Grace, de Brittas	2	4
Thos. Grace ″	1	2
James Sherrall ″	1	2
William McConnr, ″	1	2

Fig. 5.12: Extract from T. Laffan (ed.), *Tipperary's families: being the Hearth Money Records for 1665-6-7* (Dublin, 1911).

can be clearly seen, with the construction of new buildings on the properties of the Christian Brothers and the Convent of Mercy. Nos 10-16 Headfort Place were renumbered. The Bank of Ireland had been renamed the National Bank of Ireland and another Bank, the Hibernian Bank, was recently established in no. 23. The Catholic chapel was replaced by a modern church in the 1960s and a petrol station now stands on the site of the then recently enlarged Old Flaxmill.

In the valuation fieldbooks buildings valued at £5 and over were described – their age, dimensions, and condition. These are therefore good sources for architectural history. They are

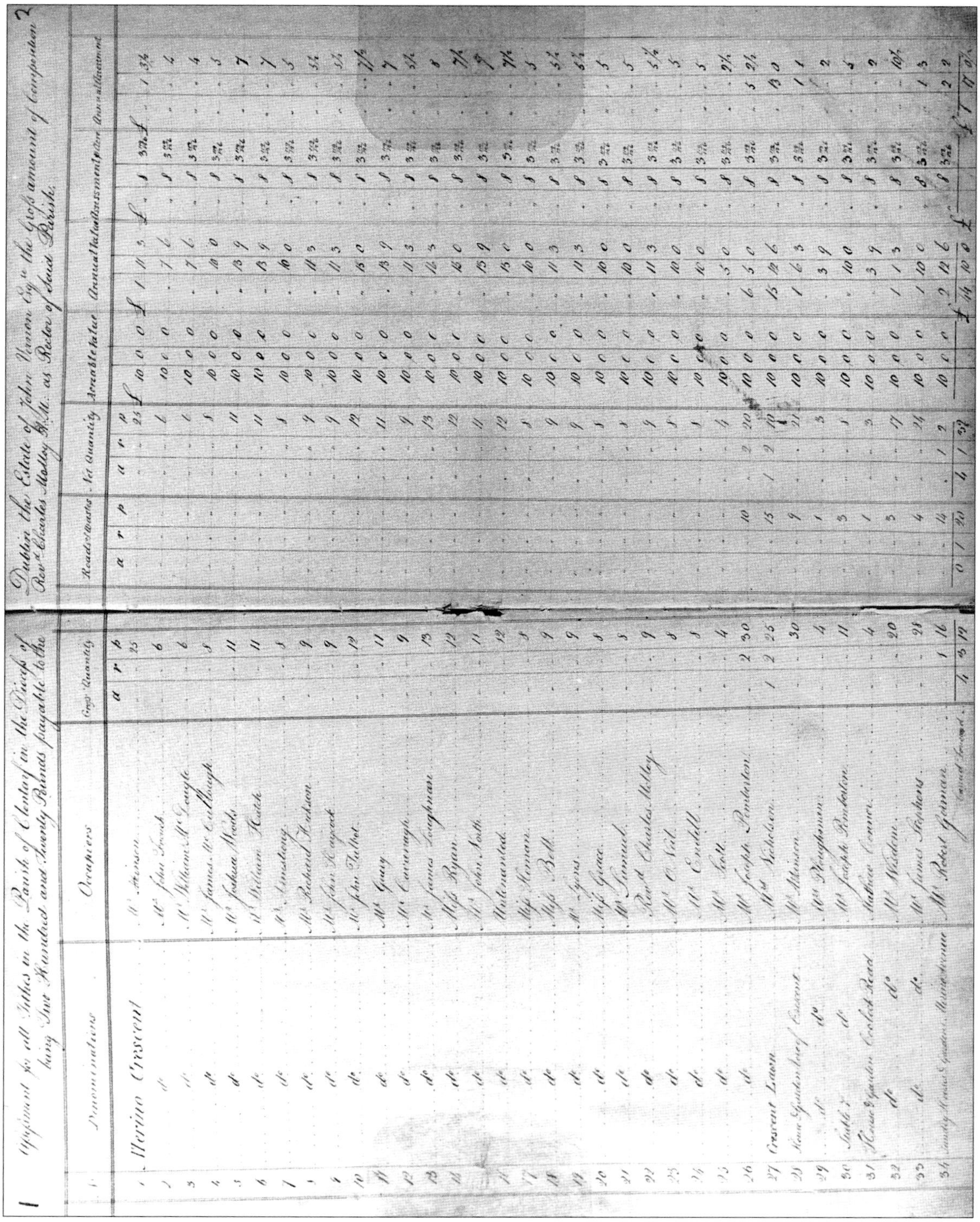

Fig. 5.13: Extract from the Tithe Applotment Books for Clontarf parish, Dublin (National Archives).

Fig. 5.14 (a) (above): Kells (County Meath) manuscript town plan, *ca.* 1854 (General Valuation Office, Dublin).

Fig. 5.14 (b) (right): Printed primary valuation of tenements for parish of Kells (Griffith's Valuation) with subsequent revisions on manuscript books in the General Valuation Office.

No. and Letters Reference to Map.	Names.		Description of Tenement.	Area.	Rateable Annual Valuation.		Total Annual Valuation of Rateable Property.
	Townlands and Occupiers.	Immediate Lessors.			Land	Buildings.	
	BACK-STREET.						
1	Christopher Tormay,	Marquis of Headfort,	House, offices, & garden,	0 0 12	0 4 0	4 6 0	4 10 0
2	Margaret Aughey, .	Same, .	House and garden, .	0 0 15	0 5 0	3 0 0	3 5 0
3	Peter M‘Mahon, .	Same, .	House, office, & garden,	0 0 18	0 6 0	5 4 0	5 10 0
4	James Reynolds, .	Same, .	House, offices, & garden,	0 0 10	0 5 0	6 15 0	7 0 0
5	James Daniel, .	—— O'Farrell, .	House, offices, & garden,	0 0 10	0 3 0	5 17 0	6 0 0
6	Cecilia Smith, .	Same, .	House, offices, & garden,	0 0 10	0 3 0	5 17 0	6 0 0
7	John Lacy, .	Patrick Macken, .	House, coach-factory, office, and garden, .	0 0 22	0 10 0	12 10 0	13 0 0
8	John Campbell, .	James Armstrong, .	House, office & garden, .	0 0 24	0 10 0	9 10 0	10 0 0
9	Michael Dunne, .	Mrs. Denning, .	House, offices, & garden,	0 0 16	0 5 0	11 15 0	12 0 0
10	Catherine Garvey, .	Marquis of Headfort,	House, office, and yard,	—	—	7 10 0	7 10 0
11	Patrick Ellis, .	Catherine Garvey, .	House, office, & garden,	0 0 31	1 0 0	9 10 0	10 10 0
12	James Maxwell, .	Marquis of Headfort,	House and yard, .	—	—	4 0 0	4 0 0
13	Bryan Hughes, .	John Christie, .	House and yard, .	—	—	2 10 0	2 10 0
14	Michael Boylan, .	James Reynolds, .	House and yard, .	—	—	1 10 0	1 10 0
15	James Reynolds, .	Marquis of Headfort,	Forge and yard, .	—	—	1 5 0	1 5 0
16	Vacant, . .	James Reynolds, .	House, office, and yard,	—	—	2 15 0	2 15 0
17	Ptk. Browne & another,	Terence O'Brien, .	House, . . .	—	—	1 10 0	1 10 0
18	Terence Murtagh, .	Same, .	House, . . .	—	—	1 10 0	1 10 0
19	George Plunket, .	Same, .	House, . . .	—	—	1 0 0	1 0 0

also useful for industrial history, as detailed accounts of commercial, and therefore taxable, enterprises, such as mills, were given. Each plot on the valuation maps was numbered in reference to the valuation listing.

Rural valuations were summarised for townlands, urban valuations by street. Valuation listings with this information were published for each barony. The valuation listing includes information on the lessee (the person who occupied the plot) and the immediate lessor (to whom the rent was paid). Major landlords can be identified, and their holdings located. Many geographers and historians have utilised Griffith's Valuation to reconstruct the social geography of towns and villages; the quality of the housing can serve as an indicator of the social status of the residents

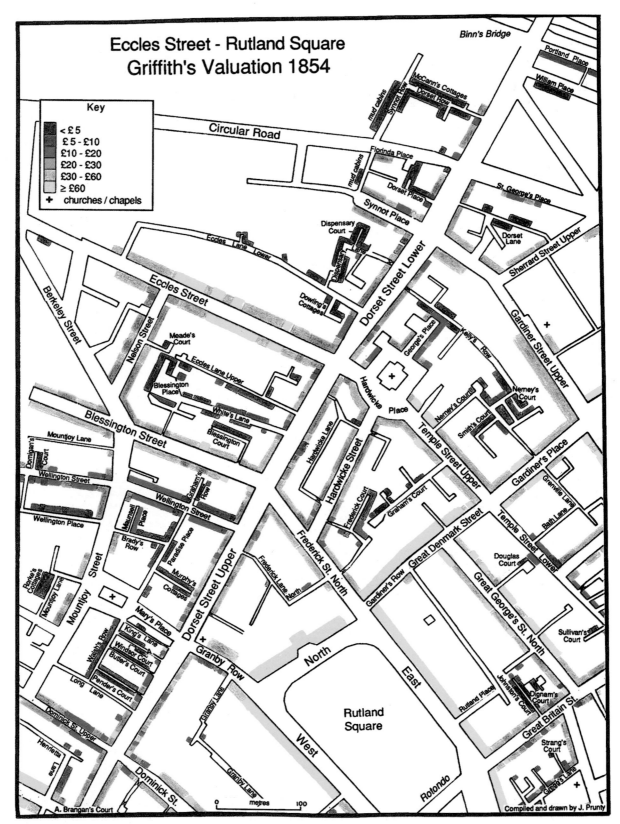

Fig. 5.15: Eccles Street – Rutland Square, Dublin, Griffith's Valuation 1854 (compiled by Jacinta Prunty).

and the countrywide coverage allows comparisons to be drawn. In fig. 5.15 the valuation of houses in the Eccles Street/Rutland Square (now Parnell Square) district in Dublin has been mapped, showing the great contrast between the magnificent houses of Rutland Square (valued between £60 and £250) and adjoining high status streets (Granby Place, Cavendish Row, Great George's Street North, Great Denmark Street, Temple Street Upper) and the huddled maze of back-street houses and cottages hidden behind the grand thoroughfares. The houses of Synott Row and the rear of Synott Place were classed as 'mud cabins' (O.S. first edition, 1838), valued at 31 and 30 shillings respectively. It should be noted that valuations will always be substantially higher in urban than in rural locations and also that the valuation of any one house is not the only guide to its status; subdivision of one family residences into tenements is not fairly represented in the valuation record which deals with each premises as a unit; so care must be taken. The valuations were summarised in the census reports from 1851 onwards. An indexed list of householders in each county between 1850 and 1860, summarised from Griffith's valuation, is available on microfilm in the National Library and in the National Archives where compiled. The National Archives and the National Library also has a surname index to Griffith's Valuation. Valuation of property has continued to the present day on an intermittent basis, but no valuation books were published after the first Primary Valuation. Manuscript annual revisions are available for consultation by arrangement in the Valuation Office in Ely Place in Dublin and scrutiny of these reveals changes in urban property ownership and amendments to property units.

The earlier Townland Valuation, commenced in 1830 in order to levy the county cess, is not as detailed, as this tax was levied by townland and thus individual information on individual tenements is not recorded. A useful exception was that all houses and buildings, including industrial, valued over £5 were recorded and their dimensions detailed.

5. School Records

Until 1831 there was no nationwide system of education, schooling being provided by religious and private institutions. Hedge schools (also known as pay schools or scoileanna scairte) were unofficial Catholic schools, voluntarily supported by pupils, were established during Penal times and lasted into the mid nineteenth century. Their unofficial nature has resulted in a dearth of documentation. Between 1831 and 1922 the commissioners of national education were responsible for the establishment and management of national schools, and the Intermediate Education Board was responsible for secondary schools between 1879 and 1918. Since 1924 all levels of education are controlled by the Department of Education, whose records are held in the National Archives. In Northern Ireland, the Ministry of Education is responsible for schools.

Reports by parliamentary commissions on education are good sources of information on the state of education in the nineteenth century. (D.H. Akenson, *The Irish education experiment* (London, 1970), is a useful guide to parliamentary papers concerning education.) In 1824 a commission of Irish education was established to inquire into the educational institutions in Ireland wholly or in part publicly funded (which included parochial and diocesan free schools) and to formulate a plan of education of the poor. Its records include School Returns 1824-5, which were forms returned to the commission by all schools in Ireland. The second report of the commission of Irish education of 1826 tabulates all Irish schools in existence at that date (including hedge schools) by county and parish, including their names, the religion and income of the schoolteacher, the number of pupils of each religious denomination and a short description of the schoolhouse. This could be compared with the 1835 *Report of the commission of public instruction* (fig. 5.16), set up by parliament to examine the state of education and religious practices in each parish and to establish what changes, if any, had occurred. This report included accounts of hedge schools in each parish, from which one could trace hedge schools serving towns. It listed the number and type of schools – for example whether a hedge school, infants school, or boys and/or girls school; the name of the teacher; the school's source of support – which indicated the sponsor and religion (i.e. schools supported by the Baptist Society); the number of children and their gender and the type of instruction received. As such, this report is a good source for understanding the social structure of a town, from which one can trace the state of education and the variety of religious practices.

Schools managed by religious or charitable organisations are recorded in their respective archives. Parliamentary reports of the commissioners of the board of education, 1809-1812, contain information on diocesan free schools, charter schools and other pre-national school institutions (*House of Commons Papers* 1813-14, v). Other useful sources are the minutes of evidence of the *Reports of the select committee on foundation schools, 1835-36* (*House of Commons Papers* 1837-38, vii), and the minutes of evidence of the *Reports of the committee of inquiry into endowed schools, 1857-58* (*House of Commons Papers* 1857-58, xxii).

Records of the commissioners of national education document every school within the national school system and are in the National Archives. All aspects, from the construction of a school building to its day-to-day management, were recorded, allowing one to trace the origins and history of the local national schools. Financial records document the financial support for schools and their purpose, whether for the erection of a new school building or the payment of a teacher's salary. School rolls give a good impression of the socio-economic backgrounds of the children attending, as the occupation of the child's father was usually entered. Annual school reports sent to the commissioners and reports of exam grades in schools also exist. The correspondence between schools, inspectors, members of the public and the commissioners is of special interest. Of note also are inspectors' reports which, as well as containing descriptions of conditions in schools visited, sometimes contain accounts of general social conditions. They are a useful source for tracing the decline of Irish as special attention was given to the 'problem' of teaching Irish-speaking students. In order to join the national school system, schools had to send in applications to the commissioners, detailing the number of pupils in the school and the subjects taught, as well as giving a description of the premises. Applications were accompanied by an inspector's report and recommendations. The commissioners' annual reports to parliament included tables of grants received by national schools and their pupil attendances.

6. Local Government Records

Local government records reveal the daily concerns of urban administrations, the particular problems experienced and the solutions proposed. Through them one can trace the development of the economy of a town and its physical infrastructure. They deal with the minutiae of local life, from rubbish collection, the provision of charity to the local needy, to minor misdeeds, and often make very lively reading.

The structure of local government has changed over the centuries, making it necessary to access a variety of records. The county council system in operation today was established by the 1898 Local Government Act and took over the responsibilities of a variety of older bodies – the grand juries, poor law unions, board of works, the lord lieutenant, the county sheriff, and Church of Ireland parishes which also undertook local administrative functions, such as the construction and maintenance of parish roads, charity work, census taking, all of which were paid for by a parish tax, called the cess. Many records dealing with local government are held locally, either in the county or town library, or in the offices of the county council. The Society of Archivists' *Directory of Irish archives* is a good means of tracking these records. Although Ireland does not yet have a comprehensive network of local record offices, several local authorities employ professional archivists who have set up archive services, so that the public can consult documents at local level. These include Cork Archives Institute (for Cork city and county), Dublin Corporation, Fingal County Council, and Limerick Regional Archives.

CLASS I.—RECTORIES AND VICARAGES.

BENEFICES.	No. of Schools.	Description of each School.	Sources of Support.	No. of Children on the Books at the time of Inspection.		Average daily Attendance.	Whether the average daily Attendance has been increasing, stationary, or diminishing, for the last five years.	Kind of Instruction.
1. **ARDAGH.** ⎯ Ardagh	1	1. Boys' and girls' school, kept by John Caldwell.	£12 per annum from the Baptist Society.	Males.. Females Total.	60 30 — 90	45	Diminishing.	Reading, writing, arithmetic, and religious instruction daily.
Ballinahaglish .	5	1. National school; Richard Flynn, master.	£8 per annum from the Board; £5 per annum from Mr. Knox, of Mount Falcon; and contributions of the children, from 1s. to 2s. 6d. per quarter each.	Males.. Females Total.	74 20 — 94	50	Stationary.	Reading, writing, arithmetic, and English grammar; religious instruction daily, and the whole of Saturday set apart for it.
		2. Boys' and girls' school; Ann Mulkerin, mistress.	£10 per annum from the Baptist Society; and a house, rent free, from the patrons of the school.	Males.. Females Total.	30 50 — 80	40	Increasing.	Reading, writing, arithmetic, needlework to the girls, and religious instruction daily.
		3. Boys' and girls' school; Ambrose Pugh, master.	£12 per annum from the Baptist Society.	Males.. Females Total.	71 42 — 113	45	Stationary.	Reading, writing, arithmetic, and religious instruction daily.
		4. School; John Pugh, master.	No support at present, as it is in contemplation to have this school in connexion with the National Board.	Males.. Females Total.	58 22 — 80	36	Ditto.	Reading, writing, arithmetic, and religious instruction each Saturday.
		5. Hedge school; James Swift, master.	Contributions of some of the children, from 1s. to 2s. per quarter each, amounting to about £6 per annum.	Males.. Females Total.	21 9 — 30	30	Increasing.	Reading, writing, arithmetic, the Irish language, and religious instruction daily.
Killbelfad . . .	4	1. Hedge school; John Kelly, master.	Contributions of the children, from 1s. to 2s. 6d. per quarter each.	Males.. Females Total.	47 17 — 64	48	Stationary.	Reading, writing, arithmetic, and religious instruction each Saturday.
		2. Hedge school; Peter M'Nulty, master.	Contributions of the children, from 1s. to 1s. 3d. per quarter each.	Males.. Females Total.	40 8 — 48	48	Ditto.	Reading, writing, arithmetic, and religious instruction mostly every day.
		3. Hedge school; Manus Cox, master.	Contributions of some of the children, from 1s. to 2s. 6d. per quarter each, amounting to about £6 10s. per annum.	Males.. Females Total.	55 6 — 61	48	Increasing.	Reading, writing, arithmetic, and religious instruction daily.
		4. Hedge school; Thomas Naughten, master.	Contributions of the children, from 1s. to 6s. 6d. per quarter each.	Males.. Females Total.	53 8 — 61	40	Ditto.	Reading, writing, arithmetic, bookkeeping, mensuration, and religious instruction daily.
Killmoremoy . .	17	1. National female school; Miss O'Connor, mistress.	£8 13s. from the Board; and £11 7s. subscriptions of private individuals, through the Rev. Mr. Costello.	Males.. Females Total.	.. 117 — 117	40	Increasing.	Reading, writing, arithmetic, needlework, religious instruction daily, and the whole of Saturday set apart for it.
		2. National male and female school; Michael Jordan, master.	£8 13s 6d. from the Board, and contributions from the children of 1d. per week each.	Males.. Females Total.	58 15 — 73	60	Ditto.	Reading, writing, and arithmetic; religious instruction daily, and the whole of Friday set apart for it.
		3. Infant school; Miss Fletcher, mistress.	£30 per annum private subscriptions, through the hands of Mr. Langley.	Males.. Females Total.	11 45 — 56	40	Ditto.	Reading, writing, arithmetic, geography, English grammar, needlework to the girls, and religious instruction daily.
		4. Boys' and girls' school; Isabella Brennan, mistress.	£16 per annum from the Baptist Society.	Males.. Females Total.	25 31 — 56	20	Ditto.	Reading, writing, and arithmetic; needlework to the girls, and religious instruction daily.
		5. Boys' school, under the superintendence of the Rev. Mr. Hueston.	£20 per annum from the Rev. Mr. Hueston.	Males.. Females Total.	25 .. — 25	25	Stationary.	Classics, the English language, and religious instruction daily.
		6. Female school; Mrs. Greghan, mistress.	£15 5s. per annum, private subscriptions, through the vicar.	Males.. Females Total.	.. 72 — 72	20	Increasing.	Reading, writing, arithmetic, and religious instruction daily.

Fig. 5.16: Extract from *Report of the commission on public instruction, Ireland, 1835* describing schools in the benefice of Ardagh, diocese of Killala reproduced in K. Hannigan, compiler, *The national school system, 1831-1924, facsimile documents* (Dublin, 1984).

Grand Jury	Destroyed by fire in 1922			Salvaged or acquired after 1922
	Query Books	Presentment Books	Schedules Abstracts, etc.	
Antrim	1787–8; 1790–1; 1807; '08; '17			
Belfast			1784–95; 1808; '12; '17;' 24	
Armagh	1790–1809; '24; '47–87	1832–87;	1811–16; 1832–87	
Carlow	1758–1824; 1826–70	1836–51; Abstracts 1780–1879; 1819–71	1807–1880	Pr. Schedules 1852–59
Cavan		1809–68; 1877–81; 83–86; Abstracts 1852–64; 1870, '72, '77, '79	1842–70; 1871, '72, '76	
Clare		1809–36; 1860–81; 1885–91; 1806–65 (various yrs)	1819–28	
Cork Co.	1779–1850	1768–1880 Account Books 1773–9	1771–1886 inc.	
Cork City				
Derry	1763–1870	1763–1870 (1st series); 1800–70 (2nd series); 1869–95 (3rd series)	1821–42; 1843–93	
Donegal	1767–1892; Query Payment Bks. 1774–94	1768–1891; 1893–9	1777–80, '88; 1827–89	Pr. Bk. 1805–6; Query Bk. 1807–20, 1834, '53, '99
Down	1796–1841; '46–70; '69–72; '91	1802–54	Road Plans 1807–61	
Dublin Co.		1845–96; Pr. Papers		
Dublin City				Some records given to National Archive in 1939 by Dublin Co. Council
Fermanagh	1800–08; 1864–70; 1881–2; 1883–6	Same as Query Bks. also 1872–5; 1880; Abstracts 1871–2; Abstracts 1873–87	1871–72; '75/6; '33–86;	
Galway		1827–75; Papers 1766–1874		Pr. Papers 1895
Kerry	No record of any books destroyed	No record of any books destroyed		Pr. Papers 1886–9 Pr. Bk. 1893–98
Kildare	1788–1882 1877–98	1879; Abstracts 1863–83 1844–60; Pr.	1782–1862; Salt Barony	Pr. Bk. North Papers 1883–99
Kilkenny				
Laois	1782–1888	1783–1803; 1789–1897		"Presentments" 1881–97; Pr. Bk. 1865, '72, '88
'98;				in Co. Lib.: Payments 1834, '73–8, '94

| Grand Jury | Destroyed by fire in 1922 | | | Salvaged or acquired after 1922 |
	Query Books	Presentment Books	Schedules Abstracts, etc.	
Leitrim		1826–87; Abstracts 1821–87	Pr. Papers 1771–1887	
Limerick	1734–1887	1756–1879; 1773–1899		Pr. Bk. 1846
Limerick City	1738–1887	1791–1887		Pr. Bk. 1885–99
Longford	1787–1887; Sec's copies: 1850–77	1787–1887; 1860–77; Presentments 1840–1849		
Louth	1779–1851	1768–1880; 1771–1886; Abstracts 1872–86	Pr. Maps 1795–1863; Acc. Bk. 1773–9	Query Bk. 1851–92; Pr. Papers 1877–9
Mayo	1779–1851 '71, '72, '88	1798–1880; 1827–70	1892–1899	Pr. Schedule Query Bk. 1866
Meath				1761/76; 1785/90; 1800–1835; '35/44; '78/99
Monaghan	1772–1884; 1730–8	1771–1886; Abstracts 1837–84; Presentments 1731–1887	Tres. Acc. 1785–1869	
Offaly	1813–87; 1757–98	1757–98; 1805–17; '19 to '87	Pr. Papers 1746–1887	Pr. Bk. 1892, '95, '96–97
Roscommon	1821–54; 1867–77; Spring 1878; Summer 1874, '82	1872; '81; '82; '83		Pr. Bk: a few between 1880 and 1898
Sligo	1806–87; 1886–7	1820–99; 1796–1878	Abst. 1872–77	
Tipperary N. Riding		Pr. Papers 1832–70; 1809/38 Co. - at-large 1839–70		
Tipperary S. Riding	1803–99	1843–54; 1860–64; 1876–84; Pr. Papers 1839–70; 1871–1887		Pr. Papers 1888–91
Tyrone	1848–86	1874–87	Pr. Papers 1846–1885	
Waterford	1760–1892	City 1859–96; Co. 1810–82	Pr. Papers 1760–1886 P. Rolls 1760–1892	Pr. 1880–82 1895–97
Westmeath	1794–1897	1767–1891; Prs. 1801–99	Pr. Maps 1815–63	
Wexford	1799–1898	1800–44; Abs. 1858–69; 1787–1890	Pr. Papers (various baronies) 1805–70 1854–5 & '69; Maps 1814–40	
Wicklow	1712–1782; 1817–82	1813–87		Pr. Abs 1859–89; Pr. Bk. 1888–98

Fig. 5.17: Reproduction of figure 3 from P. O'Keeffe and T. Simington, *Irish stone bridges, history and heritage* (Dublin, 1991) listing Grand Jury presentment documents in the National Archives.

Corporation Records

Depending on the origin of particular towns, corporation records date to the establishment, by charter, of Anglo-Norman boroughs. Many corporations were dissolved in 1841, but their records may still be available. Louth county library, for example, has records of extinct local boroughs. One should check whether a town was a borough at any time of its history through checking with the local library and local authority. The *1835 (Parliamentary) Report on the municipal corporations of Ireland* is a good starting point. It provides very good potted histories of corporate towns, noting the date of their first charter and its provisions, the rights it held in relation to fairs, tolls, customs duties, the names of corporation officers, burgesses (citizens with civic rights and privileges) in 1835 with their dates of admission to the franchise, holdings of common and corporation land and population.

Some corporation records have been calendered and published. For example the 19 volumes of Gilbert's *Calendar of the ancient records of Dublin* contain extracts from Dublin Corporation records from 1228 to 1841. The National Library has copies of published corporation records. Finding local government records will be much easier with the publication of the National Archives and Department of the Environment *Local authority record survey* which is creating a computerised database of existing records and their location.

The county council system was established in 1898 by the Local Government (Ireland) Act. Each county had an elected council, under which there are subordinate bodies for county districts – urban district councils and rural district councils (now extinct, which had responsibility for smaller towns and villages). In addition to some responsibilities inherited from earlier bodies, local authorities now include housing, transport, sanitation and physical planning within their remit. Corporation and urban district council minutes of relevant committees reveal the daily management of urban areas. For example, the housing records of Dublin Corporation, which are the annual reports of the housing committee, include lists of condemned housing and various clearance schemes, draft plans, various local government reports on housing, photographs and detailed statistical information. Local authority planning records are also excellent sources of information on the physical development of towns, and those responsible for change. Development plans, detailing local planning policy, were established under the Local Government (Planning and Development) Act 1963 and are revised at five year intervals. They consist of maps and written documents stating planning policy for development and conservation, and the objectives (specific works) of the local authority for the next five and ten years. Records of planning applications and decisions, which are usually only comprehensive for the period after 1963, can be consulted in planning departments and document in detail building changes, developers, and their interaction with the planning department.

Grand Jury Records

Grand Juries, the precursors to the county councils, have a very long history; the first being established soon after the Anglo-Norman conquest. The modern Grand Jury system was established in 1736 and was abolished by the 1898 Local Government (Ireland) Act. A detailed listing of Grand Jury records may be found in fig. 5.17, derived from P. O'Keeffe and T. Simington, *Irish stone bridges* (Dublin, 1991), pp 41-3. It is a good guide to extant and destroyed records, especially for the period before 1850. It includes a table of Grand Jury records in the National Archives. Grand Juries operated on a barony and county basis, and consisted of boards of twenty-three landowners chosen by the high sheriff. They were empowered to undertake works within the county, which were paid for by a local tax, the county cess. Until the 1840s, Grand Juries had a wide variety of functions, and carried out the miscellaneous public works of a county. They were involved in the construction and maintenance of the transport infrastructure, and their road building programmes led in part to the development of many market towns. They constructed and maintained courthouses, gave financial support to orphaned or deserted children, lunatic asylums, county infirmaries and dispensaries, and to industrial schools, such as the Artane Industrial School in Dublin. They also financed some public officials, and had some policing responsibilities. Their responsibilities gradually declined so that by the late nineteenth century they were mainly involved in road building and maintenance. Decisions were made at twice-yearly presentment sessions. Presentment books record the amount of tax collected, and the decisions made at the sessions on the uses it was put to. The following extract from a Grand Jurors abstract book records improvements undertaken to roads in Tullamore, county Offaly:

> Granted £268 to William Digan, to repair 1055 perches, road from Tullamore to Philipstown, between three roads at Earl street and barony boundary at Puttaghan (via Charles street), including Henry street, a portion of William street, from Charles street to Pound bridge, from Bury quay to three roads near Bury bridge and Store street, from Cork's bridge to three roads at Bachelor's walk: between the Hibernian Bank at Charleville square and Crow street, and 29 perches of approaches to Cornmarket, at 4s per perch, for three years.
>
> Sureties – Patrick Moran and Joseph Lynch, both of Tullamore.
>
> *Source:* National Archives of Ireland, 'Kings County Abstract Book. Ballycowan. Presentments granted and Queries respited, Summer Assizes, 1891', p. 58.

7. Deeds

Deeds are legal proofs of sale or transfer of property. As such they are important sources for the ownership of property: on the type of landownership (whether or not a freeholder and the type of tenancy); the hierarchy of property divisions; the use of the property; and changes in land-owning patterns. Deeds are useful for determining the socio-economic hierarchy of an area by showing the ownership-tenancy relationship. Omissions occur at the lower end of the socio-economic scale as poorer leaseholds such as the sub-letting of property (tenements), or the letting of smaller premises on the property (as for example slum cottages or small business premises in back lanes) may not be recorded. The varied use of deeds is well illustrated in chapter four of P.H. Gulliver and M. Silverman, *Merchants and shopkeepers: a historical anthropology of an Irish market town 1200-1991*, Toronto and London, 1995, pp 55-88. The authors used deed memorials to chart the evolution of urban property and commercial concerns in Thomastown in the eighteenth and nineteenth centuries (fig. 5.18).

Deeds are in a number of source areas. The Registry of Deeds is the official registry office but as registration was not compulsory, many deeds were not registered and the originals may be in estate records, solicitors' records or family papers. The National Archives has a good selection of deeds from the sixteenth to the twentieth century which were part of estate and solicitors' collections acquired by it. The National Library has 30,000 deeds; these can be accessed through the places volumes of Hayes, Manuscript sources, as can deeds in the National Archives.

The Registry of Deeds was established in 1708 and has over three million deeds from that period to the present (P.B. Phair, 'Guide to the Registry of Deeds', *Analecta Hibernica*, 23, 1966, pp 261-276 is a more detailed introduction to the Registry of Deeds, its records and their uses. It should be consulted before using the Registry). Until 1832, as any document signed and sealed was accepted for registration in the Registry, a variety of legal agreements – memoranda of indentures of conveyance, deeds of partition, marriage settlements, mortgages, leases and wills – were transcribed into the records of the Registry of Deeds. Although leases of less than twenty-one years were exempt from registration, they were often deposited. After 1832 only land transactions in Ireland were registered, with the exception of wills which continued to be registered until 1857. As the main reason for the establishment of the Registry was to enforce the penal codes which prevented Catholics from owning land or from holding leases for over 35 years, property transfers concerning Catholics are under-represented until after the 1780s when

The Legal History of Thomastown's Old Brewery (1765–1821)

c. 1765. The brewery was built by Richard Graves who arrived from Waterford in about 1763.

1787. James Graves, son of Richard (died 1788), mortgaged his interest to Francis Scott, gardener, Mount Juliet, for £344.

1787. A writ was taken out against James Graves and Francis Scott by Michael Kennedy, a Waterford 'gentleman,' for their debt of £48. 7s. 6d.

1787. Michael Kennedy foreclosed and assigned the brewery to Thomas Davis, a 'gentleman' from New Ross, for the residue of the lease.

1790. Thomas Davis and his kinsman, Nathaniel Davis, ran the brewery and enlarged it.

1803. Nathaniel Davis was bankrupt, and later was in gaol.

1803. Michael Duigan, William Davis (Summerhill), John McCartney (Kilkenny, Duigan's solicitor), and Edward Briscoe (Mullinahone) leased the Old Brewery to Kenny Scott, Ormonde Mills, Kilkenny, who set up Thomas Scott, his kinsman, in business. The concern was expanded.

1807. Scott was bankrupt.

1820. John Nugent (a local Catholic merchant) held the brewery.

1821. Nugent leased the brewery to Richard Keefe, farmer, of Rathduff.

Fig. 5.18: An example from P.H. Gulliver and M. Silverman, *Merchants and shopkeepers, a historical anthropology of an Irish market town, 1200-1991* (Toronto, 1995), demonstrating how Registry of Deeds material can be used to document the history of a family enterprise.

these codes were revoked. Also underdocumented were very small tenancies. Registration involved the copying of deeds. The copies are called memorials; they were sealed by the person registering the deed and stored in vaults. Memorials detailed the date of the deed (or other legal agreement), the names of involved parties and witnesses, and the property.

Transcripts of memorials were made into abstract and transcript books, organised by date. These may be consulted in the Registry of Deeds. Memorials themselves may be consulted when there is a doubt as to the authenticity of the transcript. There are two indices to the deeds. The name index lists the grantors of deeds alphabetically by county and barony in volumes ordered by date. The land index of property subject to a deed is organised by county, barony, townland and streets in volumes ordered by date, therefore allowing one to trace a deed even if the owner's name is unknown. Consult the *General topographical index* (Dublin, 1904) to find out the county, barony, townland, and civil parish in which the town is situated. Deeds for property in corporation towns are indexed separately at the back of the relevant county volumes. There is no index for grantees. One should be aware that spellings of names and places may vary from that of the present and thus look for phonetically similar names. One should also be aware whether streetnames have been changed and to search under older titles as well. Microfilm copies of the indexes are also in the National Library. The indexes make it quite straightforward to trace deeds of a town and to trace the deeds for a property back to the beginning of the registry. One should note, though, that the registration of the transaction of property may be quite some time after the transaction occurred (or in the case of wills, years before the death of the grantor). In addition, the old style calendar was in operation before 1752, and the year began on 25 March.

8. Miscellaneous Records

Prison Records

The National Archives has prison registers for over 40 penal institutions. The earliest is for Kilmainham Gaol from 1788, although most are from 1840. It also holds the general prisons board records, and prisoners' petitions (1777-1836). The transportation registers (1836-1857) list sentenced persons, the crime they were sentenced for, where they were to be transported to, and the length of sentence.

Military Records

Records relating to late eighteenth and nineteenth century local militia are held in the National Archives. Surviving ones are of use for tracing military activity in a town and are especially important for the history of garrison towns. Republic of Ireland military records are held in the Military Archives, Cathal Brugha; the Military Archives is open to the public. Much of the material here concentrated on oral records of the War of Independence 1919-1922.

Court Records

The petty sessions courts, established in the late eighteenth century, were the precursors of the district court/county registrar. Their records, held in the National Archives, mostly starting from the 1880s, contain miscellaneous local information. The records are ordered in volumes by county and are well indexed, making them quite accessible. As well as records of the proceedings of the petty sessions court and correspondence with the crown office and peace office, they may include registers for applications for licenses – blacksmith, publican, firearm, dog, the holding of fairs and markets; voters registers and jury lists, which record names and addresses and may be of some use for genealogical information between population census periods; and records of arrears in rents and eviction proceedings. They may contain records from other bodies, for example the crown court records for county Donegal include harbour commissioner records, constabulary papers and census returns. They can also contain maps and plans of local public infrastructural developments such as roads, canals, railways, harbours, piers, labourers' cottages, drainage systems, gas and waterworks, as well as maps relating to court cases. Examinations of suspects and witnesses in criminal cases preserve the minutiae of urban social existence and have been little used, which makes them even more important. These files are in the National Archives.

Harbour Authorities Records and Shipping Records

Harbour authorities or commissions were established from the early eighteenth century – the Dublin harbour authority was the earliest in 1708. The survival rate of the records is poor, but where they do exist they give a marvellous insight into the activities of port towns. Records are also widespread. They are usually held locally but may also be in the National Archives, or in Great Britain. A useful guide is the 'Maritime history sources issue' in *Irish Archives, Journal of the Irish Society of Archives* ii, No. 1 (1992), which details records and their locations.

Although there is no uniformity in the types of records, they may contain shipping ledgers, recording incoming and outgoing ships, their masters, cargo and destination; harbour charges receipt books, listing the ship, its master and the date; harbour import and export books, returns on imports or exports, the vessel, its master, cargo and consignee; harbour labour books; harbour board minute books; and correspondence. They may also include records such as maps and plans, of the development and maintenance of harbour infrastructure. From these one can reconstruct the trading links of a port town, the goods it specialised in, the size in economic terms of the port, and how it developed. Pilot log books, in which the activities of a pilot boat's shift were recorded, give an insight into the daily activities of a port as pilots noted such events as shipwrecks, life-saving missions, altercations with ship captains, and storms.

Many shipping registers from 1863 to 1921 are held in the National Archives. They cover ships

Vessel and Tonnage	BLT	Owners	Captains	Voyages
Waterford Vessels, 1766-1771				
Active			Brown, Lawson, Kirwan 7	France, Spain, Scotland
1. Ann 100	N. Eng. '61	Robert Power	Power, Connolly 12	Briston 6, NF12
1. Anne & Bridget 70	R.I. '69	Wm. & Francis Smyth	Passmore	NF
Bee			Stenger 26	Bristol, S.England 6, Rotterdam 7
2. Beresford		Thos Hill	Hill 19, Connolly 5	Bristol 23
1. Berry 30	Brit. '62	Jacob, Watson & Strangman	Owens 8	England
2. Betsy 40	Plant.		Nowlan, Gaffney, Fling 26	S. England, NF., Iberia
1. Betsy 45	Quebec '64	Peter Duron	Shaw	S. England, W.1.
3. Betty			Egan	Coasting
2. Bridget 130	N.Eng.	Paul Farrell	Berill, Shanahan, Murphy Brown	NF 4, Cadiz 6, Lisbon
Bristol Packet 60		James Wyse	Forristal 20, White, Connolly	Bristol 19, Campvere, Cadiz
1. Brothers 120	Boston '59	Dominick Farrell & Co.	Wiseman 6, Hill, Sinnott, Carberry	NF 6, Cadiz 4
1. Catherine 150	Hull '64		Welsh, Foran, Smithwick	Holland
1. Charlotte 70 (140)	Boston '62	Balfour & Co.	Gaffney 11	Milford, London, NF 6
4. Charlotte 160		Peter Duron	Curtis 10	Philadelphia 6, London, Dublin
2. Charming Molly 60	Brit.		Cherry, Roche 11	Briston, London 5, France, Cadiz
3. Charming Molly			Regan 10	Bristol, London
3. Charming Molly			Heffernan 9, Scott 10	Bordeaux 6, Cadiz, Holland
1. Cumberland 30		Wyse	Carberry	London
2. Diamond 80			Welsh	Cadiz
3. Duchess of Leinster 60		O'Neill	McCarthy	Milford, W.1.

Fig. 5.19: Reconstruction of voyages of Waterford ships in John Mannion, 'Vessels, masters and seafaring: patterns of voyages in Waterford, 1766-1771' in W. Nolan, T. Power and D. Cowman (eds), *Waterford history and society* (Dublin, 1992).

registered in the 26 counties during this period. Northern Ireland records may be held in PRONI. The National Archives also has the records of the mercantile marine office from 1922, but the permission of the office is needed before they can be inspected. John Mannion's work is perhaps the best example of how records of shipping movements and the personnel who organised and directed them can be utilised to highlight the role of maritime trade in urban economics. Mannion made use of lists published by Lloyds of London in the 1770s which name the ship, the surname of the master, where the vessel came from or where bound, the date of arrival at or departure from port. Lloyd's Register supplements this information with detailed data concerning individual ships; Mannion also used newspapers published in Waterford, Kilkenny, Dublin and Bristol to chart the shipping trade of Waterford (fig. 5.19).

SELECT BIBLIOGRAPHY

1. Official Papers

D. Englefield, *The printed records of the parliament of Ireland, 1613-1800: a survey and bibliographical guide* (London 1978)

P. and G. Ford, *Guide to parliamentary papers: what they are, how to find them, how to use them* (Shannon, 1972)

P. and G. Ford, *Select list of British parliamentary papers, 1833-1899* (Oxford, 1953; Shannon, 1970)

J.T. Gilbert (ed.), *Historic and municipal documents of Ireland, 1170-1320* (London, 1870)

A.P.W. Malcolmson, *Eighteenth century Irish official papers in Great Britain* i (Belfast, 1973), ii (Belfast, 1980)

2. Records of Government Commissions and Surveys

A. Lanigan, 'The workhouse child in Thurles, 1840-1880' in W. Corbett and W. Nolan (eds), *Thurles the Cathedral town* (Dublin, 1989), pp 55-80

M. Lyons, *Illustrated incumbered estates, Ireland, 1850-1905* (Ballinakella, 1993)

A. and I. Maltby, *Ireland in the nineteenth century: a breviate of official publications* (Oxford, 1979)

A. Maltby and B. McKenna, *Irish official publications: a guide to Republic of Ireland papers, with a breviate of reports 1922-1972* (Oxford, 1980)

— *Catalogue and breviate of Northern Ireland government publications 1922-1972* (Shannon, 1972)

E. Ó Cathaoir, 'The poor law in county Wicklow' in K. Hannigan and W. Nolan (eds), *Wicklow history and society* (Dublin, 1994), pp 503-81

A. O'Day and J. Stevenson, *Irish history documents since 1800* (Dublin, 1992)

S.C. O'Mahony, 'The poor law records of counties Limerick, Clare and Tipperary', supplement to *North Munster Antiquarian Journal*, 21 (1979)

A. Prochaska, *Irish history from 1700: the sources* (London, 1986)

H. Wood, *Guide to the records deposited in the Public Record Office of Ireland* (Dublin, 1919)

3. Census Records

C. Devine (Ó Duibhinn), 'The Irish language in county Down' in L. Proudfoot (ed.), *Down history and society* (Dublin, 1997), pp 431-87

R. Ffolliott, 'Irish census returns and census substitutes' in D. Begley (ed.), *Irish genealogy: a record finder* (Dublin, 1981), pp 51-74

S.A. Royle, 'Irish manuscript census records: a neglected source of information' in *Irish Geography*, 2 (1978), pp 110-25

B. Murnane, 'The recreation of the urban historical landscape: Mountjoy Ward, Dublin ca. 1901' in W.J. Smyth and K. Whelan (eds), *Common ground* (Cork, 1988), pp 189-207

W.J. Smyth, 'Society and settlement in seventeenth century Ireland: the evidence of the 1659 Census' in W.J. Smyth and K. Whelan (eds), *Common ground* (Cork, 1988), pp 55-81

4. Taxation Records

R.C. Simington, 'The tithe composition applotment books' in *Analecta Hibernica*, 10 (1941), pp 295-8

5. School Records

D.H. Akenson, *The Irish education experiment* (London, 1970)

Reports of the select committee on foundation schools, 1835-36 (House of Commons papers 1837-38, vii)

Reports of the committee of inquiry into endowed schools, 1857-58 (House of Commons papers 1857-58, xxii)

6. Local Government Records

P. O'Keeffe and T. Simington, *Irish stone bridges* (Dublin, 1991)

D. Roche, *Local government in Ireland* (Dublin, 1982)

7. Deeds

R. Ffolliott, 'The Registry of Deeds for genealogical purposes' in D. Begley (ed.), *Irish genealogy: a record finder* (Dublin, 1981), pp 139-56

P.H. Gulliver and M. Silverman, *Merchants and shopkeepers: a historical anthropology of an Irish market town 1200-1991* (Toronto/London, 1995)

P.B. Phair, 'Guide to the Registry of Deeds' in *Analecta Hibernica*, 23 (1966)

CHAPTER SIX

Estate Records (Jacinta Prunty)

1. Introduction

By the early eighteenth century the private landlord had become the most important influence in the creation and remodelling of Irish towns. The varied records left behind, known collectively as 'estate papers', provide invaluable insights into critical periods in the development of many towns, such as the laying out of a new quarter or the erection of an important building under landlord patronage, as well as the more mundane day-to-day management, such as the collection of rents and arrears.

Certain towns are readily identified with particular landed families, such as Maynooth, county Kildare (the Carton estate, of the Fitzgeralds, earls of Kildare) and Strokestown, county Roscommon (the Mahons of Strokestown House), both of which were remodelled as fashionable and valuable urban annexes to the 'great house' itself. Some towns such as Killarney are almost entirely landlord creations, while others exhibit various degrees of landlord influence as in Kells, county Meath and Birr. In parts of the country the landlord influence was by far the most important single factor in urbanisation; in county Monaghan, for example, all the towns were landlord-inspired. Most landlord towns and villages are associated with the largest and wealthiest estates, as indeed even minor remodelling was expensive, and buying out leases, or waiting for leases to fall out so that redevelopment could proceed, was a long process that could span more than one generation of landlord and agent. Perhaps one of the most striking examples was the case of Westport (Cathair na Mart), where from 1750 the landlord relocated the entire motley collection of cabins and houses in the shadow of his house to a new site several hundred yards south of the house at the mouth of the river; here a succession of agents acting on his behalf laid out an orderly new town and supervised its development, with wide and regular streets, meeting at one end in an octagon, lined by slated two-storey houses.

The previous discussion has indicated the importance of estate maps for the understanding of Irish towns. Recently a Leverhulme Trust funded project carried out by Brian Graham and Lindsay Proudfoot has focused on the rise of the small-town bourgeoisie as one of the most significant social changes to occur in urban Ireland. More than 750 small towns and villages have been identified as exhibiting evidence of improvement. The underlying assumption of this research is that landlords were unable to transform the landscape unilaterally, as they were constrained by tenurial and rental practices. Landlords were motivated to invest in urban improvements in the eighteenth and nineteenth centuries out of a sense of paternalistic responsibility as well as for the prestige they gained through the landscaping of their estate-towns. Furthermore, improvements in both marketing and transport infrastructure were the key

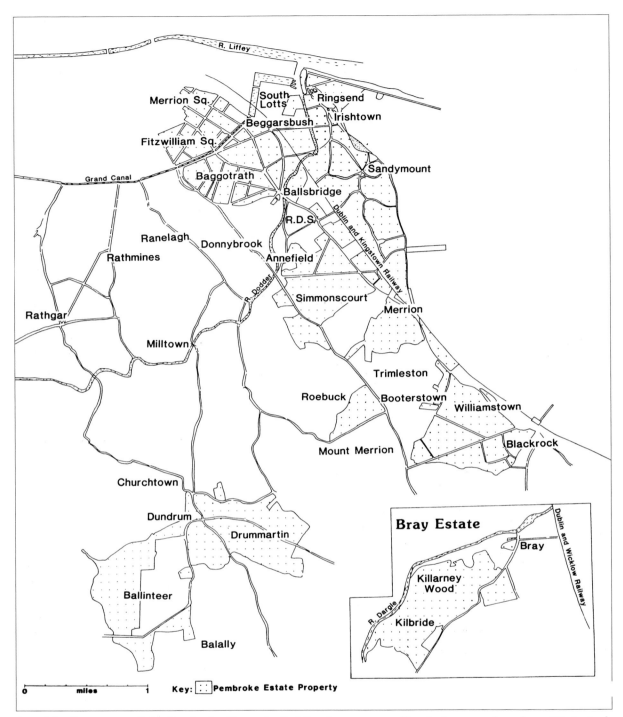

Fig. 6.1: The extent of the Pembroke Estate in Dublin, from estate office index map, based on OS six-inch 1907 edition (compiled by Jacinta Prunty).

to maximising profits from estates. Finally, landlords sometimes manipulated the leases to ensure the support of the urban electorate.

Many private landlords, such as the earl of Meath, owned urban property as part of a larger portfolio. Meath's estate included large tracts of land in county Wicklow as well as the Liberties estate in Dublin, where the family is amply recalled in a number of street names: Meath, Brabazon, Ardee, Earl, and Reginald. It is important to see the urban property as part of the overall estate. In the case of another Dublin property owner, the Fitzwilliam/Pembroke family, its portfolio consisted of a huge expanse of land extending south-eastwards from the high-class

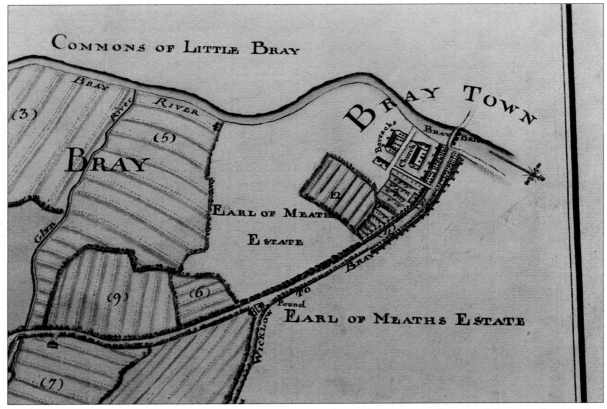

Fig. 6.2: Extract from map of Great Bray in the county of Wicklow surveyed in 1762 by Jonathan Barker (Pembroke Estate papers).

speculative developments of Merrion and Fitzwilliam Squares through to Blackrock, county Dublin, while they also owned land in county Wicklow (see fig. 6.1). In these estate records, therefore, a single letter from the local agent to the landlord would typically include ideas for future development on the urban fringe alongside discussion of the agricultural economy and how it might impact on the estate's rental income. It is also important to note that in some towns, and certainly in the larger ones, there are likely to be several significant estates involved; the records of any one private family will deal almost exclusively with matters relating to their own holdings. In the case of Bray, for example, the Fitzwilliam/Pembroke family owned a number of plots to the south of the bridge (fig. 6.2), while the earl of Meath was the principal landholder in the town; any study of Bray therefore will require access to both sets of records. Estate papers then are to be distinguished from more 'general' sources such as valuation records (Griffith's), the census or the Ordnance Survey which cover the entire area under consideration regardless of individual ownership.

2. Estate Maps

The successful management of an estate created a wide variety of records: property maps, letters, leases, building plans, inventories, rental rolls and financial accounts. Very often transfer to a new heir, or the occasion of his coming-of-age, were appropriate times were for taking stock of the property, and an estate survey, including detailed maps, provided an overview of the situation and a basis for long-term planning.

Maps were commissioned for the purposes of administration and planning; for land reclamation and drainage works; for the laying out of new roads, streets and squares; and most especially for the issuing of new leases both on existing and newly-developed property. Estate maps included both estate-wide and smaller area surveys, while the clear depiction of disputed boundaries was always a special interest. The detail on these maps varies greatly, depending on the purpose for which each was commissioned. Some engineering maps, for instance, concentrate on technical details such as tidal levels and depths, mill-races and land quality. However, the vast bulk of estate maps was produced for the purposes of identifying who was in possession of exactly which plot of land and associated buildings, the duration of occupation, the rental and the possibilities that the disposition of the property gave for increasing future income. The estate map, where each plot was clearly outlined and numbered, with the details attaching to each listed on an accompanying survey sheet, was an essential tool for good long-term estate management and, where urban property was concerned, is invaluable to an understanding of town development. In the decades before the Ordnance Survey (1830s) undertook the production of large-scale town plans (especially the five-foot and 1:2,500 sheets), estate surveys are especially valuable. Some estate surveys are outstanding for their artistic quality as well as wealth of detail, such as the Jonathan Barker survey 1762-64 which is introduced as

> a book of maps and references to the estate of the Right Honourable Richard Lord Viscount Sir William, wherein are expressed roads, rivers, bridges, mills and gentlemen's seats; the quantity and quality of ground plott and prospective view of all the new buildings thereon the whole being accurately surveyed as they were set and held in 1762.

In the maps and bound volume which comprise the Barker survey the details include lessors' names, acreage, field boundaries, dimensions of plot, street widths, tidal/river levels, lease expiry dates, value of encroachment, yearly rental, and in the case of proposed developments, areas 'as designed and laid out for building'. In a later survey of the same estate (Sherrard, Brassington, Gale, 1831) additional columns of information include description of tenement and 'observation', allowing number of storeys, land use and condition of premises to be determined therefrom.

Comparison between estate maps and later Ordnance Survey maps can yield valuable insights; they can also deepen one's appreciation of the high technical standards achieved by early surveyors. In the case of Mount Merrion, a suburb almost five miles from the centre of Dublin city and part of the Fitzwilliam/Pembroke estate, the Jonathan Barker survey of 1762 (fig. 6.3) reveals a very fine 'gentleman's seat' with coach-houses and farm buildings (as in the architectural vignette), with exactly-aligned wide North and East avenues, named fields and formal gardens: the Ash Grove to the south, the Elm Wilderness and garden to the south-west, the Shell House with its radiating lines and the Scotch Fir Grove on rising ground to the west. The modern (1939) OS 1:2,500 extract (fig. 6.4) reveals the extent to which the inherited rural landscape influenced suburban development: field boundaries and routeways are largely preserved, most notably the remarkable geometric gardens to the west, while the original complex of buildings is now in part the site of Mount Merrion church and presbytery. Sycamore Crescent preserves the line of the earlier East Avenue, meeting up with the Stillorgan Road where the abrupt change in alignment marks the former grand entrance to the house. North Avenue is recalled only in a single property line, while the fields between this avenue and the Stillorgan Road are all filled in with suburban housing, with Greenfield Road marking one of the earlier field divisions. The new road names – Greenfield Road, Sycamore Road and Crescent, and Trees Road – have some historical relevance, but unfortunately the more colourful former field names, such as the Upper and Lower Slang, Quarry Field, Pigeon Park, Shoulder of Mutton Meadow and Quicken Park have all been lost.

3. Correspondence

Estate correspondence is another invaluable source for urban history, but will often require that large numbers of letters covering extended periods of time be perused. This will allow the urban material to be extracted, but more importantly it will provide insights into how the estate operated, and the larger context within which urban developments were planned and executed. A well-

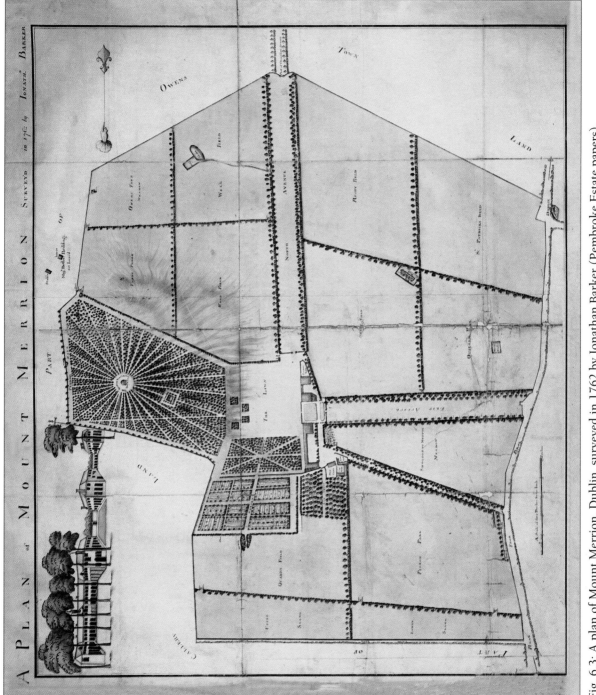

Fig. 6.3: A plan of Mount Merrion, Dublin, surveyed in 1762 by Jonathan Barker (Pembroke Estate papers).

125

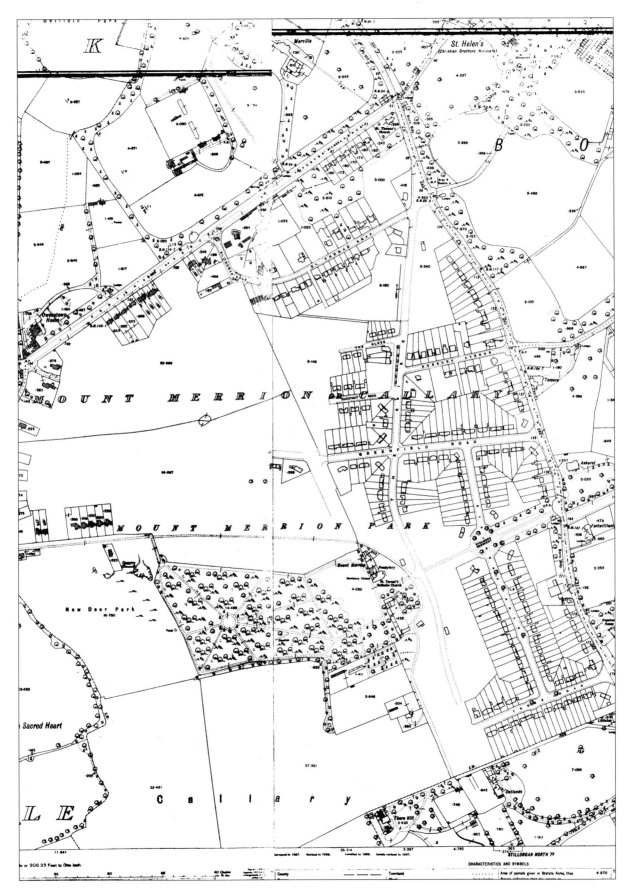

Fig. 6.4: Mount Merrion, Dublin OS 1:2,500, sheets 22, viii, 23v, revision of 1938/39.

managed enterprise such as the Fitzwilliam/Pembroke estate kept copies of all its outgoing correspondence (in bound letterbooks, from 1792) as well as carefully filing all incoming correspondence. Correspondence was kept up with outside bodies such as the corporation, poor law guardians, wide streets commissioners, commissioners of paving and lighting, ballast board, civil engineers and surveyors, and charitable associations as well as numerous individuals, mostly but not exclusively tenants or prospective tenants. Correspondence between the landlord and his/her agent is generally most informative, especially where the local agent is particularly active and voluble. A good example is the correspondence between Barbara Verschoyle, agent to the Fitzwilliam/Pembroke estate 1776-1821, who provided her employer with broad-brush policy suggestions ('to have the pleasure of seeing your Estate improved would be a greater object to you which long leases only will encourage', 19 May 1798), detail on individual tenants and holdings ('Mr Hague is from everything I can know an adventurer and deeply concerned in law', 26 October 1798), progress reports ('the [Grand] Canal as far as it goes through your ground is started on both sides and in a few years will I hope be very pretty indeed', 9 May 1801), interspersed with general rumour as it might affect her employer's interests ('government have I believe an idea of doing something with Ringsend ... there have been several people there this day and yesterday measuring it ... many think it for an artillery barracks', 8 May 1798), along with occasional chiding in cases of neglect, such as the loss of the fisheries in Ringsend ('it is now in possession of the City tho' it certainly was the property of your family and let it be of small or great value should have been preserved', 22 February 1799). The impact of major upheavals such as rebellion, crop failure and currency crises on the estate was relayed by Barbara Verschoyle to her absent employer ('wretchedness seems to stare everyone in the face – yet nothing is done to employ the Poor – no money to be had and how can it be expected that they will quietly starve?', 18 May 1797). The Act of Union, it was rightly feared, would devastate the building trade ('If you were to see how deserted the Streets look at the most Publick Hours you would not think there was sufficient [inhabitants] for those [houses] already built and I fear we shall still have fewer', 9 May 1801). In the case of Merrion and Fitzwilliam's aristocratic squares, Barbara Verschoyle's correspondence to Lord Fitzwilliam reveals many of the complications attendant on these projects, including her wish to have Fitzwilliam as 'an open paved square but I could find none of the tenants to joyen me', and her immense pride in the newly-landscaped Merrion Square, 'it looks so handsome, it is so fashionable a walk and drive there ... you have nothing in London so handsome as Merrion Square – the Irregularity of the ground forms a first part of its Beauty, and I think you will say it is well laid out', (18 May 1797). Where the estate correspondence is extensive and detailed, as in the Fitzwilliam/Pembroke example, we have an invaluable record, on an almost daily basis, of the interior workings of the estate administration, the vision behind various urban development projects, the powers of local agents of change and the constraints within which they operated.

4. Leases

leases were the principal means of regulating building in advance of late nineteenth century by-laws and later planning legislation, and were the most important controls on the development, architectural appearance and use of buildings in any town. Leases detail the length of tenure, the building materials to be used, the length of time allowed for construction to be completed, the annual rent and the permitted uses of the premises so erected, the boundaries of which are often delimited on an accompanying map. Other common specifications were distance from the road and the duty of enclosing the plot with iron railings and paving the area directly outside each house. In the case of Fitzwilliam Square, for example, specific reference is made to the duty incumbent on the residents of enclosing and embellishing the open square, which was not to be used for the herding of cattle or other agricultural pursuits but solely as a pleasure ground for the residents. The fulfilment of the covenants in leases ensured an ordered, aesthetically pleasing

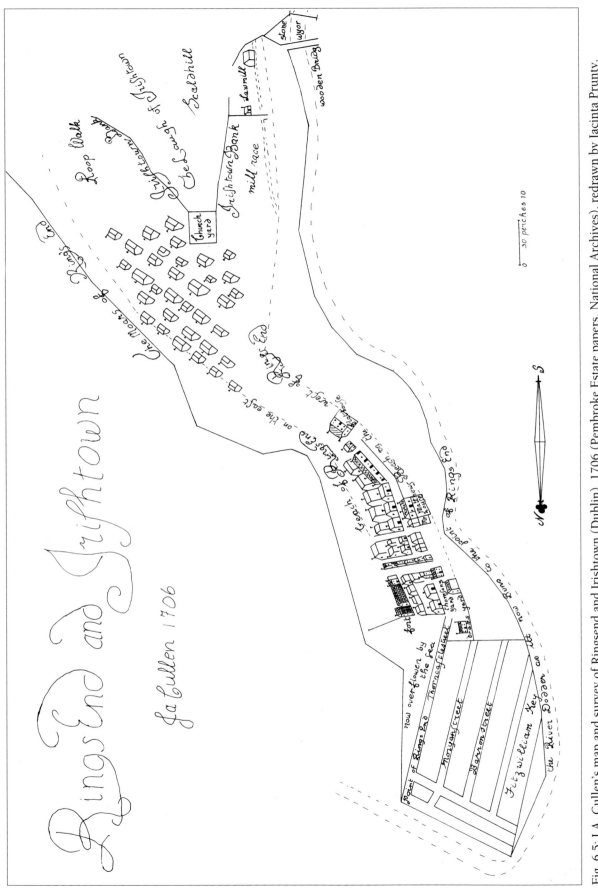

Fig. 6.5: J.A. Cullen's map and survey of Ringsend and Irishtown (Dublin), 1706 (Pembroke Estate papers, National Archives), redrawn by Jacinta Prunty.

townscape, and bears testimony to the lasting influence of the landlord and his agents. No additions or changes to the premises or their use could be made without his/her written consent. The leases issued by a single authority follow a standard formula, but nonetheless deserve very close attention· as any adaptations may point to special local circumstances. In the case of the Fitzwilliam/Pembroke estate, for example, leases for the poorer village of Ringsend allow the building of single-storey houses, while leases granted for very short periods, such as five years, point to plots if not whole streets in a stage of transition. Failure to renew leases often indicates to some strategic planning on the part of the estate, as the more usual practice of granting leases in reversion (i.e. a new lease granted to come into effect on the expiry date of the earlier one), ensured continued tenancy and an uninterrupted rent flow to the landlord. Lease details were summarised in the rent rolls, which were updated periodically, and included information such as street, lessee, date of lease, term and present rental.

5. A Case Study

The example of Irishtown in Dublin illustrates how materials grouped under the heading 'estate records' may prove invaluable in reconstructing the urban past. In the 1700s Irishtown was a small and very poor fishing village on the outskirts of Dublin city and today, although close to the commercial core and transected by major routeways, it still maintains something of its 'village' character. Extracts from the estate maps show the irregular morphology which characterised this cluster of thatched cabins before the active intervention of the landlord in the person of the estate agent Barbara Verschoyle in the 1780s.

Estate maps from 1706 (fig. 6.5) and 1762 (fig. 6.6) show the major physical influences on the development of this remote part of the Fitzwilliam/Pembroke estate: a sandy spit separated on the west from the city by extensive tidal flats, through which the River Dodder weaves an ever-changing route, and bounded on the east by 'The moars of Ring's End' (fig. 6.5) or more simply 'The Strand' (fig. 6.6). The 1706 survey (fig. 6.5) depicts Irishtown as a cluster of cabins, exhibiting little evidence of formal planning, although aligned very generally in a NW/SE direction. This is in marked contrast to its near neighbour, the industrial and tax-collecting settlement of Ringsend, where slated houses of several storeys in a regular street pattern are well established. A close-up of Irishtown in the 1762 survey (fig. 6.7) shows little change. This is the first estate map to depict the Roman Catholic chapel, although it was present from the late seventeenth century (Donnelly (1905), i, p. 52), and the irregular clustering in its immediate vicinity points to it as a focus of early settlement. Of approximately 80 plots referenced for Irishtown in the 1762 survey, no fewer than 60 are entered as 'with encroachment' or 'part encroachment', testifying to the unsupervised and disordered origins of the settlement, but also pointing to future estate policy in its regard, which was to guide regular thoroughfares through the village and work towards unifying the townscape.

Letters from the estate agent Barbara Verschoyle, to Lord Fitzwilliam, can be used to track progress in the remodelling of these two villages. In May 1798 she wrote that 'Mr Verschoyle and I frequently ride through Ringsend and Irishtown and I had several little plans for the improvement of which we had pencilled on this map' (8 May 1798). By April 1801 she could report that

> Mr Verschoyle and I have been busy in taking possession of different holdings out of lease in Ringsend and Irishtown – receiving proposals for them and endeavouring if possible to introduce a little degree of cleanlyness and decency there – they are in Irishtown wretchedly poor – and ever must be so – while they are so idle – I had no idea they were half so bad – until I went through their cabins – when I enquired for the men I was told they were at sea (for they are most all fishermen) and to the women I said what do you do – have you any way to earn bread – do you spin – do you knit – no – we gather cockles, the young ones replied – the old hawked this fish the men caught – in short it was quite

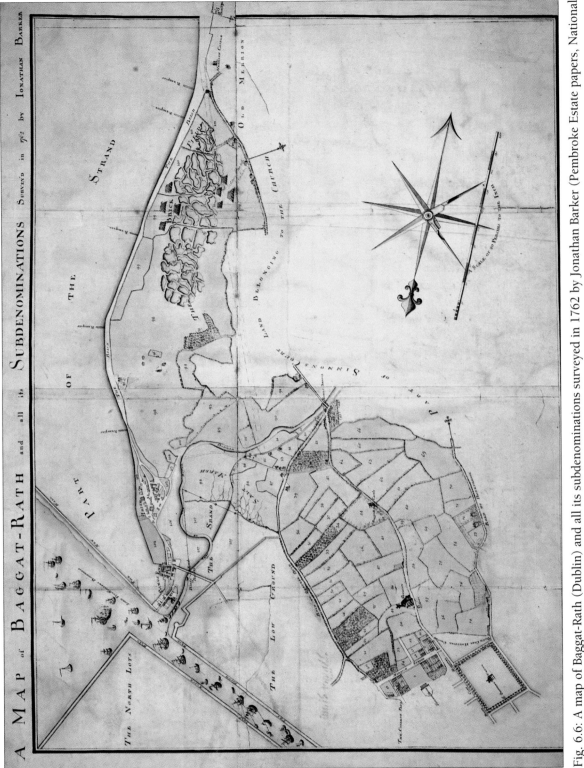

Fig. 6.6: A map of Baggat-Rath (Dublin) and all its subdenominations surveyed in 1762 by Jonathan Barker (Pembroke Estate papers, National Archives).

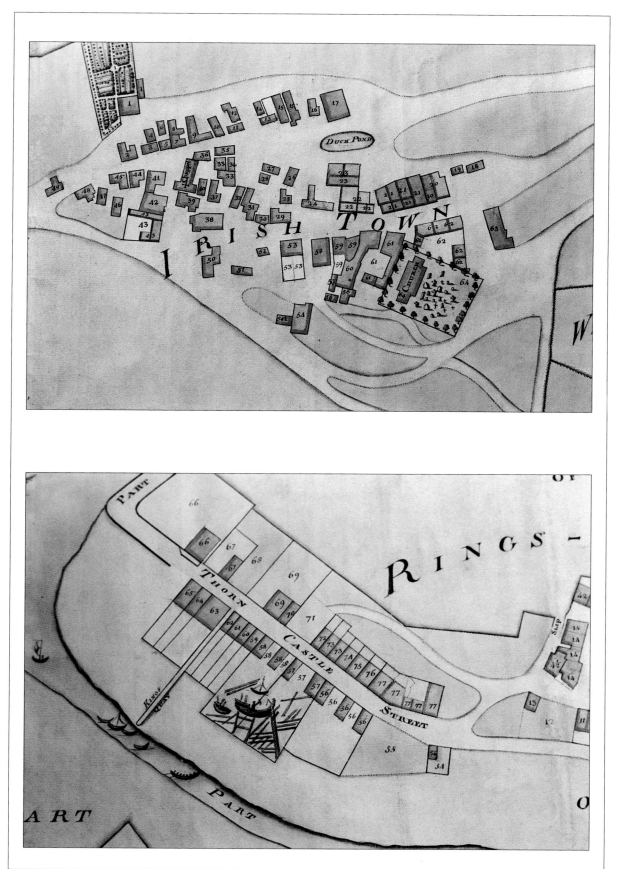

Fig. 6.7: Extracts from a plan of Ringsend and Irish-Town (Dublin), surveyed in 1762 by Jonathan Barker (Pembroke Estate papers, National Archives).

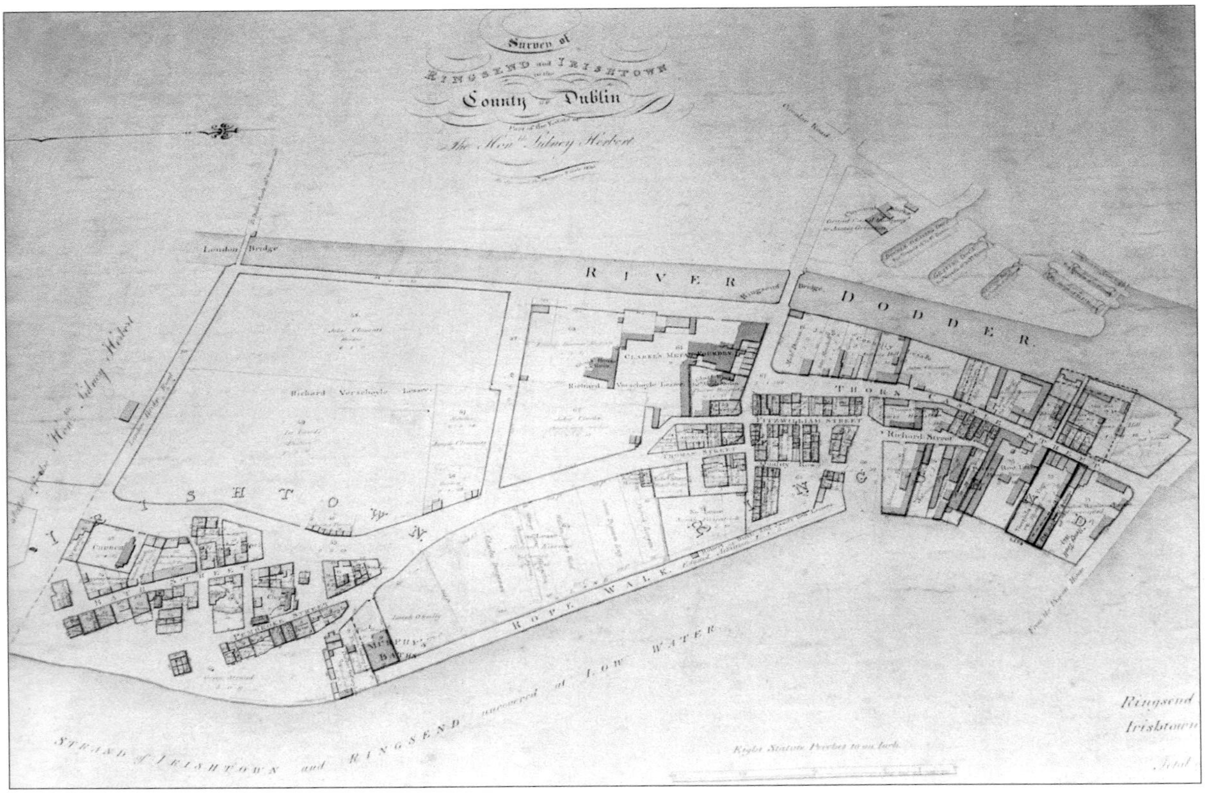

Fig. 6.8: Survey of Ringsend and Irishtown in the County of Dublin part of the estate of the Honorable Sidney Herbert, by Sherrard, Brassington and Gale, 1830 (Pembroke Estate apers, National Archives).

> shocking – the hovels they live in are partly down – some are half down – some the thatch nearly off – yet the unhappy laziness and idleness with which they are possessed prevents them from making any efforts to do better. (15 April 1801)

The improvement of this most isolated and decrepit part of the estate was undertaken in a crusading spirit:

> To get rid of some of them [the Irishtown tenants] and strike terror into others I am sure we will be obliged to throw down some of those half-fallen hovels – or a storm may destroy the lives of many. We have desired such of them as have tolerable decent houses to have them thatched and whitewashed by the first of May or they will be put out, and that if they have done that they shall get those places for 5 or 6 years – upon paying a rent for them and keeping them in order – but such as do not shall be put out at the end of 1 year. We hope this will have a good effect. When we regulate for the letting of those places that are tolerably good – for which we shall certainly try to get improveing tenants – I shall send your Lordship a list of them – as to those that I have described above – I shall let them again, in the way I mentioned, without giving you any further trouble about them (15 April 1801).

While it was relatively simple to insist on white-washing and thatching, and to evict tenants who had not paid rent, real progress could only be made as leases reverted to the control of the estate.

The major London firm of surveyors, Sherrard, Brassington and Gale, was employed by the Fitzwilliam (from 1818 known as the Pembroke) estate in 1830, and devoted close attention to the problematic areas of Ringsend and Irishtown, as well as the poor rural portion of Ticknock (1832) and other parts of the estate. Fig. 6.8 is the 1830 map for Ringsend and Irishtown; the accompanying survey book (1831), which provides detail on each of the numbered plots in this map, exposes the condition of premises (good, tolerable or poor repair/ruins) as well as number of storeys (three, two or one/cottage), and the use to which each premises is put. Irishtown

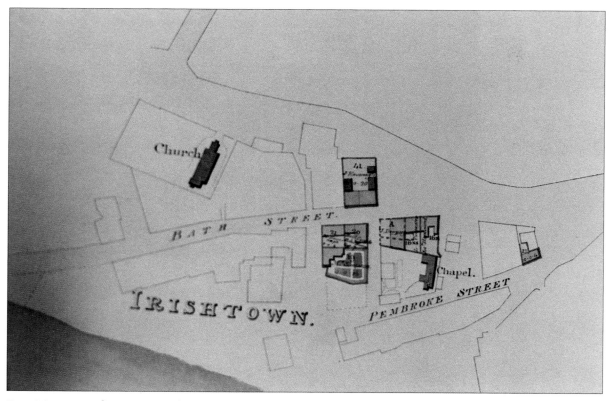

Fig. 6.9: Extract from survey of premises out of lease or to be out of lease within five years in Ringsend and Irishtown in the county of Dublin part of the estate of the Honorable Sidney Herbert, by Sherrard, Brassington and Gale, 1830 (Pembroke Estate papers, National Archives).

emerges as largely one-storey residential, generally in tolerable repair though with individual 'problem' units, The small plot standing alone to the north of the Catholic chapel (coloured in fig. 6.8, clear in fig. 6.9) is one of the many vexations Barbara Verschoyle and her successors faced, and described in the 1831 survey as 'an old house in a ruinous state occupied as a forge'. Fig. 6.9 is a small section of the Sherrard Brassington and Gale 1830 survey focusing on holdings in Irishtown which were now 'out of lease' or would be within the next five years, and for which the plot boundaries could be redrawn and new stipulations for building and use introduced before reletting. Fig. 6.10 illustrates the remodelling which had occurred by 1849. The mechanism for effecting such changes was the lease, as the sample indenture for 1859 (fig. 6.11) demonstrates.

The opportunity afforded by the termination of leases in Irishtown in 1830 (fig. 6.9) allowed the haphazard plot arrangement to be redrawn in several instances, most notably improving the Pembroke and Bath Street frontages by extending the existing plots, and by the creation of two new streets: Chapel Avenue, and Herbert Place (fig. 6.10). The lease stipulations, as illustrated in the case of William Cullen for 1859 (fig. 6.11), granted a long term lease (99 years) in return for completing within two years 'in a good and workmanlike manner' three 'good and substantial dwelling houses of the best materials well roofed and covered with slates', which were to be devoted exclusively to residential purposes. The accompanying sketch map (fig. 6.11) located the site exactly, while ensuring the new dwellings would adhere to the new street line. Comparison of fig. 6.7 (1762) and 6.10 (1849) provides a useful measure of landlord influence in directing the shape of this urban area. The confused plot pattern which persists behind the orderly frontages betrays the earlier haphazard arrangements. While Irishtown was never going to compete with high-class urban developments elsewhere in the Fitzwilliam/Pembroke estate, such as Merrion Street (fig. 6.6), it nevertheless benefited from the close attention of the estate's management, and for the urban historian and geographer this has resulted in an enviable wealth of estate records.

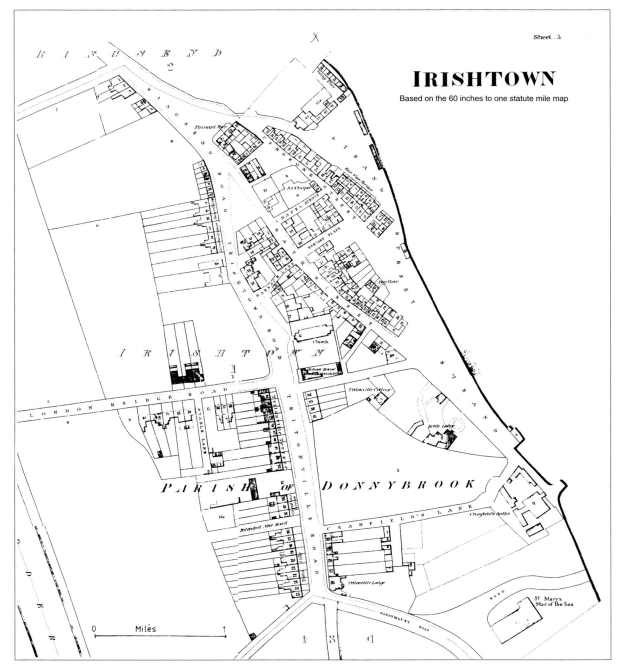

Fig. 6.10: Irishtown, valuation map, Dublin sheet 5, *c.* 1849 (General Valuation Office, Dublin).

THIS INDEMNITY made the Ninth day of April One Thousand Eight Hundred— and Fifty-Nine BETWEEN THE RIGHT HONORABLE SIDNEY HERBERT of Belgrave— Square in the Parish of Saint George Hanover Square in the County of —— Middlesex of the one part and William Cullen of Irishtown in the County — of Dublin of the other part for a term of ninety-nine years for the —— first three years to pay three pounds sterling afterwards to pay six —— pounds ————————————————————————————————————

1.   And also that he shall and will within the first two years of the — said term build and complete in a good and workmanlike manner on the —— said lot and hereby demised Premises fronting to Pembroke Street ———— aforesaid three good and substantial Dwelling Houses to the best —— materials well roofed and covered with slates shall enclose the said —— demised Premises with a stone or brick wall within the first twelve —— months of the said term and that the front of said House shall range —— in the line marked on the said Map and that the area shall be enclosed — with a stone kirb with iron pallisadoes on the top ranging uniformly —— along the said road or street and that the front of the said House(s) —— to the said road or street shall be built of stone or stock bricks ———

2.   And further that he the said William Cullen shall and will ——— insure and from time to time during the said Term keep Insured against — loss or damage by Fire in some one of the Insurance Offices in Dublin —— to be approved of by the Agent of the said Sidney Herbert or other such — person or persons aforesaid for the sum of One Hundred Pounds in joint — name of Sidney Herbert and William Cullen for the time being the House — or Houses and all other Erections and Buildings on the ground hereby —— demised or any of them shall during the said Term hereby granted be ——— destroyed or damaged by Fire and so all such sum and sums of money — as shall become payable and be received by virtue of such Insurance or — Insurance as aforesaid shall with all convenient speed, be applied to — reinstating the said Premises and making the same fit for alternation to — the satisfaction of the said Sidney Herbert or his Agent for the time —— being ————————————————————————————————————

3.   And also that he the said William Cullen shall not nor will ——— during the within term build or cause to be built on any part of the —— said demised Premises any House or Houses save the one(s) so as ——— aforesaid covenanted to be built except a Stable Coach-House or Out —— Offices and that same shall not be used as a Dwelling House or Houses — or be in any manner separated from the House so covenanted to be ——— built as aforesaid without the consent in writing of the said ——— Sidney Herbert endorsed on the back hereof ————————— And in case of or upon any breach of this Covenant the said William —— Cullen shall be subject to a further and increased rent of Twenty —— Pounds per annum to be recovered by all or any of the ways as said —— herein-before reserved Yearly Rent is recoverable —————————

4.   And moreover that the said William Cullen shall not nor will at — any time during the said Term of Ninety-Nine years employ or use or —— permit to be employed or used any part of the said demised Premises or — any Houses or Buildings thereon as a Shop or Tavern or Public House — nor for the purposes of the Trade or Business of a Soap-Boiler Chandler — Baker Butcher Distiller Sugar-baker Brewer Druggist Apothecary Tanner — Skinner Limeburner Hatter Silversmity Coppersmith Pewterer Founder —— Founder Blacksmith or any other offensive or noisy Trade Business or —— Profession whatsoever ————————————————————————

5.   And further that be the said William Cullen shall and will from — from time and at all times during the said term hereby granted at his —— and their own proper costs well and sufficiently uphold maintain repair — preserve and keep all the Houses Buildings and all Erections and ——— Improvements thereon whatsoever which at any time during the said term — shall be built erected made or done upon the said demised Premises or —— any part thereof in good and substantial repair order and condition and — so well and sufficiently repaired shall and will leave and yield up the — same unto the said Sidney Herbert at the expiration or other sooner ——— determination of this present issue in good order repair and condition —— Provided the conditions herein are fulfilled shall and may ——— peaceably and quietly have hold and enjoy all and singular the said —— hereby demises Premises. ————————————————————

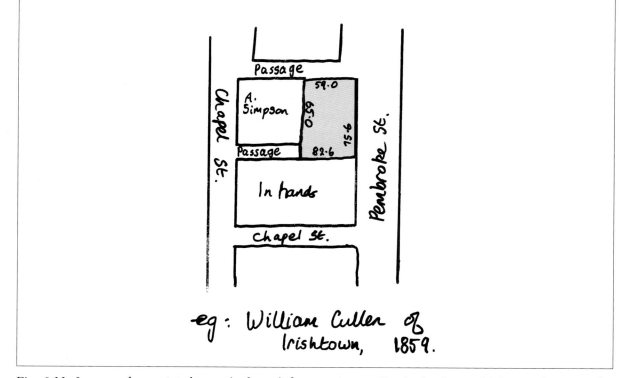

Fig. 6.11: Lease and associated map (redrawn) for premises at Pembroke Street, Irishtown, between the Right Hon. Sidney Herbert, and William Cullen, 9 April 1859 (Pembroke Estate papers).

P. J. Duffy, 'The evolution of estate properties in south Ulster 1600-1900' in W.J. Smyth and K. Whelan, (eds), *Common ground, essays on the historical geography of Ireland* (Cork, 1988), pp 84-109

B. J. Graham and L.J. Proudfoot, *Urban improvement in provincial Ireland, 1700-1840* (Athlone, 1994)

P.H. Gulliver and M. Silverman, *Merchants and shopkeepers: a historical anthropology of an Irish market town 1200-1991* (Toronto and London, 1995)

S. Hood, 'New sources for the history of estate towns in eighteenth and nineteenth century Ireland' in M.D. Evans and E. Ó Dúill (eds), *Aspects of Irish genealogy: proceedings of the first Irish genealogical congress* (Dublin, 1993) pp 150-61

S. Hood, 'The landlord influence in the development of an Irish estate town: Strokestown, county Roscommon' in *Irish Geography* 28 (2) 1995, pp 118-30

A.A. Horner, 'Maynooth' in A. Simms and J.H. Andrews, (eds), *Irish country towns* (Cork, 1994), pp. 59-70

A.A. Horner, *Maynooth, no. 7, Irish historic towns atlas* (Dublin, 1995)

T. Jones Hughes, 'The estate system of landholding in nineteenth century Ireland' in W. Nolan (ed.), *The shaping of Ireland* (Cork, 1986) pp 137-50

N. Kissane, *The landed gentry, National Library historical documents series* (Dublin, 1977)

W. A. Maguire, *Letters of a great Irish landlord* (London, 1974)

W. A. Maguire, *The Downshire estates in Ireland, 1801-1845* (Oxford, 1972)

F. Mitchell, *The shell guide to reading the Irish landscape* (Dublin, 1986) pp 188-202

W. Nolan, *Fassadinin, land, settlement and society in South-East Ireland, 1600-1850* (Dublin, 1979)

L. J. Proudfoot, 'Spatial transformation and social agency: property, society and improvement, 1700-1900' in B.J. Graham, L.J. Proudfoot (eds), *An historical geography of Ireland* (London, 1993) pp 219-57

L. J. Proudfoot and B.J. Graham, 'The nature and extent of urban and village foundation and improvement in eighteenth and nineteenth century Ireland' in *Planning perspectives,* 8 (1993), pp 259-81

L. J. Proudfoot, *Urban patronage and social authority: the management of the duke of Devonshire towns in Ireland, 1764-1891* (Washington DC, 1995)

W. J. Smyth, 'Estate Records and the making of the Irish landscape: an example from county Tipperary' in *Irish Geography,* 1976, ix, pp 29-49

K. Whelan, 'The famine and post-famine adjustment' in W. Nolan (ed.), *The shaping of Ireland* (Cork, 1986) pp 151-66

CHAPTER SEVEN

Church Records (Raymond Refaussé)

1. Archives of Local Churches

Churches, although principally centres of religious expression and experience, have also been loci for social cohesion, charitable activity and education. The churches too have been landowners and developers and, in the case of the Church of Ireland, local authorities. Inevitably, therefore, their records (registers of baptisms, marriages, and burials and related administrative records) are important sources for the study of urban life (fig. 7.1).

As the church 'by law established', the official church of the state from the Reformation until 1871, the Church of Ireland has the oldest and most extensive collection of parish registers. Registers of baptisms, marriages and burials, the earliest of which dates from 1619, survive for 637 parishes and although registers from some 1,006 parishes were destroyed in the fire in the Public Record Office of Ireland in 1922, much more of the information from these records has survived in copy form than is generally supposed. Noel Reid (ed.), *A table of Church of Ireland parochial records and copies* is the most recent listing of parish registers while appendix viii of the *Fifty-sixth report of the deputy keeper of the records ... in Ireland* (1931) contains a list of transcripts of registers, the originals of which were lost in 1922. A number of registers have been printed while the *Journal of the association for the preservation of the memorials of the dead*, which was published between 1888 and 1934, contains many gravestone inscriptions which replace or augment burial records.

Since religious activity by Roman Catholics and non-conformists was curtailed by law in the seventeenth and eighteenth centuries, Church of Ireland registers often contain records of people from other denominations. This is particularly so in the case of burials as the penal laws permitted only the established church to own graveyards and so Church of Ireland graveyards were often the burial place for all residents of a parish irrespective of their religion. Few Catholic parish registers exist before the early nineteenth century and while early Presbyterian registers are equally rare some records of Presbyterian baptisms and marriages may appear in Church of Ireland registers until the nineteenth century. Methodist ministers did not baptise until the 1830s, before which children were usually brought to the Church of Ireland to be christened, and were not enabled to perform marriages until 1845. Among the smaller non-conformist churches the Society of Friends (Quakers) has impressive records of births, deaths and marriages from the late seventeenth century, Huguenots registers from Dublin and Portarlington from the same period have been printed by the Huguenot Society of London, while the extant Moravian and Unitarian registers date mainly from the mid eighteenth century.

The PRONI *Guide to church records* is a comprehensive listing of the registers of all the christian churches in Ulster and most of the material referred to is available in original or copy

NGA No.	CIVIL PARISH	GV No.	CHURCH OF IRELAND	ROMAN CATHOLIC	PRESBYTERIAN	OTHERS
1	Agha	32		Bagenalstown 1820 Leighlinbridge 1783		
2	Aghade	43	1740	Ballon 1782		
3	Ardoyne	23		Ballon 1782		
4	Ardristan	25		Tullow 1763		
5	Ballinacarrig	6		Tinryland 1813		
6	Ballon	42		Ballon 1782		
7	Ballycrogue	7		Tinryland 1813		
8	Ballyellin	36		Bagenalstown 1820 Ballon 1782 Borris 1782		
9	Baltinglass	13		Rathvilley 1797		
10	Barragh	45	1831	Clonegall 1833		
11	Carlow	4	1744	Carlow 1769	Carlow 1820 (united with Athy 1936)	M. Carlow Q. Carlow
12	Clonmelsh	5		Carlow 1769 Leighlinbridge 1783		
13	Clonmore	22	1845 marriages	Clonmore 1813		
14	Clonygoose	37		Borris 1782		
15	Cloydagh	26		Leighlinbridge 1783		
16	Crecrin	21		Clonmore 1813		
17	Dunleckny	33	1791	Bagenalstown 1820		
18	Fennagh	24	1796 Tullow 1696	Ballon 1782 Myshall 1822 Tullow 1763		
19	Gilbertstown	40		Ballon 1782		
20	Grangeford	9		Tullow 1763		
21	Hacketstown	19	1845 marriages	Hacketstown 1820		
22	Haroldstown	18		Hacketstown 1820		
23	Kellistown	8		Ballon 1782		
24	Killerrig	3		Tullow 1763		
25	Killinane	30		Leighlinbridge 1783		
26	Kiltegan	15		Hacketstown 1820		

Fig. 7.1: From B. Mitchell, *A guide to Irish parish registers* (Baltimore, 1988). This invaluable publication gives the date of origin of registers for the various denominations. NGA no. refers to parish reference in the companion, *A new genealogical atals of Ireland* and GV no. refers to parish location in householders index to Griffith's valuation in NLI.

form in the Public Record Office in Belfast. There is no equivalent guide for the whole country but J.G. Ryan (ed.), *Irish church records* is a useful introduction. An incomplete but nevertheless useful list of Catholic parish registers was printed in *Archivium Hibernicum* vol. iii (1914) pp 366-406 while Olive C. Goodbody, *Guide to Irish Quaker records* is the most accessible catalogue of the records of the Society of Friends. Stephen ffeary-Smyrl has published a list of pre-1800 records from the non-conformist congregations in Dublin in Kevin Herlihy (ed.), *The Irish dissenting tradition*.

Registers of baptisms, marriages and burials are mainly of genealogical and demographic importance, particularly for the period before accurate censuses were taken, or between census years, and, more generally, for the period before the introduction of civil registration of births, marriages and deaths in 1864. In the particular case of the Church of Ireland, however, civil registration of marriages began in 1845.

The administrative records of the local churches are also useful sources. This is particularly so in the Church of Ireland for before the emergence of local government in the nineteenth century the vestry, the committee which oversaw the running of the parish, dealt not only with religious matters but also offered a wide range of social and economic services to all the residents of the parish (fig. 7.2). Vestry records detail activities such as church building, schools, poor relief, road repair, street cleaning and local policing; they include annual financial accounts which list those who paid and those who received, lists of cess (parish tax) payers often arranged street by street, and, occasionally, parish censuses. From the mid nineteenth century onwards preachers' books record the numbers who attended services and can provide a valuable guide to the vibrancy of local communities.

The following extract from the vestry minute book of St Kevin's Parish in south Dublin city exemplifies the varied responsibilities of the parish. Here decisions are made on supporting an abandoned child, paying parish employees, collecting a parish tax of ten pounds and introducing measures to curb vagrancy:

> A vestry at St Kevin's Church, February the 2nd 1674.
>
> It is agreed upon that the Ballore shall have fifty shills per annum and a coate, bell and shoues and that he shall continue at the pleasure of the parish. It is likewise ordered that all persons that have borne any office for five years past and are not discharged shall so appear and cleare their accounts and ( ) refusal they shall bee cited by the church-wardens for the time being. It is further ordered that all landlords and inhabitants entertaining or receiving any inmates suspected to burthen the parish shall give security to the parish for them, whereby the parish may be secured or otherwise put them out of the parish. Ordered that the child found at Sr Henry Ingoldsby doore shall be provided for at the rate of three pounds tenn shills per ann. during the parishes pleasure. Ordered that an assessm~ for the Ballore and for the repaire of the church shall bee made amounting to seven pound and for the present clerke for his paynes in serving the parish, in drawing assessm~ of all kindes forty shills, but to collect and applott ten pounds, allowing twenty shills for insolvencies to be apploted by the churchwardens according to the abilities of every person to be collected by the sidesmen and constables.
>
> Alice Lewis widdow, Sarah Edgerton widdow, Thomas Oadham,
> Roger W. Ennis Darby Cullen – at sixpence p week.
>
> *Source:* Records of St Kevin's Parish, Dublin, M5136, National Archives.

Diocesan archives can be useful in augmenting parish records particularly in relation to land and buildings. The determination of parish boundaries, and the building of churches, glebe houses, halls and schools are frequently better documented in diocesan archives which are more likely to include maps and architectural drawings. Episcopal visitations of parishes and cathedrals can be vivid accounts of physical and social conditions as well as periodic assessments of the state of religion. Many diocesan collections were destroyed in the fire in the Public Record Office of Ireland in 1922 but those for Armagh, Dublin, Ossory and Tuam, in particular, are rich sources.

COUNTY ANTRIM

Ballywillan	Connor	1710–1753

COUNTY CARLOW

Carlow	Leighlin	1669–1915
Clonmelsh	Leighlin	1855–1877
Clonmore	Leighlin	1808–1849
Dunleckney	Leighlin	1776–1855
Hacketstown	Leighlin	1816–1870
Kiltennel	Leighlin	1902–1969
Nurney	Leighlin	1846–1893
Painestown	Leighlin	1849–1916
Painestown-St Anne	Leighlin	1865–1870
Powerstown	Leighlin	1810–1850
Shankill	Leighlin	1871–1923
Timogue	Leighlin	1811–1869

COUNTY CAVAN

Arva	Kilmore	1894–1921
Kingscourt	Meath	1902–1963
Larah	Kilmore	1901–1971
Moybologue	Meath	1872–1932
Swanlinbar	Kilmore	1875–1948
Templeport	Kilmore	1817–1942

COUNTY CLARE

Clonlea	Killaloe	1883–1923
Drumcliffe	Killaloe	1873–1934
Kilfieragh	Killaloe	1850–1962
Kilmurry	Killaloe	1822–1916
Kilnaboy	Killaloe	1780–1955
Kilnasoolagh	Killaloe	1761–1957
Kilrush	Killaloe	1741–1876
Kilseily	Killaloe	1827–1907
Kiltinanlea	Killaloe	1870–1950
O'Brien's Bridge	Killaloe	1870–1928

COUNTY CORK

Abbeymahon	Ross	1864–1929
Aghada	Cloyne	1816–1924
Ballycotton	Cloyne	1879–1905
Ballymartle	Cork	1820–1920
Blackrock	Cork	1829–1975
Brinny	Cork	1910–1920
Carrigaline	Cork	1722–1880
Cork-St Nicholas	Cork	1721–1914
Cork-St Paul	Cork	1796–1927

Fig. 7.2: Extract from Raymond Refaussé, *A handlist of Church of Ireland vestry minute books in the representative church body library, Dublin* (Dublin, 1995).

The administrative records of Catholic parishes, although of a more recent vintage than those of the Church of Ireland, are important sources for the development of the nineteenth and twentieth century urban landscape for in many Irish towns the most significant buildings from this period are Catholic churches, church halls and schools. The records of parish building projects and the subsequent records of the religious, educational, social and charitable enterprises which emanated therefrom are among the most vibrant archives of modern Ireland. In the Catholic Church, as in the Church of Ireland, diocesan records are also valuable sources for urban studies and may include visitations, deeds, building and development records, charitable and fund raising papers: David Sheehy's article on Catholic archives in Réamon Ó Muirí (ed.), *Irish church history today* includes an introduction to diocesan records. Miscellaneous diocesan correspondence can divulge very useful material. For example in 1860 in preparation for the *Inquiry into the operation of the poor law in Ireland,* Paul Cullen, archbishop of Dublin, solicited reports from every part of Ireland reporting on the local workhouse situation. The replies present a picture of the prevailing social and physical conditions in the country. The following is a sample of what was returned from a Dublin priest:

> There being in Dublin very little remunerative employment for women or grown children, as a necessary consequence the maintenance of these ten thousand people almost exclusively depends on the proceeds of the <u>father's</u> labour and exertions; to such an extent is this the case that while men have been paid from nine to twelve shillings per week wages, I have frequently known able-bodied women to be most happy to be engaged at <u>manual labour</u> at <u>three pence</u> per day! It is therefore manifest that any suspension or interruption of the father's employment has the effect of depriving <u>immediately</u> the large class of persons above almost of all means of support. In consequence of this exclusive dependence on the father's labour, as well as because of the low rate of wages, the dearness of provisions and the consequent impossibility of saving, it is manifest that the stoppage of the <u>father's</u> wages through illness or other causes must always produce <u>immediate</u> and <u>absolute</u> want to all families so dependent on him. And it may be added that the illness of <u>any member</u> of a family so situated, as it always must bring additional expenses, has always the effect of inflicting great privations on those whose scanty means were already overtaxed.

Source: Fr. P. O'Neill to Dr. Cullen, 2 May 1861, DDA: file I secular clergy, 340/1 no. 70.

Presbyterian records are important sources particularly for Ulster's urban history. *The records of the General Synod of Ulster* (1890, 3 vols.) contains an abundance of local information for the period 1691 to 1820. Kirk session minutes are good sources for tracing changes in the Presbyterian population of a town as they record the names of new members of the congregation and of those who moved from it, and include subscription lists. Stipend books list people who paid into the church and pew rent book or seat lists which give the names of those who had rented seats in the church. More generally, committee minutes, dating from the eighteenth century, record the activities of the church.

In the Methodist Church membership registers (also called quarterly class rolls), dating from the mid-nineteenth century, are useful for tracing the practice of Methodism in a particular area. From the 1870s, circuit schedule books record the names and locations of Methodist societies, the number of members, the number of new members and of those leaving, as well as emigration and deaths. These are important sources for reconstructing in detail local fluctuations in the strength of Methodism. The circuit schedule books also contain information on Sunday schools, chapels, temperance associations, and details of church finances. The minutes of Methodist Conferences in Ireland since 1752 have been printed.

The Religious Society of Friends (Quakers) has had a far greater influence in Irish history than its small numbers may suggest, its philanthropic work during the Great Famine being a case in point. The Society holds very complete administrative records which, as well as detailing its charitable enterprises, include deeds, maps and plans, and school records. Membership records include lists of members, records of removal from one part of the country to another, and sufferings – factual records of imprisonments, fines and distraint of goods incurred because of religious belief.

Although considerable progress has been made in recent years in consolidating ecclesiastical archives in a number of repositories, much of the material referred to above remains in the custody of the bodies which created it. The general exception to this is the situation in Northern Ireland where most of the principal series of church records are available in original or copy form in the Public Record Office in Belfast, In the Republic of Ireland the parochial and diocesan records of the Church of Ireland are increasingly being transferred to the Representative Church Body Library in Dublin but many still remain in local custody. However, most of the older parish registers have been microfilmed by the National Archives. Roman Catholic registers have been microfilmed by the National Library and most dioceses have an archives which is usually part of the administration at the bishop's residence. The principal locations for Presbyterian records are the Presbyterian Historical Society and Assembly's College, both in Belfast, while Methodist records are to be found at the Wesley Historical Society in Belfast and Leeson Park in Dublin. The Friends' Historical Library in Dublin is the principal repository for Irish Quaker records although the papers of the Central Relief Committee of the Society of Friends, which chronicle famine relief, are in the National Archives. Details of these repositories and resumes of their collections may be had from Seamus Helferty and Raymond Refaussé (eds), *Directory of Irish Archives*.

2. Archives of Religious Congregations and Charitable Organisations

The archives of most Roman Catholic religious congregations in Ireland date from the nineteenth century at the earliest. Correspondence of individual foundations (houses and associated charities) can include very useful contemporary detail on urban centres as most religious institutions in Ireland were town-based. Land holding, social geography, disease and literacy may all be mentioned. Wealthy benefactors as well as the plight of the very poor may be recorded. Many individual houses still hold their own archives but in recent years there has been a tendency to consolidate collections in provincialate and generalate archives. Information on most of these archives is included in the *Directory of Irish Archives*.

Most Irish charitable societies were nineteenth century foundations the records of which are of immense importance in documenting the lives of the apparently insignificant who might otherwise have been untraceable (fig. 7.3). Charities looked after the poor, the orphans and the aged, the sick and insane, prisoners, prostitutes and alcoholics, and provided food, clothing, housing, education and employment. Conspicuous features of many Irish streetscapes are schools, orphanages and asylums which were erected by charitable bodies, many of which had a particular religious orientation. Fund-raising missionary publications such as the one below were designed to attract support throughout Great Britain for the cause of converting Irish Catholics. They also provide interesting insights into the sectarian struggles which were of importance in delimiting urban religious territory especially in the period 1850-1880.

> [The Catholics] took two houses in the neighbourhood of the Weavers' Hall, and ordered breakfast of tea and bread and butter, and dinner of cabbage and bacon, to be prepared for any children who would leave the schools. Some poor hungry things were induced to go, but not many: and in a short time, the houses were closed. A shop was then opened, to which parents, who promised to keep their children from school, were provided with orders for groceries, &c. The rations of food in the Roman Catholic schools were raised to four times the usual quantity; and boys were sent out into the streets with boxes of silver money to entice the children to the Roman Catholic schools. Then mobs were raised, if possible by force, to prevent the attendance; women and boys filled the windows armed with stones to throw at the poor children, locking the doors to keep out the police.
>
> *Source*: Irish Church Missions (Dublin, 1875).

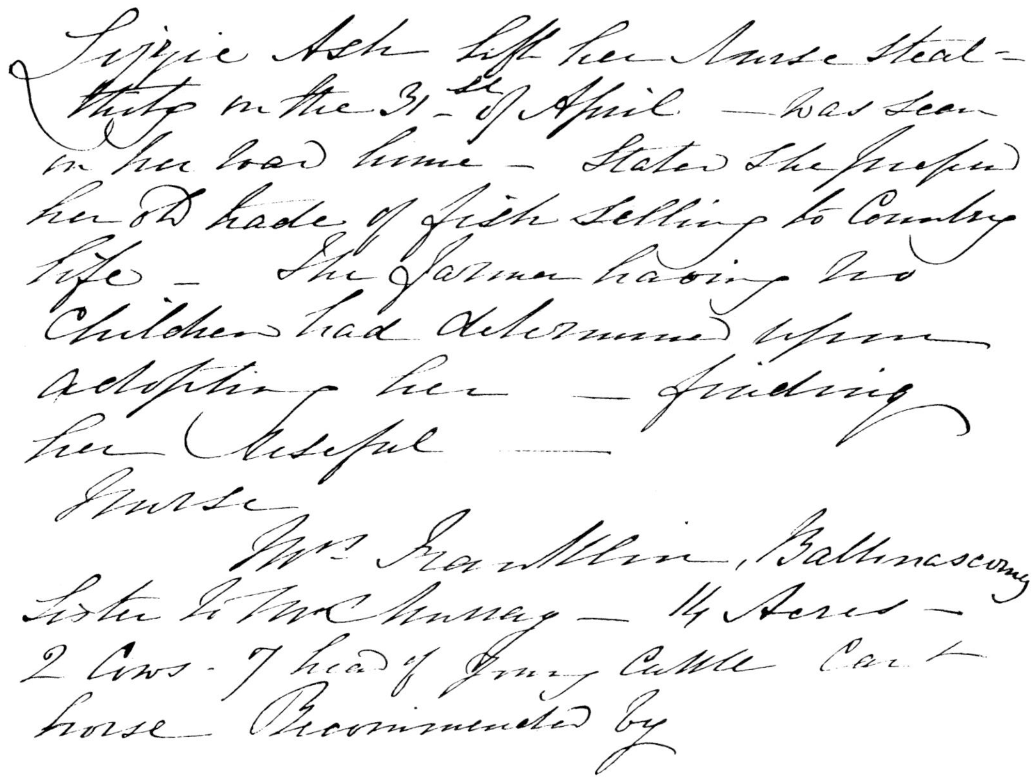

No. 60 March 20 1858

Lizzie Ashe – Age 10 or 11 years – residence Stocking Lane 126 Townsend Street – Child totally uninstructed – upon Miss Lentaigne's recomd. this girl was received mainly – she having contributed generously – also upon Miss Lynch's Mountjoy Place – a subscriber who promised to get one or more pound subscribers – the girl is too old to take – City children when advanced in years will hardly content themselves in the country – She has been received in the hope that it may be her salvation – & that she may be provided for in the country.

Lizzie Ashe left her Nurse stealthily on the 31st of April – was seen on her road home – Stated she preferred her old trade of fish selling to country life – the farmer having no children had determined upon adopting her – finding her useful – Nurse Mrs Franklin, Ballyscorney, sister to Mrs Murray – 14 acres and 2 cows – 7 head of young cattle, cart horse. Recommended by

Fig. 7.3: Extract from Register of St. Brigid's Orphanage, Holy Faith Archives, Glasnevin, Dublin, detailing the case of Lizzie Ashe who 'preferred her old trade of fish selling to country life'.

Most of the relief societies provide graphic accounts of the situation of the poor in their care, often including addresses.

> In one of the narrow lanes of St Michan's parish, they sought a poor woman to whom they brought relief. On a damp, earthen floor a few particles of straw were strewn to serve as a bed for this poor widow: her tattered garments and the squalid appearance of her son, a lad earning three or four shillings a week, almost the sole support of his mother and little sister, sufficiently indicated the poverty of the whole.
>
> *Source*: Ladies of Charity, 1855, Fourth report, p. 10, Holy Faith Archives, Glasnevin.

A similar picture is built up by the reports of charities and missions of other denominations working in these parishes. One bible woman reports:

> Have you ever passed through any of the narrow streets in the neighbourhood of the Law Courts? If so, you have doubtless remarked upon the dismal, dirty aspect of the houses, and had you entered you would have found that each room was the abode of a whole family. The highest ambition, as far as this world goes, of these much-to-be respected poor seems to be embraced in that negative happiness to 'get along' – not to perish – to open eyes, however wearily, on a new morning, to satisfy with something, no matter what, a craving appetite, to close eyes at night under some shadow or shade.
>
> *Source*: Annual Report of the Dublin bible woman mission in connection with the Church of Ireland (Dublin, 1877) p. 16.

The National Archives and the Representative Church Body Library in Dublin and the Public Record Office of Northern Ireland are the main sources for records of Protestant charitable institutions. Records of Catholic organisations, such as the Society of St Vincent de Paul and the Legion of Mary, may still be in the offices of the societies while others may be in the local diocesan archives. A valuable guide to the range of charitable institutions in Dublin is G.D. Williams, *Dublin charities*.

3. Testamentary Records

Wills, as well as being valuable social documents, are important sources for tracing the disposition of real and moveable property (land, buildings, personal possessions and, of course, money) and for estimating the wealth of communities and individuals.

Following the Reformation, testamentary jurisdiction in Ireland was exercised by the Church of Ireland, as the established church, and wills were proved in the consistorial court of the diocese in which the testator had lived. However, if the estate had a value of over £5 in a second diocese probate was granted by the Prerogative Court of the archbishop of Armagh which sat in Dublin. In 1857 testamentary jurisdiction was transferred from the Church of Ireland to a newly established court of probate and following the establishment of the Public Record Office of Ireland in 1867 the records of wills and administrations from the consistorial courts and the prerogative court were transferred there for safe-keeping. These records, together with much of the post-1857 testamentary material, were destroyed in 1922. Since then the National Archives (formerly the Public Record Office of Ireland) and the Public Record Office of Northern Ireland have been assiduous in acquiring copy wills and their collections are now considerable. Important collections are also to be found in the National Library, Royal Irish Academy, Representative Church Body Library, Trinity College Library, the Friends Historical Library and among the Carrigan MSS in St Kieran's College, Kilkenny. In addition, the Registry of Deeds has accepted wills as well as deeds since its foundation in 1708 and three volumes of abstracts from this collection have been published by the Irish Manuscripts Commission (fig. 7.4). Abstracts of Quaker wills were published as P.B. Eustace and O.C. Goodbody, *Quaker records, Dublin, abstract of wills*. In addition the indexes to a number of the collections which were destroyed in 1922 have

702 ASHBORNER, RICHARD,[1] Dublin, merchant.
25 June 1743. Narrate, 2¼ p., 10 July 1744.

Jas. Bibby, Co. Dublin, gent., trustee. His first cousin John Ashborner, second son of his late uncle George Ashborner, late of Co. of Cumberland, deceased. Richard Ashborner, eldest son of his said uncle George Ashborner. Thos. Ashborner Parker, eldest son of his niece Ann Parker otherwise Thompson, wife of Paul Parker of Temple Barr, Dublin, merchant. Richard Parker second son, Isaac Parker third son, Wm. Parker fourth son, Paul Parker fifth son of said niece Ann Parker. Elizabeth Dulap[1] otherwise Ashborner daughter of his late uncle George Ashborner and wife of Robert Dunlap, Dublin, *upholder*. Said John Ashborner and said Eliz. Dunlap exors.

To Mary Malone otherwise Gernon, wife of Joseph Malone of Cork Hill, Dublin, hosier, he left his first wife's picture, etc. Susanna Hendrick, spinster. His tenant the widow Lyons. Andrew Craig, a poor lame man that lived on the Batchelor's Walk. Legacy to poor of St. Mary's Parish and St. Aude[o]n's parish. His servant Elizth. Brownrigg, her sister Mary Brownrigg. His sister Ann Thompson. Mary Ashborner his uncle George's youngest daughter. His niece Mary Brookbank otherwise Thompson. Dorothy Ashborner, his uncle George's widow. Samuel Gernon his first wife's son. His niece Ann Parker. His sister-in-law Susanna Burleigh.

Ground in Francis Street, Dublin, on which there was three or four houses built and the College of Dublin were his tenants. Two houses near St. Aude[o]n's Arch adjoining the Carpenter's Hall. Two houses, warehouses etc. on Merchant's Quay, Dublin. Ground in Chamber Street and Clothworkers Square. Ground fronting Dolphin's Barn Lane " joining to the water course that runs from Roper's Rest on which ground six new houses and the Anabaptist dipping Place did stand." Several leases in liberties of Thos. Court and Donore. Ground in Back Lane, Dublin. Holding on Hawkins Quay in parish of St. Mark's, Dublin. Holdings on Jervis Quay otherwise the Batchelor's Walk, Union Street and Abby Street, Dublin.

Witnesses : Stephen Robinson, Castle Street, Dublin, grocer, John Sumner, Dublin, confectioner, Wm. Sumner, Dublin, public notary.

Memorial witnessed by : John Kathrens, Dublin, public notary, Henry Steevens Reily his clerk.

117, 8, 79412   James Bibby (seal)

---

[1] This surname appears as Ashburner in Vicars *Index of the Prerogative Wills of Ireland*, and in *Betham's Will Pedigrees*, Genealogical office.

Fig. 7.4: Example of a Dublin city will from P. Beryl Eustace, (ed.), *Registry of Deeds, Dublin. Abstracts of wills*, i, 1708-1745 (Dublin, 1956), no. 702.

been published and these are listed in the most authoritative guide to Irish testamentary collections: Rosemary ffoliott and Eileen O'Byrne, 'Wills and Administrations' in D.F. Begley (ed.), *Irish genealogy: a record finder.*

SELECT BIBLIOGRAPHY

D.F. Begley (ed.), *Irish genealogy: a record finder* (Dublin, 1981)

E. Ellis and P.B. Eustace (eds), *Registry of deeds, Dublin, abstracts of wills, vol. iii, 1785-1832* (Dublin, 1984)

P.B. Eustace (ed.), *Registry of deeds, Dublin, abstracts of wills, ii, 1746-1785* (Dublin, 1954)

P.B. Eustace (ed.), *Registry of deeds, Dublin, abstracts of wills, i, 1708-1745* (Dublin, 1956)

P.B. Eustace and O.C. Goodbody, *Quaker records, Dublin, abstracts of wills* (Dublin, 1957)

O.C. Goodbody and B.G. Hutton, *Guide to Irish Quaker records, 1654-1860* (Dublin, 1967)

S. Helferty and R. Refaussé (eds), *Directory of Irish archives* (2nd ed., Dublin, 1993)

K. Herlihy (ed.), The *Irish dissenting tradition, 1650-1750* (Dublin, 1995)

J.J. Digges La Touche (ed.), *Registers of the French conformed churches of St Patrick and St Mary, Dublin* (Dublin, 1893)

T.P. Le Fanu (ed.), *Registers of the French church of Portarlington, Ireland* (London, 1908)

T.P. Le Fanu (ed.), *Registers of the French non-conformist churches of Lucy Lane and Peter Street, Dublin* (Aberdeen, 1901)

R. Ó Muirí (ed.), *Irish church history today* (Armagh 1991).

PRONI, *Guide to church records* (Belfast, 1994)

N. Reid (ed.), *A table of Church of Ireland parochial records and copies* (Naas, 1994)

J.G. Ryan (ed.), *Irish church records. Their history, availability and use in family and local history research* (Dublin, 1992)

G.D. Williams (comp.), *Dublin charities, being a handbook of Dublin philanthropic organisations and charities* (Dublin, 1902)

CHAPTER EIGHT

Newspapers, Directories and Gazetteers (Arnold Horner)

Introduction

Newspapers, directories and gazetteers, in their own distinctive and very different ways, may provide a wide variety of local information which may be otherwise unobtainable or, at least, not easily obtained. Each is significant as a source from the eighteenth century onwards, providing valuable insights on the local social scene and on local commercial activity. Newspapers developed in the main cities during the eighteenth century and in most of the main country towns during the nineteenth century. The information available from their news reports and advertisements is frequently unique. It may be complemented by the outline descriptions offered in gazetteers and by the increasingly comprehensive listings of commercial activity in the main cities and in many smaller centres which appeared in directories for Dublin, the country at large, and for individual counties and localities. The range of possible material of interest to urban historians in these sources is dauntingly large. The following paragraphs can give only a flavour of the material which may ultimately prove fruitful.

1. Newspapers

The earliest newsheets appeared in Dublin during the late seventeenth century but most survived only a few issues. Newspapers – usually appearing weekly or twice weekly to start with and of two to four sides in length – took firmer root during the early decades of the eighteenth century. Newspapers are known to have been published in Dublin, Cork, Limerick and Waterford before 1730. The most durable of these early papers was the *Dublin Journal* published by the Faulkner family. It lasted a hundred years until 1825. However, its longevity seems short compared to that of the *Belfast Newsletter*, first issued in 1737 and still publishing.

A comprehensive listing of these and other newspapers appears in *Newsplan – report of the Newsplan project in Ireland*, by James O'Toole (1992). This report attempts to list all newspapers held by the main public libraries in Ireland and by the British Library. Newspapers are listed by title and are cross-referenced by county or place of publication. Under the title heading, details are given of its life-span, its availability in microfilm and the location and extent of hard-copy runs. This work is an indispensable introduction to the period and indicates the degree to which a particular locality may have been served by local newspapers. It can be complemented by the published general histories of Irish newspapers (notably Munter, 1967; Oram, 1983) and by Rosemary ffolliott's excellent overview (1981). In the National Library of Ireland, the yellow-coloured 'newspaper book' available at the issue desk provides an invaluable, much-thumbed list

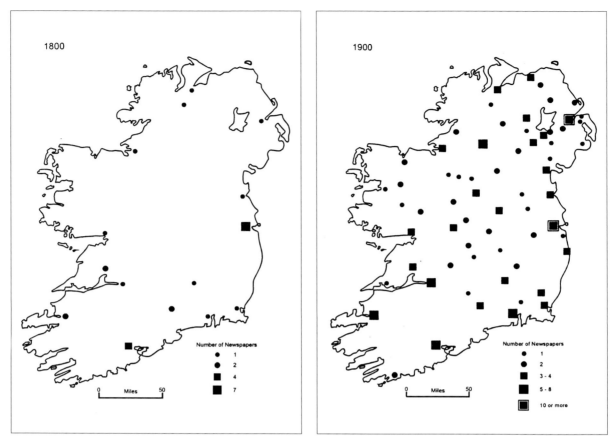

Fig. 8.1: Places where newspapers were published, 1800 and 1900 (Source: Derived from O'Toole (1992). Covers papers publishing at least once a week. Where more than one place of publication is recorded, only the main place of printing is shown. Weekly editions of daily papers not included.

of the newspapers held by the NLI. Besides the NLI and other Dublin repositories, a growing number of regional and county genealogical centres (many attached to local libraries) have microfilm runs of newspapers relevant to their localities. Where possible, microfilm should be used in consultation; the hard copies of many newspapers, especially those produced on poor quality paper since the mid nineteenth century, are worn from intensive use and are now deteriorating quite rapidly.

From the *Newsplan* report the spread of newspapers during the nineteenth century can be readily traced. In 1800, newspapers were being published only in fifteen of the larger urban centres. By 1900 there were five times as many places publishing at least one newspaper once a week or more frequently (fig. 8.1). This diffusion goes apace with the modernisation of Irish society, and is complementary to such developments as the growing local significance of commercial activity, the spread of mass literacy, and the emergence of new forms of local politics reflected in both institutions and attitudes. By 1900, local newspapers were not only more numerous, they had more and larger pages, and appealed to a wider populace than a century earlier.

The Eighteenth century Newspaper as Source-Material

Early newspapers carried a range of information, usually including reports from outside Ireland, accounts of local incidents and a selection of recent births, marriages and deaths. News reports and advertisements particularly reflected the preoccupations of property owners and commercial interests in the place of publication and its surrounding hinterland. However, this did not necessarily mean that the content was narrow. The eighteenth century *Dublin Journal* (*DJ*)

The Earl of Mountrath, being resolv'd to encourage good Tenants to inhabit the Town of Jamestown in the County of Leitrim, a Market Town beautifully situated on the River Shannon, and fit for any Manufacture, over which is lately built a new Stone Bridge, has set out the same in Plots for Houses and Gardens, of which he will make Leases for Lives renewable for ever, and to the said Plotts has appointed certain Parcels or Lands adjoining to the said Town, of which he will make leases for 3 Lives, or for a Term of Years. Whoever is minded to take any of the said Plots and Lands let them apply in Writing to Doctor STAUNTON in Jervis Street Dublin; to CARNCROSS NISBET, Esq at Aghuane, near Longford, or to the Earl of MOUNTRATH in Grosvenor Square, London.

N.B. A Map of the Town and Lands is to be seen at Doctor STAUNTON's in Dublin.

Fig. 8.2: Advertisement (reset) promoting Jamestown, County Leitrim in the *Dublin Journal* 18-21/3/1731-2.

produces a steady run of news reports on the problems posed by beggars, the activities of highwaymen and the problems of vice. For example, successive issues of the *DJ* during October 1781 report how (a) on the Dublin quays a mob had attacked the cart bringing beggars to the House of Industry, forcing the beadles to open fire, with the result that two men were brought to Inns Quay infirmary, and (b) a young woman had been beaten to death at a 'house of ill-fame in Little Booter Lane [Dublin] kept by Ann McDonagh'. Certainly not all of the historically most significant events are fully covered (the swirl of events marking the turmoil of 1798 is intriguingly yet incompletely captured due to censorship, and to perceptual and communications problems), yet there may be numerous references to social and economic conditions which can complement or corroborate other sources. To give another example, a *DJ* for the famine year of 1741 includes a letter commenting on the miserable condition of the 'common people' in the town of Enniscorthy: 'they die in great numbers, without distinction of ages, of the fever and bloody flux'.

The advertisement columns may be of particular interest to the urban historian. Proposed new developments and property for sale, lease or letting are frequently featured. For example, the availability of building lots along the new Dominick Street in Dublin is advertised in the *Dublin Journal* during June 1753 while five months later there is a notice of lots for building near St George's church. Advertisements are also to be found for property in many parts of the city's near countrywide hinterland. Town inns are frequently advertised and described, some of them being new developments, others because a new tenant is needed. Individual houses, including new ones speculatively built, are also featured, and occasionally there appear ads for one of the many ambitious (but not always successful) schemes for new villages or towns (fig. 8.2).

Other advertisements may give information on spa towns and nascent resorts; for example a notice of May 1746 refers to 'Swadlingbar Spaw' (county Cavan). Forty years later, in the *Dublin Evening Post (DEP)* of 1788, Christie's hotel and tavern at Bray, and lodgings for sea-bathing at Westport and Bundoran receive a mention. Fairs and markets, industrial activity such as flour mills, breweries and malt houses, boarding houses, and schools may be featured. New initiatives in coaching and communications services are also advertised and may give information on the journey as well as the proprietor's name and the precise places of departure and arrival. Thus, the *DEP* of 1788 includes a reference to a new mail coach being exhibited in the yard of Dublin Castle, and advertisements, *inter allii,* for the 'Granard Fly[-coach]', the 'Drumsna Fly' and the Ballinasloe route journey involving a canal journey from Dublin to Monasterevan and the remainder by stagecoach.

Topics close to the hearts of the gentry include gentlemen's societies and clubs (e.g. in the 1770s/1780s, the Anna Liffey Club, meetings of the 'knots' of the Friendly Brothers of St Patrick), cock-fights, stallions, race meetings, balls and suppers. In the late 1770s-1780s, there are notices of the formation of volunteer companies. A decade later, there are notices of meetings of the Roman Catholics of particular areas (usually parishes) to press for emancipation or to pledge loyalty. Rising tensions are signified in notices of the formation of yeomanry cavalry and local militias. There are also references to the activities of the Whiteboys and other secret organisations.

Enough has perhaps been said to suggest the economic and social potential of the eighteenth century newspaper in local studies. However, it must be noted too that newspapers provide a patchy coverage of developments, with some small towns appearing much less frequently than others. Unless the newspaper has been well indexed by some archive, it may be time-consuming, and not always directly rewarding, to search for material relevant to a particular town or village. The value of the search may be mainly in building up a general perspective.

Nineteenth century Papers as Source Material

Besides the kind of topics already described, early nineteenth century papers contain advertisements on such matters as the building and provision of new barracks and – foreshadowing the growing significance of community institutions – the provision of dispensaries and fever hospitals. There are many advertisements for small boarding schools in country towns, for example Portarlington and Mullingar. Other notices are for free schools, charity schools and charity sermons. The transport revolution brought about by the steamship is clearly signalled in the 1820s with notices of new routes, for example Dublin to Bristol in 22-24 hours, while early hints of leisure being more significant appear in the *Dublin Evening Post* during 1828 in notices for 'aquatics' and a regatta at Kingstown (now Dun Laoghaire), and in the announcement of a one-day 'marine excursion' to Anglesey for the price of £1. Twenty-one years later there are notices of an excursion to London and back for two guineas and the comment that railway travel has brought Dublin and Paris within twenty-six hours of each other.

Alongside these items heralding developments of general significance there is the detail which becomes the lifeblood of local newspapers. Lists of names appear in records of attendances at funerals, in reports of local political and other meetings, in accounts of court proceedings against those involved in unrest such as the rising of 1848, and in accounts of subscribers to various types of memorial. Not only can such material provide information on particular individuals; taken over a longer period and in aggregate it may offer a major insight into the changing social structure of a place. So Gulliver and Silverman (1995) in their magnificent 'biography' of Thomastown, county Kilkenny, meticulously explore the contemporary local press to produce an unrivalled analysis of the social structure of this small town during the late eighteenth and nineteenth centuries (fig. 8.3).

By the later decades of the nineteenth century many more local newspapers had been established – each county had at least one newspaper, usually more. Individual papers could now be said to be truly local, although their emphases could vary, particularly in relation to their political sympathies. For the urban historian, local newspapers may afford invaluable perspectives on local political change as the franchise widened and as the unionist-nationalist dichotomy hardened. The preoccupations of the various local authorities, the poor law unions and town commissions, and later the county, urban and rural district councils may be recorded in what is sometimes merciless detail in local newspapers. Embedded in all this is material which may be of profound interest to the urban historian, for example about housing conditions, water supply and sewage disposal issues.

At the same time the continuing modernisation of the country is extensively, if still patchily, recorded. The *Kildare Observer* of 1886-7 records the establishment of sub-offices of the Ulster Bank at Blessington and Dunlavin. There is also news of local concerts and of a formalisation and

No.	Date	Meeting
1. June 1830:		anti-stamp and spirit duty meeting
2. December 1830:		repeal of the Union meeting
3. January 1831:		repeal of the Union meeting
4. May 1832:		anti-tithe meeting
5. June 1833:		subscription list for a reward fund
6. July 1833:		subscriptions for Charleston Catholics
7. March 1835:		magistrates meeting
8. May 1836:		anti-tithe, pro-election meeting
9. July 1838:		anti-tithe meeting
10. October 1838:		Precursor Society meeting
11. July 1839:		candidates and seconders for Kilkenny Union elections
12. July 1842:		subscriptions to improve Thomastown's navigation
13. October 1842:		subscriptions for a new cathedral in Kilkenny city
14. January 1844:		parochial meeting – O'Connell trial
15. June 1844:		meeting to appoint collectors for 'repeal rent'
16. March 1845:		subscriptions – O'Connell (repeal) tribute
17. March 1846:		petition to secure funds for improving navigation
18. April 1846:		meeting of the Thomastown Poor Relief Committee
19. April 1846:		subscriptions to the Poor Relief Fund

Political Coalitions, Events and Agents, 1830–46

Event no:	(1)	(2)	(3)	(4)	(5)	(6)	(7)	(8)	(9)	(10)	(11)	(12)	(13)	(14)	(15)	(16)	(17)	(18)	(19)
Year:	1830	1830	1831	1832	1833	1835	1835	1836	1838	1838	1839	1842	1842	1844	1844	1845	1846	1846	1846
Artisans:†																			
Bryan, Edw.(mas)																x			
Carroll, T.(c)			x																
Comerford, Th.(b)			x																
Cullen, E.(st-c)			x																
Cullen, Jms(sh)	x	x	x																
Delaney, Dan (t)																x			
Delaney, Pat (mil)																x			
Dillon, Owen(br)			x																
Doyle, C.(sm)			x																
Drea, Martin(sh)			x																
Drennan, Pat(mas)			x																
Gane, Rich(t)																x			
Landrigan, T.(-)			x																
Murphy, Edw.(bm)																x			
Murphy, Wm.(v)			x																
Neil, P.(sh)			x																
Shea, J.(sh)			x																
Tracey, Ed.(pl)																x			
Retailers:																			
Aylward, Wm.(i,p)				x		x		x											
Bishop, Th.(p,g,htl)												x				x			
Cahill, Th.(p,g)												x				x	x		
Candler, Pat(dr)																x			

Fig. 8.3: Attendances at public meetings in Thomastown, County Kilkenny 1830-46. Compiled from newspaper records by Gulliver and Silverman (1995).

growing range of sports activity. The formation of an Athy boat club is noted in 1886, and Athy rugby football club is reported in 1888 as is the inaugural meeting of Naas cycling club. The *Irish Times* of the same period records many of the new rugby, cricket, tennis, golf and other clubs being established around suburban Dublin. The emerging Gaelic Athletic Association is also recorded. The *Kildare Observer* of 1888 contains extensive accounts of a Maynooth football tournament. A year earlier, the establishment of the GAA in Naas and Newbridge is reported. In these and other records, large numbers of personal names appear, many of which can be found only rarely elsewhere.

By the dawn of the new century, local papers carry news of the Irish language revival and of the establishment in many small towns of Irish language classes organised by the Gaelic League. Elsewhere there may be reports of the establishment of new medical halls and of the new

Fig. 8.4: Advertisement for new housing at Mount Merrion, Dublin in *The Irish Times*, 15 April 1937.

significance of the motor car. So The *Kildare Observer* for 1901 carries a display from the Dublin Laundry Co, owners of the Dartry Dye Works, to announce that they have purchased 'a powerful Daimler motor van' and that they will now collect custom from as far away as Wicklow, Newbridge, Trim and Drogheda.

Other more sombre aspects of Irish life are also recorded. *The Kildare Observer* in 1900 reported how a Jewish pedlar, Wolf Wachmann, was robbed in Monasterevan. This paper also has a continuing preoccupation with what it calls the 'tramp problem', noting for example that 'the tramps are always to the front in Celbridge. It is their first resting place out of Dublin...' but adding that each 'casual' who boards overnight at the Union must break five hundredweight of stone before he is let out next morning. In 1902 there is a graphic description (9 August) of the state of Dunlavin, county Wicklow, offering a reminder that contemporary housing conditions in some small towns were as bad as in the larger cities; a month later the problems of back street Maynooth are described in comparably withering language.

Newspapers as Sources in the Twentieth Century

The fortunes of newspapers have been mixed over the twentieth century. A range of factors – changing economics, demographic change, new media, and the decline of old rivalries – have combined to force amalgamations and closures, but there have also been new ventures, most

Land Purchase Orders Opposed

"More Ready Money From Playfields": Factory's Position

CORPORATION CRITICISED

OBJECTIONS to the acquisition of lands in the Crumlin area on the grounds that they were being used as sports fields or were required for existing business enterprises, which would be seriously disturbed if the Corporation's orders became effective, were made when the housing inquiry, conducted by Mr. Denis J. Hickie, Local Government Inspector, was resumed in the Dublin City Hall, yesterday.

"So great is the scarcity of playing fields that we could get more ready money by letting the land for that purpose than if it were used for house building," said Mr. E. J. Kelly, K.C., who represented the Meade Estate.

He added that they were, like the other citizens of Dublin, most anxious to see the slums abolished and the working classes properly housed, but he maintained that the land which the Corporation sought to acquire could be a great deal more usefully employed than by devoting it to the relief of the slum problem.

Mr. D. J. O'Sullivan solr., who appeared for the Drimnagh Lawn Tennis Club, whose grounds are on the estate, said that "the Corporation seemed to feel that its back was against the wall and that it had to defend itself."

Fig. 8.5: Extract (reset) from *The Irish Press*, 23 October 1936.

notably the free suburban papers of recent decades. Outside the main cities, well over sixty local papers continue to occupy distinctive niches as media of local expression. New media have emerged such as regional radio, yet local newspapers continue to generate interest and command strong support. As such they remain important as records of events which may not be covered elsewhere. The incidents of various 'troubles', new roads and housing, sports matches and other club activities, births and deaths are all recorded. In both local and countrywide papers, a diverse range of advertisements may also provide important information on, for example, property development and land acquisition (figs. 8.4 and 8.5).

Summary

The material in any newspaper is variable in its coverage. In local papers, mad dogs and the purchase of old false teeth may as easily get a mention as matters of government policy or the Boer War. But, with patience, an enormous range of material of significance to a wide range of history specialisms can be extracted. Part of their attraction is the extent to which they contain items such as those itemised above, many of which are as yet unanalysed by historians. When the local history of late nineteenth and twentieth century Ireland receives sustained attention, newspapers, especially local papers, must be an indispensable, central source.

2. Directories

Directories evolved during the eighteenth century as collections of information which might be useful to a range of interests: government, the military and the gentry, political, ecclesiastical, legal and commercial interests, and communications. Many also incorporated listings which had appeared in earlier almanacks, giving a calendar of events, including such matters as the tides, the rising and setting of the sun, and the dates and locations of the main fairs. While some of their data appear to cover the whole country (e.g. listings about the legal profession), from the point of view of the urban historian the particular appeal of directories lies in their growing range of more specific locational information.

In the course of a wide-ranging overview, the guide to Irish directories produced by Rosemary ffolliott and Donal Begley (1981) lists Dublin, provincial and professional directories chronologically. An invaluable county-by-county cross-reference is also included. This assessment must be regarded as essential reading for anyone concerned with this source, although the review of early Irish directories and almanacks published by Edward Evans in 1895 (reprinted 1980) may also be of interest as it identifies many short-lived publications and bibliographical nuances which cannot be considered here.

For many local studies, however, a departure point may be provided by the *Gentleman and citizen's almanack* ('Watson's') which appeared annually from 1729 and Wilson's *Dublin directory* which first appeared in 1752. Among much else, the former includes lists of post towns and other communications data while the latter includes lists of Dublin merchants and traders from its 1755 edition and publishes a street map of the city from the 1780s. From the 1760s onward, these publications had a complementary role and may usually be found bound together with *The English registry* as a compendium providing a more general information repository on many topics of political, economic and social significance in Ireland and Britain. The complementary nature of the three publications is formalised in the name *Treble almanack* to describe the omnibus edition for thirty years after 1801.

In the 1830s the *Treble almanack* gave way to newer, more co-ordinated directories. The *post Office Dublin directory* first appeared in 1832. Besides an extensive alphabetical listing of 'nobility, gentry, merchants and traders' editions of the 1840s contained a Dublin street directory and (among other items) a listing of the principal residents and activities in each of the Dublin suburbs; a banking directory, listings of mail coach and railway times and listings of the arrival and departure times of mails from each post town are among other features. Other near-contemporaneous directories were Pettigrew and Oulton's *Dublin almanack and directory* (1834-48) and the ambitious single issue, Henry Shaw's *Dublin pictorial guide and directory* (1850, reprinted in 1988), which included an unusual series of perspective views of major streets. However, the directory that has ultimately proved most durable was Alexander Thom's *Irish directory and official almanack*, initiated in 1844. Incorporating many of the features of the *Post Office directory* noted above, 'Thom's' appeared annually and extended to over 1,000 pages. A general section covering a wide range of topics relevant to the country as a whole included short sections on the administration of towns (fig. 8.6). It was supplemented by a Dublin section providing a list of the householders along each street and an alphabetical listing of 'nobility, gentry, merchants and traders'. From 1927, the general section included listings of the commercial activities in the principal towns of each county in the twenty-six county state. In 1959 'Thom's' was split into separate Dublin and commercial directories, which were to be published at 2-3 year intervals. In recent years, both directories have again been published annually, with street listings now extended to other major cities and with listings of the commercial activities in over 150 towns.

In Ulster, at least a dozen directories covering the Belfast area were published during the first half of the nineteenth century. The two earliest, produced by the firm of Smyth and Lyons (who had issued the first Belfast almanack four years earlier), appeared in 1807 and 1808 and have recently been reprinted (Adams, 1991). In 1852, there followed the *Belfast and Province of Ulster directory*, of which a further fifteen editions were produced by 1900. This publication now continues as the annual *Belfast and Northern Ireland directory*.

While directory data have been most regularly published and are most comprehensive for Dublin and Belfast, listings of trades and professions in various smaller centres can be found in dedicated commercial directories published at intervals from the 1820s (fig. 8.7). The edition of *Pigot's* directory which appeared in 1820 covered twenty-six Irish cities and towns, a total which was greatly expanded in the 1824 and 1846 editions and in the 1856, 1870, 1881 and 1894 editions of the succeeding *Slater's* directory. *Kelly's* two volume Irish directory of 1905 is also in this idiom. By the end of the century these publications had extended to most of the smaller towns and villages. Because of their comprehensiveness, the 1894 *Slater* and 1905 *Kelly* offer a unique, as yet not really appreciated, source of information on turn of century commercial life at the beginnings of the motor era.

In addition, some more localised directories – generally published as 'once-off' ventures – appeared from the late eighteenth century and may provide important, possibly unique, perspectives on the commercial activity of some country towns. A Limerick directory was produced by John Ferrar in 1769, while Richard Lucas's two volume *Cork directory* (1787-8) provides listings of merchants and traders in thirty-four urban centres of Munster and south Leinster; there are well over 200 entries for Kilkenny, and over 150 for Clonmel. Other early examples listed by ffolliott and Begley (1981) include directories of the Newry area (1819), the Sligo area (1839) and Waterford-Kilkenny-Carlow (also 1839). Many more were produced during the second half of the nineteenth century, most notably the directories of Cork (1875, 1889) and Munster (1886, 1893) by Francis Guy and the series of county directories by George H. Bassett for Limerick (1866, 1879), Kilkenny (1884), Wexford (1885), Louth (1886), Antrim (1888) and Tipperary (1889). Publications not listed by ffolliott and Begley include directories for King's County (now Offaly – 1890) and those produced during the twentieth century, for example those by Frank Porter for Kildare (1910) and Kingstown (1911).

Other more specialised directories may also be relevant to the urban historian, for example the long-running *Catholic* (first issued 1836) and *Irish Church* (Church of Ireland – first issued 1862) directories which contain extensive lists of clergy. Medical directories, the first of which appeared in 1843, may also prove of value. In the later twentieth century, there may be considerable, though yet underexploited, potential associated with the *Golden Pages* telephone directory (issued

BOROUGH OF CLONMEL.

CLONMEL, an inland town and parliamentary borough, partly in the S. Riding of Tipperary, and partly in Waterford county, Munster province, 104 miles S.W. from Dublin; comprising 331 acres. Population in 1834, 17,835; of which 1,737 were of the Established Church, 250 Protestant Dissenters, and 15,848 Roman Catholics: population in 1841, 13,505, inhabiting 1,455 houses, averaging 9 persons to a house. It is built on both sides of the Suir, and on Moore and Long Islands, which are connected with the mainland by 3 bridges. The public buildings are, the Parish Church, 3 Roman Catholic Chapels, a Presbyterian, an Independent, a Unitarian, a Baptist, a Friends', and 2 Methodist Meeting-houses, 1 Christian Brethren Community, 2 Convents, an Endowed School, a Mechanics' Institute, the Court House and Prison for the S. Riding, a Fever Hospital and Dispensary, the District Lunatic Asylum for Tipperary county, which maintains 121 patients, at an annual expense, in 1845, of £2,059, being at the rate of £17 each; a Market House, and Barracks for cavalry, infantry, and artillery. The woollen manufacture was carried on here extensively till the Union in 1800; flour is largely manufactured; there is a brewery and a distillery in the town. The Corporation, styled "The Mayor, Free Burgesses, and Commonalty of the Town of Clonmel," returns 1 member to Parliament; constituency on 1st February, 1846, 539. The corporation estates comprise 4,800 Irish acres, producing in 1845, £588 which is expended chiefly in salaries and pensions to municipal officers, in municipal elections, and in public works and repairs. The Mayor and Bailiffs hold an annual Court Leet; the Mayor's Court decides pleas of debt under 40s. Irish. The paving and cleansing of the streets is in charge of the Corporation; the lighting, watching, supplying pipe-water, and abating nuisances, are vested in commissioners under the 9th Geo. IV., c. 82, for which latter purposes there were, in 1843, 470 houses valued at £20 and upwards, and rated at 8d. in the pound; 270 at £10 and under £20, rated at 6d.; and 472 at £5 and under £10, rated at 4d.; total amount of rate for the year, £822. The Assizes for the S. Riding are held here, also Quarter Sessions; a Petty Sessions Court sits weekly. Fairs are held on 5th May, 5th Nov., and the first Wednesday in every alternate month; Markets on Tuesdays and Saturdays. The Excise duties of the district of Clonmel in 1834 amounted to £76,514; in 1838, to £91,206; and in 1845, to £51,698. The amount of postage collected in the town of Clonmel was, in 1841, £950 19s. 10d.; in 1842, £1,050 6s. 3d.; in 1843, £1,152 2s. 11d.; in 1844, £1,192, and in 1845, £1,003. Grain, provisions, cattle, and butter are largely exported. The river is navigable for barges of 50 tons to Waterford; and the town is the centre of a system of conveyance of travellers on light cars, established by Mr. Bianconi, extending over a great part of Leinster, Munster, and Connaught. The Tipperary Joint Stock Bank was established in this town in 1842; and the Bank of Ireland, the Provincial and the National Banks have branches here. The Savings' Bank, established in 1823, had 1,600 depositors in November, 1845; total amount deposited, £47,074, averaging £29 3s. 6d., at a rate of £2 17s. 1d. per cent. The Loan Fund in 1845 had a capital of £3,873, which circulated £17,086 during the year, with a gross profit of £449; the expenses of management were £196; interest paid on capital, £118; nett profit on the year, £135. The amount of property valued for the Poor Law Union is £89,831. The Workhouse was opened on 1st January, 1841; and the expenditure in 1844 amounted to £2,793. The town is the station for the Constabulary Inspector of the S. Riding, and the head-quarters of the force of the Clonmel district, which comprises the 8 stations of Clonmel, Donegal, Fethard, Kilsheelan, Kiltynan, Marlfield, Knockeevan, and Lisronagh. There are two newspapers in Clonmel, The Tipperary Free Press, published on Wednesdays and Saturdays,—Alderman Hacket, proprietor; and The Tipperary Constitution, published on Wednesdays and Saturdays,—Henry Townsend, esq., proprietor.

Member for the Borough—The Hon. CECIL LAWLESS, son of the Right Hon. Lord Cloncurry, Lyons House, Rathcoole.

CORPORATION.

Mayor, John Luther, esq.

ALDERMEN.

East Ward, Wm. Byrne, Patrick Fennelly, John Lacy.
West Ward, John Hackett, William Kiely, P. Quinn.

TOWN COUNCILLORS.

East Ward, Charles Bianconi, John Dunphy, James Gill, Patrick Grady, Joseph Kenny, John Luther, Patrick O'Neill, Edward Phelan, William Singleton.
West Ward, Richard Barrett, David Clancy, Patrick Corcoran, William Hogan, Martin Kennedy, Thomas Prendergast, Francis Ryan, John Shanahan, Thomas Stokes.
Borough Assessors, Peter M'Swiney, Cornelius Denehy.
East Ward, Michael Guiry, Jeremiah Moriarty.
West Ward, Richard Creane, William Ryan.
Auditors, Patrick Daniel, James Meyers.
Town Clerk, Michael Glisson.
Mayor's Secretary, Thomas Dorney.
Solicitor, Dominick F. Ronayne.

COMMISSIONERS FOR LIGHTING AND WATERING.

Chairman, Joseph Kenny, Joseph Grubb, Bernard P. Phelan, Patrick Egan, Samuel Fayle, Thomas Prendergast, Patrick Quinn, Robert Malcomson, Jas. O'Farrel, William Smith, Patrick O'Neill, Patrick Fennelly, John Hackett, John Lacy, Chas. Bianconi, Robert Sparrow, Thos. Stokes, Edw. Phelan, M.D., Henry Sterne.

REVENUE DEPARTMENT.

Distributer of Stamps, John Luther, esq.
Postmaster, Wm. P. Worrall, esq.

BANKS.

Branch Bank of Ireland.—Agent, Thomas Roberts, esq.; Sub-Agent, Mr. Jos. Chaytor; Notary, Wm. P. Worrall, esq.
Provincial Bank.—Director, Sam. Gordon, esq.; Manager, W. Sibbald, esq.; Notary, W. P. Worrall, esq.
National Bank.—Directors, Charles Bianconi, esq., Thomas Stokes, esq., John Dunphy, esq.; Manager, James Gill, esq.
Tipperary Joint Stock Bank.—Director, W. Kennedy, esq.; Manager, James Sadleir, esq.
Clonmel Savings' Bank.—Treasurer, Provincial Bank; Clerk, Thomas Chaytor; Assistant, Richard Legge. Office open on Mondays, from 12 to 3 o'clock.
Notaries Public, John Luther, William P. Worrall.
Clonmel Mechanics' Institute, Warren-street.—For the diffusion of knowledge, by means of a Library, Reading-rooms, Lectures, and Schools. Subscription, 10s. per annum; members, apprentices, and children are admitted to the schools at half the charge of strangers.
Treasurer, Richard Graham, esq.; Honorary Secretary, William Nunan, esq.; Teacher, Mr. Philip Kean, Secretary and Librarian, James Cuddihy.
Dispensary and Fever Hospital.—Physician, John W. Dowsley, M.D.; Apothecary, Dutton M. Hewetson; Treasurer, Edward Jones.

CLUBS AND NEWSROOMS.

The Tipperary County Club, Bagwell-street.
Chamber of Commerce, Duncan-street.
Liberal News-room, Main-street.
Conciliation Hall, Mary-street.
Literary Society, Johnstone-street, lower.

DISTRICT LUNATIC ASYLUM.

Established in 1835 for the relief of the poor of the County of Tipperary, pursuant to Act of Parliament. The Board meet on the 1st Tuesday of each month or oftener if required.
Governors, Right Hon. Earl Glengall; Right Hon. Lord Viscount Lismore; Right Hon. Lord Hawarden; Right Hon. Lord Dunally; Right Hon. Lord Bloomfield; Right Hon. Lord Gough; John Bagwell, esq., D.L.; S. Moore, esq., D.L.; S. W. Barton, esq.; S. O. Meagher, esq., D.L.; William Perry, esq., D.L.; George Ryan, esq., D.L.; Count D'Alton, D.L.; M. C. Moore, esq., D.L.; R. B. H. Lowe, esq., D.L.; E. Lalor, esq., J.P.; H. Prittie, esq., J.P.; C. Bianconi, esq., J.P.; E. Phelan, esq., M.D.; James Scully, esq., J.P.; W. H. Riall, esq., J.P.; Lieutenant-Colonel Phipps, J.P.; Rev. J. B. Palliser; Very Rev. Dr. Burke, V.G.; Rev. W. Giles; Rev. J. Baldwin; Rev. J. Dill; Rev. J. P. Rhones; Denis Phelan, esq.; H. Scott, esq.
Manager, James Flynn, esq., M.B.
Physician, William James Sheill, M.D., F.R.C.S.I.
Apothecary, Richard Graham, esq.

UNION WORKHOUSE AND OFFICERS.

The CLONMEL UNION is situated partly in the county of Tipperary, and partly in the county of Waterford; it contains 89,958 acres, about 140 square miles, and has a population of 37,301. There are 10 Electoral Divisions, represented by 21 elected and 7 ex-officio Guardians. The Workhouse is built for the reception of 600 paupers, to which additional accommodation for 100 has been made; it was opened on the 1st of January, 1841. The Board of Guardians meets at the Workhouse on every Thursday.

Chairman, Lieutenant Colonel Phipps, Oaklands, Clonmel.
Vice-Chairman, Wm. Moore, esq., Loughtally.
Deputy Vice-Chairman, Wm. Smyth, esq.
Treasurer, The National Bank.
Clerk and Returning Officer, Patk. J. Keily.
Master and Matron, Wm. Geoghegan and Ellen Mahony.
Chaplains, { Established Church, Rev. Daniel Foley.
            { Roman Catholic, Rev. John Baldwin.
Medical Officer, Thomas Scully, M.D.

Fig. 8.6: Extract from *Thom's directory* 1848 for the borough of Clonmel.

KILBEGGAN

Is a small market and fair town situated on the banks of the river Brusna, in the county of Westmeath, 44 miles west of Dublin, 8 east of Moate, 15 east of Athlone, and 5 north of Tullamore. It was formerly a borough town, and sent two members to the Irish parliament. Its municipal governors are a portreeve and burgesses. The church stands on the bank of the river and is a neat stone building, with a square tower and one bell. There is also a Roman Catholic chapel. The only charitable institution of this town is a dispensary. There is no manufactory carried on here, but during the butter season a great deal of business is done in that article, and here are two extensive breweries, belonging to A. and B. M'Manus and Mr. John Fallon. The market-day is on Saturday, and fairs are held on March 25th, June 16th, and October 28th.—Population about 1800.

POST OFFICE.—*Post Master*, Mr. Laughlin M'Laughlin. The Dublin Mail arrives at four in the morning, and is despatched at half-past nine in the evening. The Galway Mail arrives at half-past nine in the evening, and is despatched at four in the morning. The Mails from Clara, Ferbane, Cloghan, Banagher, Eyrecourt and Portumna, arrive at nine in the evening, and return at five in the morning. The bags for Tullamore, Ballyboy and Kinnety, arrive at eight in the evening, and are sent at half-past four in the morning. The Mails to and from Tyrell's Pass, Kinnegad, Clonard, Enfield, Kilcock, Maynooth and Leixlip, go by the Dublin Mail. Moat, Athlone and Ballinasloe letters, with the Galway Mail. Letters for England and Scotland by the Dublin Mail.

GENTRY AND CLERGY

Batersby H. W. esq. Ballard
Bennett Captain H. P. 5th regiment of foot
Cantwell Rev. John
Carr Miss
Codd Mrs.
Cuffe Wm. esq.
Daniel Henry, esq. New Forest
Dillon Edward, esq. Horselep

Dowling James, esq.
Dowling Rev. Edward, Castletown
Dowling Lieutenant Wm. H. P. King's County militia
Geoghean Wm. esq.
Gresson Rev. George, Horselep
Handy Samuel W. esq. Coolalough
Hearn Colonel, Coria
Martin Samuel D. esq. chief constable of police

Marshall Rev. Wm. Glebe House
North Peter, esq.
Palmer George, esq.
Robinson Mrs.
Smith S. W. esq. Middleton
Stepney Mrs. Durrow
Walsh Rev. Wm. Spencer
Whitfield Mrs.
Wilson Jas. esq. under sheriff for the county

MERCHANTS, TRADESMEN, &c.

PROFESSIONAL GENTLEMEN
Briscoe John Wm. attorney
Duigan S. A. surgeon
Flood John, Apothecary
M'Guire Bernard, attorney
Walsh Laurence, physician
Willson John, revenue officer

BREWERS.
Fallon John
M'Manus Andrew
M'Manus Bernard

SHOPKEEPERS, TRADERS, &c
Barnett Charles, leather seller
Berry John, linen-draper
Booth Jeremiah, grocer
Carey David, grocer & chandler

Fletcher Edward, joiner
Fullarton Hugh, baker
Galvin Timothy, grocer
Geoghean Daniel, baker
Kelly John, tallow chandler and soap boiler
Kelly Mary, linen-draper
Mulready Wm. grocer & leather seller
Rourke Thomas, baker
Ward Lawrence, grocer
Whitfield John, miller
Whitfield Edwd. linen & woollen draper

PUBLICANS.
Barnett Joseph
Daly Michael
Digan Mary

Doolan Thomas
Robins Michael
Sheridan John
Stoney John
Whitfield Edward, Hotel

COACHES.
DUBLIN, the Mail at half-past nine in the evening, through Tyrell's Pass, Kinnegad and Leixlip.
GALWAY, the Mail at four in the morning, through Moat, Athlone, Ballinasloe and Loughrea.
DUBLIN, the Day Coach, at ten in the morning, through the same towns as the Mail, on Mondays, Wednesdays and Fridays.
DUBLIN, the Day Coach, to Ballinasloe, on Tuesdays, Thurs. and Saturdays at two in the afternoon, through Moat and Athlone.

Fig. 8.7: Extract from *Pigot's directory* (1824) for Kilbeggan, County Westmeath.

since 1970 and expanding on the classified section previously included in the general telephone directory) containing classified lists of commercial activities. Coverage is naturally confined to activities with telephones and the listings in early editions of this publication cannot be considered fully representative. There are also some classification problems, yet this source must have a value not least because the whole country is covered in a few volumes. This is also an important attribute of the general household telephone directory and the more recent fax directory. Few libraries have maintained runs of these publications which are usually seen as space-consuming ephemera, yet in each there is a valuable record, not only of where individuals lived, but of how a major innovation diffused socially and spatially.

Directories as Source Material

Directories are not without problems for the urban historian. Issues of interpretation as to the consistency, completeness and up-to-dateness of the material included cannot always be easily resolved. There may be puzzling omissions and it is not always easy to spot double entries. Yet it can also be claimed that directories may have considerable potential for the urban historian whether in relation to family history, an individual town or the changing fortunes of a group of towns. A particularly appealing feature is that so much is contained in a single volume and that long runs can usually be fairly easily consulted.

In city studies, for example, much can be done with the listings of the merchants and traders by name, trade and address which are available for Dublin from the 1750s and with the more comprehensive later listings of the householders and traders along the main, and many of the lesser, streets. Not only can such information provide important data on individual families and on particular sites, it may also be reviewed in relation to more general topics such as the concentration of particular trades within the city and the changing character of particular streets. For the mid twentieth century Michael Bannon (1973) made use of directory data to map the extensive changes in the location of professional and business services within central Dublin between 1940 and 1970. A similar approach can be applied in earlier periods, although before *ca.*1830 it may be possible to locate functions only to a particular street, not to a specific house. In Cork city, Angela Fahy (1984) used directories with great effect to examine the emergence of what she termed 'functional and social segregation' between 1787 and 1863.

Table 8.1
Most commonly listed types of commercial and professional activity,
44 towns in central Leinster 1824

Publicans, spirit dealers	551
Grocers, Shopkeepers	307
Drapers	184
Bakers	152
Boot and shoe makers	99
Physicians and surgeons	76
Apothecaries	70
Inns, hotels	69
Attornies, barristers, solicitors	62
Tallow chandlers, soap boilers	60
Tailors	56
Leather sellers, leather cutters	53
Hardware, Ironmonger	49
Painter and glazier	43
Saddler	42

Table 8.2
Recorded total numbers (A), and number of different types
(B) of services in selected towns of mid-Leinster, 1824 and 1894

	1824		1894	
	A	B	A	B
Carlow	171	34	256	52
Birr	114	34	202	42
Portarlington	72	23	107	30
Mountmellick	68	20	127	32
Mountrath	45	15	89	24
Maryborough	43	17	136	40
Rathdowney	*	*	76	27

* = not recorded in 1824
Source: Compiled by the author from Pigot (1824) and Slater (1894).

With smaller urban centres, directories may give only limited address information. For mapping of activities, they may therefore have to be supplemented by other sources, for example the valuation books. Nonetheless they offer a readily-available measure of the scale and range of local services (table 8.1). Gulliver and Silverman (1995) demonstrated how directory data can feed into the wider study of a nineteenth century small town (in this instance, Thomastown, county Kilkenny). Subject to caution over possible variations in coverage, this measure may be comparable over time and/or with other urban centres. Table 8.2 shows how directories record the expansion and diversification of services in each of five towns during the nineteenth century. At the same time, the data suggest how the rank order of towns changed, as the communications centre of Maryborough (Portlaoise) expanded faster than neighbouring Mountrath and Mountmellick.

3. Gazetteers

Gazetteers can be considered as ready reference sources offering, for a large number of localities, a relatively-standardised range of general historical, administrative and economic information about their local circumstances. The information is usually presented with each place being listed alphabetically under counties or in relation to the whole country. In contrast to newspapers or directories, the information in gazetteers is less specific, and was intended for general orientation. In a local studies context, it may be of most value for a few, usually brief, comments on the general conditions in a locality.

Two major late eighteenth century examples of gazetteers are *Topographia Hibernica* by W.W. Seward (1795) and the *Post chaise companion* which ran to several editions from 1784. A descriptive explosion followed during the first half of the nineteenth century, including E. Wakefield's two volume account of Ireland (1812), the sample parish surveys in W. Shaw Mason's three volume *Statistical account* (1814-19), the two volume *Topographical dictionary* of Samuel Lewis (1837) and the three volume *Parliamentary gazetteer of Ireland* of 1846. Some impression of the kind of information to be found in these volumes is given by the entry which appeared in 'Lewis' for the small town of Caherciveen, county Kerry (fig. 8.8); the improvements of recent decades are described and the prospect, then under active discussion, of the town being on 'a great western railway', is noted. However, possibly because of the daunting compilation task involved, nothing comparable to Lewis or the *Parliamentary gazetteer* appears to exist for later periods.

The inventory-type approach of the gazetteer is also evident in some countrywide surveys such as Daniel Augustus Beaufort's *Memoir of a map of Ireland* (1792) and in many of the local (usually county) surveys which have been compiled for many parts of the country since the late sixteenth century. The latter include the material collected for various Dublin-based societies, the Dublin Philosophical Society 1680-1710 (part unpublished), the Physico-Historical Society in the 1740s and 1750s, and the Dublin Society, 1801-1832. Informative general town descriptions may appear in these reviews, for example the account of Mullingar which appears in the description of Westmeath by Sir Henry Piers (1682, printed 1780s and reprinted 1979). Part of it reads as follows:

> '... The ancient buildings here were old fashionable castles, some of which remain yet, and some are demolished, and better or at least more commodious houses are built in their room. Here are held continually, all assizes and sessions, four fairs yearly, and all public meetings of the county. It is also a great thorough fare or road from Dublin to Connaught, all houses here are ale houses, yet some of the richer sort drive at other trades also; they sell all sorts of commodities to the gentry abroad in the country, and some besides have large farms abroad. Here is a new goal (sic) built on the county's cost, for the old one was very weak; the old session house also, being very narrow and inconvenient in all respects, a new one is framing, very large and spacious according to the modes of modern architecture; the church also of this town is handsomely rebuilt ...'.

(1979 reprint, p. 78)

CAHIRCIVEEN, a market and post-town, in the parish of CAHIR, barony of IVERAGH, county of KERRY, and province of MUNSTER, 36 miles (S. W.) from Tralee, and 183 (S. W. by W.) from Dublin; containing 1192 inhabitants. This town, of which the greater portion has arisen since the formation of the new line of road along the coast of Castlemaine bay and through the Iveragh mountains to Valencia, is pleasantly situated at the base of the Cahirciveen mountain, and on the high road from Tralee to Valencia. In 1815 there were only five houses in the entire village, but within the last ten years it has rapidly increased, and consists of one principal street stretching along the main road, and of two smaller streets branching from it at right angles, one of which leads down to the quay, and the other to the upper road or old village of Cahir, which consists only of mud cabins. The houses on the new road are neatly built and roofed with slate; the town has a lively and cheerful appearance; the approaches are all by good roads kept in excellent order, and great improvements have been made in the neighbourhood. A subscription news-room upon a small scale has been established, also an agency for transacting business with the National Bank of Ireland. The chief trade carried on is the importation of timber, salt, and iron; oats and flour from some mills to the east of the town are occasionally exported. The flour-mills were erected at an expense exceeding £4000, and from the increasing cultivation of wheat in this district, are now extensively worked. A pier and a small quay were constructed in 1822, which are much used, but would have been more beneficial to the town had they been built a little below the present site; the quay is accessible to vessels of considerable burden. About 400 persons are employed in the fishery, but being also engaged in agriculture they neglect the best seasons for fishing. At Renard Point, immediately opposite to the "foot" of Valencia island, is a small quay, from which is a ferry to Valencia. It is supposed that Renard, which is about 2½ miles to the west of Cahir-civeen, will be the commencement of the great western railway, should that work be carried into execution. The market is on Saturday; and fairs are held on the 1st of September and 13th of December, besides which, several others have been recently established. A constabulary police force has been stationed here; and petty sessions are held in the town every alternate week. The bridewell is a neat and well-arranged building. The parish church and the R. C. chapel (the latter a handsome building), and a fever hospital and dispensary, are situated in the town. Here is also a national school.— See CAHIR.

Fig. 8.8: Extract from *Lewis's Topographical dictionary* i (1837), p. 239 for Caherciveen, County Kerry.

Seventy years later, Charles Smith in his *Ancient and present state of ... Waterford* (1756) describes Dungarvan at some length, noting (among much else) that 'forty or fifty coasting boats belong to the place', and that

> ... This place is visited every Summer by numbers of people from distant parts of the inland country, in order to bathe in the Sea-Water for Rheumatic complaints, and other disorders, for which the cold bath is useful ...

Such comments, embedded in a recitation of more widely-available fact, may be what give surveys, and gazetteers, a particular added value for local studies.

SELECT BIBLIOGRAPHY

Newspapers

J.R.R. Adams, *Northern Ireland newspapers: checklist with locations* (Belfast, 1979)

R. ffolliott, 'Newspapers as a genealogical source' in D.F. Begley (ed.), *Irish genealogy: a record finder* (Dublin, 1981), pp 117-38

P.H. Gulliver and M. Silverman, *Merchants and shopkeepers: a historical anthropology of an Irish market town 1200-1991* (Toronto, 1995)

J.P. Haughton, 'Irish local newspapers: a geographical study' in *Irish Geography*, 2 (1950), 52-8

N. Kissane, *The past from the press* (Dublin, 1985)

R. McCutcheon, 'Pue's Occurrences 1744-9' in *The Irish Genealogist* (1996), 9, 305-80
[Abstracts of births, deaths and marriages from a mid-eighteenth century newspaper]

R.L. Munter, *The history of the Irish newspaper 1685-1760* (Cambridge, 1967)

H. Oram, *The newspaper book: a history of newspapers in Ireland 1649-1983* (Dublin, 1983)

J. O'Toole, *Newsplan: report of the Newsplan project in Ireland* (London, Dublin, 1992)

Directories

J.R.R. Adams, *Merchants in plenty: Joseph Smyth's Belfast directories of 1807 and 1808, with an historical introduction and bibliography of Belfast directories to 1900* (Belfast, 1991)

M. Bannon, *Office location in Ireland: the role of central Dublin* (Dublin, 1973)

E. Evans, *Historical and bibliographical account of almanacks, directories, etc., etc., published in Ireland from the sixteenth century ... with jottings of their compilers and printers* (Dublin 1897, reprinted, 1980)

A.M. Fahy, 'The spatial differentiation of commercial and residential functions in Cork city 1787-1863' in *Irish Geography* (1984), 17, pp 14-26

R. Ffolliott and D.F. Begley, 'Guide to Irish directories' in D.F. Begley (ed.), *Irish genealogy: a record finder* (Dublin, 1981), pp 75-106

CHAPTER NINE

Literary Sources (William Nolan)

1. Introduction

This chapter assesses the ways in which literature in Irish and English conveys images of towns. Literature is generously defined to incorporate diaries, biography, travel writing and novels. The dimension of scale is introduced by citing examples from the village through to the capital city. In order to 'show things as they really are' (or were) it may be beneficial for the student of urban worlds to go beyond the map and the official record and to delve into the rich vein of literature. The Belfast poet Ciaran Carson suggests (*The Irish Times*, 13 October, 1990), that there is a dynamic in literature which conveys a sense of engagement with urban places that goes beyond received documentary images. Literature connects habitant and habited: it may also reveal things which are only visible to the engaged. Seamus Heaney in his introduction to Maurice Hayes, *Sweet Killough let go your anchor* (Belfast, 1994) gives us an inkling as to why such books constitute valuable resources:

> This is a book about life in a seaside village in county Down during the 1930s, a mine of vivid information, partly a census, partly an inventory; but it is also a book about what it felt like to be a particularly attentive child in a family that had 'observer status' because of its recent arrival into the local community. Either way it is a triumph of recollection and re-creation.

In a recent analysis of the spatial dimension in writings associated with county Galway 'The road, the house and the grave. A poetics of Galway space 1900-1970' in G. Moran and R. Gillespie (eds), *Galway history and society* (Dublin, 1996), Patrick Sheeran is concerned with how 'the spatial language of Galway's literary texts can help to gather something about the world model of a culture, become aware of underlying tensions, and learn a little about where the sources of identity lie.'

There are three indispensable reference works relating to Irish writers. *The dictionary of Irish literature* (London, 1996) edited by Robert Hogan has detailed biographical – when applicable – and bibliographical data on some 1,200 subjects. *The Field Day anthology of Irish writing*, 3 vols (Derry, 1991), edited by Seamus Deane, Andrew Carpenter and Jonathan Williams is a rich reservoir of biography and bibliography replete with copious selections spanning the centuries; a fourth volume focussed on women authors is in preparation. Perhaps the two more significant chapters in the *Field Day anthology* for our purposes are Alan Harrison, 'Literature in Irish, 1600-1800' in i, pp 274 to 325 and Seamus Deane, 'Autobiography and memoirs 1890 to 1988' in iii, pp 380 to 560. Irish language sources are also revealed in *1882-1982 Beathaisnéis*, five parts, co-authored by Diarmuid Breathnach and Máire Ní Mhurchú. This remarkable project is almost equivalent to a dictionary of national biography with respect to people who contributed in some way to the Irish language.

2. A Planned Village: New Birmingham, County Tipperary

Personal diaries and letters add significantly to our understanding of the processes of urbanisation and may reveal, for example, why a landlord embarked on town foundation. An unpublished diary belonging to Vere Hunt landlord of Curragh Chase, county Limerick in the early nineteenth century is particularly relevant as it chronicles his attempts to build a new town on a small property owned by him in the barony of Slieveardagh, county Tipperary. This material fortunately survived the accidental fire which destroyed Curragh Chase House in 1946 and is now in Limerick City Library; microfilm copies are available in the National Library of Ireland. New Birmingham (Glengoole, *Gleann an Guail*) is today a small, street village with a Catholic church, parochial hall, primary school, two public houses, a post office and a grocery shop. Hunt's ambitions were inspired by the coal deposits of the Slieveardagh Hills; his misplaced hopes for a canal connection; his assumed connections in the Dublin administration who would, he believed, favourably respond to his request for public buildings; and the inflated war economy *c*. 1813.

In May 1813, Vere Hunt was in Dublin lobbying government officers and people of influence: 'Call on Colonel Bagwell and his daughter and son-in-law, Mr and Mrs Langley, and hint about his power of getting me a barrack at New Birmingham.' Hunt was allowed build a post office after agreeing 'to provide a postmaster and to run free for a year unless the produce warrants the payment by the Postmaster General'. Hunt's quest for a barracks, however, was not successful and the diary records his frustration and annoyance:

> left the castle after reading the humbug letter (rejecting his barracks) in utter contempt of the weakness of an administration, imbecile, evasive and mouldering into contempt, and every loss of public opinion and respect ever must attend the paltry pretended adminis-tration of this despicable and degraded country governed as it is now by outcast English peers and their upstart coadjutors.

Building a new town was a wearisome business judging from Hunt's diaries and correspon-dence. He himself had to take personal responsibility for every building and to suffer the financial consequences of failure. Hunt was either unable to get a responsible person to delegate to or he attempted to do everything himself. Returning from Dublin in late 1813 he found his house surrounds and new town in a lamentable state:

> Joe Hunt's cows on my lawn, the entire of it ploughed with unrung swine, geese dragging the remnants for grass and ducks repasting on the worms. The town filthy, dung heaps in every quarter and turf ricks made in the street.

New Birmingham survived but not on the grand scale which Hunt had desired. His summary of the year 1815 suggests why his ambitions were unrealised:

> Sunday 31st December 1815 – last day of old year and which to me was a year of trouble, vexation and uneasiness. God almighty send the next year and succeeding ones may be more smooth. I experienced every want of money my tenants being unable to pay their rents in consequence of the general fall of every article, wheat from 3/- now 1/3, Oats 2/- now 6d, beef 8d now 2d, pork £3 a hundred now 18/-. It is however some consolation to me that others are suffering equal privations in consequence of the fall of times and that Buonaparte himself has experienced a greater downfall, hurled from an Imperial Throne to an insular incarceration.

Diaries and personal correspondence of town developers will not be available for every town. After checking the Hayes *Catalogue* it is essential to examine local archives and solicitors' offices and to talk with informed locals to establish if papers are held in private collections. Indeed many diaries relevant to Irish towns may be in archives in Britain or elsewhere.

3. The Medieval Town: Callan, County Kilkenny

Literature is most revealing when we have contrasting word pictures of the same place written at roughly similar times. Callan, a medieval borough in mid-west Kilkenny, has significant relict features, moated site, parish church, Augustinian friary. It also has some surviving documentary records for its corporation (held by the Royal Society of Antiquaries of Ireland, Dublin) and poor-law union workhouse (some held by Kilkenny County Council). In 1834 the fair-minded Henry Inglis visited the town in the course of his Irish tour. His eyewitness account (Inglis, *Ireland in 1834*, i, pp 55-6), carrying the convincing 'All this I saw and cannot be deceived' is a damming indictment of the absentee proprietor, Lord Clifden:

> I had not yet seen in Ireland, any town in so wretched a condition as this. I arrived in it very early in the morning: and having been promised breakfast at a grocer's shop (for there is no inn in Callan), I walked through the outskirts of the town, and round a little common which lies close to it, and there I saw the people crawling out of their hovels, they and their hovels not one shade better than I have seen in the sierras of Granada, where the people live in holes excavated in the banks. Their cabins were mere holes, with nothing within them (I speak of two which I entered) excepting a little straw, and one or two broken stools. And all the other outskirts of the town, are in nearly a similar condition: ranges of hovels, without a ray of comfort or a trace of civilization about them: and people either in a state of actual starvation, or barely keeping body and soul together. All this I saw, and cannot be deceived; and from the inquiries which I made of intelligent persons, the protestant clergyman among the number, I may state, that in this town, containing between four and five thousand inhabitants, at least one thousand are without regular employment; six or seven hundred entirely destitute; and that there are upwards of two hundred actual mendicants in the town – persons incapable of work. Is there any one so blind as to contend, that this is a state of things which ought to continue; and that an absentee nobleman should be permitted to draw, without deduction for the support of the infirm poor, the splendid income which he wrings out of a people left to starvation or crime?

If this and the reports of the various poor-law commissions were all we had for Callan we would have little option but to regard it as a rather deplorable place in the early nineteenth century. Fortunately, Inglis's account of his day-trip can be qualified by the evidence of Amhlaoibh Ó Súilleabháin, a local shopkeeper of Kerry extraction, who kept a diary in Irish for the period 1827 to 1835. There were, it is true, poverty and wretchedness, unemployment, hunger, infectious diseases and great political instability but there were also gaiety and music, hurling matches on the fair green, rumbuctious faction fights and intensive drinking sessions (fig. 9.1).

For the later nineteenth century Callan has the documentary texts of valuation, census and administration common to most Irish towns. Callan, however, was revealed more intimately through a series of libel cases which arose from the decision of the parish priest, Rev James O'Keeffe, to re-organise education in the town without first receiving episcopal approval. Not only was there a paper conflict but Callan was riven by internal factions who either supported parish priest or bishop.

(The evidence in the various cases involving Fr. O'Keeffe is given in H. Kirkpatrick, *Report of the action for libel brought by the Rev Robert O'Keeffe P.P. against His Eminence Cardinal Cullen* (London, 1874); details of the state's involvement in the context of the schools and workhouse are recorded in *Miscellaneous parliamentary papers relative to Rev Robert O'Keeffe of Callan 1872-1873* (London, 1873).

Although ostensibly about the disciplinary code of the Catholic Church and its relationship with the common law the conflict may have had its origins in commercial jealousy and the participants may have been divided along older Caravat and Shanavest alingments. These were factions which proliferated in early-nineteenth century Ireland. Their origins are unclear but it appears their purpose was to influence the regulation of property and work. Shanavests were

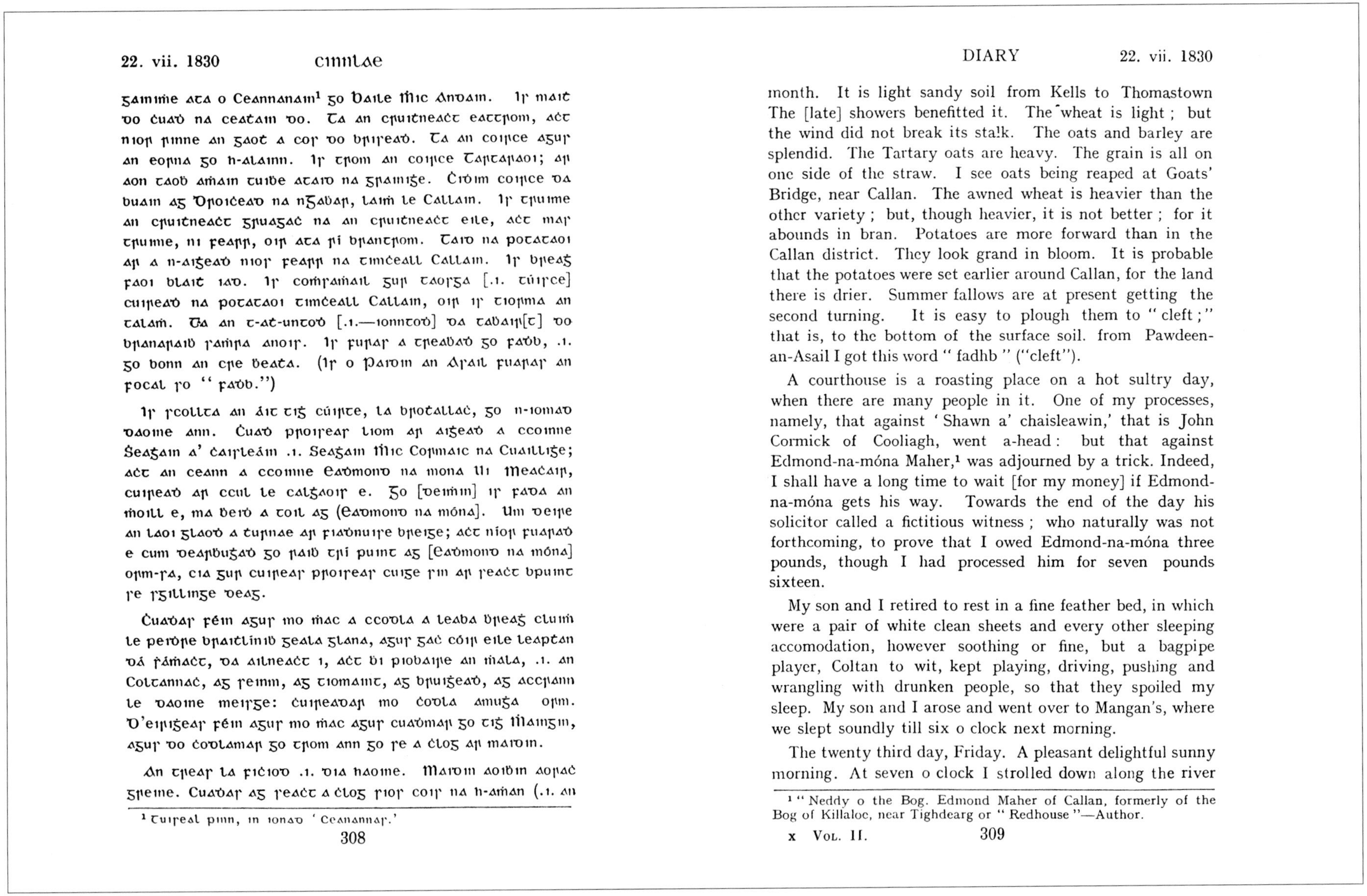

Fig. 9.1: Extract from M. McGrath (ed.), *Cinnlae Amhlaoibh Uí Shúilleabháin*, parts i–iv (Dublin, 1926–31).

---

22. vii. 1830 — CINNLAE

Ġaiṁe ata o Ceannanraoi¹ ġo baile ṁic Anḋaṁ. Is ṁaiṫ do ċuaḋ na ceaṫaṁ do. Ta an ċruiṫneact eatrom, act nior ṫinne an ġaoṫ a cor do ḃruiread. Ta an eorna ġo h-alainn. Is trom an coirce Tartaraoi; an aon taoḃ aṁain tuiḋe ata do na ġráinne. Ċim coirce da buain aġ Droiceaḋ na nGaḃar, laiṁ le Callan. Is truiṁe an ċruiṫneact ġránaiġac na an ċruiṫneact eile, act mar truiṁe, ni fearr, oir ata ri ḃrantrom. Tato na potataoi ar a n-aiġeaḋ nios fearr na tmċeall Callan. Is breaġ faoi blat iad. Is comḋanail ġur taoirsa [.i. tuirce] cuiread na potataoi tmċeall Callan, oir is tiorma an talaṁ. Ta an t-at-uncod [.i.—tontcod] da taḃair[t] do talaṁ, .i. ḃranaraiḋ raṁra anoir. Is fusar a treaḃaḋ ġo faḋḃ, .i. ġo bonn an cre beata. (Is o Paṫṁin an Asail fuaṫar an focal so "faḋḃ.")

Is tsoolta an ait tiġ cuirte, la ḃroṫallac, ġo n-ioṁaḋ daoine ann. Ċuaḋ broirear liom ar aiġead a ccoṁne Seaġán a' ċairteaṁ .i. Seaġán ṁic Cormaic na Cualluiġe; act an ceaṁ a ccoṁne Eaḋṁonḋ na ṁóna Ui Meaċair, cuiread ar ccul le caṫġaoir e. Ġo [ḋeiṁin] is fada an ṁoill e, ma beiḋ a toil aġ (Eaḋṁonḋ na ṁóna). Um ḋeire an laoi ġlaoḋ a ṫurnae ar fiaḋnuire ḃreiġe; act nior fuaraḋ e cum beaġḃuġaḋ ġo raiḃ trí puint aġ (Eaḋṁonḋ na ṁóna) orm-sa, cia ġur cuirear proirear cuiġe rin ar react bpunt re rġillinġe ḋeaġ.

Ċuaḋar féin aġur mo ṁac a ccoḋla a leaba ḃreaġ cluiṁ le peiṫe ḃraitlinḃ ġeala ġlana, aġur ġac coir eile leaṗtan ḋá fáṁact, ḋa aiṫneaċt i, act bi piobaire an ṁala, .i. an Coltanac, aġ reinm, aġ tiomaint, aġ ḃruiġeaḋ, aġ accraṁ le daoine meirġe: cuiread ar mo ċoḋla amuġa orm. D'eiriġear féin aġur mo ṁac cuaḋṁar ġo tiġ Ṁanġin, aġur do coolaṁar ġo trom ann ġo re a ċloġ ar maroṁ.

An treas la ficiod .i. Dia haoine. Maroṁ aoiḃṁ aoṁac ġreṁe. Cuaḋar aġ react a ċloġ rior coir na h-aṁain (.i. an

308

DIARY — 22. vii. 1830

month. It is light sandy soil from Kells to Thomastown The [late] showers benefitted it. The wheat is light ; but the wind did not break its stalk. The oats and barley are splendid. The Tartary oats are heavy. The grain is all on one side of the straw. I see oats being reaped at Goats' Bridge, near Callan. The awned wheat is heavier than the other variety ; but, though heavier, it is not better ; for it abounds in bran. Potatoes are more forward than in the Callan district. They look grand in bloom. It is probable that the potatoes were set earlier around Callan, for the land there is drier. Summer fallows are at present getting the second turning. It is easy to plough them to " cleft ;" that is, to the bottom of the surface soil. from Pawdeen-an-Asail I got this word "fadhb" ("cleft").

A courthouse is a roasting place on a hot sultry day, when there are many people in it. One of my processes, namely, that against 'Shawn a' chaisleawin', that is John Cormick of Cooliagh, went a-head : but that against Edmond-na-móna Maher,¹ was adjourned by a trick. Indeed, I shall have a long time to wait [for my money] if Edmond-na-móna gets his way. Towards the end of the day his solicitor called a fictitious witness ; who naturally was not forthcoming, to prove that I owed Edmond-na-móna three pounds, though I had processed him for seven pounds sixteen.

My son and I retired to rest in a fine feather bed, in which were a pair of white clean sheets and every other sleeping accomodation, however soothing or fine, but a bagpipe player, Coltan to wit, kept playing, driving, pushing and wrangling with drunken people, so that they spoiled my sleep. My son and I arose and went over to Mangan's, where we slept soundly till six o clock next morning.

The twenty third day, Friday. A pleasant delightful sunny morning. At seven o clock I strolled down along the river

---

¹ "Neddy o the Bog, Edmond Maher of Callan, formerly of the Bog of Killaloe, near Tighdearg or "Redhouse."—Author.

apparently representative of the wealthier farmers while the Caravats are presumed to have been labourers. Such hidden geographies are difficult to encounter in official texts but subsequent social and economic networks, church affiliations and the general life of the town were shaped by these turbulent events.

The image of the town in ferment caught the imagination of twentieth century Kilkenny novelists, Francis McManus and Tom Kilroy. McManus published *The greatest of these* in 1943 and Kilroy's *The big chapel* emerged in 1971. *The greatest of these* is set mainly in Kilkenny city and McManus describes the ecclesiastical buildings of Callan in a somewhat laconic manner:

> A church here with iron railings set in limestone around it, then the Christian Brothers, then another church up farther, then the mellowed Protestant church with its old surrounding trees, then the Augustinians, the Convent bright with new stone.

As a citizen of Kilkenny city he was rather dismissive of Callan (Bannow in the novel) with the bitter east wind 'blowing across the flat, stony fields'. Noting that the railway disregarded the existence of Bannow, he penned this rather striking simile: 'So Bannow was like a sorry beast that had tried to crawl from sodden land to the distant Linny Hills in the north-west, beyond which the main road lay and forked to Ossory and Cashel; but Bannow had laid down exhausted and slept.' (For a more detailed analysis of this and the other Kilkenny novels of Francis MacManus see W. Nolan, 'In the mind's eye: Kilkenny in the novels of Francis MacManus' in John Kirwan (ed.), *Kilkenny. Studies in honour of Margaret M. Phelan* (Kilkenny, 1997), pp 205-20.)

Tom Kilroy's *The big chapel* (London, 1971), has more to say about Callan (Kyle in the novel). His description of the Commons (Kilroy, *Big chapel*, p. 12), and its inhabitants evokes the threatening world of small town transients and re-creates the raw edges of a nineteenth century town:

> One or two places in the town had a special significance in the priest's struggle. They ought to be mentioned now. Like the Commons. The Commons was situated a mile and a half below the town, just where the Kilkenny road twisted away towards the north. Here, a warren of British army cottages built after the Napoleonic Wars and added to since then. There was little disloyalist feeling against the British in the area but some special attitude, between fear and contempt, was reserved for these veterans of the Imperial Army and their breed who lived on the Commons. They were held to be different as their names were different, outlandish names like Stukely or Winkle, common but foreign names like Baker or Thomson or Grainger and the Irish among them Connors or Reilly having sold themselves away from the town into the licentious marriages of the cottages with women who seemed to come and go, unsettled and unsettling with their English accents standing apart from the men and children even in the same houses.
>
> Before the revolt of Father Lanigan the contacts between the Commons and the town, while sometimes sinister, were at least tolerable. One-armed men appeared and disappeared with the change of seasons. At one time or another every kind of mutilation exhibited itself on the Kilkenny road or River Street or around the timber yards and sawmills near the bridge. The children, lice-ridden and ashen with hunger, walked back and forth to town to beg in streels of four or five holding hands across the width of the common highway, hardly moving from the feet of fretful horses and the raised whip of the angry driver.

The diaries of Patrick Moran, bishop of Ossory from 1872 to 1884 when he became archbishop of Sydney, are now in St Mary's Catholic Cathedral, Sydney. Moran was not a committed diarist but his involvement in the O'Keeffe controversy is detailed in the diaries. Additional material in the Moran Papers has many pertinent references to Kilkenny.

Individual towns are part of a system of urbanism and comparisons can highlight either similarities or differences. Tony O'Malley, the painter, was born in Callan, spent his early working years as a bank clerk in Irish country towns and then moved to St Ives in Cornwall; he is now back living near his native place. O'Malley was able to read Callan because as a bankman he had comparative knowledge of rather similar towns. For O'Malley the most expressive elements in his natal place were its mills and forges. Mills feature in many of his paintings because:

Mills were part of an ancient cycle – farm, grain food, brewing, work and sun – vital to the whole people. I remember corn going to the mill, the bags, the weighing, the ground corn go gushing down the chutes. There was a mill at the end of our garden in Callan. I loved its solemn growl as it started up. The mill to me was a life centre – a centre of food and culture.

O'Malley provides a twentieth century counterpart of Ó Súilleabháin's rich evocations of town life:

> Callan to me was people, characters and talkers. I used to see the town itself from the top of the Kilkenny road in wintertime and Slievenamon away off in the distance. That was Callan then – it was a physical place. I saw it as a unit but I knew there were internal differences. I knew the streets – Green Street, Mill Street, West Street and Bridge Street – each of which had its own character. Callan people were observers and if they had something to say, it would be very short. The cross was the unifying place for north, south, east and west – that was the centre. In the days when the Confraternity was in full swing in Callan in the twenties, the cross at the four corners would be full of men from each street gathering there, because the pubs were shut (no pubs opened on a Sunday that time at all).

4. A Market Town: Swinford, county Mayo

George Moore who was a Mayo man writing about Dublin (see below, page 170) may be contrasted to John Millington Synge, a Wicklow-Dublin man writing about Mayo. Synge's description of Swinford (*The works of J.M.S. 4 vols, iv In Wicklow In West Kerry. In the Congested Districts. Under ether* (Dublin, 1910), pp 234-5) suggests the small town's intermittent market day vibrancy and captures the essential central-place functions of a town built to cater for its rural hinterland:

> The life and peculiarities of the neighbourhood – the harvesting and the potato blight, for instance – are made curiously apparent by the selection of these articles. Over nearly every shop door we could see, as we wandered through the town, two scythe blades fixed at right angles over the doorways, with the points and edges uppermost, and in the street below them there were numbers of hay-rakes standing in barrels, scythe-handles, scythe-blades bound in straw rope, reaping-hooks, scythe stones, and other things of the kind. In a smith's forge at the end of the town we found a smith fixing blades and hand-grips to scythe-handles for a crowd of men who stood round him with the blades and handles, which they had bought elsewhere, ready in their hands. In front of many shops also one could see old farmers bargaining eagerly for second-hand spraying machines, or buying supplies of the blue sulphate of copper that was displayed in open sacks all down the street. In other places large packing-cases were set up, with small trunks on top of them, and pasted over with advertisements of the various Atlantic lines that are used by emigrants, and large pictures of the Oceanic and other vessels. Inside many of the shops and in the windows one could see an extraordinary collection of objects – saddles, fiddles, rosaries, rat-traps, the Shorter Catechism, castor-oil, rings, razors, rhyme-books, fashion plates, nit-killer, and fine-tooth combs.

5. Cities: Dublin

In their book of essays *Literary landscapes of the British Isles: a narrative atlas* (Harmondsworth, 1979) David Daiches and John Flowers, despite the title of the book, include a chapter on the 'Dublin of Yeats and Joyce'. *Ulysses* is described by them as probably the most 'conscientiously topographical novel ever written' and it is the novel which has given Dublin shape for thousands who will never see the city. Drawing on memory, newspapers, Thom's Dublin directory of 1904 and a mass of detailed information supplied by his Aunt Josephine, Joyce re-created Dublin city and environs for 16 June 1904. Joyce's insistence on topographical clarity is revealed in a letter written by him from Trieste on 5 January 1920 requesting information from his aunt in Dublin: 'Another thing I wanted to know is whether there are trees (and what kind) behind the Star of the Sea Church in Sandymount visible from the shore and also whether there are steps leading down at the side of it from Leahy's terrace.' (Quoted in *Literary landscapes*, pp 221-2).

The following extract (Daiches and Flowers, *Literary landscapes*, p. 224) is the author's reconstruction of episode six in *Ulysses* when Bloom and others are in a cab on the way to Glasnevin cemetery:

> We first see the cab on Tritonville Road which connects Sandymount with Irishtown. It proceeds along Irishtown Road, turns left across Dodder Bridge to go along Ringsend Road. It crosses the Grand Canal where it stops for a moment and Bloom puts his head out of the window to report where they are then proceeds along Great Brunswick Street. They pass the Ancient Concert Rooms at no. 42. St. Mark's Church at no.40. the Queen's Theatre at no. 209. Plasto's at no. 1 where Bloom had bought his hat and 'Sir Philip Crampton's memorial fountain' at the corner of College Street. They catch a glimpse of Blazes Boylan who has an assignation with Bloom's wife Molly later in the day. They pass the statue of Smith O'Brien by Farrell ('Farrell's statue') at the corner of Westmoreland Street and D'Olier Street, then cross O'Connell Bridge to pass the statue of Daniel O'Connell ('They passed under the huge cloaked Liberator's form') at the entrance to Sackville Street, which is now O'Connell Street. They go up Sackville Street past Nelson's pillar to the Rotunda Corner. On the way they pass the 'temperance hotel' (which was at 56 Sackville Street), 'Falconer's railway guide' (i.e. the publishers of that work at no. 53) the 'civil service college' (at no. 51), Gill's the bookseller's (at no. 51), the 'catholic club' (at no. 42), and the foundation for 'the industrious blind' (no. 41). Past the Rotunda the carriage 'climbed more slowly the hill of Rutland square' (now Parnell Square). They turn into Berkeley Street (Berkeley Road) and go past the top of Eccles Street ('My house down there' thinks Bloom) past the 'ward for incurables' and Our Lady's Hospice for the Dying (34-8 Eccles Street) by the North Circular Road to turn into Phibsborough Road.

Seán O'Casey's dramas and his autobiography, and Oliver St John Gogarty's *As I was going down Sackville Street* (Dublin, 1937), create their own sense of Dublin. Austin Clarke's biographical musings in *Twice round the Black Church* (London, 1962) is a personal geography of north inner-city Dublin in the first years of the twentieth century as seen from the 1950s. Clarke's early poetic engagement was with heroic Ireland but his later work (Clarke, *Black Church*, p. 13) is a mirror of changing Dublin:

> As a child, I knew Watling Street well, for twice a year, my sisters brought me with them to the store nearby in Thomas Street, where they bought a stone of salt for the large wooden seller at home; and there were many ways by which we could reach the ancient part of the city, with its stalls, its big and little shops. Sometimes we went underneath the last part of the old town-wall, by the fourteenth century tower of St. Audoen's, and by the distillery. We passed Francis Street where our poor relatives lived in rooms, came down Watling Street or under the arch of Winetavern Street to the Quays again.

> Many of these old hilly streets are changing and new working-men's flats have been built along them. The Guinness Brewery has long since spread on its monstrous way; vast offices of Victorian ugliness replaced the houses of James's Street, in one of which my mother was born; all day there is the sound of machinery, clanking small trains, and escaping steam. But at evening all is still. Recently I walked through the slums, clearances, tumble-downs of Pimlico, from which I could see, at every turn, the Dublin Mountains, went down shadowy lanes under the walls of the brewery which seemed a mighty stronghold of grain. Suddenly above a queer structure like a ziggurat I saw a wisp of hot vapour rising with religious persistency, and thought how the prophets of the Chosen Race had railed against the worship of the Gentiles.

In many respects much of the writing about Dublin has elements of the backward nostalgic look which is so characteristic of rural centred literature, particularly in the Irish language.

George Moore's *Drama in muslin* (reprint Gerrards Cross, 1981), captured the shabby, rather melancholy facade of Dublin in 1882. This extract (Moore, *Drama*, p. 158) conveys the creative writer's skill in describing and, peopling the houses on the square:

> The weary, the woebegone, the threadbare streets – yes, threadbare conveys the moral idea of Dublin in 1882. Stephen's Green, recently embellished by a wealthy nobleman with gravel walks, mounds and ponds, looked like a school treat set out for the entertainment of charity children. And melancholy Merrion square! broken pavements, unpainted hall doors, rusty area railings, meagre outside curs hidden almost out of sight in the deep gutters – how infinitely pitiful!
>
> The Dublin streets stare the vacant and helpless stare of a beggar selling matches on a doorstep, and the feeble cries for amusement are like those of the child beneath the ragged shawl for the gleam of a passing soldier's coat. On either side of you, there is a bawling ignorance of plaintive decay. Look at the houses! Like crones in borrowed bonnets some are fashionable with flowers in the rotting window frames – others languish in silly cheerfulness like women living on the proceeds of the pawnshop; others – those with brass plates on the doors – are evil smelling as the prescriptions of the thread bare doctor, bald as the bill of costs of the servile attorney. And the souls of the Dubliners blend and harmonise with their connatural surroundings.

6. Cities: Irish Language Literature

Sir John Davies, the seventeenth century attorney-general and architect of British policy in Ireland, observed that the 'natives of Ireland never performed so good a work as to build a city' (J. Davies, *Historical tracts of Sir John Davies, attorney-general and speaker in the House of Commons in Ireland 1600-1616* (Dublin, 1767). Although there has been some revision of this statement with respect to urban origins in Ireland, the perception that urbanism is non-indigenous is prevalent. Daniel Corkery, champion of the hidden Ireland, noted the evidence for the widespread use of Irish in cities and town but he essentially agreed with Davies ... 'the Gaels never made their own of the cities and towns – they were little more than exiles among the citizens.' (Daniel Corkery, *The hidden Ireland; a study of Gaelic Munster in the eighteenth century* (Dublin, 1924), p. 22).

A number of studies have focussed on the Irish language in specific urban contexts, for example, Breandán Ó Madagáin, *An ghailge i Luimneach 1700-1900* (Baile Átha Cliath, 1974), Breandán Ó Buachalla, *I mBéal Feirste cois cuain* (Baile Átha Cliath, 1968), Liam Mac Mathúna, *Dúchas agus dóchas: scéal na gaeilge i mBaile Átha Cliath* (Baile Átha Cliath, 1985). Cornelius Buttimer's article('Gaelic literature and contemporary life in Cork, 1700-1840' in Patrick O'Flanagan and Cornelius Buttimer (eds), *Cork history and society* (Dublin, 1995), pp 585-655) is a model of how surviving manuscripts of poetry and prose in Irish can be used to reconstruct a most credible picture of socio-cultural and economic life in a city. Buttimer, using the internal evidence of the manuscripts, places Cork very firmly in a European context as an outward-looking dynamic city. His work illustrates the dangers of uncritically accepting the dictats of either Corkery or Davies concerning urbanism.

Because writers in Irish were invariably migrants from rural areas their perspective on towns can be different than those referred to above. In much of their work the city features as an alien place far removed from the urban village of *Ulysses*. Máirtín Ó Direáin, an islandman from Aran, first migrated to work in the post office in Galway and then subsequently to become a civil servant in Dublin. He always kept Aran in his mind's eye. Reared in a tradition which recognised in the clear limestone landscape the signatures of past generations in fieldnames, fields, stone walls, gaps, paths and houses, Ó Direáin lamented that in the urban world of Dublin his mark would be only in the dusty paper files of a government office:

170

Beidh cuimhne orainn go fóill
Beidh carnán trodán
Faoi ualach deannaigh
Inár ndiaidh in oifig Stáit.

Máirtín Ó Direáin, *Selected poems: Tacar dánta. Selected and translated by Tomás Mac Síomóin and Douglas Sealy* (Droichead Nua, 1984), pp 12-13.

Seosamh Mac Grianna from the north Donegal Gaeltacht migrated to Dublin and we find him in the 1930s in a lodging house in Mountjoy Square. Alienation from the bleak impersonal world of the city is Mac Grianna's lot and eventually he is forced to leave Dublin for his native county. One of the more compelling images of the city as prison in a psychological sense is located in *Mo bhealach féin* (Baile Átha Cliath, 1940). In the following passage (*Mo bhealach féin*, lgh 14-15), Mac Grianna relates how on returning to his shabby, wallpapered domicile in the third floor of the lodging he found a seagull trapped within the room. The caged wild bird becomes a metaphor for the despair of the incarcerated person. Wallpaper for Mac Grianna, perhaps remembering sturdier whitewashed walls in Donegal, symbolised the inanity of urban life:

> Bhí mé sa teach sin i rith geimhridh. Is iomaí duine a tháinig amach is isteach i rith an ama sin. Ach tugadh cuairt ormsa thuas i mbarr an tí nach raibh cosúil le cuairteanna coitianta. Tháing teachtaire chugam as an aer. Oíche amháin ag dul suas a luí dom, agus mé ag meabhrú go mór fá mo chroí, fuair mé colman ina sheasamh os cion m'fhuinneoige. Bhí sé cosúil le teachtaire ó shaol eile, saol fairsing a raibh scáilí air agus contúirt ann, saol a mheallfadh thú mar bhéadh ceol a chluinnfeá i bhfad uait agus a dheas duit, saol an tslua sí. Dá bhfeicfeá colman ina shuí ós cionn na fuinneoige istigh í seomra agus an solas lasta, í lár na hoíche, thuigfeá an scéal. Bhéarfá fá dear chom fiáin agus bhí a shúile agus gheofá amharc eile ar a chluimhreach agus mhothófá an crith beo a bhí ar a cholainn. Ní chuirfeá sonrú ar bith ann i ngarraí agus duilliúr ar a chúl. Ach ní raibh istigh anseo ach leaba agus prios agus pictiúir beag saor, agus bhí páipéar ar na ballaí, agus is é páipéar ballaí an rud is neamhdhúchasaí a rinne an duine. D'imigh mo sheomra beag seascair suarach mar scoiltfeadh splanc é agus réabhfadh séidean na farraige móire tríd. Chonaic mé leige mílte den spéir i súile an cholmain sin agus chuaigh cathracha agus cuibhrinn agus línnte mara thart fúm agus mé ag fáil tormáis orthu, i mo rí ar ríocht leitheadach na gaoithe.
>
> B'Fhéidir gurbh é an dúchas é, b'fhéidir gurbh é an oiliúint é, ach is é an chéad rud a rinne mé iarraidh a thabhairt an colman sin a cheapadh. Ba sin an uair a bhí an seomra cúng. Bhí sé chomh cúng agus go roinnfeadh an colman a chnámha air ach go bé gur oscail mé an fhuinneóg. Thug sé léim fhada anonn trasna na sráide agus chuaigh sé le trí bhuille dá eiteóga gur sheasaigh sé thall ar crann. Mhair an léim fhada sin a bhí chomh huasal le toinn, mhair sí im aigne ó shin agus cnap bróin in aice léi.

For a comprehensive assessment of writings in Irish relating to Dublin city see: Eoghan Ó hAnluain, 'Baile Átha Cliath i nua litríocht na Gaeilge' i Seán Ó Mordha (eag.), *Scríobh* (1970), lgh 25-46.

Muiris Ó Súilleabháin has a rather different perspective of Dublin in his *Fiche bliain ag fás* (Baile Átha Cliath, 1933). Dublin to him is the bright city of lights, traffic filled streets and awesome scale (*Fiche bliain*, ltc. 344 and especially lgh 341-51):

> Nach ar mo chroídhe a tháinig an gliondar nuair a bhog an gluaisteán amach tríd an sráid, nár mhór an t-atharú radairce é, nár mhór an scóp é in am mhairbh na hóidhche. D'fhéachas amach ar an sráid, agus dar fia ní raibh ag baint na radhairce dhíom ach na céadta mílte soillse; soillse ar gach taobh díom, soillse ós mo chomhair, soillse ós mo chionn ar bharr bata. Is gearr go bhféaca soluisín chugham fé mar bheadh réalt tríd an gceo agus i gceann leath-nóimint do bhí sé gabtha tharm — cad a bhéadh ann ach gluaisteán, darnó — ceann eile 'na dhiaidh sin and ceann eile — bólga báisín á dhéanamh ag ár ngluaisteán féin timpeall na gcinní agus an adharc á shéideadh gan aon stad — ní fheadar an domhan an i dtromluighe atáim, nó, marab eadh, is í tír-na-nÓg atá ann gan aon bhréag.

Cork

Apart from Buttimer's work, modern Cork city is wonderfully scanned in the writings of Seán Ó Riordáin who observed its nuances of class. In the following passage Ó Riordáin, bitingly sardonic as usual, dismisses Cork's upper middle-class as gentry posers beyond the Pale (*The Irish Times*, 11 Aibreán, 1970):

> Foirmiúlacht ar fad is ea iad. Ta foirmle mhéasúil acu d'imeachtaí uile an duine. Ní fheadair siad cad is bheith leathscéalach ann. Conaíonn siad i Montenotte nó í mBothar na Dughlaise nó í mBaile na Manach. Tugann siad turasanna ar Londain, ar na Stáit, ar Phárais. Ní haighearálann siad éadach feistis. Bíonn a lá leagatha amach go foirmiúil. Baill de Chumann an Daichid a bhformhór. Bíonn linn snámha phríobháideach acu. Ólann siad uisce beatha istóiche. Cabhraíonn siad le mná a gcótaí a chur umpú. Is iad na dechosaigh is dechosaí ar domhan iad. Rud *infra dig,* dar leo, ab ea fealsunú. Votálann siad d'Fine Gael.
>
> Táid an-láidir ar bhróga svaeide agus stocaí buí. Seilg searcanna a seilg. Níl aon eolas acu ar Dhónal Ó Corcora. Tá Garrán na mBráthar chomh fada ó bhaile le Mars. Bíonn rúnaithe agus oifigí acu ar an Meall Teas. Maidir le náisiúntacht ní fheadar siad aon ní mar gheall uirthí ach gur Sasanaigh Éireannacha iad agus *Jolly good chaps.* Caitheann siad spéaclaí gréine agus spéaclaí *opera.* Chífeá iad ag fágaint an Oyster istóiche agus láracha bán ar adhastar acu.

Galway

The relationship between Galway city and the Irish language is considered by Patrick Sheeran, 'Cathair na Gaillimhe agus litríocht na hathbheochána', pp 97-111 and Liam Ó Dochartaigh 'Gaillimh na Gaeilge', lgh 69-96 (both in *Macalla, Journal of the Student's Irish Society,* UCG, 1984).

Breandán Ó hÉithir's *Lig sinn i gcathú* (Baile Átha Cliath, 1976) is perhaps the finest evocation of urban life in the Irish language: it has that dimension of intense engagement which reveals every facet of Galway life. Baile an Chaisil (Galway) has taken on the personality of its hinterland and this now rural town has been superimposed on an edifice which was once so set apart. The reading in tandem of Ó hÉithir's novel and Paul Walsh's brillant re-creation of Galway's morphology gives a vivid perspective of the city then and now. This is Ó hEithir's analysis (*Lig sinn i gcathú,* lch 24) as to why a new Catholic cathedral was built on the site of the old jail:

> Is minic a dúradh i dtaobh Bhaile an Chaisil nach ndearna sé a intinn suas riamh an baile mór tuaithe nó cathair mheánaoiseach a bhéadh ann. Ceann de na cúiseanna a bhí leis an mbreithiúnas, go raibh comharthaí soirt na seanchathrach le tabhairt faoi deara fós i lár an bhaile. Bhí dhá cheann de na seangheataí fós ina seasamh, má ba ar éigean féin é, agus fothracha lucht gnó an seú agus an seachtú céad déag fós ina seasamh sna sráideanna gnó ba mhó. Bhí cearnóg fhairsing in aice lár an bhaile agus in aice leis bhí an Árdeaglais ar a raibh an clog a choinníodh am leis an bpobal go leir. Ach ní raibh Baile an Chaisil roshásta leis an Ardeaglais. Cé go raibh sí fíorshéanda agus stair cheatach ag baint léi, ba leis na Protastúin í, pobal beag a bhí ag imeacht as an saol chomh tapa sin go mba dheacair radharc níos uaigní a shamhlú ná an pobal go léir cruinnithe i bhfolús na hÁrdeaglaise agus a nguthanna fána ag dúiseacht macallaí míllteacha sna frathacha, baite i ndord an orgain.

What one can arrive at in the context of Galway is the direction and content of interaction between the city and its Irish speaking countryside. This is particularly revealed for the Menlo district just north of the city on the shores of Lough Corrib – Galway's great water spine. The memoirs of Tomás Láighléis were edited by Tomás de Bhaldraithe and published in 1977. They are particularly pertinent today as the city gradually moves northward to capture the once independent Irish speaking clachan. Láighléis chronicles traffic of goods and people between city and country. The coming together of county and town (Tomás de Bhaldraite (ed.), *Seanchas Thomáis Laighleis* (Baile Átha Cliath, 1977), lch 17) wasn't always cordial.

Ag deanamh anuas ón tSráid Árd go dtí an Seamlas a casadh ar a chéile iad. Thosaigh an obair agus chuir muintir an Chladaigh i ndiaidh a gcúil chomh fada le Bóithrín an Teampaill Mhóir, Bóithrín an Chraein Mhóir agus Bóithrín na Blathaí iad. Sheas siad dushlánach ina n-aghaidh ansin agus chuir siad an ruaig siar go Droichead an Chladaigh orthu. Chuir an Cladach aniar arís iad go dtí an áit chéanna. Bhí siad ag cur a chéile siar is aniar ar feadh a trí nó a ceathair de bhabhtaí go bhfuair Mionlach an ceann is fearr orthu is gur chonnigh siad thiar iad. Ní troid dibheirg nó díoltas a bhí inti ná ag baint sásaimh amach ar sheanrudaí a bhí marbh ach troid ghlan lena lámha gan cloch ná buidéal a gcaitheamh intí ach ag triail cé acu ab fhearr. Bhí an dá bhaile chomh múintireach le chéile ina diaidh agus a bhí siad roimpi.

SELECT BIBLIOGRAPHY

D. Breathnach and M. Ní Mhurchú, *1882-1982, Beathaisnéis, cúig imleabhar* (Baile Átha Cliath, 1986-1997)

A. Clarke, *Twice round the Blackchurch* (London, 1962)

D. Daiches and J. Flowers, *Literary landscapes of the British Isles, a narrative atlas* (Harmondsworth, 1979)

T. O'Malley, 'Inscape: life and landscape in Callan and county Kilkenny' in W. Nolan and K. Whelan (eds), *Kilkenny history and society* (Dublin, 1990), pp 617-32

S. Deane, *Reading in the dark* (London, 1996)

S. Deane, A. Carpenter and J. Williams (eds), *The Field Day anthology of Irish writing*, 3 vols (Derry, 1991)

R. Hogan (ed.), *The dictionary of Irish literature* (London, 1996)

H.D. Inglis, *Ireland in 1834. A journey through Ireland during the spring, summer and autumn of 1834*, 2 vols (London, 1834)

T. Kilroy, *The big chapel* (London, 1971)

J. Kirwan (ed.), *Kilkenny. Studies in honour of Margaret M. Phelan* (Kilkenny, 1997)

F. McCourt, *Angela's ashes* (London, 1997)

B. Ó Buachalla, *I mBéal Feirste cois cuain* (Baile Átha Cliath, 1968)

E. Ó hAnluain, 'Baile Átha Cliath i nua litriocht na Gaeilge' in S. Ó Mordha (eag.), *Scríobh* (1970)

B. Ó hÉithir, *Lig sinn i gcathú* (Baile Átha Cliath, 1976)

CHAPTER TEN

Researching towns

Each town's history is unique, and there is no one way to undertake an urban study. Two case studies are presented here: the first by the author recalling her work on Kells (county Meath) and the second a review of McCorry's work on Lurgan (county Armagh).

1. Kells (Anngret Simms)

How then do you go about researching your town? My advice is to begin by looking up *The Shell guide to Ireland* by Lord Killanin and Michael V. Duignan (London, 1967), for an overview of your town's history. It is excellent on the early period. Then look up Samuel Lewis's *A topographical dictionary of Ireland* (2 vols with atlas, London, 1837, reprint, 1970), which will supply you with detailed information on the social and economic history of your town in the eighteenth and nineteenth centuries. Having acquired a historical framework, you will enjoy exploring your town by walking around it and getting to know its shape and character.

When I started my work on Kells in county Meath for the *Irish historic towns atlas* project, I took the early morning bus, which also delivers newspapers, and, equipped with a large-scale map, I got off in Kells. Somewhat apprehensive about what lay before me, I was drawn by a large open gate into the garden of the convent of the Sisters of Mercy beside the bus-stop. I walked over to a grotto, noticed how the garden bordered on the fields beyond the town, and that there was a lovely stone-cut private chapel surrounded by flower-beds. By then I had been spotted and a friendly but definite sister brought me into the house. Who was I and why was I in their garden? I explained my mission and I was no longer alone. The sisters brought me to the parish clerk of the nearby Catholic church, who turned out to be one of my former students. He sent me to the town-clerk in the town-hall on the opposite side of the road, who sent me to the lady in the glebe-house on the Dublin Road, who was prepared to share her considerable knowledge of the history of Kells with me. By now the day was not long enough to follow up all the leads I was given. I had made friends and the next time I got off the bus I felt no need to hide in the convent garden.

Local historians may have already written about your town, and such books and articles will be useful to begin with. However, in order to validate your research, you need to go back to the primary sources. As you can see from flicking through the pages of this guidebook, there are many different sources to be used. The most important ones are held in state-run institutions such as the National Library and the National Archives in Dublin. For example, the National Archives holds the first manuscript census of your town in 1901, including details on who lived in which house at the time, and what their economic and cultural background was. In the National Library you will find back numbers of local newspapers which will tell you when the

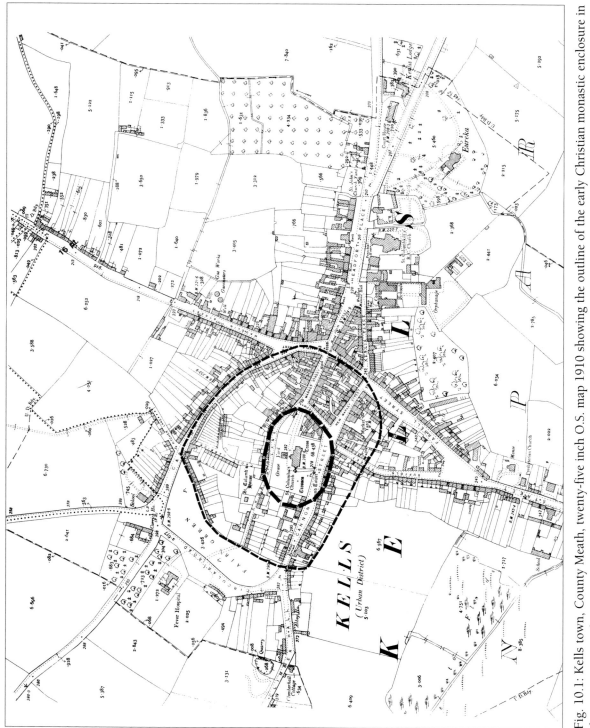

Fig. 10.1: Kells town, County Meath, twenty-five inch O.S. map 1910 showing the outline of the early Christian monastic enclosure in the present town plan.

water supply and gas came to your town. But there are also important sources held locally as, for example, the town council minutes books, usually held in the county libraries. All of these sources have been compiled for a particular purpose and it is your task to extract what is important for the story which you wish to tell.

Each town has a specific location and hinterland, but its early history and pattern of development are shared by other towns as well. While at the centre of their immediate district, they are also part of an urban network, and therefore tied in with countrywide developments, which can only be understood within a historical framework. That is why this book opens with a short chapter on the history and geography of Irish towns.

The Use of Large-scale Maps

Next I suggest that you buy a large-scale topographical map from the Ordnance Survey in the Phoenix Park in Dublin. Because of its scale, which shows individual house plots, the early twentieth century twenty-five inches to one mile map (scale at 1: 2500) is well suited for your purpose (fig. 10.1). Many towns also have unpublished manuscript town plans (scale at 1: 1056) for the early nineteenth century and/or published town plans (scale at 1: 1056 or at 1: 500) for the second half of the nineteenth century. You should also have access to the much smaller scale early nineteenth century first six-inches: one mile map (1: 10560). Try to find these maps in your local council office or county library, or even better buy a copy, if you can afford it. Look at these maps as a historical document and study the town-plan as an arrangement of streets, plots and buildings forming the topographical pattern of the built environment.

The town plan will give you the most important clue to urban origins, while it will also serve to anchor and organise your research. Once you have familiarised yourself with the detail of the town-plan try to understand its evolution. What are its dominant features? Which roads are curved, which straight, and why? In Kells the most striking feature is the circular alignment of the roads following the former monastic enclosure. In fact, we can distinguish the alignment of an inner enclosure along Church Lane, Church Street and Canon Street, and of the outer enclosure along Carrick Street, Castle Street, Cross Street and along the eastern edge of the Fair Green. The church in the middle of the former enclosure is dedicated to St Columba in honour of the Columban monastery, which was founded here in AD 807 according to the Annals of Ulster. The round tower, built before 1076, when it is mentioned in the Annals of Ulster, and the high crosses in the churchyard and on the market place dating into the eighth and ninth centuries (H.M. Roe, *The high crosses of Kells*, Dublin, 1959) form part of the story of an early Christian monastery.

And what do the street-names tell us? In Kells for example we find a Cross Street near the famous market-cross. There is a Castle Street, where the 1807 estate map and a water colour from *c.* 1800 show a tower house, which has vanished without trace; there is a Maudlin Street leading out of town to where the medieval hospital of St Magdalen stood. Then there is a Cannon Street, leading to the site of an important Augustinian monastery just outside the medieval gates to the west of the town (fig. 10.2); and finally there is a John's Street, leading out of town to the ruined site of a medieval church and church-yard established by the order of St John Hospitallers, providing hospital services at the edge of the town. Headfort Place recalls the fact that the head of the Taylor family, whose predecessor had been granted extensive lands in Meath in 1706, was elevated to the Irish peerage as Baron Headfort in 1760 and lived in a big house on Headfort Place. The family moved into Headfort House in 1770, a Georgian mansion to the east of the town (*Burke's Peerage and baronetage*, London, 1912, pp 964-65). The Headfort family owned the town until the early twentieth century. You can continue the analysis of the town plan by thinking about the different sizes and patterns of building plots, the varying street widths, and the location of individual buildings, such as the Catholic church, which uncharacteristically is found in Kells in the middle of the landlord quarter!

Categories to Help you Organise your Research

Having familiarised yourself with the general layout of your town by field-walking and by

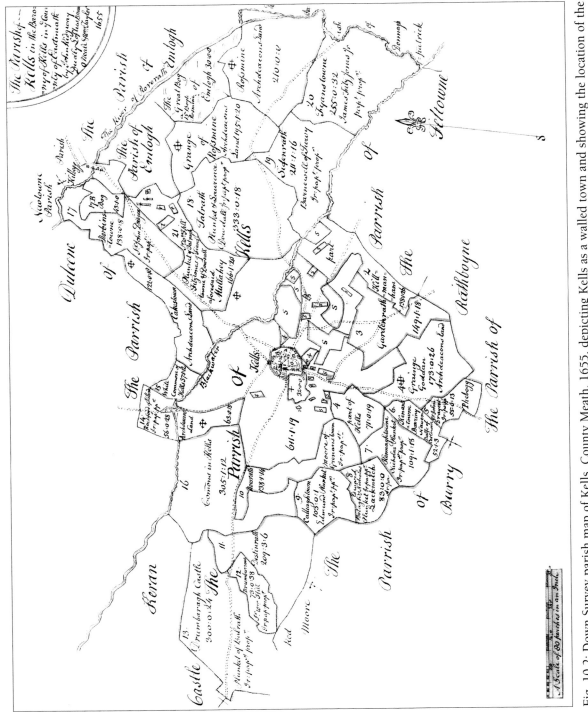

Fig. 10.2: Down Survey parish map of Kells, County Meath, 1655, depicting Kells as a walled town and showing the location of the former Augustinian monastery within a 32 acre site to the west of the town (National Library of Ireland).

studying topographical maps, you may at this point decide to organise the information which you have already collected and which is still to come, into a number of major categories. A simplified version of the topographical information section of the *Irish historic towns atlas* series might assist you. So let's say that you decide on the following headings:

- **Name:** What were the early spellings and what is the meaning of the name?
- **Legal status:** Which words were used to describe your town, its people and form of local government in early documents? Was it *civitas*, burgesses, charter, town commission, corporation?
- **Administrative location:** In which county is your town located, in which barony and townland? Which Poor Law Union and Poor Law Electoral Division did it belong to? When was the Urban District founded?
- **Population:** The ten year censuses from 1821 onwards will give you information on population numbers and from 1841 on quality of housing.
- **Streets:** The OS map at 1: 2500, for Kells dated 1910, will give you the present street names with the exception of those which may have changed since 1922! Can you interpret their meanings?
- **Religion:** The OS map at 1:2500, 1910, will give you the name of the churches. Which denominations do they belong to and when were they founded?
- **Defence:** Are there any remnants of a former town-wall, of towers, gates? Early maps will give some information, particularly the seventeenth century Down Survey and estate maps.
- **Administration:** Look for a courthouse, post office, police barracks, bridewell, union workhouse.
- **Manufacturing:** Are there mills, malt houses, forges, tanyards, coach houses on any of the nineteenth century maps which you have obtained? The street-directories will give some information.
- **Trades and services:** Are there different types of markets – butter, fish, fowl markets – on the nineteenth century maps? What about fairs, hotels and banks?
- **Transport:** Look for a railway station, canal harbour. When were they built?
- **Utilities:** Do the nineteenth century maps indicate public wells and pumps? When were sewers laid, when did gas and street lighting come?
- **Health:** Where were the dispensaries and fever hospitals in the nineteenth century?
- **Education:** Where were the first schools? The street directories will give you some information as do the *Reports from the commissioners of the board of education in Ireland*, H.C. 1813.
- **Leisure:** Is there any information on ball alleys, parks, ball-rooms, theatres, cinemas?

You will find it useful to enter these categories with their numbers on a separate sheet or card, or directly into a computer file. Then begin to study the large-scale topographical map of your town and transfer any information relevant to your different categories on the appropriate sheet or into the computer. Always give a precise reference as to where the information came from.

Important Growth-Phases of your Town

In order to interpret the layout of your town, you need to know something about its history. If your town was founded in the medieval period, you should try to find a copy of its charter. Gearóid Mac Niocaill has collected all available medieval charters of Irish towns and published them in Latin with a commentary in Irish in two volumes called *Na buirgéisí* (Dublin, 1964). A charter is such an important cornerstone for the history of your town that you should find a learned friend who will translate the short text for you. For example, the Latin charter issued by Walter de Lacy for Kells in the thirteenth century granted the burgesses the law of Breteuil (a small town in Normandy) to be free of customs through all his lands and to be free from attending any courts except his own. He also granted each burgess three acres in the fields outside the town (*Na buirgéisí*, vol. 1, 1964, pp 124-125).

The other most important medieval source is the *Calendar of documents relating to Ireland* (5 volumes, London, 1875-86). They were originally written in Latin and a summarised version has been translated into English. You will find them on open shelf access in the National Library. Check

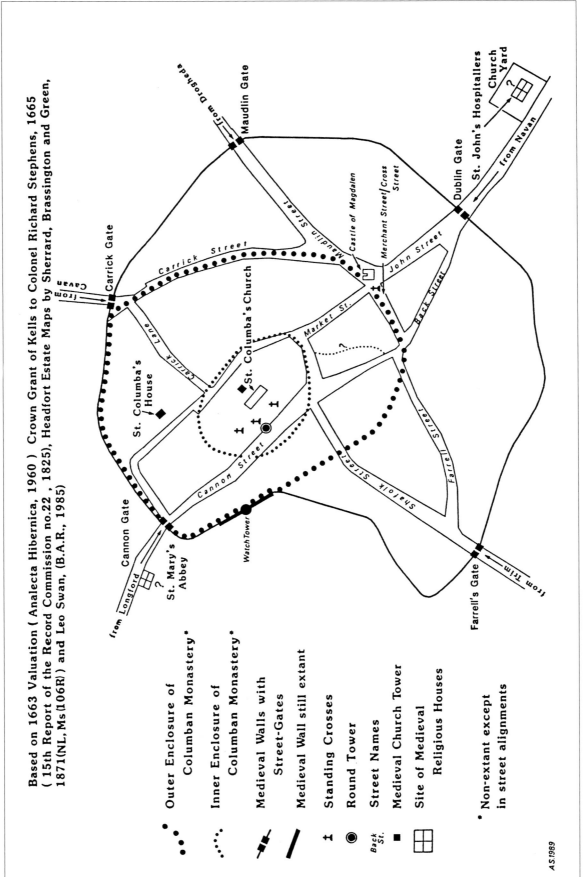

Based on 1663 Valuation (Analecta Hibernica, 1960) Crown Grant of Kells to Colonel Richard Stephens, 1665 (15th Report of the Record Commission no.22, 1825), Headfort Estate Maps by Sherrard, Brassington and Green, 1871(NL, Ms(106R) and Leo Swan, (B.A.R., 1985)

Outer Enclosure of
Columban Monastery*

Inner Enclosure of
Columban Monastery*

Medieval Walls with
Street-Gates

Medieval Wall still extant

✝ Standing Crosses

◉ Round Tower

Back St. Street Names

■ Medieval Church Tower

⊞ Site of Medieval
Religious Houses

* Non-extant except
in street alignments

AS.1989

Fig. 10.3: Reconstruction of medieval Kells, County Meath, by A. Simms.

the index and write down all the references to your town and then look them up one by one and put the information down under the relevant category. Also important is the *Calendar of the justiciary rolls of proceedings in the court of the justiciar of Ireland* (3 vols, Dublin, 1905-52). We learn indirectly from this document (1307-1314, p. 152), that there must have been a tavern in Kells in 1310, as it is mentioned that some gentry were discovered by their enemies drinking in the town of Kells!

An important issue for any medieval town were the foundations of religious houses. There is an excellent reference book by A.O. Gwynn and R.N. Hadcock, *Medieval religious houses: Ireland* (London, 1970). For Kells it records the Columban Monastery built in AD 807 (AU), believed to have occupied the site of the present-day St Columba's Churchyard. It also recorded St Mary's Abbey (canons regular of St Augustine), founded in the 1140s, which was located just outside the western end of the town, but there are no traces left. And finally it mentions the Priory or Hospital of Crutched Friars of St John the Baptist at the eastern end of the town, where only the churchyard remains.

If there have been excavations in your town you should make contact with the archaeologist in charge and ask to see the excavation report. If you cannot establish any personal contact, ask the Office of Public Works in St Stephen's Green in Dublin, whether you may see the specific excavation report. The OPW also holds a copy of the Urban Archaeology Survey compiled under the direction of John Bradley. This survey provides an inventory of building fabric prior to 1600 in the twenty-six counties.

Excellent sources that cast light on the medieval period are the mid seventeenth century Civil Survey and the Down Survey. On the Down Survey barony map of Kells (Headfort Collection, National Archives of Ireland) Kells is depicted as a walled town, as it would have been in the middle ages. On the basis of information on the churches of Kells in the medieval period and with the help of the Down Survey I was able to produce a reconstruction of medieval Kells (fig. 10.3).

When you think about the eighteenth century, ask yourself if your town was part of a major estate. While we most often associate landlords with the big house surrounded by a walled demesne, many landlords were heavily involved in urban improvement, some even creating entirely new towns. For their specific purposes they created maps, estate maps, which predate the earliest OS maps of the 1830s. If estate maps exist for your town, you may be able to locate them in the National Library. They are a great bonus as they often show important features of the built environment. The Kells estate maps, dating to 1817, produced by the famous estate cartographers Sherrard, Brassington and Green, show medieval gates, where the streets leave the built-up areas, and a tower-house castle close to the crossroads where Market, Carrick, Cross and John Streets join (fig. 10.4). They also show road building plans by the turnpike trust, which luckily in the case of Kells did not have enough money to drive a road right through the present churchyard in order to shorten the way through town! More than likely the estate-maps also contain lists of tenants in the town with the description of their property. You will find these a goldmine for your detective mind. The Kells estate maps contained a detailed survey of 1817 recording for each household who lived in it, what the fabric was like (thatched or slate roof) and what the rental value was. This information was mapped and helps to explain the social geography of the early nineteenth century town (fig. 10.5).

The nineteenth century has many sources, because central government began to accept responsibility for collecting taxes, organising the health service and national school system, and attempting to improve transport. In order to establish a record of the ownership and occupancy of each house a survey was carried out in the 1850s, which also established the valuation of each house. In the case of Kells this valuation showed that in the 1840s almost all of the town was owned by the Headfort family and that the houses nearest to the market-cross had the highest valuation. Connected with the Griffith Valuation are the manuscript maps compiled at the same time or soon after by the General Valuation Office. They provide you with the names of alleys and back courts and they refer to specialised markets as for example in Kells to an egg market, poultry market or butter market and to commercial sites like breweries and tanneries. You will find these maps in the Valuation Office in Ely Place in Dublin.

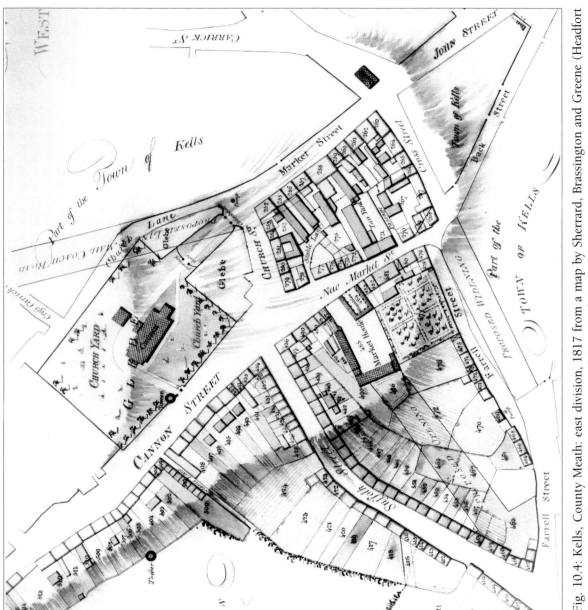

Fig. 10.4: Kells, County Meath: east division, 1817 from a map by Sherrard, Brassington and Greene (Headfort Papers, National Library of Ireland, courtesy of the earl of Bective).

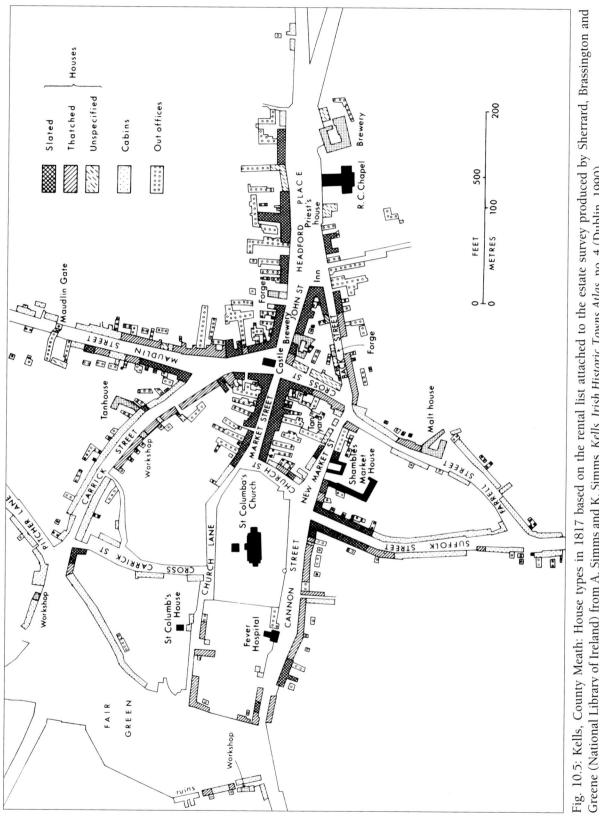

Fig. 10.5: Kells, County Meath: House types in 1817 based on the rental list attached to the estate survey produced by Sherrard, Brassington and Greene (National Library of Ireland) from A. Simms and K. Simms, *Kells, Irish Historic Towns Atlas*, no. 4 (Dublin, 1990).

Also in the National Library you find the nineteenth century street directories, Slater and Pigot, which tell you who the gentlemen in the town were (very rarely do they mention the ladies), which shops were located in which street, and where the coach office was located. In the National Library you will also find under government papers the published reports of markets and fairs, which give some insight into what was sold in the market of your town.

A really delightful source are the nineteenth century travel books. Listen to what Isaac Butler wrote about Kells in 1892:

> Kells or Kenlis 29 miles from Dublin is pleasantly situated on a rising ground not far from the banks of the Blackwater. It forms an agreeable prospect for two miles in a gradual ascent to the town. It was formerly larger and walled with gates and towers by the English soon after their arrival and was deemed amongst the cities of the first rank in Ireland and was the key of those parts of Meath against the incursions of the Ulster men. The castle built by the English in 1178 is in the market place, on the right entering the Main Street, which had some fashionable houses in it. Opposite to the castle is a large cross of one entire stone erect, adorned with several figures in bass relief with Irish inscriptions altogether unintelligible, of great antiquity.
>
> I. Butler, 'A journey to Lough Derg' in *Journal of the Royal Society of Antiquaries of Ireland*, xxii (1892), pp 128-9, spelling modernised

A particularly colourful source, if you can find them, are the municipal records. For Kells I found the records of the corporation of Kells, 1685-1787, in the Headfort Estate Papers in the National Library, and I found seven volumes (1839-1922) of the Kells corporation and town commissioners' minute books in the cellar of the Meath County Library in Navan. I was fortunate to receive good guidance from the librarian. These minutes record the stark reality of life in eighteenth and nineteenth century Kells. For example, in 1711 women of questionable repute were expelled from the town. In 1718 it was forbidden to erect pig-sties in the streets. In 1742 every respective inhabitant of Market Street had to find six loads of stones towards paving the said street. In the 1880s penalties are recorded for people who kept furze bushes in front of their houses as firewood, which was a fire hazard. Penalties were also recorded for people who produced soap without a chimney, which was another fire hazard. On 20 April 1891 the minutes record a report by the medical officer to the town-council, which gives a bleak impression of the living-condition of the poorer classes at the time:

> As medical officer of health I beg to report that the hovels in Bective Street owned by Mr Thomas Nelson in the occupation of weekly tenants are wholly unfit for human habitation and I consider it really dreadful at a time when so much is being done for the Housing of the Working Classes that such structures should be allowed to exist in any town. These hovels consist of the most part of one small dark apartment in which persons of various ages and different sexes live by both day and night.

But we must not forget that the nineteenth century was also the time when most towns were connected to a railway line and commercial institutions were established. The Great Northern Railway was extended from Dublin to Kells in 1853. The first savings bank was established in Kells in the courthouse in 1837, the first Hibernian Bank was set up in 1844 and the first National Bank in 1853, all three located in Headfort Place.

When you have come so far, it will be very helpful to transfer all the information on your town from the sources mentioned above and from the many others discussed in the text of this book on to a large-scale map. You will find that the major growth-phases of the town become recognisable. Now you begin to understand the development of your town. Your story will be an important one, because it tells about the trials and tribulations and the successes of the people who lived in the town before you. If you run into difficulties do not hesitate to ask for help from people who have worked with sources before you. The more you can quote from the original sources the more authentic your own story will be.

Fig. 10.6: Kells, County Meath, view from the east, ca. 1800 (in private ownership).

SELECT BIBLIOGRAPHY FOR THE STUDY OF KELLS

(taken from: A. Simms with K. Simms: *Kells, Irish historic towns atlas*, no. 4 (Dublin 1990), pp 11-12.)

R. Atkinson (ed.), *Book of Ballymote* (Dublin, 1887)

R.I. Best and others (eds), *The book of Leinster, formerly Lebar na nuachongbala*, 6 vols (Dublin, 1954-83)

R.I. Best and O. Bergin (eds), *Lebor na hUidre, Book of the dun cow* (Dublin, 1929)

J. Bradley, 'The medieval towns of county Meath' in *Ríocht na Mídhe*, viii (1988-9), pp 30-49

J. Bradley, 'The role of town-plan analysis in the study of the medieval Irish town' in T.R. Slater (ed.), *The built form of western cities* (Leicester and London, 1990), pp 39-59

J. Brady, *A short history of the parishes of the diocese of Meath, 1867-1983*, no. 4 (Navan, 1938)
 Books of survey and distribution. East Meath and Louth c. 1690, National Archives of Ireland, Dublin

E. St J. Brooks (ed.), *The Irish cartularies of Llanthony Prima and Secunda* (Dublin, 1953)

Burke's peerage, barontage and knightage (London, 1939), pp 1106-1108

I. Butler, 'A journey to Lough Derg' in *Journal of the Royal Society of Antiquaries*, xxii (1892), pp 126-36
 Castle and part of John Street, Kells. Artist unknown, inscribed 'E.B. 1874'. Location of original unknown

M.V. Clarke (ed.), *Register of the priory of the Blessed Virgin Mary at Tristernagh* (Dublin, 1941)

A. Cogan, *The diocese of Meath, ancient and modern*, 3 vols (Dublin, 1862-70)

Crown grant of Kells to Colonel Richard Stephens, *Fifteenth annual report of the Irish record commission*, HC 1825 (428), xvi, pp 197-8

Crown rental, County of East Meath, Kells barony, 1706, pp 90-98, National Archives of Ireland, Dublin

O. Davies and D.B. Quinn, 'The Irish pipe roll of 14 John, 1211-1212, in *Ulster Journal of Archaeology*, 3rd series, iv, supplement (1941), pp 1-76

Down Survey, 1655. Parish and barony maps of Kells. Reeves collection, NLI, MS 723, Headfort Collection, National Archives of Ireland, Dublin

G.V. Du Noyer, View of round tower, Kells, *c.* 1857, in: Kells drawings, iii, p. 32; *RSAI*, Dublin; by the same artist: View of church spire, round tower and part of the old fortifications of Kells in Meath, 1865, in: Kells drawings, x, p. 40, Royal Society of Antiquaries of Ireland, Dublin. C.C. Ellison, 'Bishop Dopping's visitation book, 1682-1685' in *Ríocht na Mídhe*, v (1973-4), pp 3-11

P. Ferguson, Kells in 1865: a case study, unpublished B.A. thesis, Geography Department, University College, 1987

A.M. Freeman (ed.), *Annála Connacht: the Annals of Connacht (AD 1224-1544)* (Dublin, 1944)

E.J. Gwynn (ed.), *Book of Armagh: the Patrician documents* (Dublin, 1937)

A. Gwynn, *The medieval province of Armagh, 1470-1545* (Dundalk, 1946)

A. Gwynn, 'Some notes on the history of the Book of Kells' in *Irish Historical Studies*, ix (1954), pp 131-61

Headfort estate maps: 'Town and lands of Kells' by John O'Brien, 1762, scale ten Irish perches to one inch (1:2520); 'Town and lands of Kells' (maps 1-4,7,8 and terriers) by Sherrard, Brassington and Greene, 1817, scale four Irish perches to one inch (1;1008), National Library of Ireland, Headfort papers

Headfort estate papers. National Library of Ireland, MSS 25,300-453, 26,679-739

J. Healy, *Historical guide to Kells (Ceanannus Mór), county Meath* (Dublin, 1930)
 Headfort estate papers. National Library of Ireland, MSS 25, 300-453, 26, 679-739

T.K. Henderson, *Henderson's post office directory for the counties of Meath and Louth* (Trim, 1861)

W.M. Hennessy and B. MacCarthy (eds), *Annála Uladh, Annals of Ulster; otherwise Annála Senait, Annals of Senat: a chronicle of Irish affairs, 431-1131, 1155-1541*, 4 vols (Dublin, 1887-1901)

M. Herbert, *Iona, Kells and Derry: the history and hagiography of the monastic familia of Columba* (Oxford, 1988)

M. Herity, 'The lay-out of Irish early-Christian monasteries' in P. Ní Chatáin and M. Richter (eds), *Ireland and Europe* (Stuttgart, 1984), pp 105-16

R.C. Hoare, *Journal of a tour in Ireland, AD 1806* (London, 1807)

J. Hunt, *Irish medieval figure sculpture, 1200-1600*, 2 vols. (Dublin, 1974)

G. Keating, *Foras Feasa ar Éirinn; the history of Ireland*, ed. by D. Comyn and P.S. Dinneen, 4 vols (Dublin, 1902-14)

Kells corporation common council book, 1711-1829. Headfort Estate Papers, National Library of Ireland, MS 25 447

Kells turnpike journal, 1734-6; Account of Kells and Navan turnpikes, 1738-58. Headfort Estate Papers, National Library of Ireland, MS 25, 450

Kells, view from the east Watercolour. Artist unknown, inscribed 'Kells, L.E.W., July 1803' (in private ownership)

M.B. Kelly, 'Short history of the convent of Mercy' in *Ceanannus Credit Union, silver jubilee* (Navan, 1986), p. 28

R.A.S. Macalister (ed.), *Lebor Gabala Erenn; The book of the taking of Ireland*, 5 vols. (Dublin, 1938-56)

Maps of the Headfort Estate, County Meath, 1758-62. National Archives of Ireland, M 442/15, 17, 18

A.D.S. McDonald, 'Aspects of the monastery and monastic life in Adomnan's Life of Columba' in *Peritia,* iii (1984), pp 271-302

Meath county council, *Draft development plan for Kells* (Kells, 1986)

C. McNeill (ed.), *Calender of Archbishop Alen's register, c. 1175-1534* (Dublin, 1950)

C. McNeill and A.J. Otway-Ruthven (eds), *Dowdell deeds* (Dublin, 1960)

G. Mac Niocaill (ed.), *Notitiae as Leabhar Cheanannais, 1033-1161* (Blackrock, 1961)

L. Miller and E. Power (eds), *Holinshed's chronicle: Ireland 1577* (Dublin, 1979)

J. Mills and M.J. McEnery (eds), *Calender of the Gormanston register* (Dublin, 1916)

An abstract of the presentments of the grand jury of the County Meath at summer assizes, 1804, Royal Irish Academy, Haliday pamphlets, 865, 12

Murray collection of architectural drawings. Kells R.C. Church, 1846; Kells Savings Bank, 1846; Kells Session House, rear elevation, 1802 (by Francis Johnson). Irish Architectural Archive, Dublin

B. Nic Aongusa, The charters in the Book of Kells: a historical analysis, University College, Dublin unpublished M.Phil. thesis (1988)

P. O'Connell, 'Kells, early and medieval' in *Ríocht na Mídhe*, ii, no. 1 (1959), pp 18-36; no. 2 (1960), pp 8-22

J. O'Donovan, Letters containing information relative to the antiquities of the county of Meath, collected during the progress of the Ordnance Survey in 1836 (typescript copies Dublin, 1928)

J. O'Donovan, 'The Irish charters in the Book of Kells' in *Irish Archaeological Society's Miscellany* (Dublin, 1848), pp 127-58

J. O'Donovan (ed.), *Annála rioghachta Éireann; Annals of the kingdom of Ireland by the Four Masters from the earliest period to the year 1616.* 7 vols.(Dublin, 1851 reprint 1992)

D. O'Neill, Kells: the seventeenth and nineteenth centuries, Geography Department, University of Dublin, unpublished B.A. thesis (1986)

Ordnance Survey. Large-scale map of Kells: scale 1:1056, manuscript, 1836 Ordnance Survey office, Dublin. Maps of County Meath, scale 1:10,560, printed, 1836, 1882; scale 1:2500, printed, 1910, 1974

M. O'Reilly, The development of Kells: a study in town plan analysis. Geography Department, University College, Dublin, unpublished B.A. thesis (1982)

G.H. Orpen, *Ireland under the Normans, 1169-1333,* 4 vols (Oxford, 1911-20)

A.J. Otway-Ruthven, 'The partition of the de Verdon lands in Ireland in 1332', in *Proceedings of the Royal Irish Academy,* lxvi, C (1968), pp 401-55

C. Plummer (ed.), *Bethada naem nErenn: Lives of Irish saints,* 2 vols (Oxford, 1922)

*Rawlinson B 502: a collection of pieces in prose and verse in the Irish language from the original MS in the Bodleia*n. With an introduction by Kuno Meyer (Oxford, 1909)

Records of the Corporation of Kells, 1685-1787. Headfort Estate Papers, National Library of Ireland, MS 25,446 (1-8). Kells corporation and town commissioners' minute books, 7 vols., August 1839 to June 1922. Meath County Library, Navan

Report of local government and taxation of towns inquiry commission (Ireland), pt 3, HC 1877 (C.-1787), xl

Reports of royal commission on market rights and tolls, pp 208-13, HC 1889 (C.-5888), xxxvii.

Report of the municipal boundaries commission (Ireland), pt 3, pp 467-71, HC 1881 (C.-3039), 1

Returns from all schools receiving grants from the commissioners of national education in Ireland, HC 1892 (23), ix

M. Reynolds, 'Kells lace' in *Irish Arts Review,* ii (1985), pp 50-55

H.M. Roe, *The high crosses of Kells* (Dublin, 1959)

Returns from all schools receiving grants from the commissioners of national education in Ireland, HC 1892 (23), ix

Royal commission on primary education (Ireland). Returns showing the number of children in each primary school, HC 1870 (C.-6.v.), xxviii (v)

Second report of the commissioners appointed to consider and recommend a general system of railways for Ireland, HC 1837-8 (145), xxxv

M.P. Sheehy (ed.), *Pontificia Hibernica: medieval papal chancery documents concerning Ireland, 640-1261,* 2 vols (Dublin, 1962)

R.C. Simington (ed.), 'Valuation of Kells (1663), with note on map drawn by Robert Johnston' in *Analecta Hibernica,* xxii (1960), pp 231-68

H. Simmonds, Census of the town and parks of Kells, January 1865, Headfort Estate Papers, National Library of Ireland, MS 25, 423

D.L. Swan, 'Monastic proto-towns in early medieval Ireland: the evidence from photography, plan analysis and survey' in H.B. Clarke and A. Simms (eds), *The comparative history of urban origins in non-Roman Europe, British Archaeological Reports International Series,* 255 (Oxford, 1985), i, pp 77-102

Valuation. Records of the General Valuation Office relating to Kells. (1) Early manuscript valuation book, 1837, and manuscript town plan, *c.* 1837. Valuation Office, Dublin. (2) Printed tenement valuation, Kells Union, 1854, and manuscript town plan, *c.* 1854. Valuation Office, Dublin. (3) Manuscript revision books and related maps, Kells District Electoral Division, 1855 to present. Valuation Office, Dublin. (4) Records of the circuit court: general valuation and applotment books. National Archives of Ireland, Dublin

N.B. White (ed.), *Irish monastic and episcopal deeds, AD 1200-1600* (Dublin, 1936), appendix 3, The register of Kells, pp 300-13

W.R. Wilde, *The beauties of the Boyne and its tributary, the Blackwater* (Dublin, 1849)

2. Lurgan (Frank McCorry)

Lurgan: An Irish provincial town, 1610-1970 (Lurgan, 1993), provides a valuable case study of a northern plantation town. This book is not so much concerned with urban morphology as with the interplay of a range of interests which shaped Lurgan. Foremost among these were the Brownlows, scions of an astute legal-commercial family, who had established a bawn, market house and windmill here by the 1620s (fig. 10.7). The Brownlows have left an impressive paper record which kept pace with the town. Apart from the landlord family, Lurgan became home to a number of religious groupings who through their exclusiveness and cohesiveness provided a key dynamic for industrial development. The development of weaving based on the production of high quality linen, initially home located and subsequently in large factory units, is in many respects the story of Lurgan. But the town was host and sometimes hostage to its rural hinterland and traces of rurality were visible in the town confines up until the 1960s. Although never a garrison town, Lurgan was always a soldiering town. It competed with the regional centres of Portadown and Armagh for state patronage when the canal, road and rail networks integrated north-eastern Ireland into the urban hinterland of Belfast.

The Plantation of Ulster brought the Brownlows to the old territory of Clanbrassil which had been incorporated by Mountjoy into the newly formed county Armagh in 1605, a decision disputed by the Magennises, Irish lords of nearby Iveagh. John Brownlow, a native of Bashford close to the city of Nottingham, was allotted the manor of Dowcoran and his son William the manor of Ballynamoney. By 1611 they were in residence with a retinue of six carpenters, one mason, a tailor and six workmen. Clanbrassil on the southern shore of Lough Neagh was a land of promise. Lough Neagh had vast resources of fish and wildfowl. There were massive peat deposits and the derry (doire, oak-wood) lands along the lough shore were full of oak, ash and willow, suitable for building and tanning and raw material for linen loom manufacture. Native black cattle ranged freely on shrubby pasture; clay and sand were in plentiful supply for the construction of settler houses.

McCorry utilised the earlier plantation surveys of Pynnar (1619) and Caulfield (1622) to estimate the scale and appearance of the new settlement. Neither survey was satisfactory, the former being very inaccurate. Foundation patents had a formative influence on ethnic and religious differentiation. On 22 June 1629 the patent of Charles 1 formally recognised Sir William Brownlow's town of BallyLurgan (fig. 10.8). Brownlow was given local jurisdiction through courts baron and leet and economic status through fairs and markets and the power to erect tanyards. Tenancies at the core were restricted to English and the Irish were permitted farms in thirteen named townlands which detached them from ancient ceremonial and sacred grounds. analysis of Brownlow rentals for 1622 and 1635/6 suggests that there was a large turnover of early settlers. Indeed this study demonstrates that in the context of Lurgan, comings and goings were to exert a profound influence on the urban character throughout the town's history. Evidence from the depositions concerning the 1641 rebellion shows that Lurgan was retaken by the Magennises and their local proteges, the McCanns. Some of the settlers were killed but the landlord was given safe passage to Armagh and subsequently to Dungannon. The status of his Irish wife was the key factor in his survival. Uneasy peace fashioned by the Parliamentarians ushered in a new era for Lurgan and by 1649 Brownlow was back shaping his estate town through the significant medium of freehold leases. Tenements in front steads were long narrow strips of land stretching from the high street ridge to either the Derry Bog or the Pound River which then marked the restricted physical limits of Lurgan town. Each tenement was divided by an eight feet right-of-way and these features can be detected in the street patterns of modern Lurgan in much the same way as burgage plots from the medieval period are revealed in Anglo-Norman foundations (figs. 10.9, 10.10). William Brownlow's will dated 1660 refers to a debt of £3,600 to English financier Robert Parkhurst of Pirford, Surrey, which suggests that landlord development in Irish towns was often paid for by English money.

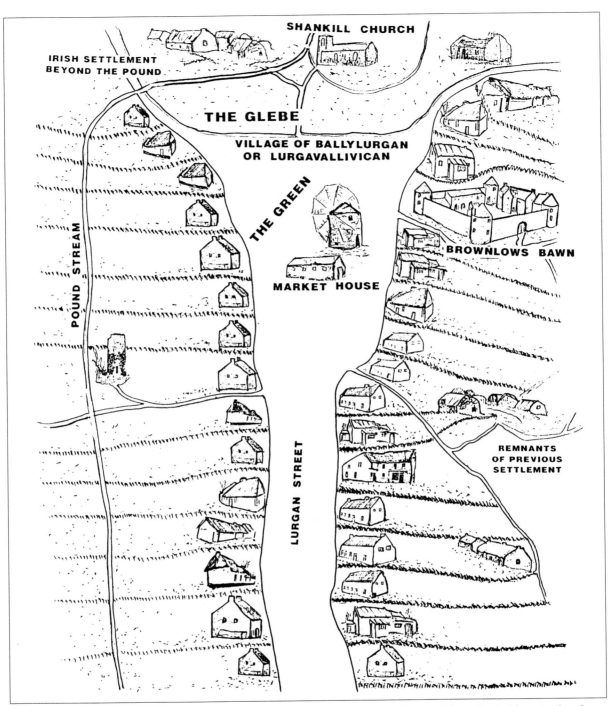

Fig. 10.7: Artist's impression of Lurgan village prior to the rebellion of 1641. The raised ridge site has been subdivided into elongated tenements, headed by detached dwellings. In broad Market Street a market house and windmill stand close to Brownlow's defensive bawn. The tiny Pound river winds its way down past the refurbished Shankill church. Remnants of the earlier Irish settlement stand in or near the village, F. McCorry, *Lurgan*.

In 1652 six Montiagh townlands close to Lough Neagh were leased to a group of tanners who inevitably set about the exploitation of the woodlands. The commercialisation of the timber trade had ripple effects in the local economy, stimulating trade and generating a range of specialist skills with Lurgan the clearing house for produce and capital. Another event central to Lurgan's development was the coming of the Quakers in 1654; they brought with them the skill and

We do give and grant full and absolute power and authority unto the aforesaid Sir William Brownlow, his heirs and assigns for ever that the said Sir William Brownlow, his heirs and assigns and every one of them shall or may for ever hereafter have and hold at the aforesaid Town of Bally Lurgan one free market to be held there weekly upon every Friday for ever, and two fairs there yearly the one to begin to be held upon the Feast Day of St. James, the other upon the Feast Day of St. Martin yearly for ever, each of the said fairs to routine for two days repectively.

....do grant to the said Sir William Brownlow his heirs and assigns, several courts of Pipowders and all things belonging to the Courts of Pipowders to be held in or within the aforesaid several fairs

.... and all singular tolls, profits, commodities, emoluments, liberties, free customs, meritorious or privileges whatsoever belonging to aforesaid fairs, markets and Courts rendering and paying yearly unto our heirs 20 shillings of current and lawful money. And further we will to the said Sir William Brownlow all figures that our said grant of the aforesaid several fairs.

And we will that the said Sir William Brownlow shall not grant or demise the aforesaid Castle Townland of Derry otherwise called Brownlow's Derry, the aforesaid townlands of Toberhewny, the aforesaid townland of Ballyblagh, the aforesaid townland of Killaenargett, the aforesaid townland of Turmoyra....or any part of them to any one of ones being mere Irish or who shall not be of English or British race.

....five several freeholders, said freeholders shall have 50 acres of arable land, meadow or pasture....their tenants being in fee payable, fee simple or fee farm....every of them being of British or English race, build or erect their dwelling houses together in Town as near to the principal dwelling house or mansion of the said Sir William Brownlow.

....and further the aforesaid Sir William Brownlow may lawfully grant Kinago, Clanrolla, Clankillvoragh, Drumnakerne, Derrytagh, Ballinary, Derryadd, Derryinver, Derrytrasna, Ardmore, Derrytagh, Ballinamoney and a moiety of Monbrief unto any person or persons being mere Irish for any term not exceeding 41 years or three lives, such tenants of the Irish Nation to build and erect their dwelling houses together and in town reeds and not dispersedly or solitary and to conform themselves with that usage after the manner of England.

22nd. June, 1629   Fifth Charles I   9th. July, 1629

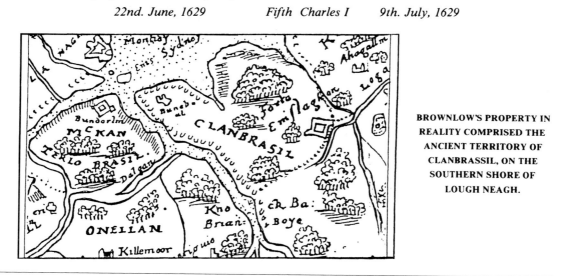

BROWNLOW'S PROPERTY IN REALITY COMPRISED THE ANCIENT TERRITORY OF CLANBRASSIL, ON THE SOUTHERN SHORE OF LOUGH NEAGH.

Fig. 10.8: Extracts from the patent of Brownlow's Derry, 1629, F. McCorry, *Lurgan.*

culture of linen weaving and the cohesion which champions self-interest for mutual benefit. Minority religions are usually good record keepers and there is extant for Lurgan a complete list of the subscribers to the building fund of the new Quaker meeting house in 1696 (G.R. Chapman, 'Quaker meeting places in the Lurgan area in the seventeenth century' in *Review Journal of the Craigavon Historical Society,* 1992). The Quakers established their meeting house and graveyard close to the river at the opposite end of the town to the Church of Ireland's central buildings. Their strategy in Lurgan had two significant dimensions: urban based members engaged in linen finishing – bleaching, processing and marketing – while those on rural farms provided the raw materials and the early spinning and weaving.

Lease of Tenement by Arthur Brownlow, alias Chamberlain, of Brownlows Derry, to Abell Porter of Lurgan, Linen Draper, 2nd. September 1703.

.... all that part or proportion of that tenement in Lurgan, now in the possession of William Porter, containing about 36 yards of Fronstead, butted and bounded by Robert Hoope's Tenement on one side and Robert Douglass's Tenement on the other side, and extending down to the little river or stream at the foot of the orchard (one acre) near the south-east end of the Town of Lurgan. Arthur reserves free liberty of a clear passage or way from the Street of Lurgan of the breadth of 8 feet all along the premises to that of the said tenement or land beyond the River or Stream to pass and trespass with horses, cows and Carrs. And provided always the said Abell Porter does not assign or sell away the Interest of the premises but to such as be of British race or descent, nor into such before the first offer or refusal given to the said Arthur Brownlow. And that the said Abell Porter shall within the next two years have built at least 45 feet in the front street of the premises next Hoope's wall, at least 10 feet high, and within 5 years to wall the old house where it is not already done with good lime and stone or brickwork. And that the said Abell Porter shall give service to the Court Leet and Courts Baron. Rental, £3.10s.0d. yearly, during Abell's life, rising to £4.0s.0d. yearly, after Abell's death.

Fig. 10.9: Brownlow lease 1703, F. McCorry, *Lurgan*.

The Church of Ireland vestry functioned as a town government collecting tithes, relieving the poor, catering for orphans, burying the dead and organising church and road construction. It was dominated in this period by rural landholders. Fragmentary parish records and church cess returns enable us to identify phases of immigration. The published hearth money rolls of county Armagh (*Archivium Hibernicum*, viii 1941) provide a guide to relative prosperity as measured by building scale and it confirms the success of Brownlow's original patent restricting access to the Irish. It also suggests that incoming migrants could begin their life in Lurgan as residents of low-status houses but could, as the Quaker Robert Hope did, progress through property acquisition and business acumen to become key players in Lurgan's development.

Apart from the records of churches and state there are the voluminous Brownlow papers and in particular the leasebooks of Arthur Brownlow 1667 to 1708, which chart the key dynamic period in the town's growth. By 1700 Lurgan's religious groupings had carved out or were given specific niches in its social and economic life. The raw materials for the tanning industry were in possession of rural Church of Ireland landholders; the Presbyterian community was in weaving and trade; the Quakers controlled the fine linen industry; the Catholics were at the base of the social pyramid invariably residing in the less valuable rural townlands and providing turf, fish and farm produce for the developing town. By 1703 Lurgan was described as

> a large village consisting of a great many stone houses well shingled and finished and abounding with a great number of British inhabitants who are industrious and trading people who have considerably advanced and improved the general manufactures and especially the linen market there (PRONI, T2942).

The linen industry was the catalyst which transformed Lurgan. An Act of 1697 encouraged its development and Louis Crommelin, a French Huguenot linen expert, came to the region in 1698. Not all the innovators were from outside. Using the lease-book of Arthur Brownlow it is possible to reconstruct the role of a local Quaker family, the Bradshaws, in developing the linen industry (PRONI T.970). Beginning as farmers the Bradshaws leased part of the strategic townland of Drumnakelly in 1670. In 1711 James Bradshaw then described as a linen draper renewed the lease; a year later he was licensed by the Linen Board as an inspector. By 1720 Bradshaw was a

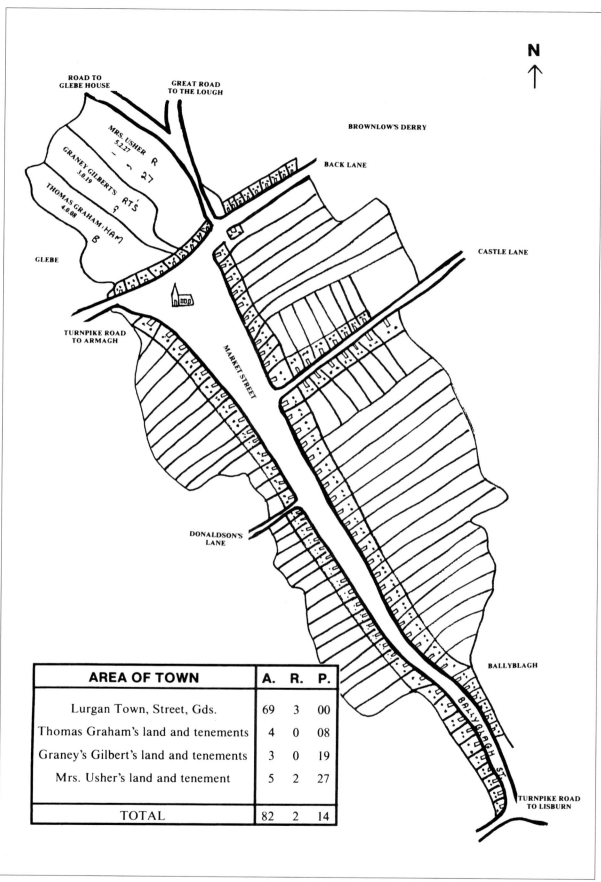

AREA OF TOWN	A.	R.	P.
Lurgan Town, Street, Gds.	69	3	00
Thomas Graham's land and tenements	4	0	08
Graney's Gilbert's land and tenements	3	0	19
Mrs. Usher's land and tenement	5	2	27
TOTAL	82	2	14

Fig. 10.10: Reconstruction of Dougan's map of Lurgan, 1751 (original in private ownership).

flax and hemp dresser for county Armagh and retailed flax in a Lurgan shop. In 1728, subsequent to visiting Holland to study Dutch techniques, he presented an improved version of the sleying table for looms to the Linen Board. Bradshaw's success was marked by his ability to secure a freehold lease for his Lurgan property on payment of seventy guineas to the landlord thereby enabling him to divert the millrace through his land and construct a proper bleachyard. Brownlow lease renewals make it possible to construct business, family, social and religious networks in early-eighteenth century Lurgan. A manuscript map from the Brownlow papers reveals the shape of the town in 1751 and a late-nineteenth century photograph illustrates a commercial building constructed *ca.* 1750 (fig. 10.11). The demand for prime urban sites encouraged the landlord to subdivide the large frontages of earlier leaseholds and in the period from 1696 to 1723 wealthy merchant families were permitted to build in a strategic location adjoining the market house thereby inserting a somewhat incongruous middle row into the main street. All of the lessees were members of the Church of Ireland vestry which suggests that this middle group had major influence in the town: they, more than the landlord, were to control the shape of the town behind the main streets.

Changes of ownership undoubtedly had important repercussions in urban arenas. William Brownlow who succeeded his innovative father in 1710 built upon the basic manufacturing and commercial enterprises already established and became very wealthy. The estate account books 1752 to 1754 show that Brownlow spent considerable money entertaining freeholders, buying spinning wheels, purchasing books and musical scores, sponsoring race-meetings, enlarging and ornamenting the demesne and castle and making expensive forays into parliament.

Three valuations of Lurgan's housing stock in the years 1782, 1795 and 1821, respectively, enable us to assess urban growth and identify patterns within the town. These valuations – essentially assessments for cess payment – recorded in the Church of Ireland Vestry records highlight the significance of local sources particularly for the era prior to state census and taxation records. Two things emerge from an analysis of the valuation lists. Firstly, continuity of occupancy by individual families was much more pronounced for more highly valued houses; between 1782 and 1795, eighty-one of the one hundred and fifty-nine houses with relatively low valuations had occupancy changes. Secondly, the evidence from surnames suggests that in Lurgan's lower valued houses, Scots were replacing Irish occupiers. Apart from stipulations in leases, Lurgan's growth was supervised by the Court Leet which met irregularly.

Towns shared the population surge evident in rural areas from the 1780s. The question remains as to the nature and origin of this growth. Was it commercial investment, growth in trade, the role of philantrophic landlords or was it perhaps the influx of poverty stricken rural migrants? Were towns provision centres or dynamic growth cores? There are a number of secondary sources now available to supplement estate and other records. Arthur Young visited Lurgan and recorded data on its linen trade; Coote's *Statistical survey of county Armagh* enables us to place Lurgan in its regional context and the Linen Board for Ireland produced annual statistics. All the data indicates regional specialisation within the linen industry: Lurgan's working population was predominantly female and the town's occupational structure was not as diversified as that of either Armagh or Portadown. The Ordnance Survey Memoirs are particularly valuable for northern counties and trade inventories are by now flourishing. Landlord agents such as the remarkable John Hancock who served forty-seven years as agent to the Brownlow property reveal a conscious urban policy. Hancock was also keeper of the Brownlow accounts, seneschal, justice of the peace, grand juror, poor law guardian and chairman of the town's commissioners. His letter books in the Brownlow papers are important commentaries on the state of Lurgan in the nineteenth century.

Trade directories need to be used with caution as their classificatory system is oftentimes suspiciously tidy. Multiple rather than single occupations were more characteristic of provincial towns. There are also problems with parish registers insofar as many urban marriages went unrecorded. Neither can censal occupational data in the period from 1871 to 1911 be taken as

Fig. 10.11: The White Thorn Inn, Lurgan, erected ca. 1740. Photographed from the original plate (in private ownership) by Kieran Clendenning, Lurgan.

objective. It is apparent that people, particularly rural migrants, sometimes listed occupations which they were in twenty years before the taking of the particular census. In 1901, for example, ninety-seven per cent of Lurgan's male adults stated an occupation. This percentage included 184 men of 70 years and over. The information returned depends on how people interpreted the instructions or followed the pattern table which the enumerator had. Occupied females may not have listed an occupation whereas male migrants may have entered their rural occupation prior to moving.

Grand Jury presentments from 1801 to 1898 helped identify Lurgan's leading property owners and businessmen as well as detailing both structural defects and improvements within the town. County council records for the twentieth century fulfilled a similar role. The heart and soul of Lurgan emerge from a direct comparison of inter-denominational trends constructed from nineteenth century parish registers and then placing this data alongside comparative findings from contiguous rural parishes. Unfortunately one local denomination had the registers for the pre-1846 period destroyed. The workhouse admission registers were fortuitously recovered in 1948 from their damp home within Lurgan's workhouse thereby facilitating mortality rates to be established for the famine years. Without these registers such a task would have been impossible. A recurring theme in McCorry's work is the comparative disadvantage of Lurgan in respect of its neighbour, Portadown, and his analysis of unemployment figures for the town from different and sometimes contradictory sources for the period 1948 to 1963 suggests that the pattern established in the seventeenth century has persisted. Fig. 10.12 reproduces McCorry's bibliography which indicates the variety of source material available for Lurgan.

ORIGINAL SOURCES - MANUSCRIPT MATERIAL

(i) Researched in the office of Mr. James Neill, Solicitor, Lurgan.

The Patent of Brownlow's Derry, from the King to Sir William Brownlow, 1629.

Alexander Gill's Counterpart of Deed of Bargain and Sale, May 1648.

Will of Sir William Brownlow, 1660.

A hand-written genealogical account of the Brownlow family, from c.1600 to 1860.

Original town leases, numbered according to Charles Brownlow's lease book.

Individual town leases from 1670 to 1723, and subsequent renewals to c.1870.

Will of Mrs. Jane Brownlow, widow of Arthur Brownlow, 1720.

Estate Deed Books of Lord Lurgan.

Deed of Sale drawn up for the joint purchase of the Manor of Richmount from the Waldron family by Robert Hoope and Arthur Brownlow, 1703.

Cash Books, covering the greater part of the 18th. and 19th. centuries.

Declaration of Trust, 17th. May, 1808, for the formation of a bank in Lurgan, under the partnership of William Brownlow, William Burke, Joseph Malcomson, Henry McVeagh, John Cuppage and John Waite.

Lease of the Bank in Lurgan, May 1808: Indenture between William Brownlow and William Burke, Gentleman and Attorney-at-law.

Much of the Brownlow material previously retained in the office of Mr. James Neill, Lurgan, has recently been deposited in the Public Records Office of Northern Ireland, Belfast. The material is entitled:- Brownlow Papers. D.1928. Deposited by Watson and Neill, Solicitors, Lurgan, on behalf of John Desmond Cavendish Brownlow, 5th Baron Lurgan. The Brownlow Papers consist of 520 volumes and 9,300 numbered documents. Within the numbered documents are bundles of documents which bring the overall total number of items to 25,000 - 30,000.

(ii) Parish registers and related sources.

Parish of Shankill, Lurgan; Church of Ireland Parish Registers and Vestry Minutes. Baptisms, from 1681; Marriages, from 1676; Burials, from 1675; Vestry Minutes, from 1672, containing Rent Rolls, House Classifications of Lurgan Town, and Lists of Poor in Lurgan.

Parish of Shankill, Lurgan; Catholic Parish Registers; Baptisms, from 1822; Marriages, from 1866; Funerals, from 1866.

Marriage Register, Presbyterian Church, High Street, Lurgan.

Burial Register, Parish of Donaghcloney, Waringstown, near Lurgan.

Parish of the Montiaghs (Church of Ireland jurisdiction); Church of Ireland Parish Registers, catering for the Derrymacash-Derrytrasna area.

Parish of Seagoe (which, under Catholic jurisdiction, caters for the Derrymacash-Derrytrasna area); Baptism, Marriage and Funeral Registers.

Minutes of Lurgan's Men's Montly Meeting, Quaker Records, Lisburn Meeting House.

(iii) Public Records Office of Northern Ireland. (P.R.O.N.I.)

The Proceedings of the Court Leet, Brownlow's Derry, Lurgan. D 1817/1.

Poor List, Shankill Parish, 1810-4. Brownlow Papers. D 1928/5/1/1.

Letter of introduction concerning Francis Watson from William Armstrong, Lurgan, to George Smith and Son, Belfast. D 2516/1.

Ordnance Survey Memoir, Parish of Shankill, County Armagh. MIC/6/104.

Ordnance Survey Memoir, Parish of Shankill, County Down section. MIC/6/171.

Book of payments to weavers, 1837-9. D 2516/4.

Letter-book of John Hancock, Agent of the Brownlow Estate. D 1817/2.

Admission Registers of Lurgan Union Workhouse. BG/22/G/1-3.

Minutes of the Board of Guardians for Lurgan Poor Law Union. BG 22/A/4-9.

Evidence taken before the Commissioners appointed to inquire into the Occupation of Land in Ireland. Devon Commission. Evidence taken in Lurgan, March 1844. DA 189/69/1.

Report of field-work in the flooded lands along the Upper Bann by John McMahon, 1845. FIN 9/1/23.

Will Books, 1840 and onwards, Armagh District Registry. MIC 15C/1/1.

Extract from Address to the Rt. Hon. Baron Lurgan, K.P., from the town Commissioners of Lurgan, on his resigning the chairmanship of that Board. T 3077/1/1-13.

Linen order book, 1871-1930, and book of prices and wages, 1891-1930, of William Livingstone and Company, Linen Merchants, Lurgan. D 1619/7.

Fig. 10.12: Bibliography extract from F. McCorry, *Lurgan: an Irish provincial town, 1610-1970* (Lurgan, 1993).

Original Sources - Printed Material (contd)

Summaries of the Trade of Northern Ireland for the years, 1936, 1937, 1938, 1943, 1944 and 1945. Loosely-bound booklets issued by the Statistics Branch, Ministry of Commerce of Northern Ireland.

Northern Ireland Housing Trust, First Annual Report, 1945-46. Belfast, 1946.

Report on the Census of Production of Northern Ireland, 1951. Belfast, 1955.

Local Authority Financial Returns, 1953-54. Belfast, 1955.

Census of Population of Northern Ireland, 1951. General Report, Part II. Belfast, 1955.

Census of Population of Northern Ireland, 1961. Fertility Report. Belfast, 1965.

New City Northern Ireland: First Report. Belfast, 1964. Social and Economic Trends in Northern Ireland. No.1. Belfast, 1975.

(iii) County and local official and municipal records.

Annual Reports of the Lurgan Town Commissioners, 1856-72.

Fourth Annual Report: Society for Nursing the Sick Poor of Lurgan. Lurgan, 1897.

Armagh County Health Committee: Annual Reports of the County Medical Officer of Health, for the years, 1948-63.

Presentments of the Grand Jury of County Armagh, 1821-98. (Armagh County Museum).

Minutes of Proceedings of the Finance and General Purpose Committee, Armagh County Council, 1917-53. (In Armagh County Museum).

Official Guides to Lurgan, for the years, 1958-9, 1961-2, 1966.

(iv) Maps

The Map of the Glan Bogg lying between the Counties of Down and Armagh ...... to show the whole extent between Lough Neagh and Newry ...... by Francis Nevil, 1703. P.R.O.N.I. D695/M1.

Maps of the Brownlow Estate, 1751, by Patrick Dougan. In the office of Mr. J. Neill, Lurgan.

Map of County Armagh, 1760, by John Rocque. One of the three original copies is held in Armagh County Museum.

Taylor and Skinner's Maps of the Roads of Ireland: Surveyed in 1777, and corrected down to 1783. London, 1783.

Map of Lurgan, 1832, by Alex Richmond. In the office of Mr. J. Neill, Lurgan.

Map of Lurgan, 1834. P.R.O.N.I. VAL 1D/2/11, and T 2933/4/81.

Map of Lurgan, 1859. P.R.O.N.I. VAL 2D/2/8.

Map of Lurgan, 1862. P.R.O.N.I. VAL 2A/2/6A, and T 2933/3/503.

Map of Lurgan, revised 1889. P.R.O.N.I. OS 8/39/1.

Fig. 10.12 (contd.): Bibliography from F. McCorry's *Lurgan.*

Original Sources - Manuscript Material (contd)

(iii) Miscellaneous

Census of Lurgan, 1856, taken by the Lurgan Town Commissioners. Retained in Craigavon Civic Centre.

Power-loom tenter's apprenticeship contract. Relating to, and in the possession of James Boston, Parkmore, Craigavon.

Notes referring to post-War handloom weaving practices. Relating to the linen concern of John McCollum, and in the possession of his widow, Mrs. Vera McCollum, Lurgan.

Notebook containing sample mathematical calculations relating to linen manufacture in the Limited factory, Lurgan, and also to silk weavers' wages. Formerly used by, and in the possession of, Samuel Chambers, Waringstown Road, Lurgan.

ORIGINAL SOURCES - PRINTED MATERIAL

(i) Parliamentary Papers and Records.

Census of the population, 1821, with comparative abstract as taken in 1813. H.C.1822 (36), xiv.

Census of the population, 1831, with comparative abstract as taken in 1821. H.C.1833 (23), xxxxix, 3-41.

An account in detail, of the expenses incurred under the Population Act in Ireland. Supplement to Appendix (E), First Report. H.C.1836 (36), xxxi.

Reports of the Assistant Commissioners on Hand-Loom Weavers. H.C.1840 (43-II), xxiii, 367.

Census of Ireland, 1841. H.C.1843 (459), li.

Correspondence relating to the state of Union Workhouses in Ireland. H.C.1847 (766), LV.ii, and H.C.1847 (790), LV.ii.

Report to the Board of Health on Lurgan Union Workhouse, by Dr. Smith. H.C.1847 (257), LV.ii, 11-16.

Returns of the Number of Factories, H.C.1850 (745), xlii, 455; H.C.1857 (7-Sess.1), xiv, 173; H.C.1862 (23) LV, 629; H.C.1867-8 (453), lxiv, 811.

Census of Ireland, 1851. H.C.1852-53 (various), lxxxxii. Vol.III. Ulster.

Census of Ireland, 1861. H.C.1863 (3204-III), lix, lx.

Return of the Number of Manufacturing Establishments in which the Hours of Work are regulated by an Act of Parliament. H.C.1871 (440), lxii, 105.

Census of Ireland, 1871. H.C.1871 (375), lix.

Census of Ireland, 1881. H.C.1882 (3204), lxxiix.

Census of Ireland, 1891, H.C.1892 (6626), lxxxxii.

Return of the Number of Flax and Linen Factories in the United Kingdom. H.C.1905 (290), lxxii, 543.

Report from the Select Committee on Adulterated Wine, together with Proceedings of the Committee and Minutes of Evidence and Appendices. House of Commons of North Ireland. N.I.H.C. 450, 1938.

First and Final Reports from the Select Committee on Public Accounts, ... for the financial year, 1938-9, together with Proceedings of the Committee and Minutes of Evidence and Appendices. N.I.H.C. 514, 1939.

First and Second Interim Reports and a Special Report from the Select Committee on Unemployment in Northern Ireland, together with Proceedings of the Committee, Appendices and Minutes of Evidence. N.I.H.C. 537m 1941.

Parliamentary Debates. N.I.H.C. Vol.52, Session 1962-3.

Census of Northern Ireland, 1926, 1937, 1951, 1961, 1966, from Books of Abstracts, P.R.O.N.I.

(ii) Government-related Reports.

Calendar of State Papers, Ireland 1615-1625. Published by V.W. Treadwell, in Ulster Journal of Archaeology, xxiii, 1960, pp.126-37, and xxvii, 1964, pp.140-54.

Entry Book of reports of the Commissioners for Ireland, appointed by James I in 1622, and of letters from the king and Council to the Lord Deputy, Oliver St. John, and the Council of Ireland; 1616-1621. British Library, Additional MS 4756. Milles Collection, Vol.11.

Copy of the Cromwellian Inquisition as to Parishes in County Armagh in 1657. In the Armagh Papers of William Reeves, in Armagh Library.

Reports of the Secretary of the Trustees of the Linen and Hempen Manufactories of Ireland, 1816. Dublin, 1817.

Municipal Corporation Boundaries (Ireland): Reports and Plans. Vol.4. 1836.

General Valuation of Rateable Property in Ireland. Union of Lurgan (part of). Valuation of the Several Tenements situated in the County of Armagh. Dublin, 1864. ...... situated in the County of Antrim. Dublin, 1862. ...... situated in the County of Down. Dublin, 1864.

Report of the Commissioners appointed to inquire into the state of the Fairs and Markets in Ireland. Dublin, 1853.

Reports from Commissioners: Royal Commission on Railways. London, 1867. (Irish University Press Series Of British Parliamentary Papers).

Report on the Administration of Local Government Services, 1926-27. Belfast, 1928.

Report on the Administration of Local Government Services, 1932-33. Belfast, 1934.

Report on the Administration of Local Government Services, 1934-35. Belfast, 1936.

Report on the Administration of Local Government Services, 1935-36. Belfast, 1937.

Report on Health and Local Government Administration in Northern Ireland, 1938-46. Belfast, 1948.

Fig. 10.12 (contd.): Bibliography from F. McCorry's *Lurgan*.

BIBLIOGRAPHY:

Select Bibliography of Publications printed between 1969 and 1993 on Irish Towns in the period 1500 to 1980 (D. McCabe)

First published in W. Prevenier and P. Stabel (eds), *Bibliographies on European Urban History: Belgium, Ireland, Spain* (Gent, 1996).

Introduction

This list of books, articles, theses and dissertations, is an 'interim' bibliography. It attempts to list and classify published and unpublished writings, completed between *1969 and 1993*, on the history of Irish urban centres between *1500 and 1980*. It thus helps to supplement the catalogue of material of Irish interest, in manuscript and printed form, compiled under the supervision of Richard Hayes in the 1960s and 1970s (R.J. Hayes (ed.), *Manuscript sources for the history of Irish civilisation*, 11 vols (Boston, 1965), 3 vols supplement, ed. D. Ó Luanaigh (Dublin, 1979) and R.J. Hayes (ed.), *Guide to the periodical sources for the history of Irish civilisation*, 9 vols (Boston, 1970).

The towns included are those whose populations exceeded 2,000 at any of the censuses between 1821 and 1971. This is the same criterion adopted with respect to the urban listing in W. E. Vaughan and A. J. Fitzpatrick, *Irish historical statistics: population, 1821-1971* (Dublin, 1978). The proportion of unpublished writings (Ph.D. and M.A. theses and B.A. dissertations) taken from the large number of such works produced in recent decades at Irish, U.K., American and Canadian third level institutions is not exhaustive.

The bibliography consists of a simple classification of these writings. Every effort was made to place each text under the heading of a particular town or city. General works, or works more difficult to classify, were placed under the headings of 'Urban Settlement and Society', 'Transport and Infrastructure', 'Industry', 'Commerce', etc. These subject headings were defined in the following way. 'Urbanisation: Settlement and Society' includes general works on the development of urban society in Ireland from 1500 to 1993 (though certain works that range into the middle ages are also included). Writings on the subjects of the railway network, roads, bridges, or passenger and goods services by road, sea or river, come under the heading of 'Transport and Infrastructure'. The heading 'Industry' is devoted primarily to writings on manufacturing industry; 'Commerce' refers to the matters of banking, circulation of money, the merchant community or the financial system generally. Writings under the heading of 'Labour' refer principally to the history of trade unions in the country. The heading 'Architecture' is self-explanatory, as is 'Art', 'Demography', 'Maritime Ports' and 'Bibliographies and Guides to Sources'. Aspects of the school system at all levels, together with reformatories, are covered under 'Education'. 'Institutions of State' encompasses departments of state and the military services. Finally, works on printing, newspapers, and the postal service come under the heading of 'Communications/Media'.

This work was produced when Desmond McCabe (University College Dublin) was an E.U. Fellow under the Human Capital and Mobility Programme at the Centre for Urban History Leicester, engaged in the international *EUROCIT* project on European urbanisation in the modern and contemporary periods. We are very grateful to the European Union for its support of the *EUROCIT* project. Neil Wood, who was involved in the editing and formatting of the work, is a researcher at the Centre for Urban History and the Economic and Social History Department, Leicester University.

1. Irish Towns in General

Administration

Brady, C., 'Court, castle and country: the framework of government in Tudor Ireland', in Brady, C. and Gillespie R. (eds), *Natives and newcomers: the making of Irish colonial society 1534-1641* (Dublin, 1986).

Brynn, E., *Crown and castle: British rule in Ireland, 1800-1830* (Dublin, 1978).

Burke, H., *The people and the poor law in nineteenth century Ireland* (Littlehampton, 1987).

Feingold, W.F., *The revolt of the tenantry: the transformation of local government in Ireland 1872-1886* (Boston, 1984).

Gibbons, J., 'Some root causes of failure in Irish local government: a Mayo perspective' in *Cathair na Mart*, i (1981), pp 13-19.

Megehen, P.J., 'The administrative work of the Grand Jury' in *Administration*, 6 (1958-9), pp 247-264.

Wilson, T. M., 'Local government and local power in Meath 1925-1942' in *Riocht na Midhe*, vii, 4 (1985-6), pp 66-78.

Jupp, P., 'Urban politics in Ireland, 1801-1831' in Harkness, D. and O'Dowd, M., *The town in Ireland*, pp 103-124 (Belfast, 1981).

Architecture

Brett, C.E.B., *Court houses and market houses of the province of Ulster* (Belfast, 1973).

Brett, C.E.B., *Historic buildings, groups of buildings, and areas of architectural importance in the towns and villages of East Down* (Belfast, 1973).

Brett, C.E.B., *Historic buildings, groups of buildings and areas of architectural importance in the towns and villages of Mid-Down* (Belfast, 1974).

Casey, C. and Rowan, A., *North Leinster: the counties of Longford, Louth, Meath and Westmeath* (The buildings of Ireland), (London, 1993).

Craig, M., *Architecture in Ireland* (Dublin, 1978).

Craig, M., *The architecture of Ireland from earliest times to1880* (Dublin and London, 1982).

Craig, M., *The architecture of Ireland from earliest times to 1880* (Dublin, 1989).

Craig, M., 'Architecture: before 1850' in Edwards, O. D. (ed.), *Conor Cruise O'Brien introduces Ireland*, pp 214-20 (London, 1969).

Cruikshank, D., *A guide to the Georgian buildings of Britain and Ireland* (London, 1985).

Dixon, H., *An introduction to Ulster architecture* (Belfast, 1975).

Dixon, H., *Ulster architecture, 1800-1900: an exhibition of architectural drawings* (Belfast, 1972).

Evans, D, *An introduction to modern Ulster architecture* (Belfast, 1977).

Foley, N., 'The Irish architectural archive' in *Irish Archives Bulletin*, viii (1978), pp 21-7.

Graby, J. (ed), *150 years of architecture in Ireland: the Royal Institute of the Architects of Ireland, 1839-1989* (Dublin, 1989).

Guinness, D., *The Irish house* (Dublin, 1975).

Guinness, D. and Sadler, J.T., *The Palladian style in England, Ireland and America* (London, 1977).

Harbison, P., Potterton, H. and Sheehy, J., *Irish art and architecture: from pre-history to the present* (London, 1978).

Jackson, R. W., *Cathedrals of the Church of Ireland* (Dublin, 1971).

Kennedy, T. P., *The church since emancipation: church building* (Dublin, 1970).

Kingdon, D.P., 'Irish Baptist churches – 100 years ago and today' in *Irish Baptist Historical Society Journal*, ii (1972), pp 22-36.

Larmour, P., *The arts and crafts movement in Ireland* (Belfast, 1992).

Loeber, R., 'Early classicism in Ireland: architecture before the Georgian era' in *Architectural History*, xxii (1979), pp 49-63.

McParland, E., 'A bibliography of Irish architectural history' in *Irish Historical Studies*, xxvi, 102 (1988), pp 161-212.

McParland, E., 'Francis Johnston, architect, 1760-1829' in *Irish Georgian Society Bulletin*, xii (1969), pp 61-139.

McParland, E., 'James Gandon and the Royal Exchange Competition, 1768-69' in *Royal Society of Antiquaries of Ireland Journal*, cii (1972), pp 58-71.

Mulvaney, T. J., *The life of James Gandon* (Dublin, 1846, reprint, London, 1969).

Office of Public Works, *The architecture of the Office of Public Works 1831-1987* (Dublin, 1987).

Richardson, D.S., *Gothic revival architecture in Ireland* (London, 1984).

Rothery, S., *The shops of Ireland* (Dublin, 1978).

Rowan, A., *The buildings of Ireland 1: north-west Ulster, the counties of Londonderry, Donegal, Fermanagh and Tyrone* (London, 1979).

Ruch, J., 'Coade Stone in Ireland' in *Irish Georgian Society Bulletin*, xiii, 4 (1970), pp 1-12.

Sheehy, J., 'Railway architecture: its heyday' in *Irish Railway Record Society Journal*, xii, 68 (1975), pp 125-38.

Sheehy, J., *J.J. McCarthy and the Gothic revival in Ireland* (Belfast, 1977).

Stokstad, M. and Gill, L., 'Antiquarianism and architecture in eighteenth century Ireland' in Orel, H. (ed), *Irish history and culture: aspects of a people's heritage* (University Press of Kansas, 1976), pp 165-88.

Arts

Angelsea, M., *The Royal Ulster academy of arts: a centennial history* (Belfast, 1981).

Bell, S. H., *The theatre in Ulster* (Dublin, 1972).

Grindle, H., *Irish cathedral music: a history of music at the cathedrals of the Church of Ireland* (Belfast, 1989).

Ó hAodha, M., *Theatre in Ireland* (Oxford, 1974).

Bibliographies and Guides to Sources

Anderson, R. and McDonald, T., *Memories in focus: N.E. Ulster from old photographs 1860-1960* (Coleraine, 1986).

Andrews, J.H., 'Ireland in maps' in *Irish Geography* (The Geographical Society of Ireland Golden Jubilee 1934-1984), supplement to *Irish Geography*, 17 (1984), pp 280-92.

Antrim County Library, *A subject catalogue of books and some other material relating to county Antrim* (Ballymena, 1969).

Bell, J.B., 'Contemporary Irish archival resources' in *Administration*, xviii (1970), pp 174-8.

Brady, D., 'A select bibliography of county Waterford' in Nolan, W., Power, T.P. and Cowman, D. (eds), *Waterford history and society: interdisciplinary essays on the history of an Irish county* (Dublin, 1992), pp 733-45.

Byrne, M., *Sources for Offaly history* (Tullamore, 1977).

Byrne, M., *Select bibliography of writings on Offaly history since 1960* (Tullamore, 1980).

Clarke, A., Gillespie, R. and McGuire, J., *New history of Ireland, iii, 1534-1691: bibliographical supplement* (Oxford, 1991).

Connolly, S.J., *The public record: sources for local studies in the Public Record Office of Ireland* (Dublin, 1982).

Cullen, L.M., 'Private sources for economic and social history' in *Irish Archives Bulletin*, ii, 1 (1972), pp 5-25.

Deutsch, R., *Northern Ireland 1921-74: a select bibliography* (London, 1975).

Ferguson, P., *Irish map history: a select bibliography of secondary works, 1850-1983, on the history of cartography in Ireland* (Dublin, 1983).

Flynn, M. E., 'A retrospective bibliography of Irish labour history, 1960-1972' in *Saothar*, xvi (1991), pp 144-58.

Helferty, S. and Refaussé, R., *Directory of Irish archives* (Dublin, 1993).

Humphreys, A., *A handbook to county bibliography: being a bibliography of bibliographies relating to the county towns of Great Britain and Ireland, 1917* (London, 1974 reprint).

Johnston, E. M., *Irish history: a select bibliography* (London, 1969).

Kavanagh, M.V., *A bibliography of the history of county Kildare* (Kildare, 1976).

Keaney, M., *Westmeath local studies: a guide to sources* (Mullingar, 1982).

Martin, G. H. and MacIntyre, S.A., *A bibliography of British and Irish municipal history, i, general works* (Leicester, 1972).

McCann, W., 'Bibliographical studies in Ulster – an historical survey' in *Linen Hall Review*, vi, no. 1 (1989), pp 16-7.

Nolan, W., *Tracing the past: sources for local studies in the Republic of Ireland* (Dublin, 1982).

O'Connor, L., *Lost Ireland: a photographic record at the turn of the century* (Dublin, 1985).

Ó Dufaigh, S., 'Irish local historical and archaeological journals' in *Eire/Ireland*, v (1970), pp 90-9.

O'Dwyer, M., 'A select bibliography of county Kilkenny' in Nolan, W. and Whelan, K. (eds), *Kilkenny history and society: interdisciplinary essays on the history of an Irish county* (Dublin, 1990), pp 633-6.

Prochaska, A., *Irish history from 1700: a guide to sources in the Public Record Office* (London, 1985).

Ryan, J. G., *Irish church records: their history, availability and use in family and local history research* (Dublin, 1992).

Commerce

Barrow, L., 'The use of money in mid-nineteenth century Ireland' in *Studies*, lix (1970), pp 81-8.

Barrow, L., 'Kilkenny private banks' in *Old Kilkenny Review*, xxiii (1971), pp 36-40.

Cullen, L.M., 'Irish Manuscripts Commission survey of business records' in *Irish Economic and Social History*, x (1983), pp 81-91.

Cullen, L.M., 'Landlords, bankers and merchants: the early Irish banking world 1700-1820' in *Hermathena*, cxxxv (1983), pp 22-44.

Daly, M.E., 'An Irish-Ireland for business?: the control of manufactures acts, 1932 and 1934' in *Irish Historical Studies*, xxiv, 94 (1984), pp 246-72.

de Breffny, B., 'Businessmen who issued tokens in Ireland 1653-1679' in *Irish Ancestor*, x, 1 (1978), pp 51-60.

Donnelly, B., 'Irish Manuscripts Commission survey of business records' in *Irish Economic and Social History*, xvii (1990), pp 93-44.

Dowle, A, and Finn, P., *The guide book to the coinage of Ireland from 995 A..D. to the present day* (London, 1969).

Harrison, R. S., *Irish insurance: historical perspectives, 1650-1939* (Cork, 1992).

Josset, C. R., *Money in Great Britain and Ireland* (Newton Abbot, 1971).

Logan, P., *Fair day: the story of Irish fairs and markets* (Belfast, 1986).

Lyons, F.S.L. (ed.), *The Bank of Ireland 1783-1983: bicentenary essays* (Dublin, 1983).

McMillan, D.S., 'Commercial and industrial society in Great Britain and Ireland 1812-24; a study of Australian immigration applications' in *Social History* (Ottawa), vi, 12 (1973), pp 65-107.

O'Brien, J., 'Business history' in *Irish Archives Bulletin*, ii, 1 (1972), pp 50-7.

Ollerenshaw, P., 'Banking in Ulster 1808-1820' in *Moirae*, 8 (1984), pp 126-153.

Ollerenshaw, P., *Banking in nineteenth century Ireland: the Belfast banks 1825-1914* (Manchester, 1987).

Parkhill, T., 'Business records in county Kildare' in *Kildare Archaeological Society Journal*, xv, 3, pp 262-7.

Parkhill, T., 'Business records survey in county Longford' in *Teathba*, i, 3 (1973), pp 226-7.

Robinson, H.W., *A history of accountants in Ireland* (Dublin, 1983).

Seaby, W.A., 'Catalogue of Ulster tokens, tickets, vouchers, checks, passes etc.,' in *Ulster Journal of Archaeology*, xxxiv (1972), pp 96-106.

Share, B. (ed), *Root and branch: Allied Irish Banks yesterday, today, tomorrow* (Dublin, 1979).

Thomas, W.A., *The stock exchanges of Ireland* (Liverpool, 1986).

Ulster Bank, *Ulster Bank 1836-1986: the history* (Belfast, 1989).

Yeats, W. B., *The designing of Ireland's coinage* (Dublin, 1972).

Young, D., *Guide to the currency of Ireland: legal tender notes, 1928-1972* (Dublin, 1972).

Communications/Media

Castleleyn, M.A., *A history of literacy and libraries in Ireland. The long traced pedigree* (Aldershot, 1984).

Dixon, F.E., 'Irish postal history' in *Dublin Historical Record*, xxiii (1970), pp 127-36.

Farrell, B. (ed), *Communications and community in Ireland* (Dublin and Cork, 1984).

Oram, H., *The newspaper book: a history of newspapers in Ireland, 1649-1983* (Dublin, 1983).

O'Toole, J., *Newsplan: report of the newsplan project in Ireland* (Dublin, 1992).

Reynolds, M., *A history of the Irish post office* (Dublin, 1983).

Wheeler, W.G., 'The spread of provincial printing in Ireland up to 1850' in *Irish Booklore*, iv, I (1978), pp 48-52.

Demography

Clarkson, L.A., 'Population change and urbanisation, 1821-1911' in Kennedy, L., and Ollerenshaw, P. (eds), *An economic history of Ulster 1820-1939* (Manchester, 1985), pp 137-57.

Drake, M., 'Population growth and the Irish economy' in Cullen, L.M. (ed.), *The formation of the Irish economy* (Cork, 1969), pp 65-87.

Houston, R.A., *The population history of Britain and Ireland, 1500-1750* (London, 1991).

Lee, J. (ed.), *The population of Ireland before the nineteenth century* (Farnborough, Hants, 1973).

Walsh, B.M., *Ireland's changing demographic structure* (Dublin, 1989).

Walsh, B. M., 'A perspective on Irish population patterns' in *Eire/Ireland*, iv, 3 (1969), pp 3-21.

Walsh, B. M., 'Marriage rates and population pressure: Ireland 1871 and 1911' in *Economic History Review*, xxiii (1970), pp 146-62.

Economy

Childs, W., 'Ireland's trade with England in the later middle ages' in *Irish Economic and Social History*, ix (1982), pp 5-33.

Cochrane, L.E., 'Scottish-Irish trade in the eighteenth century' in Devine, T M. and Dickson, D. (eds), *Ireland and Scotland, 1600-1850: parallels and contrasts in economic and social development* (Edinburgh, 1983), pp 151-9.

Cochrane, L.E., *Scottish trade with Ireland in the eighteenth century* (Edinburgh, 1985).

Cox, J.M., 'Local economies in the Clogher valley, 1790-1811' in *Clogher record*, vii (1970), pp 236-50.

Cullen, L.M., 'Incomes, social classes, and economic growth in Ireland and Scotland, 1600-1900' in Devine, T.M. and Dickson, D. (eds), *Ireland and Scotland, 1600-1850: parallels and contrasts in economic and social development* (Edinburgh, 1983), pp 248-60.

Cullen, L.M., 'Irish economic history: fact and myth' in Cullen, L.M. (ed.), *The formation of the Irish economy* (Cork, 1969), pp 113-24.

Cullen, L.M., 'The Irish economy in the eighteenth century' in Cullen, L.M. (ed.), *The formation of the Irish economy* (Cork, 1969), pp 9-21.

Cullen, L.M. (ed.), *The formation of the Irish economy* (Cork, 1969).

Cullen, L.M., *An economic history of Ireland since 1660* (London, 1972).

Cullen, L.M., *Merchants, ships and trade, 1660-1830* (Dublin, 1971).

Daly, M.E., 'Government finance for industry in the Irish Free State: The Trade Loans (Guarantee) Acts' in *Irish Economic and Social History*, xi (1984), pp 73-92.

Gillespie, R., *The transformation of the Irish economy, 1550-1700* (Dublin, 1991).

Gillmor, D.A., *Economic activities in the Republic of Ireland: a geographical perspective* (Dublin, 1985).

Lee, J., 'Capital in the Irish economy' in Cullen, L.M. (ed.), *The formation of the Irish economy* (Cork, 1969), pp 53-63.

Lee, J., 'The dual economy in Ireland, 1800-50' in *Historical Studies*, viiii (1971), pp 191-200.

Lynch, P., 'The Irish economy since the war, 1946-51' in Nowlan, K.B. and Williams, T.D. (eds), *Ireland in the war years and after, 1939-51* (Dublin, 1969), pp 185-200.

Mitchison, R. and Roebuck, P. (eds), *Economy and society in Scotland and Ireland 1500-1939* (Edinburgh, 1988).

Mokyr, J., *Why Ireland starved: a quantitative and analytical history of the Irish economy, 1800-1850* (London, 1983).

Ó Gráda, C., *Ireland before and after the Famine. Explorations in economic history, 1800-1925* (Manchester, 1988).

Ó Gráda, C. *Ireland: A new Economic history, 1780-1939* (Oxford, 1994).

Othick, J., 'The economic history of Ulster: a perspective' in Kennedy, L. and Ollerenshaw, P. (eds), *An economic history of Ulster 1820-1939* (Manchester, 1985), pp 129-47.

Raymond, R.J., 'A reinterpretation of Irish Economic history (1730-1850)' in *Journal of European Economic History*, xi, 3 (1982), pp 651-64.

Solar, P., 'The reconstruction of Irish external trade. Statistics for the nineteenth century' in *Irish Economic and Social History*, xii (1985), pp 63-78.

Truxes, T. M., *Irish-American trade, 1660-1783* (Cambridge, 1989).

Education

Akenson, D. H., *The Irish education experiment: the national system of education in the nineteenth century* (London, 1970).

Durcan, T. J., *History of Irish education from 1800* (Merioneth, 1972).

Milne, K., 'Irish charter schools' in *Irish Journal of Education*, viiii, 1/2 (1974), pp 3-29.

Morton, R. G., 'Mechanics institutes and the attempted diffusion of useful knowledge in Ireland, 1825-79' in *Irish Booklore*, ii (1972), pp 59-74.

Rusling, G.W., 'The schools of the Baptist Irish society' in *Baptist Quarterly*, xxii, 8 (1968), pp 429-42.

Health

Barrington, R., *Health, medicine and politics in Ireland 1900-1970* (Dublin, 1987).

O'Kelly, P., From workhouse to hospital: medical relief in Ireland, 1838-1921, unpublished M.A. thesis, University College Galway (1972).

Scanlan, P., *The Irish nurse: a study of nursing in Ireland, history and education, 1718-1981* (Manorhamilton, 1991).

Williamson, A. P., The origins of the Irish mental hospital service, 1800-35, unpublished M.Litt. thesis, Trinity College Dublin (1971).

Industry

Bottomley, P., *The Ulster textile industry: a catalogue of business records* in P.R.O.N.I. *relating particularly to the linen industry in Ulster* (Belfast, 1978).

Bowie, G., Watermills, windmills and stationary steam engines in Ireland, with special reference to problems of conservation, unpublished Ph.D. thesis, Queen's University, Belfast (1975).

Boyle, G.E., and Sloane, P.D., 'The demand for labour and capital inputs in Irish manufacturing industries, 1953-1973' in *Economic and Social Review*, xiii, 3 (1982), pp 153-70.

Brooks, C.M., 'Aspects of the sugar-refining industry from the sixteenth to the nineteenth century' in *Post-Medieval Archaeology*, 17 (1983), pp 1-14.

Brophy, S., *The strategic management of Irish enterprise 1934-1984: case studies from leading Irish companies* (Dublin, 1985).

Burnett, J.E. and Morrison-Low, A.D., '*Vulgar and mechanick': the scientific instrument trade in Ireland, 1650-1921* (Dublin, 1989).

Caskey, A., Entrepeneurs and industrial development in Ulster, 1850-1914: a study in business history, unpublished M.Phil. thesis, New University of Ulster (1983).

Clark, W., *Linen on the green: an Irish mill village 1730-1982* (Hythe, Kent, 1982).

Coe, W., *The engineering industry in the north of Ireland* (Newton Abbot, 1969).

Cowman, D., 'Life and labour in three Irish mining communities c.1840' in *Saothar*, ix (1983), pp 10-9.

Crawford, W.H., 'Drapers and bleachers in the early Ulster linen industry' in Cullen L.M. and Butel P. (eds), *Négoce et industrie en France et en Irlande aux xviiii et xix siecles: actes de colloque Franco-Irlandais d'histoire* Bordeaux, 1978 (Paris, 1980), pp 113-19.

Crawford, W.H., *The Irish linen industry* (Cultra, 1987).

Crawford, W.H., 'The rise of the linen industry' in Cullen, L.M. (ed.), *The formation of the Irish conomy* (Cork, 1969), pp 23-35.

Crawford, W.H., *Domestic industry in Ireland: the experience of the linen industry* (Dublin, 1972).

Crawford, W.H., 'The origins of the linen industry in north Armagh and the Lagan valley' in *Ulster Folklife*, xviii (1971), pp 42-51.

Dick, W. (ed.), 'Industrial archaeology' in *Technology Ireland*, vii, 8 (1975), pp 41-2.

Farley, N.J.J.,'The functional distribution of income in Ireland's manufacturing sector 1956-1973' in *Economic and Social Review*, xii, 2 (1981), pp 73-95.

Gailey, A., 'Bricks and brick-making in Ulster in the 1830s' in *Ulster Folklife*, xxviiii (1982), pp 61-4.

Glen, R., 'Industrial wayfarers: Benjamin Franklin and a case of machine smuggling in the 1780s' in *Business History*, xxiii, 3 (1981), pp 309-26.

Goldstrom, J M., 'The industrialisation of the north-east' in Cullen, L M. (ed.), *The formation of the Irish economy* (Cork, 1969), pp 101-12.

Green, E.R.R., 'Industrial decline in the nineteenth century' in Cullen, L.M. (ed.), *The formation of the Irish economy* (Cork, 1969), pp 89-100.

Harrison, R.T., *Industrial organisation and changing technology in U.K shipbuilding: historical development and future implications* (Aldershot, 1990).

Hogan, S., *A history of Irish steel* (Dublin, 1980).

Industries of the north, one hundred years ago: industrial and commercial life in the north of Ireland, 1888-1891 (Belfast, 1986).

Kelly, E.T., 'A bridge of fish: the Irish connection with Newfoundland, 1500-1630' in *Eire/Ireland*, iv, 2 (1969), pp 37-51.

Kennedy, L., *The modern industrialisation of Ireland 1940-1988* (Dublin, 1989).

Manning, M. and McDowell, M., *Electricity supply in Ireland: the history of the E.S.B.* (Dublin, 1985).

McCabe, B., 'History of the town gas industry in Ireland, 1823-1980' in *Dublin Historical Record*, xlv, 1 (1992), pp 28-40.

McCutcheon, W.A., *Wheel and spindle: aspects of Irish industrial history* (Belfast, 1977).

McCutcheon, W.A., *The industrial archaeology of Northern Ireland* (Belfast, 1980).

McGuire, E.B., *Irish whiskey: a history of distilling, the spirit trade and excise controls in Ireland* (Dublin, 1973).

McKernan, A., The dynamics of the linen triangle: factor, family, and farm in rural Ulster, 1740 to 1825, unpublished Ph.D. thesis, University of Michigan (1990).

Messenger, B., *Picking up the linen threads: a study in industrial folklore* (Austin, 1978).

Messenger, B., ' "You will easy know a doffer": the folklore of the linen industry in Northern Ireland' in *Éire/Ireland*, xiv, 1 (1979), pp 6-15.

McNeice, D., 'Industrial villages of Ulster, 1890-1900' in P. Roebuck (ed.), *Plantation to partition* (Belfast, 1981), pp 172-90.

McNeice, D., Factory workers housing in counties Down and Armagh, unpublished P.hd. thesis, Queens University Belfast (1981).

O'Hagan, J.W. and McStay, K.P., *The evolution of manufacturing industry in Ireland* (Dublin, 1981).

O'Malley, E., 'The decline of Irish industry in the nineteenth century' in *Economic and Social Review*, xiii, 1 (1981), pp 21-42.

O'Sullivan, C., *The gasmakers: historical perspectives of the Irish gas industry* (Dublin, 1987).

Ollerenshaw, P., 'Industry 1820-1914' in Kennedy, L. and Ollerenshaw, P. (eds), *An economic history of Ulster 1820-1939* (Manchester, 1985), pp 62-108.

Pollock, V., 'The seafishing industry in county Down and its Scottish connections, 1860-1939' in Mitchison, R. and Roebuck, P. (eds), *Economy and society in Scotland and Ireland 1500-1939* (Edinburgh, 1988), pp 255-66.

Pollock, V., The seafishing industry in Co. Down, 1860-1939, unpublished D.Phil. thesis, University of Ulster.

Press, J.P., 'Protectionism and the Irish footwear industry 1932-39' in *Irish Economic and Social History*, xiii (1986), pp 74-89.

Press, J., *Irish shoes: the footwear industry in Ireland, 1922-1973* (Blackrock, 1989).

Smiley, J.A., 'Factory children in nineteenth century Ireland' in *Pace*, vii, 4 (1974), pp 8-14.

Smiley, J.A., 'The social and historical background to the Irish linen trade' in *Pace*, viii, ix (1974), pp 22-7, pp 15-20.

Solar, P., 'The Irish linen trade, 1820-1952' in *Textile History*, xxi (1991), pp 57-85.

Solar, P., 'The Irish butter trade in the nineteenth century: new estimates and their implications' in *Studia Hibernica*, xxv (1989-90), pp 134-61.

Swift, J., 'The baker's records' in *Saothar*, iii (1977), pp 1-5.

Turpin, J., 'Exhibitions of arts and industries in victorian Ireland, part 1: the Irish arts and industries exhibition movement, 1834-1864' in *Dublin Historical Record*, xxxv, 1 (1981), pp 2-13.

Turpin, J., 'Exhibitions of art and industries in Victorian Ireland, part II: Dublin exhibitions of art and industries 1865-1885' in *Dublin Historical Record*, xxxv, 2 (1982), pp 42-51.

Ulster Folk and Transport Museum, 'Illustrations of the linen industry in 1783 by William Hicks' in *Ulster Folklife*, xxiii (1977), pp 1-32.

Warren, P., *Irish glass: the age of exuberance* (London,1970).

Institutions of State

Arnold, M. and Laskey, H., *Children of the Poor Clares: the story of an Irish orphanage* (Belfast, 1985).

Crossman, V., 'Irish barracks in the 1820s and 1830s: a political perspective' in *Irish Sword*, xviii, 68 (1989), pp 210-13.

Finnane, M., *Insanity and the insane in post-famine Ireland* (London, 1981).

Gould, M., *The workhouses of Ulster* (Belfast, 1983).

Hoctor, D., *The department's story: a history of the department of agriculture* (Dublin, 1971).

Kerrigan, P.M., 'Garrisons and barracks in the Irish midlands, 1704-1828' in *Journal of the Old Athlone Society*, xi, 6 (1985), pp 100-8.

Réamonn, S., *History of the revenue commissioners* (Dublin, 1981).

Robins, J., *The lost children – a study of charity children in Ireland 1700-1900* (Dublin, 1980).

Robins, J., *Fools and mad: a history of the insane in Ireland* (Dublin, 1986).

Labour

Beecher, S., *The historical basis of socialism in Ireland* (Cork, 1909).

Boyd, A., *The rise of the Irish trade unions, 1729-1970* (Tralee, 1972).

Browne, M., Trade boards in Northern Ireland, 1909-45, unpublished Ph.D. thesis, Queen's University Belfast (1989).

Cradden, T., *Trade unionism, socialism and partition: the labour movement in Northern Ireland, 1939-1953* (Belfast, 1993).

D'Arcy, F.A. and Hannigan, K., *Workers in union: documents and commentaries on the history of Irish labour* (Dublin, 1988).

Ellis, P. B., *A history of the Irish working class* (London, 1972).

Girvan, B., 'Industrialisation and the Irish working class since 1922' in *Saothar*, x (1984), pp 31-42.

Greaves, C.D., *The Irish transport and general workers' union. The formative years* (Dublin, 1982).

Hannigan, K.., 'Labour records in the Public Record Office of Ireland' in *Saothar*, vii (1980), pp 93-9.

Hannigan, K., 'British based unions in Ireland: building workers and the split in congress' in *Saothar*, viii (1981), pp 40-9.

Hannigan, K., 'Trade union records in Ireland' in *Archivum*, xxviii (1980), pp 73-9.

Keaney, B., 'Irish chartism in Britain and Ireland: rescuing the rank and file' in *Saothar*, x (1984), pp 94-103.

Loftus, B., *Marching workers: a catalogue of an exhibition of Irish trade banners and regalia* (Dublin and Belfast, 1978).

McCarthy, C., *Trade unions in Ireland 1894-1960* (Dublin, 1977).

McLernon, D.S., 'Trade union organisation in the south of Ireland in the nineteenth century' in *Journal of European Economic History*, x, 1 (1981), pp 145-52.

Millotte, M., *Communism in modern Ireland: the pursuit of the worker's republic since 1916* (Dublin, 1984).

Nevin, D., 'Industry and labour' in Nowlan, K.B. and Williams, T.D. (eds), *Ireland in the war years and after, 1939-51* (Dublin, 1969), pp 94-108.

Newsinger, J., 'The Irish transport and general workers union' in *Society for the Study of Labour History Bulletin*, 49 (1984), pp 69-71.

O'Connell, T.J., *History of the Irish national teachers' organisation, 1868-1968* (Dublin, 1968).

O'Connor, E., 'The influence of Redmondism on the development of the labour movement in Waterford in the 1890s' in *Decies*, x (1979), pp 37-42.

O'Connor, E., 'Active sabotage in industrial conflict 1917-1923' in *Irish Economic and Social History*, xi (1985), pp 50-62.

O'Connor, E., *A labour history of Ireland, 1824-1960* (Dublin, 1992).

O'Connor Lysaght, D.R., 'The Munster Soviet creameries' in *Irish History Workshop*, I (1981), pp 36-49.

O'Sullivan, M., 'The Irish munitions strike of 1920' in *Cathair na Mart*, xi (1991), pp 132-36.

Parkhill, T., 'Labour records in the Public Record Office of Northern Ireland' in *Saothar*, viii (1981), pp 100-6.

Patterson, H., 'Industrial labour and the labour movement 1820-1914' in Kennedy, L. and Ollerenshaw, P. (eds), *An economic history of Ulster 1820-1939* (Manchester, 1985), pp 258-83.

Pollock, H.M., 'The Irish labour history society archive' in *Saothar*, vii (1980), pp 90-3.

Redmond, S., *The Irish municipal employees trade union 1883-1983* (Dublin, 1983).

Sweeney, G., *In public service: a history of the public service executive union, 1890-1990* (Dublin, 1990).

Walter, G., *The politics of frustration: Harry Midgeley and the failure of labour in Northern Ireland* (Manchester, 1985).

Maritime Ports

Anderson, R. and Wilson, I., *Ships and quaysides of Ulster: historic maritime photographs* (Belfast, 1990).

de Courcy Ireland, J., *Ireland's maritime heritage* (Dublin, 1992).

de Courcy Ireland, J., *Ireland and the Irish in maritime history* (Dun Laoghaire, 1985).

Transport and Infrastructure

Arnold, R.M., *The golden years of the great northern railway*, part 1 (Belfast, 1977).

Baker, H.C., *The railways of the Republic of Ireland. a pictorial survey of the G.S.R. and C.I.E. 1925-75* (Truro, 1975).

Baker, M., *Irish railways since 1916* (London, 1972).

Balty, M., *Across deep waters: bridges of Ireland* (Dublin, 1985).

Blair, M., *Once upon the Lagan: the story of the Lagan canal* (Belfast, 1981).

Boyd, J.I.C., *The Londonderry and Lough Swilly railway* (Truro, n.d.).

Brady-Deutsch, C., 'The railway question 1902' in *Galway Archaeological Society Journal*, xxxv (1976), pp 100-4.

Burns, A., 'The Bagenalstown and Wexford railway' in *Carloviana*, i, 18 (1969), pp 12-8.

Casserly, H.C., *Outline of Irish railway history* (Newton Abbot, 1974).

Clarke, P., 'The Royal Canal, 1798-1993' in *Dublin Historical Record*, xlvii, 1 (1993), pp 5-14.

Corcoran, M., 'Six decades of Irish road transport' in *Capuchin Annual* (1977), pp 325-39.

Cox, R.C., *Engineering Ireland 1778-1878* (Dublin, 1978).

Currie, J.R.L., *The northern counties railway, i: beginnings and development, 1845-1903* (Newton Abbot, 1973).

Currie, J.R.L., *The northern counties railway, ii: heyday and decline 1903-72* (Newton Abbot, 1974).

D'Arcy, G., *Portrait of the Grand Canal* (Dublin, 1969).

Delaney, R., *Ireland's inland waterways* (Belfast, 1985).

Delaney, R., 'John Trail, Grand Canal engineer' in *Kildare Archaeological Society Journal*, viiv (1970), pp 626-30.

Delaney, R., *The Grand Canal of Ireland* (Newton Abbot, 1973).

Doyle, O. and Hirsch, S., *Railways in Ireland 1934-1984* (Dublin, 1983).

Doyle, O. and Hirsch, S., *Railway lines of Coras lompair Éireann and Northern Ireland railways* (Dublin, 1985).

Dunne, J. J., 'The first Irish railway' in *Dublin Historical Record*, xliii, 1 (1990), pp 44-6.

Fayle, H., *Narrow gauge railways of Ireland* (London, 1970).

Ferris, T., *The Irish narrow gauge, a pictorial history*, i: *from Cork to Cavan* (Belfast, 1993).

Ferris, T., *The Irish narrow gauge, a pictorial history*, ii: *the Ulster lines* (Belfast, 1993).

Flanagan, P., 'The Ballinamore and Ballyconnell canal, part 1, the years of construction' in *Breifne*, iii (1968), pp 347-86.

Flanagan, P., 'The Ballinamore and Ballyconnell canal: II, the awards and acts and their implications' in *Breifne*, iii (1969), pp 492-527.

Flanagan, P., 'The Ballinamore and Ballyconnell canal' in *Breifne*, iv (1970), pp 131-80.

Flanagan, P., *Transport in Ireland 1880-1910* (Dublin, 1969).

Flanagan, P., *The Ballinamore and Ballyconnell canal* (Newton Abbot, 1972).

Gamble, N.E., 'The Dublin and Drogheda railway, part 1 & 2' in *Irish Railway Record Society Journal*, xi (1974), 64, pp 224-34; 65, pp 282-93.

Gamble, N.E., 'The Dublin and Drogheda railway 1844-1847' in *Irish Railway Record Society Journal*, xiv, 84 (1981), pp 162-70; xiv, 85 (1981), pp 228-35; xiv, 86 (1981), pp 278-82; xiv, 87.

Gamble, N. E., 'The Dublin and Belfast junction railway 1844-55' in *Irish Railway Record Society Journal*, xviiii, 117 (1992), pp 28-38; 118 (1992), pp 54-64; 119 (1992), pp 116-23.

Greer, P. E., The transport problem in Northern Ireland, 1921-48: A study of government policy, unpublished M.A. thesis, New University of Ulster (1977).

Greer, P.E., *Road versus rail: documents on the history of public transport in Northern Ireland, 1921-48* (Belfast, 1982).

Hajducki, S.M., *A railway atlas of Ireland* (Newton Abbot, 1974).

Harcourt, F., 'Charles Wye Williams and Irish steam shipping, 1820-1850' in *Journal of Transport History*, xiii, 2 (1992), pp 141-62.

Hardy, G., *The Londonderry railway* (Norwich, 1973).

Hanery, J., 'The Cork-Rosslare express in the days of steam' in *Decies*, xxxiii (1986), pp 50-53.

Horner, A.A., 'Planning the Irish transport network: parallels in nineteenth and twentieth century proposals' in *Irish Geography*, x (1977), pp 44-57.

Hughes, N.J., *Irish engineering 1760-1960* (Dublin, 1982).

Hutchins, P., 'The old roads of Bantry and Bere' in *Ireland of the Welcomes*, xxvii, 4 (1977), pp 36-8.

Jacobson, D.S., 'The motor industry in Ireland' in *Irish Economic and Social History*, xii (1985), pp 109-16.

Johnston, J., 'Communications in the Clogher Valley, 1700-1900' in *Clogher Record*, ix, 3 (1978), pp 310-25.

Leckey, J.J. and Rigney, P., *Irish railway record society archival collections, D1-DIO*, xii (Dublin, 1976) (occasional publications no. 4).

Leckey, J.J., 'A classification of Irish railway records' in *Irish Archives Bulletin*, iii, 2 (1973), pp 5-9.

Leckey, J.J., *Nineteenth century railway politics in the Belfast-Dublin-Enniskillen triangle* (Dublin, 1973).

Leckey, J.J., 'The railway servants strike in County Cork 1898' in *Saothar*, ii (1976), pp 39-45.

Leckey, J.J., *The records of the Grand Canal Company* (Belfast, 1980).

Leckey, J.J., The organisation and capital structure of the Irish north western railway, unpublished M.Sc.(Econ.) thesis, Queen's University, Belfast (1974).

Leckey, J.J., 'The end of the road: the Kilcullen turnpike 1844-1848, compared with 1787-1792' in *Royal Society of Antiquaries of Ireland Journal*, 113 (1983), pp 106-20.

Leckey, J.J., *The records of the county Donegal railways* (Belfast, 1980).

Lee, J.J., 'Merchants and enterprise: the case of early Irish railways, 1830-55' in Cullen, L M. and Butel, P. (eds), *Négoce et industrie en France et en Irlande aux xviii et xix siecles: actes de colloque Franco-lrlandais d'histoire Bordeaux, Mai 1978* (Paris, 1980), pp 143-58.

Loeber, R., 'Biographical dictionary of engineers in Ireland 1600-1730' in *Irish Sword*, xiii, 51 (1977), pp 19-54.

Loeber, R., 'Biographical dictionary of engineers in Ireland 1600-1730 (ctd)' in *Irish Sword*, xiii (1979), pp 283-314.

Loeber, R., 'Biographical dictionary of engineers in Ireland 1660-1730' in *Irish Sword*, xiii (1979), pp 230-55.

Mahon, G.R, 'Irish railways in 1872' in *Irish Railway Record Society Journal*, xii (1975), pp 36-43, 87-95, 139-50.

Mahon, G.R., 'Irish railways in 1869' in *Irish Railway Record Society Journal*, x (1971), pp 29-39, 72-80, 123-31.

Mahon, G.R., 'Irish railways in 1870' in *Irish Railway Record Society Journal*, xi (1972), pp 219-25.

Mahon, G.R., 'Irish railways in 1873' in *Irish Railway Record Society Journal*, xii (1976), pp 189-200, 227-33.

Mahon, G.R., 'Irish railways in 1877' in *Irish Railway Record Society Journal*, xiv, 84 (1981), pp 182-90; xiv, 88, pp 365-78; xiv, 89, pp 422-32.

Mahon, G.R., 'The Birth of the GNR' in *Irish Railway Record Society Journal*, xii (1976), pp 276-80.

McCutcheon, A., *Ireland: railway history in pictures*, i (Newton Abbot, 1969).

McCutcheon, Alan, *Ireland: railway history in pictures*, ii (Newton Abbot, 1970).

McCutcheon, W.A., 'Transport 1820-1914' in Kennedy, L. and Ollerenshaw, P.G. (eds), *An Economic History of Ulster 1820-1939* (Manchester, 1985), pp 109-36.

McDonald, B., 'The Newry and Armagh railway' in *Irish Railway Record Society Journal*, xv, 98 (1985), pp 422-28.

McDonald, B., 'Newry, Warrenpoint and Rostrevor railway' in *Irish Railway Record Society Journal*, xv, 91 (1983), pp 88-95.

McGrath, W., 'Cork's narrow gauge' in *Irish Railway Record Society Journal*, xi, 64 (1974), pp 210-23.

McNeill, D. B., *Coastal passenger steamers and inland navigations in the south of Ireland* (Belfast, 1965).

McNeill, D.B., 'Mail services by rail' in *Irish Railway Records Society Journal*, xxi, 100 (1986), pp 58-69.

McNeill, D.B., 'Public transport in Fermanagh, part 3, rail' in *Clogher Record*, xi, 3 (1984), pp 326-41.

McNeill, D.B., 'The Waterford and central Ireland railway' in *Irish Railway Record Society Journal*, xiii, 74 (1977), pp 114-24.

McNeill, D.B., 'The Waterford, Dungarvan and Lismore railway' in *Irish Railway Record Society Journal*, xiv, 88 (1982), pp 356-64.

McNeill, D. B., *Irish passenger steamship services*, i, *north of Ireland* (Newton Abbot, 1969).

McNeill, D. B., *Irish passenger steamship services*, ii, *south of Ireland* (Newton Abbot, 1971).

Middlemass, T., *Irish standard gauge railways* (Newton Abbot, 1981).

Moore, J., *Motor makers in Ireland* (Belfast, 1982).

Morton, G., *Railways in Ulster: historic photographs of the age of steam* (Belfast, 1989).

Mulligan, F., *One hundred and fifty years of Irish railways* (Belfast, 1983).

Murnane, B., Public transport and changing travel times: Ireland, 1891-1976, unpublished B.A. dissertation, U.C.D. (1976).

Murphy, C., 'The Limerick navigation company, 1697-1836' in *North Munster Antiquarian Journal*, xxii (1980), pp 43-61.

Murphy, C., 'The Limerick to Killaloe canal' in, *The Other Clare*, 8 (1984), pp 45-6.

Murphy, I., 'Projected railways to Limerick, 1825-1827' in *North Munster Antiquarian Journal*, xxiii (1981), pp 95-6.

Murphy, I., 'Pre-famine passenger services on the lower Shannon' in *North Munster Antiquarian Journal*, xvii (1973-74), pp 70-83.

Murray, K.A., and McNeill, D.B., *The great southern and western railway* (Dublin, 1976).

Newham, A.T., *The Cork and Muskerry light railway* (Lingfield, 1968).

Newham, A.T., *The Cork, Blackrock and Passage railway* (Lingfield, 1970).

Ní Chinnéide, S., 'A journey from Mullingar to Loughrea in 1791' in *Old Athlone Society Journal*, ii, 5 (1978), pp 15-23.

Nowlan, K.B. (ed.)., *Travel and transport in Ireland* (Dublin, 1973).

Ó Cuimín, P., *The baronial lines of M.G.W.R.: the Loughrea and Attymon light railway; the Ballinrobe and Claremorris light railway* (Dublin, 1972).

O'Dea, J.P., 'Broadstone to Clonsilla junction' in *Irish Railway Record Society Journal*, xvii, 2 (1987), pp 214-26.

O'Dea, J.P., 'Clara to Banagher, Part 1' in *Irish Railway Record Society Journal*, xi, 62 (1973), pp 127-39.

O'Dea, J.P., 'Clara to Banagher, Part 2' in *Irish Railway Record Society Journal*, xi, 63 (1974), pp 171-8.

O'Dea, J.P., 'Sligo to Ballaghadereen' in *Irish Railway Record Society Journal*, xii (1976), pp 179-88, 218-26.

O'Donovan, J., *Wheels and deals: people and places in Irish motoring* (Dublin, 1983).

Ó Gráda, D., 'The rocky road to Dublin: transport modes and urban growth in the Georgian age with particular reference to the turnpike roads' in *Studia Hibernica* (1982-3), pp 128-48.

O'Keefe, P. and Simington, T., *Irish stone bridges: history and heritage* (Dublin, 1992).

Ó Lúing, S., 'Richard Griffith and the roads of Kerry, part II' in *Kerry Archaeological and Historical Society Journal,* ix (1976), pp 92-124.

Patterson, E.M., *The Belfast and county Down railway* (Newton Abbot, 1982).

Patterson, E. M., *The Clogher valley railway* (Newton Abbot, 1972).

Phelan, J.A., 'The Kerry railways' in *Irish Railway Record Society Journal,* xviii, 113 (1990), pp 282-90.

Prideaux, J.D.C.A., *The Irish narrow gauge railway: a pictorial history* (Newton Abbot, 1981).

Rowlands, D.G., *The Tralee and Dingle railway* (Truro, 1977).

Shepherd, W.E., 'Athenry to Ennis' in *Irish Railway Record Society Journal,* xviii, 111 (1990), pp 159-71.

Shepherd, W.E., *The Dublin and south-eastern railway* (Newton Abbot, 1974).

Sprinks, N.W., *Sligo, Leitrim and northern counties railway* (Essex, 1970).

Townshend, C., 'The Irish railway strike of 1920: industrial action and civil resistance in the struggle for independence' in *Irish Historical Studies,* xxi, 83 (1979), pp 265-282.

Tucker, D.G., 'The Listowel and Ballybunion railway: some revisions and additions to its story' in *Journal of the Railway & Canal History Society,* xxviii, 1 (1984), pp 2-13.

Woods, D., 'The Portadown to Dungannon railway, 1914-1965' in *Dúiche Néill: Journal of the O'Neill Country Historical Society,* 7 (1992), pp 88-100.

Urbanisation: settlement and society

Andrews, J.H., 'An Elizabethan map of Kilmallock' in *North Munster Antiquarian Journal,* xi (1968), pp 27-35.

Bannon, M.J., *A hundred years of Irish planning* (Dublin, 1984).

Bannon, M.J., *Planning: the Irish experience 1920-1988* (Dublin, 1989).

Breen, R., Hannan, D., Rothman, D. and Whelan, C., *Understanding contemporary Ireland: state, class and development in the Republic of Ireland* (Dublin, 1990).

Buchanan, R.H., 'Historical Geography of Ireland pre-1700' in *Irish Geography: The Geographical Society of Ireland golden jubilee 1934-1984,* supplement to *Irish Geography,* 17 (1984), pp 129-48.

Buchanan, R.H., 'Towns and plantations 1500-1700' in Nolan, W. (ed.), *The shaping of Ireland: the geographical perspective* (Cork and Dublin, 1986).

Butel, P. and Cullen, L.M. (eds), *Cities and merchants: French and Irish perspectives on urban development, 1500-1900* (Dublin, 1986).

Butlin, R.A. (ed.), *The development of the Irish town* (London, 1978).

Clancy, P. (ed.), *Ireland: a sociological profile* (Dublin, 1986).

Clarkson, L.A., 'Population change and urbanisation 1821-191' in Kennedy, L. and Ollerenshaw, P.G. (eds), *An economic history of Ulster 1820-1939* (Manchester, 1985), pp 137-58.

Crawford, W.H., 'The evolution of Ulster towns, 1750-1850' in Roebuck, P. (ed.), *Plantation to partition: essays in Ulster history in honour of J.L. McCracken* (Belfast, 1981).

Crawford, W.H., 'Markets and fairs in county Cavan' in *Breifne,* ii, 3 (1984), pp 55-65.

Cullen, L.M., *Irish towns and villages* (Dublin, 1979).

Cullen, L.M., *Town life* (Dublin, 1974).

Curriculum Development Unit, Trinity College Dublin, *Urban Ireland: development of towns and villages* (Dublin, 1982).

Curtin, C. and Ryan, C., 'Clubs, pubs and private houses in a Clare town' in Curtin, C. and Wilson, T.M. (eds), *Ireland: Social change from above and below local communities* (Galway, 1989), pp 128-43.

Curtin, C., Donnan, H. and Wilson, T. A. (eds), *Irish urban cultures* (Belfast, 1993).

Daly, M.E., 'An alien institution: attitudes towards the city in nineteenth and twentieth-century Irish society' in *Etudes Irlandaises,* 10 (1985), pp 181-94.

Daly, M.A., 'Irish urban history: a survey' in *Urban History Yearbook* (Leicester, 1986), pp 61-72.

Darley, G., *Villages of vision* (London, 1975).

Dickson, D., 'Large-scale developers and the growth of eighteenth century Irish cities, in Butel, P. and Cullen, L.M. (eds), *Cities and merchants: French and Irish perspectives on urban development, 1500-1900* (Dublin, 1986), pp 109-24.

Dickson, D., 'Centres of motion: Irish cities and the origins of popular politics' in *Culture et pratiques politiques en France et en Irlande, xviie xviiiie siecle: actes du colloque de Marseille, 1988* (Paris, 1991), pp 101-22.

Fagan, P., *The origins and development of villages in county Dublin*, unpublished M.A. thesis, University College Dublin (1987).

Ffolliott, R., 'Houses in provincial towns' in *Irish Ancestor*, viii, 2 (1975), pp 97-9.

Ffolliott, R., 'Proviincial town life in Munster' in *Irish Ancestor*, v, I (1973), pp 34-7.

Freeman, T.W., *Pre-Famine Ireland: a study in historical geography* (Manchester, 1957).

Galloway, P., *The cathedrals of Ireland* (Belfast, 1992).

Garrett, M., Municipal and central government in Ireland under Charles II, unpublished M.A. thesis, University College Dublin (1972).

Gillespie, R., 'The origins and development of an Ulster urban network, 1600-164' in *Irish Historical Studies*, xxi, 93 (1984), pp 15-29.

Gillespie, R., *Colonial Ulster: the settlement of East Ulster 1600-1641* (Cork, 1985).

Gillespie, R., 'The small towns of Ulster, 1600-1700' in *Ulster Folklife*, xxxvii (1990), pp 23-31.

Gillespie, R., 'Urban oligarchies and popular protest in the early seventeenth century: two Ulster examples' in *Retrospect* (new series), II (1982), pp 54-6.

Graham, B.J., 'The town of medieval Ireland' in Butlin, R.A. (ed.), *The development of the Irish town* (London, 1977).

Graham, B.J., 'The evolution of urbanisation in medieval Ireland' in *Journal of Historical Geography*, v, 2 (1979), pp 111-26.

Graham, B.J., 'The definition and classification of medieval Irish towns' in *Irish Geography*, xxi (1988), pp 20-32.

Graham, B.J. and Proudfoot, L.J., 'Landlords, planning and urban growth in eighteenth and early nineteenth century Ireland' in *Journal of Urban History*, xviii, 3 (1992), pp 308-29.

Gulliver, P.H., 'Shopkeepers and farmers in south Kilkenny, 1840-1981' in Silverman, M. and Gulliver, P.H. (eds), *Approaching the past: historical anthropology through Irish case studies* (New York, 1992), pp 176-204.

Hamilton, G., *Northern Ireland town plans, 1828-1966: a catalogue of large scale town plans prepared by the Ordnance Survey and deposited in P.R.O.N.I.* (Belfast, 1981).

Healy, J., *The death of an Irish town* (Cork, 1968).

Higgins, M.D. and Gibbons, J.P., 'Shopkeeper-graziers and land agitation in Ireland, 1895-1900' in Drudy, P.J. (ed.), *Ireland: land, politics and people, Irish studies*, ii (Cambridge, 1982), pp 93-118.

Hoppen, K.T., *Elections, politics and society in Ireland 1832-1885* (Oxford, 1984).

Horner, A.A., Stability and change in the towns and villages west of Dublin, unpublished Ph.D. thesis, University of Dublin (1974).

Horner, A.A., 'The pre-famine population of some Kildare towns' in *Kildare Archaeological Society Journal*, xiv (1969), pp 444-51.

Hourihan, K., 'Urban population density patterns and change in Ireland, 1901-1979' in *Economic and Social Review*, xiii, 2 (1982), pp 125-47.

Hunter, R.J., 'Ulster plantation towns, 1609-41' in Harkness, D. and O'Dowd, M. (eds), *The town in Ireland: historical studies*, xiii (Belfast, 1981), pp 55-80.

Hunter, R. J., 'Towns in the Ulster plantation' in *Studia Hibernica*, xi (1971), pp 40-79.

Jenkins, R., 'Beyond ethnography: primary data sources in the urban anthropology of Northern Ireland' in Curtin, C., Donnan, Hastings and Wilson, T. A. (eds), *Irish urban cultures* (Belfast, 1993), pp 243-62.

Johnston, J.D., 'Settlement and architecture in county Fermanagh, 1610-41' in *Ulster Journal of Archaeology*, xiii (1980), pp 79-89.

Jones Hughes, T., 'Town and baile in Irish place-names' in Stephens, N. and Glasscock, R.E. (eds), *Irish geographical studies in honour of Emyr Estyn Evans* (Belfast, 1970), pp 244-58.

Jones Hughes, T., 'Village and town in mid-nineteenth century Ireland' in *Irish Geography*, xiv (1981), pp 99-106.

Jones Hughes, T., 'Historical geography of Ireland from c.1700' in *Irish Geography: The Geographical Society of Ireland golden jubilee 1934-1984*, supplement to *Irish Geography*, 17 (1984), pp 149-66.

Lockhart, D.G., 'The linen industry and the advertising of towns and villages in Ireland 1700-1750' in *Textile History*, viii (1977), pp 163-66.

Lockhart, D.G., 'Planned village development in Scotland and Ireland, 1700-1850' in Devine, T.M. and Dickson, D. (eds), *Ireland and Scotland, 1600-1850: parallels and contrasts in economic and social development* (Edinburgh, 1983), pp 132-45.

Loeber, R., 'Civilization through plantation: the projects of Mathew de Renzi' in Murtagh, H. (ed.), *Irish midland studies: essays in commemoration of N.W. English* (Athlone, 1980), pp 121-35.

Luddy, M., 'Prostitution and rescue work in nineteenth century Ireland' in Luddy, M. and Murphy, C. (eds),

Women surviving: studies in Irish women's history in the 19th and 20th centuries (Swords, 1989), pp 51-84.

MacCarthy-Murrough, M., *The Munster plantation, English migration to southern Ireland, 1583-1641* (Oxford, 1986).

MacNeice, D.S., 'Industrial villages of Ulster, 1800-1900' in Roebuck, P. (ed.), *Plantation to partition: essays in Ulster history in honour of J.L. McCracken* (Belfast, 1981), pp 172-90.

MacNiocaill, G., 'Socio-Economic problems of the late medieval Irish town' in Harkness, D. and O'Dowd, M. (eds), *The town in Ireland: historical studies xiii* (Belfast, 1981), pp 722.

Martin, G., 'Plantation boroughs in medieval Ireland with a handlist of boroughs to c. 1500, in Harkness D. and O'Dowd, M. (eds), *The town in Ireland* (Belfast, 1981), pp 23-54.

McCrystal, R.M., Aspects of the urban settlement in county Fermanagh, unpublished B.A. dissertation, U.C.D. (1963).

McFarlane, G., 'Dimensions of Protestantism: the working of Protestant identity in a northern Irish village, in Curtin, C. and Wilson, T M. (eds), *Ireland: social change from above and below local communities* (Galway, 1989), pp 23-45.

McManus, M., 'The functions of small Ulster settlements in 1854, 1899, and 1916' in *Ulster Folklife*, xxiv (1993), pp 50-72.

Morris, J., 'Recording an urban life style' in *Ulster Folk and Transport Museum Yearbook 1976-77* (1978), pp 15-7.

Nolan, W. (ed.), *The shaping of Ireland: the geographical perspective* (Cork and Dublin, 1986).

O'Connor, P.J., *Exploring Limerick's past: an historical geography of urban development in county and city* (Newcastlewest, 1987).

O'Connor, P.J., 'Maturation of town and village life in county Limerick 1700-1900' in Smyth, W.J. and Whelan, K. (eds), *Common ground: essays on the historical geography of Ireland* (Cork, 1988), pp 149-72.

O'Connor, L., Settlement in county Carlow: a geographical perspective, unpublished B.A. dissertation, U.C.D. (1970).

O'Doherty, M., Development of the grid iron street pattern in Ulster, unpublished B.A. dissertation, U.C.D. (1977).

O'Dowd, L., 'Towards a structural analysis of Irish urbanisation' in *Proceedings of Fourth Annual Conference, Sociological Association of Ireland* (Belfast, 1978).

O'Flanagan, P., 'Settlement development and trading in Ireland, 1600-1800: a preliminary investigation' in Devine, T.M. and Dickson, D. (eds), *Ireland and Scotland, 1600-1850: parallels and contrasts in economic and social development* (Edinburgh, 1983), pp 146-50.

O'Flanagan, P., 'Markets and fairs in Ireland 1600-1800: index of economic development and regional growth' in *Journal of Historical geography*, xi, 4 (1985), pp 364-78.

O'Flanagan, P., 'Urban minorities and majorities: Catholics and Protestants in Munster towns c. 1659-1850' in Smyth, W.J. and Whelan, K.(eds), *Common ground: essays on the historical geography of Ireland* (Cork, 1988), pp 124-48.

O'Flanagan, P., 'Three hundred years of urban life: villages and towns in county Cork, c. 1600-1901' in O'Flanagan, P. and Buttimer, C. G. (eds), *Cork history and society: interdisciplinary essays on the history of an Irish county* (Dublin, 1993), pp 391-468.

O'Leary, L., *Cinema Ireland, 1896-1950* (Dublin, 1990).

Poole, M.A., 'Religious residential segregation in urban northern Ireland' in Boal, F.W. and Douglas, J.N.H. (eds), *Integration and division: geographical perspectives on the Northern Ireland problem* (London, 1982), pp 281-308.

Proudfoot, L., 'Landlord motivation and urban improvement on the duke of Devonshire's Irish estates, c.1792-1832' in *Irish Economic and Social History*, xviii (1991), pp 5-23.

Proudfoot, L., Urban patronage and estate management on the Duke of Devonshire's Irish estates, c.1792-1832, unpublished Ph.D., thesis, Queen's University Belfast (1989).

Proudfoot, L., and Graham, B.J., 'The nature and extent of urban and village foundation and improvement in eighteenth and early nineteenth century Ireland' in *Planning perspectives*, 8 (1993), pp 259-81.

Rafter, D.O., 'Irish urban policy in an anti-urban society' in *Eire/Ireland*, xxvii, 3 (1992), pp 110-21.

Robinson, P., 'Urbanisation in north-west Ulster, 1609-1670' in *Irish Geography*, xv (1982), pp 35-50.

Royle, S.A., 'Industrialisation, urbanisation, and urban society in post-famine Ireland' in Graham, B.J. and Proudfoot, L. (eds), *An historical geography of Ireland* (London, 1993), pp 258-92.

Shaffrey, P., *The Irish town – an approach to survival* (Dublin, 1975).

Shaffrey, P. and Shaffrey, M., *Buildings of Irish towns: treasures of everyday architecture* (Dublin, 1983).

Sheehan, A., 'Irish towns in a period of change 1558-1625' in Brady, C. and Gillespie, R. (eds), *Natives and newcomers: the making of Irish colonial society 1534-1641* (Dublin, 1986), pp 93-119.

Silverman, M., 'An urban place in rural Ireland: an historical ethnography of domination, 1841-1989' in Curtin, C., Donnan, H. and Wilson, T. A. (eds), *Irish urban cultures* (Belfast, 1993), pp 203-26.

Simms, A., 'Cartographic representation of diachronic analysis: the example of the origins of towns' in Baker, A.R.H. and Bilinge, M. (eds), *Period and place: research methods in historical geography* (Cambridge, 1982).

Simms, A. and Fagan, P., 'Villages in county Dublin: their origins and inheritance' in Aalen, F.H. and Whelan, K. (eds), *Dublin city and county from prehistory to the present: studies in honour of J.H. Andrews* (Dublin, 1992), pp 79-119.

Smyth, W. J., 'Towns and town life in mid-seventeenth century Tipperary' in *Tipperary Historical Journal*, iv (1991), pp 163-69.

Spellissy, S. and O'Brien, J., *Clare: county of contrasts* (Castlebar, 1987).

Webb, J. J., *Municipal government in Ireland-medieval Ireland and modern* (Dublin, 1918).

Whelan, K., 'The Catholic parish, the Catholic chapel and village development in Ireland' in *Irish Geography*, 16 (1983), pp 115.

Whelan, K., A geography of society and culture in Ireland since 1800, unpublished Ph.D. thesis, University College Dublin (1981).

Whelan, K., 'Settlement and society in eighteenth century Ireland' in Dawe, G. and Foster, J.W. (eds), *The poet's place, Ulster literature and society* (Belfast, 1991), pp 45-62.

2. Bibliography of Individual Towns

Antrim, County Antrim

Malcolmson, A.P.W., 'Election politics in the borough of Antrim, 1750-1800' in *Irish Historical Studies*, xvii (1970), pp 32-57.

Ardee, County Louth

Geraghty, P.J., 'Ardee and its Market Square 1790-1870' in *County Louth Archaeological and Historical Society Journal*, xxii, 1 (1989), pp 54-66.

Mac Iomhar, D., 'The Carmelites in Ardee' in *County Louth Archaeological and Historical Society Journal*, xx (1983), pp 180-89.

Quane, M., 'Erasmus Smith School, Ardee' in *County Louth Archaeological and Historical Society Journal*, xvii (1969), pp 10-8.

Arklow, County Wicklow

Andrews, J., 'Arklow's early chemical industry c.1770-1853' in *Arklow Historical Society Journal* (1988-9), pp 8-12.

Fitzgerald, M., 'Acetylene works in Arklow' in *Arklow Historical Society Journal* (1992-3), pp 12-4.

Forde, F., *Maritime Arklow* (Dublin, 1988).

Martin, J., Arklow port: a historical and functional study, unpublished B.A. dissertation, U.C.D. (1971).

Mulhall, D., 'Arklow pottery: working in the clay end, 1955-1959' in *Arklow Historical Society Journal* (1990-91), pp 37-42.

O'Duinn, S., 'The manor of Arklow in the sixteenth century' in *Arklow Historical Society Journal* (1986), pp 44-9.

Power, P.J., *The Arklow calendar: a chronicle of events from earliest times to 1900 A.D.* (Arklow, 1981).

Rees, J. and Charlton, L., *Arklow – the last stronghold of sail: Arklow ships 1850-1985* (Arklow, 1985).

Tansey, M., The growth and development of Arklow, as east coast port town between 1850 and 1910, unpublished B.A. dissertation, U.C.D. (1990).

Armagh, County Armagh

Cassidy, H., 'Armagh Public Library' in *Dúiche Néill*, no. 8 (1993), pp 133-39.

Clarkson, L.A., 'An anatomy of an Irish town: the economy of Armagh 1770' in *Irish Economic and Social History*, v (1978), pp 27-45.

Clarkson, L.A., 'Household and family structure in Armagh city, 1770' in *Local Population Studies*, xx (1978), pp 14-31.

Clarkson, L.A., 'Armagh 1770: portrait of an urban community' in Harkness, D. and O'Dowd, M. (eds), *The town in Ireland: historical studies,* xiii (Belfast, 1981), pp 81-102.

O'Neill, C.P. and O'Neill, S.P, *Armagh post office: its history and post-marks* (Dundalk, 1983).

Simms, G. O., 'The founder of Armagh public library: Primate Robinson among his books' in *Irish Booklore,* i (1971), pp 138-49.

Smyth, W.J., The social and economic geography of nineteenth century Armagh, unpublished M.A. thesis, University College Dublin (1972).

Thompson, F., 'The Armagh elections of 1885-6' in *Seanchas Ardmhacha,* vii (1977), pp 360-85.

Weatherup, D.R.M., 'Armagh County Museum – the reference library' in *Irish Booklore,* ii (1972), pp 44-53.

Weatherup, D.R.M., 'The Armagh public library 1771-1973' in *Irish Booklore,* ii, 2 (1976), pp 268-99.

Williamson, A.P., 'Armagh district lunatic asylum' in *Seanchas Ardmhacha,* viii, i (1976), pp 111-20.

Athlone, County Westmeath

Casey, P., 'Epidemic ophthalmia at Athlone, 1850' in *Old Athlone Society Journal,* i, 2 (1971), pp 112-5.

Claffey, J.A., 'The medieval castle of Athlone' in *Old Athlone Society Journal,* i, 2, pp 55-60.

Conlan, P., 'The "outlaw" friars of Athlone 1916' in *Old Athlone Society Journal,* ii, 5 (1978), pp 39-44.

Cox, L., 'Athlone in the Civil War, 1641-1652' in *Irish Sword,* xx (1971), pp 159-70.

Curley, S., Social and economic differentiation of nineteenth century Athlone, unpublished B.A. dissertation, University College Dublin (1988).

Delaney, R., 'Athlone navigation works, 1757-1849' in Murtagh, H. (ed.), *Irish midland studies: essays in commemoration of N.W.English* (Athlone, 1980), pp 193-204, 239-49.

English, N.W., 'The Burgess papers of Athlone' in *Old Athlone Society Journal,* i, 4 (1975), pp 254-62.

English, N.W., 'The Burgess papers of Athlone' in *Old Athlone Society Journal,* ii, 5 (1978), pp 71-4.

Finnegan, F., 'The Jesuits and Athlone in the seventeenth. and eighteenth centuries' in *Old Athlone Society Journal,* i, 2 (1971), pp 77-83.

Hanley, M.K., *The story of Custume Barracks, Athlone, 1697-1974* (Athlone, 1974).

Kerrigan, P., 'The defence of the Shannon: Portumna to Athlone, 1793-1815' in Murtagh, H. (ed.), *Irish midland studies: essays in commemoration of N.W. English* (Athlone, 1980), pp 168-192.

Murtagh, H., 'Horse racing in Georgian Athlone' in *Old Athlone Society Journal,* xi, 6 (1985), pp 85-88.

Murtagh, H., 'Thomas Phillip's plan of Athlone' in *Old Athlone Society Journal,* xi, 6 (1985), pp 133-5.

Murtagh, H. and O'Dwyer, M. (eds), *Athlone besieged: eyewitness and other contemporary accounts of the sieges of Athlone, 1690 and 1691* (Athlone, 1991).

Murtagh, H., 'The siege of Athlone 1690' in *Old Athlone Society Journal,* x (1971), pp 10-28.

Murtagh, H., 'Vicissitudes of a garrison town: Athlone at the end of the seventeenth century' in *Old Athlone Society Journal,* i (1969), pp 17-22.

O'Brien, B., 'When the circus came to Athlone' in *Old Athlone Society Journal,* xi, 6 (1985), pp 109-115.

O'Brien, B., 'Earliest memories of the theatre in Athlone' in *Old Athlone Society Journal,* i (1969), pp 35-7.

O'Brien, B., 'Athlone's Repeal demonstration' in *Old Athlone Society Journal,* i, 2 (1971) pp 107-11.

O'Brien, G., *St. Mary's parish, Athlone: a history* (Longford, 1989).

Quane, M., 'Ranelagh Endowed School, Athlone' in *Old Athlone Society Journal,* i (1969), pp 23-34.

Quane, M., 'Athlone classical school' in *Old Athlone Society Journal,* i, 2 (1971), pp 90-9.

Athy, County Kildare

Carberry, P., Athy, County Kildare: growth and development, unpublished B.A. dissertation, University College Dublin (1968).

Bagenalstown, County Carlow

Kavanagh, P.J., 'St. Joseph's Academy, Mhuine Bheag 1896-1926' in *Carloviana,* vol. 28 (1980), pp 19-22.

Ballina, County Mayo

McGuire, J., 'The private schools of Ballina' in *North Mayo Historical Journal,* xi, 5 (1992), pp 25-30.

McGuire, J., *Steeple and people: the story of Ballina and its cathedral* (Ballina, 1993).

Reilly, T., *The goal of victory: history of Ballina Stephenites 1886-1986* (Ballina, 1986).

Reilly, T., *Dear old Ballina* (Ballina, 1993).

Ballinasloe, County Galway

McLoughlin, T., *Ballinasloe inniu agus inné: a story of a community over the past two hundred years* (Galway, 1972).

Collins, P., 'Analysing division: two different approaches to the history of Belfast' in *Saothar*, xvi (1991), pp 67-72 (review essay).

Conroy, J., *War as a way of life* (London, 1988).

Costello, M., *Titanic town. Memoirs of a Belfast childhood* (London, 1992).

Crawford, W.H., 'The Belfast middle classes in the late eighteenth century' in Dickson, D., Keogh, D. and Whelan, K. (eds), *The United Irishmen, republicanism, radicalism and rebellion* (Dublin, 1993), pp 62-73.

Cunningham, M.W., 'Victoria college: the early years' in *Pace*, x, 3 (1978), pp 3-7.

Curran, D., *The story of St.Paul's, Falls Road, Belfast: 1887-1987* (Belfast, 1987).

Davies, A.C., 'Roofing Belfast and Dublin 1896-8: American penetration of the Irish market for Welsh slate' in *Irish Economic and Social History*, iv (1977), pp 5-25.

Davis, M., *The struggle for worker's unity in Belfast, 1930-1935*, unpublished M.Sc. thesis, University of California (1975).

Davison, R.S., 'The Belfast blitz' in *Irish Sword*, xvi, 63 (1985), pp 65-83.

de Baróid, C., *Ballymurphy and the Irish war* (London, 1989).

Dixon, H., *No mean city: Belfast 1880-1914* (Belfast, 1983).

Doherty, J., *Post 381: The memoirs of a Belfast air raid warden* (Belfast, 1989).

Donald, P., *Yes matron: a history of nurses and nursing at the Royal Victoria Hospital, Belfast* (Dundonald, 1989).

Doyle, M., 'Belfast and Tolpuddle: attempts at strengthening a trade union presence 1833-4' in *Saothar*, ii (1976), pp 2-12.

Duncan, T.S., *'Cautious, Belfast': the story of the first fifty years of Harris, Marrion and Company Ltd.* (Belfast, 1975).

Farrell, M., *The poor law and the workhouse in Belfast, 1838-1938* (Belfast, 1978).

Froggat, P., 'Industrialisation and health in Belfast in the early nineteenth century' in Harkness, D. and O'Dowd, M. (eds), *The town in Ireland: historical studies xiii* (Belfast, 1981), pp 155-86.

Gallagher, E., *At points of need: the story of the Belfast central mission, Grosvenor Hall 1889-1989* (Belfast, 1989).

Gallagher, C., *All around the Loney-O* (Belfast, 1978).

Gamble, N.E., The business community and trade of Belfast, 1767-1800, unpublished Ph.D. thesis, University of Dublin (1978).

Geary, F., 'The rise and fall of the Belfast cotton industry: some problems' in *Irish Economic and Social History Journal*, viii (1981), pp 30-49.

Geary, F. and Johnson, W., 'Shipbuilding in Belfast 1861-1986' in *Irish Economic and Social History*, xvi, pp 42-64.

Geary, F. and Johnson, W., 'The Belfast cotton industry revisited' in *Irish Historical Studies*, xxvi, no.103 (1989), pp 250-67.

Goldring, M., *Belfast: From loyalty to rebellion* (London, 1991).

Gray, J., *City in revolt: James Larkin and the Belfast dock strike of 1907* (Belfast, 1985).

Gray, J., 'Reporting the great Belfast debates of 1792' in *Linen Hall Review*, ix, no. 1 (1992), pp 4-8.

Green, E.R.R., 'Belfast entrepeneurship in the nineteenth century' in Cullen L.M. and Butel P. (eds), *Négoce et industrie en France et en Irlande aux xviii et xix siecles: actes de colloque Franco-Irlandais d'histoire, Bordeaux, Mai 1978* (Paris, 1980), pp 137-42.

Gribbon, S., 'An Irish city: Belfast 1911' in Harkness, D. and O'Dowd, M. (eds), *The town in Ireland: historical studies xiii* (Belfast, 1981), pp 203-20.

Gribbon, S., *Edwardian Belfast: a social profile* (Belfast, 1982).

Hamilton, P., *Up the Shankill* (Belfast, 1979).

Hammond, D., *Steelchest, nail in the boot and the barking dog: the Belfast shipyard, a story of the people by the people* (Belfast, 1986).

Harbison, J., 'The Belfast harper's meeting, 1792: the legacy' in *Ulster Folklife*, xxxv (1989), pp 113-28.

Heatley, F., *The story of St. Patrick's, Belfast 1815-1977* (Portglenone, 1977).

Hepburn, A.C. and Collins, B.,, 'Industrial society: the structure of Belfast, 1901' in Roebuck, P. (ed.), *Plantation to partition: essays in Ulster history in honour of J.L McCracken* (Belfast, 1981), pp 210-28.

Hepburn, A.C., *Employment and religion in Belfast 1901-1971* (Belfast, 1982).

Hepburn, A.C., 'Employment and religion in Belfast' in Cormack, R. J. and Osborne, R. D. (eds), *Religion, education and employment: aspects of equal opportunity in Northern Ireland* (Belfast, 1983), pp 42-63.

Hepburn, A.C., 'Work, class and religion in Belfast, 1871-1911' in *Irish Economic and Social History*, x (1983), pp 33-50.

Hepburn, A.C., 'The Belfast riots of 1935' in *Social History*, xv (1990), pp 75-96.

Johnson, D.S., 'The Belfast boycott, 1920-1922' in Goldstrom, J.M. and Clarkson, L.A. (eds), *Irish population, economy and society: essays in honour of the late K. H. Connell* (Oxford, 1981), pp 287-308.

Jones, G., 'Eugenics in Ireland: the Belfast eugenics society 1911-1915' in *Irish Historical Studies*, xxivvv, no. 109 (1992), pp 81-95.

Jordan, A., *Who cared? charity in Victorian and Edwardian Belfast* (Belfast, 1992).

Jordan, A., Voluntary societies in Victorian and Edwardian Belfast, unpublished Ph.D. thesis, Queen's University Belfast (1989).

Kelly, V., '"History around us": the experience of four Belfast schools' in *Teaching History*, xxxiv (1982), pp 14-7.

Kennedy, J., *Belfast Celtic* (Belfast, 1989).

Killen, J., *A history of the Linen Hall library, 1788-1988* (Belfast, 1991).

Larmour, P., *An illustrated guide to Belfast* (Belfast, 1987).

MacLoughlin, A., *The city of Belfast* (Dublin, 1982).

Magee, J., *The Linen Hall library and the cultural life of Georgian Belfast* (Belfast, 1982).

Maguire, W.A., 'Lord Donegall and the sale of Belfast: a case history from the encumbered estates court' in *Economic History Review*, xxxix, 4 (1976), pp 570-84.

Maguire, W.A., 'Ormeau house' in *Ulster Journal of archaeology*, xlii (1979), pp 66-71.

Maguire, W.A., 'Absentees, architects and agitators: the fifth earl of Donegall and the building of Fisherwick Park' in McNeilly, N. (ed.), *Belfast natural history and philosophical society: selections from 150 years of proceedings* (Belfast, 1981), pp 237-62.

Maguire, W.A., *Living like a lord: the second marquis of Donegall, 1769-1844* (Belfast, 1984).

Maguire, W.A., *Caught in time: the photographs of Alexander Hogg of Belfast 1870-1939* (Belfast, 1986).

Maguire, W.A., 'The Verner rape trial, 1813: James Barnes v. the Belfast establishment' in *Ulster Local Studies*, xv, 1, 1993, pp 47-57.

Maguire, W. A., *Belfast* (Keele, 1993).

Marshall, R., *Methodist college, Belfast: the first hundred years* (Belfast, 1968).

Maybin, J M., *Belfast corporation tramways, 1905-54* (Broxbourne, 1981).

Mc Caughan, M., 'Lord Templetown: a Belfast barque' in *Ulster Folk and Transport Museum Year Book 1974-75* (1977), pp 14-6.

McAllister, J. (ed.), *1789: A Belfast chronicle: a compilation from the Belfast Newsletter* (Belfast, 1989).

McCabe, B., *From Linenhall to Lopbridge: the story of McCaw, Stevenson and Orr Ltd., Printers 1876-1990* (Antrim, 1990).

McCann, M., 'Belfast ceilidhes – the heyday' in *Ulster Folklife*, xxix (1983), pp 55-69.

McCaughan, M. and Appleby, John (eds), *The Irish sea: aspects of maritime history* (Belfast, 1989).

McCaughan, M. and Appleby, John (eds), *Steel and iron, ships and men: shipbuilding in Belfast, 1894-1912* (Belfast, 1989).

McCaughan, M., 'An account of life in late nineteenth century east Belfast' in *Ulster Folklife*, xix, pp 3-12.

McClelland, A., 'Thomson of the Tays and the Belfast beggars' in *Ulster Folk and Transport Museum Year Book 1976-77* (1978), pp 30-2.

McClelland, A., 'Reminiscenses of Robert Young' in *Irish Booklore*, i (1971), pp 4-20, 235-42.

McEwen, A., 'Half-timing in Belfast' in *Northern Teacher*, xiv, 1 (1983), pp 1-5.

McHugh, J., 'The Belfast labour dispute and riots of 1907' in *International review of social history*, xxii, 1 (1977), pp 1-20.

McIvor, P., 'The rise and fall of Belfast's white linen hall' in *Long Room*, 26/27 (1983), pp 7-14.

McNeilly, N., *Exactly fifty years: the Belfast education authority and its work* (Belfast, 1974).

Merrick, A.C.W., *Old Belfast families and the new burying ground from gravestone inscriptions with wills and biographical notes* (Belfast, 1991).

Milton, K., 'Belfast: whose city?' in Curtin, C., Donnan, H. and Wilson, T. A. (eds), *Irish urban cultures* (Belfast, 1993), pp 23-38.

Moore, A. S., *Belfast today: official guide and souvenir* (Belfast, 1910).

Morgan, A., *Labour and partition. The Belfast working class 1905-23* (London, 1991).

Morgan, M., 'Belfast's forgotten bicentennial' in *Etudes Irlandaises*, xvii (1992), pp 209-18.

Moss, M.S. and Hume, J.R., *Shipbuilders to the world: 125 years of Harland and Wolff Belfast 1861-1986* (Belfast, 1985).

Munck, R. and Rolston, W., 'Belfast in the 1930s' in *Oral History*, xii, 1 (1984), pp 15-9.

Munck, R., 'Class and religion in Belfast: a historical perspective' in *Journal of Contemporary History*, xx, 2 (1985), pp 241-60.

Munck, R., 'The formation of the working class in Belfast, 1788-1881' in *Saothar*, ii (1986), pp 75-89.

Munck, R. and Rolston, B., *Belfast in the thirties: an oral history* (Belfast, 1987).

Murray, S., *The city mission story – Belfast city mission* (Belfast, 1970).

Nesbitt, N., *A museum in Belfast: a history of the Ulster Museum and its predecessors* (Belfast, 1979).

Nesbitt, N., *The changing face of Belfast: a booklet of photographs* (Belfast, 1969).

Ó Buachalla, B., *I mBéal Feirste cois cuan* (Dublin, 1968).

O'Connor, E. and Parkhill, T. (eds), *A life in Linenopolis: the memoirs of William Topping, Belfast damask weaver, 1903-1956* (Belfast, 1992).

O'Leary, C., 'Belfast urban government in the age of reform' in Harkness, D. and O'Dowd, M. (eds), *The town in Ireland: historical studies* xiii (Belfast, 1981), pp 187-202.

Ó Muirí, P., 'Irish in Belfast' in *Irish Review*, no. 14 (1993), pp 82-7.

O'Reilly, C.C., 'The development of the Irish language in Belfast: a brief historical background' in *Ulster Local Studies*, xv, no. 1 (1993), pp 72-9.

Ollerenshaw, P.G., 'The rise of the Belfast banks, 1825-1900' in *Moirae* (Ulster Polytechnic), v (1980) pp 132-48.

Ollerenshaw, P., The Belfast banks 1820-1900: aspects of banking in nineteenth century Ireland, unpublished Ph.D. thesis, University of Sheffield (1982).

P.R.O.N.I., 'Church of Ireland and Roman Catholic Church registers in Belfast' in *Ulster genealogical and historical guild newsletter*, i, 6 (1981), pp 174-84.

P.R.O.N.I., 'Presbyterian and non-subscribing Presbyterian church registers in Belfast' in *Ulster genealogical and historical guild newsletter*, i, 8 (1982), pp 265-70.

P.R.O.N.I., *Problems of a growing city: Belfast, 1780-1870* (Belfast, 1973).

Parker, T., *May the Lord in His mercy be kind to Belfast* (London, 1993).

Patterson, H.H., 'Conservative politics and class conflict in Belfast' in *Saothar*, ii (1976), pp 22-32.

Patterson, H., 'Independent orangeism and class conflict in Edwardian Belfast: a reinterpretation' in *Proceedings of the Royal Irish Academy*, 80C (1980), pp 1-27.

Patterson, H., *Class conflict and sectarianism: the Protestant working class and the Belfast labour movement, 1868-1920* (Belfast, 1980).

Patton, M., *Central Belfast: an historical gazetteer* (Belfast, 1993).

Phoenix, E., *Using the evidence series: two acres of Irish history: A study through time of Friars Bush and Belfast 1570-1914* (Belfast, 1988).

Purdie, B., 'Red hand or red flag? loyalism and workers in Belfast' in *Saothar*, viii (1982), pp 64-9.

Reid, A., 'Skilled workers in the shipbuilding industry, 1850-1920: a labour aristocracy?' in Morgan, A., and Purdie, B. (eds), *Ireland: divided nation, divided class* (London, 1980).

Robinson, P., 'A stabling yard at Millfield, Belfast in 1912' *in Ulster Folk and Transport Museum Yearbook 1974-75* (1977), pp 1-3.

Roebuck, P., 'The Donegall family and the development of Belfast, 1600-1850, in Butel, P. and Cullen, L.M. (eds), *Cities and merchants: French and Irish perspectives on urban development, 1500-1900* (Dublin, 1986), pp 125-38.

Rogers, P. and Macaulay, A., *Old St. Mary's, Chapel Lane, Belfast, 1784-1984* (Belfast, 1984.)

Scullion, F., 'R.L.O'Mealy: Belfast uilleann pipe maker' in *Ulster Folk and Transport Museum Yearbook 1975-76* (1977), pp 8-10.

Simms, J. Young, *Farewell to the hammer: a Shankill boyhood* (Belfast, 1992).

Simpson, N., *The Belfast bank 1827-1970: 150 Years of banking in Ireland* (Belfast, 1976).

Sinclair, R. C., *Across the Irish Sea: Belfast-Liverpool shipping since 1819* (London, 1990).

Smyth, D., *Days of unity in the dock lands of Sailortown, 1907-1969* (Belfast, 1986).

Tuohy, M., *Belfast Celtic* (Belfast, 1978).

Walker, B. and Dixon, H., *In Belfast town 1864-1880: early photographs from the Lawrence Collection* (Belfast, 1984).

Warke, J., 'Baptists in Belfast the twentieth century challenge of urban growth and decline' in *Irish Baptist Historical Society Journal*, xx (1987-88), pp 12-19.

Yeats, G., *Feile na gcruitiri Beal Feirste/Belfast harp hestival, 1792* (Dublin, 1980).

Yeats, G., *The harp of Ireland: the Belfast harper's festival 1792 and the saving of Ireland's harp music by Edward Bunting* (Belfast, 1992).

Young, R.M., *Historical notices of old Belfast and its vicinity* (Belfast, 1896).

Birr, County Offaly

Ryan, M., A social and economic analysis of Birr, county Offaly, in 1901 unpublished B.A. dissertation, University College Dublin (1990).

Blackrock, County Dublin

Brady, A., 'Blackrock' in *Dun Laoghaire Journal*, iii (1993), pp 12-20.

MacCoil, L., *The book of Blackrock: the story of the town of Blackrock county Dublin through the ages* (Blackrock, 1977).

Blarney, County Cork

O'Mahoney, C., 'Bygone industries of Blarney and Dripsey' in *Journal of Cork Historical and Archaeological Society*, lxxxix (1984), pp 77-87.

Bray, County Wicklow

Brophy, J., *'By the banks of the Dargle': a history of Bray Emmetts G.A.A. club 1885-1985* (Bray, 1985).

Davies, K.M., 'For health and pleasure in the British fashion: Bray as a holiday resort, 1750-1914' in O'Connor, B. (ed.), *Tourism in Ireland: a critical analysis* (Cork, 1993), pp 29-48.

Flynn, A., *History of Bray (Cork and Dublin, 1986).*

Moylan, I., The development and growth of Bray, 1750-1900, unpublished B.A. dissertation, Trinity College Dublin (1972).

O'Cathaoir, E., 'Loughlinstown workhouse 1839-1849' in *Bray Historical record*, i, 2 (1986), pp 5-15.

O'Malley, M., 'Killruddery, the Brabazons and Bray' in *Bray Historical Record*, i, 2 (1986), pp 23-34.

O'Sullivan, J., Dunne, T., and Cannon, S. (eds), *The book of Bray* (Blackrock, 1989).

Scott, G.D., *The stones of Bray* (Dublin, 1913, reprint, Bray, 1984).

Seymour, F.J., *A hundred years of Bray and its neighbourhood. from 1770 to 1870 by an old inhabitant* (Blackrock, 1978, reprint of 1907 edition).

Buncrana, County Donegal

Dickson, D., 'Buncrana and Derry in 1744' in *Donegal Annual*, viii (1970), pp 233-7.

Bundoran, County Donegal

Commins, M., *St. Joseph's orphanage*, Bundoran, Clogher.

Cahir, County Tipperary

Luddy, M., 'The lives of the poor in Cahir in 1821' in *Tipperary Historical Journal*, iv (1991), pp 73-79.

Callan, County Kilkenny

Kennedy, J., 'Thomas Shelly of Callan' in *Old Kilkenny Review*, iii, no. 5 (1988), pp 492-501.

Kennedy, J., 'Callan – A corporate town 1700-1800' in Nolan, W. and Whelan, K. (eds), *Kilkenny history and society: interdisciplinary essays on the history of an Irish county* (Dublin, 1990), pp 289-304.

O'Doherty, S., 'Repeal' in Callan Workhouse' in *Old Kilkenny Review*, ii, 3 (1981), pp 226-30.

O'Malley, T., 'Inscape: life and landscape in Callan and county Kilkenny' in Nolan, W. and Whelan, K. (eds), *Kilkenny history and society: interdisciplinary essays on the history of an Irish county* (Dublin, 1990), pp 617-32.

Carlow, County Carlow

Bagenal, J.S., 'The County Carlow cricket club in the 1870s' in *Carloviana*, i, 19 (1970), pp 13-6.

Bergin, P., 'A labour consciousness in Carlow: the young Paddy Bergin: (1916-50)' in *Saothar*, vi (1980), pp 109-17.

Clark, T., 'Seventeenth century Carlow leases' in *Carloviana*, 37 (1989-90), pp 25-9.

Crowe, A., 'Merchant and tradesmen's tokens of Carlow, Bagenalstown, and Tullow' in *Carloviana*, ii, 25 (1976-77), pp 24-6.

Duggan, M., 'The foundation of Carlow College' in *Carloviana*, ii (1972), pp 40-1.

Ellis, J., 'History of bands in Carlow town from 1900-50' in *Carloviana*, ii, 29 (1981), pp 18-9.

Ellis, W., 'Electricity comes to Carlow' in *Carloviana*, 39 (1991), pp 24-7.

Hadden, W.V., 'The election of 1841 and the reign of terror in Carlow' in *Carloviana*, i, 19 (1970), pp 214.

Horner, A.A., 'Two eighteenth century maps of Carlow town' in *Proceedings of the Royal Irish Academy*, C, lxxviii, 5 (1978), pp 115-26.

Kavanagh, P.J., The political scene: Carlow county and borough, 1831-1841, unpublished M.A. thesis, University College Dublin (1974).

Lee, T.A., Carlow town: historical development and problems of an inherited legacy, unpublished B.A. dissertation, University College Dublin (1972).

Mac Suibhne, P., *Carloviana* (Carlow, 1977).

McEvoy, J., *Carlow College, 1793-1993* (Carlow, 1993).

Pyle, H., 'William Baillie of Carlow, engraver' in *Carloviana*, i, 18 (1969), pp 26-7.

Robins, J.A., 'Carlow workhouse during the Famine years' in *Administration*, xx (1972), pp 63-70.

Carrick-on-Suir, County Tipperary

Clarkson, L.M., 'The demography of Carrick-on-Suir, 1799' in *Proceedings of the Royal Irish Academy*, lxxxvii, C, 2 (1987), pp 2-36.

Clarkson, L.M., 'The Carrick-on-Suir woollen industry in the eighteenth century' *in Irish Economic and Social History*, xvi (1989), pp 23-41.

Clarkson, L.A. and Crawford, E M., 'Life after death: widows in Carrick-on-Suir, 1799' in MacCurtain, M. and O'Dowd, M. (eds), *Women in early modern Ireland* (Edinburgh, 1991), pp 236-51.

Clarkson, L.A., 'Love, labour and life: women in Carrick-on-Suir in the late eighteenth century' in *Irish Economic and Social History*, xx (1993), pp 18-34.

Maher, J. (ed.), *Ormonde castle, Carrick-on-Suir: an anthology* (Clonmel, 1970).

Power, P.C., *Carrick-on-Suir and its people* (Dublin, 1977).

Carrickfergus, Antrim

Brereton, W., 'Carrickfergus visited in 1635' in *Carrickfergus and District Historical Journal*, iv (1988-89), pp 11-6.

Calwell, H.G., 'John Moore of Carrickfergus, Part ii' in *Carrickfergus and District Historical Journal*, ii (1986), pp 5-8.

Campbell, G. and Crowther, S. (eds), *Historic buildings, groups of buildings, areas of architectural importance in the town of Carrickfergus* (Belfast, 1978).

de Breffny, B., 'Caters of the Irish Quarter: Carrickfergus, Co. Antrim' in *Irish Ancestor*, x, 1 (1978), pp 31-3.

Rankin, D. H. and Nelson, E. C. (eds), *Curious in everything: the career of Arthur Dobbs of 1689-1765* (Carrickfergus, 1990).

Robinson, P., *Carrickfergus: Irish historic towns atlas, no. 2* (Dublin, 1986).

Speers, S., 'The imprint of the past; the divisions of Carrickfergus' in *Carrickfergus and District Historical Journal*, ii (1986), pp 29-37.

Thompson, J, 'Memories of childhood in Carrickfergus' in *Carrickfergus and District Historical Journal*, iv (1988-9), pp 6-10.

Carrickmacross, County Monaghan

Ó Cléirigh, N., *Carrickmacross lace: Irish embroidered net lace* (Mountrath/London, 1985).

Castleblayney, County Monaghan

Conlon, P., Two Monaghan towns: a study of Castleblayney and Carrickmacross, unpublished B.A. thesis, University College Dublin (1975).

Livingstone, P., 'Castleblayney rent book, 1772' in *Clogher Record*, x, 3 (1981), pp 414-18.

Castlecomer, County Kilkenny

Lyng, T., *Castlecomer connections* (Castlecomer, 1985).

Nolan, W., *Fassadinin: land settlement and society in south-east Ireland 1600-1850* (Dublin, 1979)

Cavan, County Cavan

Cunningham, T.P., 'Cavan town in 1838' in *Breifne*, iii (1969), pp 528-51.

Cunningham, T.P., 'The Cavan tenant-right meeting of 1850' in *Breifne*, iii (1969), pp 417-42.

Cunningham, T. P., 'Cavan Town in 1838' in *Breifne*, iv (1970), pp 96-130.

Cunningham, T.P., 'Cavan Town in 1838' in *Breifne*, v (1971), pp 289-317.

Garner, W., *Historic buildings, groups of buildings, areas of architectural importance in the town of Cavan* (Belfast, 1978).

Smyth, T.S., 'Markets and fairs of the town of Cavan' in *Breifne*, v, 18 (1977-78), pp 259-65.

Smyth, T.S., 'Phases of the history of the town of Cavan' in *Breifne*, v, 19 (1979), pp 358-68.

Celbridge, County Kildare

Quane, M., *Celbridge Collegiate School* (Kildare).

Charleville, County Cork

Harrison, R. S., 'The Quakers of Charleville, 1661-1742' in *Journal of the Cork Historical and Archaeological Society*, xcv, 254 (1990), pp 55-63.

Clonakilty, County Cork

O'Donovan, D., 'Clonakilty Junction, 1886-1961' in *Bandon Historical Journal*, 7 (1991), pp 6-10.

Clones, County Monaghan

O'Mordha, P., 'The linen industry in the Clones area 1660-84' in *Clogher Record*, x (1979), pp 144-53.
O'Mordha, P., 'Clones in the Williamite Wars 1689-92' in *Clogher Record*, x, 2 (1980), pp 258-62.
O'Mordha, P., 'Clones rent roll 1821' in *Clogher Record*, xiii, 1 (1988), pp 32-7.

Clonmel, Tipperary

Ahern, M., 'The Quaker schools in Clonmel' in *Tipperary Historical Journal*, iii (1990), pp 128-132.
Ahern, M., 'Clonmel mechanics institute' in *Tipperary Historical Journal*, iv (1991), pp 159-162.
Burke, W.P., *History of Clonmel* (Clonmel, 1907, reprint, Kilkenny, 1983).
Luddy, M., 'Women and work in Clonmel: evidence from the 1881 Census' in *Tipperary Historical Journal* (1993), pp 62-101.
O'Donnell, S., 'The first election to the reformed Clonmel Corporation 150 years ago' in *Tipperary Historical Journal* (1992), pp 75-80.
Pyke, D., *Parish priests and churches of St. Mary's, 1320-1984* (Clonmel, 1984).

Cobh, County Cork

Garner, W., *Cobh architectural heritage* (Dublin, 1979).

Coleraine, County Londonderry

Anderson, R., *The port of Coleraine* (Coleraine, 1977).
Anderson, R., *The port of Coleraine: a short history*, n.d.
Coleraine historical society, *Ordnance survey memoir for the parish of Coleraine*, county Londonderry (Coleraine, 1986).
Mullin, T.H., *Coleraine in by-gone centuries* (Belfast, 1977).
Mullin, T.H., *Coleraine in Georgian times* (Belfast, 1977).
Mullin, T.H., *Coleraine in modern times* (Coleraine, 1979).
Mullin, J., *The presbytery of Coleraine* (Coleraine, 1979).
Robinson, P., 'Some late survivals of box-framed 'Plantation' houses in Coleraine, county Londonderry' in *Ulster Journal of Archaeology*, xlvi (1983), pp 129-36.
Thomas, C., 'Twenty years-a-growing: geography at Coleraine 1968-88' in *Irish Geography*, xxi, no. 1 (1990), pp 56-61.

Cork, County Cork

Andrews, J.H., 'A Cork cartographer's advertising campaign' in *Journal of Cork Historical and Archaeological Society*, lxxxiv, 240 (1979), pp 112-18.
Bielenberg, A., *Cork's industrial revolution, 1780-1880: development or decline* (Cork, 1991).
Bolster, A., *A history of the diocese of Cork from the earliest times to the Reformation* (Shannon, 1972).
Bolster, E., *A history of the diocese of Cork: from the reformation to the penal era* (Cork, 1982).
Bolster, E., 'A Landgable Roll of Cork City' in *Collectanea Hibernica*, xiii (1970), pp 7-20.
Bradshaw, B., 'The Reformation in the cities: Cork, Limerick and Galway, 1534-1603' in Bradley, J. (ed.), *Settlement and society in medieval Ireland. Studies presented to F.X. Martin, O.S.A.*(Kilkenny, 1990).
Buttimer, C.G., 'A Paul Street Poem, c.1760' in *Journal of the Cork Historical and Archaeological Society*, xcii, no. 252 (1988), pp 126-37.
Byrne, K R., 'The provision of technical education in the City of Cork' in *Irish Educational Studies*, v, 2 (1985), pp 243-60.
Casey, D. P., 'Cork harbour in retrospect, 1910-1920' in *Capuchin Annual*, xxxv (1968), pp 227-39.
Cooke, R.T. and Scanlon, M., *Cooke and Scanlon's guide to the history of Cork* (Cork, 1985).
Coughlan, C., *Old Cork: historical, theatrical, commercial* (Cork, 1975).
Coughlan, S., *Picture that: a century of Cork memories* (Cork, 1985).
Cronin, M., 'Work and workers in Cork city and county, 1800-1900' in O'Flanagan, P. and Buttimer, C. G.

(eds), *Cork history and society: interdisciplinary essays on the history of an Irish county* (Dublin, 1993), pp 721-54.

Cussen, R., 'A list of Catholic merchants in Cork in 1762' in *Irish Ancestor*, iii (1971), pp 39-40.

D'Alton, I., *Protestant society and politics in Cork 1812-1844* (Cork, 1980).

D'Alton, I., 'Keeping faith: an evocation of the Cork Protestant character, 1820-1920' in O'Flanagan, P. and Buttimer, C. G. (eds), *Cork history and society: interdisciplinary essays on the history of an Irish county* (Dublin, 1993), pp 755-92.

Daly, S., *A city in crisis: a history of labour conflict and social misery 1870-1872* (Cork, 1978).

Davies, A.C., 'The first Irish industrial exhibition: Cork 1852' in *Irish Economic & Social History*, ii (1975), pp 46-59.

Dickson, D., 'The Cork merchant community in the eighteenth century: a regional perspective' in Cullen, LM. and Furet, F. (eds), *Ireland and France, 17th – 20th centuries: towards a comparative study of rural history. Proceedings of the first Franco-lrish symposium on social and economic history* (Paris, 1979), pp 45-50.

Fahy, A.M., 'The spatial differentiation of commercial and residential functions in Cork City 1787-1863' in *Irish Geography*, xvii (1984), pp 14-26.

Fahy, A., 'Residence, workplace and patterns of change, Cork 1787-1863' in Butel, P. and Cullen, L.M., *Cities and merchants: French and Irish perspectives on urban development, 1500-1900* (Dublin, 1986), pp 41-52.

Fahy, A M., 'Place and class in Cork' in O'Flanagan, P. and Buttimer, C. G. (eds), *Cork history and society: interdisciplinary essays on the history of an Irish county* (Dublin, 1993), pp 793-812.

Ffolliott, R., 'Extracts from the account books of St. Peter's parish in Cork city, 1770-1814' in *Irish Ancestor*, xvii, 1 (1986), pp 32-7.

Gamble, R.G., *History of the Cork dental hospital and school from 1913-1982* (Cork, 1985).

Harrison, R. S., 'The Cork anti-slavery society: its antecedents and Quaker background' in *Journal of the Cork Historical and Archaeological Society*, xcvii (1992), pp 69-79.

Harrison, R. S., *Cork city Quakers 1655-1939: a brief history* (Skibbereen, 1991).

Hayes, J., 'The Trants: an enterprising Catholic family in 18th century Cork' in *Cork Historical and Archaeological Society Journal*, lxxxiv, 243 (1981), pp 21-9.

Holohan, P., 'The Cork Historical and Archaeological Society: foundation and consolidation, 1891-1943' in *Journal of the Cork Historical and Archaeological Society*, xcvi, pp 19-42.

Hourihan, K., 'The Evolution and Influence of Town Planning in Cork' in O'Flanagan, P. and Buttimer, C. G. (eds), *Cork history and society: interdisciplinary essays on the history of an Irish county* (Dublin, 1993), pp 943-62.

Inglis, K., 'Father Mathew's statue: the making of a monurnent in Cork, in MacDonough, O. and Mandle, W F. (eds), *Ireland and Irish-Australia: studies in cultural and political history* (London and Sydney, 1986), pp 119-36.

Irwin, L., 'Politics, religion and economy: Cork in the 17th century' in *Cork Historical and Archaeological Society Journal*, lxxxv, 241-2 (1980), pp 7-25.

Jacobsen, D.S., 'The political economy of industrial location: the Ford motor company at Cork, 1912-26' in *Irish Economic and Social History Journal*, iv (1977), pp 36-55.

Kennedy, M., 'The Cork library society of 1801' in *Cork Historical and Archaeological Society Journal*, xciv, no. 253 (1989), pp 56-73.

Keogh, D., 'Michael J. O'Lehane organises the draper's assistants' in *Capuchin Annual* (1976), pp 234-40.

Keogh, D., 'Michael J. O'Lehane and the organisation of the linen draper's assistants' in *Saothar*, iii (1977), pp 33-43.

Kerrigan, P.M., 'The defences of Ireland 1793-1815: part 10: Cork harbour and Kinsale' in *An Cosantoir*, xxxviii, 5 (1978), pp 145-60.

Larkin, Paschal, 'The Capuchins in Cork' in *Capuchin Annual* (1976), pp 173-8.

Lincoln, C., *Steps and steeples: Cork at the turn of the century* (Dublin, 1980).

Longfield, A.K., 'Blarney and Cork: printing on linen, cotton and paper in the eighteenth and early nineteenth centuries' in *Journal of the Royal Society of Antiquaries of Ireland*, cxi (1981), pp 81-101.

Lucey, D. J., Cork public opinion and the First World War, unpublished M.A. thesis, University College Cork (1972).

Martin, G.E.D., 'A visitor to Cork in 1775' in *Cork Historical and Archaeological Society Journal*, xcviii (1993), pp 141-3.

McCann, P., 'Cork city's eighteenth century charity schools: origins and early history' in *Cork Historical and Archaeological Society Journal*, lxxxiv, 240 (1979), pp 102-11.

McCann, P., 'Charity schooling in Cork city in the late 18th and early 19th centuries (ctd)' in *Cork Historical and Archaeological Society Journal*, lxxxvii, 245 (1982), pp 51-7; lxxxvii, 246 (1982), pp 133-41.

McCarthy, J.P., 'Journeying to a journal: the society's predecessors' in *Cork Historical and Archaeological Society Journal*, xcvi (1991), pp 1-18.

McElligott, T., *Six o'clock all over Cork* (Dublin, 1992).

McGrath, W., *Tram tracks through Cork: an illustrated history* (Cork, 1981).

McKenna, T. J. and Moore, C., *The modest men of Christ Church, Cork* (Naas, 1970).

Mooney, C. and E., Bartholemew, *The friars of Broad Lane: the story of a Franciscan friary in Cork* (Cork, 1977).

Murphy, M., 'Municipal reform and the Repeal movement in Cork 1833-1844' in *Cork Archaeological and Historical Society Journal*, lxxxi (1976), pp 1-18.

Murphy, M., 'Repeal, popular politics and the Catholic clergy of Cork 1840-50' in *Cork Historical and Archaeological Society Journal*, lxxxii (1977), pp 39-48.

Murphy, M., 'Fenianism, Parnellism and the Cork trades 1860-1900' in *Saothar*, v (1979), pp 27-38.

Murphy, M., 'The economic and social structure of nineteenth century Cork' in Harkness, D. and O' Dowd, M. (eds), *The town in Ireland: historical studies xiii* (Belfast, 1981), pp 125-54.

Murphy, M., 'The working classes of 19th century Cork' in *Cork Historical and Archaeological Society Journal*, lxxxv (1980), pp 26-51.

Murphy, M., 'Cork commercial society 1850-1899: politics and problems' in Butel, P. and Cullen, L.M., *Cities and merchants: French and Irish perspectives on urban development, 1500-1900* (Dublin, 1986), pp 233-46.

Murphy, J. A., 'Cork: anatomy and essence' in O'Flanagan, P. and Buttimer, C. G. (eds), *Cork history and society: interdisciplinary essays on the history of an Irish county* (Dublin, 1993), pp 1-14.

Murphy, M., The role of organised labour in the political and economic life of Cork city in the nineteenth century, unpublished Ph.D. thesis, University of Leicester (1980).

Ní Chinnéide, S., 'A new view of Cork city in 1790' in *Journal of the Cork Historical and Archaeological Society*, lxxviii, 227 (1973), pp 1-13.

Nolan, D., The Cork grand jury, 1836-1899, unpublished M.A. thesis, University College Galway (1974).

O'Brien, J.B., 'Agricultural prices and living costs in pre-famine Cork' in *Journal of the Cork Historical and Archaeological Society*, lxxxii (1977), pp 1-10.

O'Brien, J.B., 'Sadlier's Bank' in *Journal of the Cork Historical and Archaeological Society*, lxxxii (1977), pp 33-8.

O'Brien, J., *The Catholic middle-class in pre-famine Cork* (Dublin, 1980).

O'Brien, J.B., 'The Hacketts: glimpses of entrepeneurial life in Cork 1800-1870' in *Journal of the Cork Historical and Archaeological Society*, xl, 249 (1985), pp 150-57.

O'Brien, J.B., 'Merchants in Cork before the famine' in Butel, P. and Cullen, L.M., *Cities and merchants: French and Irish perspectives on urban development, 1500-1900* (Dublin, 1986), pp 221-32.

O'Brien, J.B., 'The council books of the Corporation of the city of Cork' in *Journal of the Cork Historical and Archaeological Society*, xcii (1987), pp 24-6.

O'Brien, J. B., 'Population, politics and society in Cork, 1780-1900' in O'Flanagan, P. and Buttimer, C. G. (eds), *Cork history and society: interdisciplinary essays on the history of an Irish county* (Dublin, 1993), pp 699-720.

O'Mahoney, C., 'Shipbuilding and repairing in nineteenth century Cork' in *Journal of the Cork Historical and Archaeological Society*, xciv, 253 (1989), pp 74-87.

O'Murchada, D., 'The siege of Cork in 1690' in *Journal of the Cork Historical and Archaeological Society*, xcv, 254 (1990), pp 1-19.

Pettit, S.F., 'The royal Cork institution: a reflection of the cultural life of a city' in *Journal of the Cork Historical and Archaeological Society*, lxxxi, 233/4 (1976), pp 70-90.

Pettit, S F., *This city of Cork 1700-1900* (Cork, 1977).

Read, H., 'The Penroses of Woodhill, Cork: an account of their property in the city' in *Cork Historical and Archaeological Society Journal*, lxxxv, 241-2 (1980), pp 78-98.

Rudd, D., *Rochelle: the history of a school in Cork 1829-1979* (Naas, 1979).

Russell, L., 'Some activities in Cork city, 1920-21' in *Capuchin Annual*, xxxvii (1970), pp 332-50.

Sessions, W. K., *The first printers in Waterford, Cork and Kilkenny, pre-1700* (York, 1990).

Simms, J.G., 'Marlborough's siege of Cork, 1690' in *Irish Sword*, ix (1969), pp 113-23.

St. Leger, A., *Silver sails and silk: Huguenots in Cork, 1685-1850* (Cork, 1991).

Turpin, J., 'Daniel Maclise and Cork society' in *Cork Historical and Archaeological Society Journal*, lxxxv, 241-2 (1980), pp 66-78.

Craigavon, County Armagh
O'Dowd, L., 'Craigavon: locality, economy and the state in a failed "new city" in Curtin, C., Donnan, H. and Wilson, T. A. (eds), *Irish urban cultures* (Belfast, 1993), pp 39-62.

Derry/Londonderry, County Londonderry
Bartlett, I. and Hamilton, R., 'Thomas Ash – author of a circumstantial journal of the siege of Londonderry' in *Templemore*, iii (1990), pp 2-38.

Bonner, B., *Derry: an outline history of the diocese* (Dublin, 1982).

Carson, W.R.H., *Vanishing Derry* (Ballyshannon, 1978).

Carson, W.R.H., *A bibliography of printed material relating to the county and county borough of Londonderry*, High Wycombe (1969).

Curran, F., *Derry: countdown to disaster* (Dublin, 1986).

Doherty, R., 'The siege of Derry' in *Templemore*, iii (1990), pp 3-13.

Finlay, A., 'Politics, sectarianism and the 'failure' of trade unionisrn in Northern Ireland: the case of the garment workers in Derry, 1945-1968' in *Saothar*, xvii (1992), pp 78-86.

Gray, T., *No surrender!: the siege of Londonderry, 1689* (London, 1975).

Hempton, J. (ed.), *The siege and history of Londonderry* (Derry, 1861).

Kingsley, P., *Londonderry revisited: a Loyalist analysis of the civil rights controversy* (Belfast, 1989).

Lacy, B., 'Two seventeenth-century houses at Linenhall Street, Londonderry' in *Ulster Folklife*, xxvii (1981), pp 57-62.

Lacy, B., *Historic Derry* (Dublin, 1988).

Lacy, B., *The siege of Derry* (Dublin, 1989).

Lampen, J. and Sperou, A., *If stones could speak: glimpses of a city over three hundred years* (Derry, 1985).

Ledwidge, J, *The brow, the brothers and the Bogside: a history of the Christian Brother's school, Derry, 1854-1990* (Derry, 1993).

MacAteer, S., 'The 'New Unionism' in Derry, 1889-1892: a demonstration of its inclusive nature' in *Saothar*, xvi (1991), pp 11-22.

MacRory, P., *The siege of Derry* (London, 1980, reprint Oxford, 1989).

McCann, E., *War and an Irish town* (London, 1980).

McCarter, G, *Derry's shirt tale* (Derry, 1991).

McLaughlin, E., 'Women and work in Derry city: a survey' in *Saothar*, xvi (1989), pp 35-45.

Mitchell, B., *The making of Derry: an economic history* (Derry, 1992).

Moody, T.W. and Simms, J.G. (eds), *The bishopric of Derry and the Irish society of London, 1602-1705*, ii, 1670-1705 (Dublin, 1983).

Mullin, T.H., *Ulster's historic city* Derry/Londonderry (Coleraine, 1986).

Murphy, D., *Derry, Donegal and modern Ulster, 1790-1921* (Londonderry, 1981).

Ó Dúibhlin, D., 'Hearth money rolls (1663): city and county of Derry' in *Derriana, Journal of the Derry Diocesan Historical Society*, ii (1979), pp 41-91.

Rankin, R.A., 'Recollections of past days in Londonderry' in *Irish Baptist Historical Society Journal*, viii (1976), pp 27-42.

Tetler, R., *The battle of Bogside: the politics of violence in Northern Ireland* (London, 1970).

Dingle, County Kerry
Davies, M., 'To Dingle in 1951' in *Journal of the Irish railway record society*, xvi (1987), pp 188-193.

McDonagh, S., *The wrenboys of Dingle* (Dingle, 1983).

McKenna J., *Dingle: some of its story* (Tralee, n.d).

O'Donoghue, M., The historical development of an Irish town Dingle, unpublished B.A. dissertation, University College Dublin (1972).

Ó Lúing, S., 'Local government in Dingle, Ardfert and Tralee in 1833' in *Kerry Archaeological and Historical Society Journal*, xii (1979), pp 119-58.

Doneraile, County Cork
Crowley, S., 'An 1807 map of Doneraile town' in *Mallow Field Club Journal*, 8 (1990), pp 74-81.

Gaughan, J. A., *Doneraile* (Dublin, 1970).

Power, D. and Sleeman, M., 'The Church of Ireland, Doneraile' in *Mallow Field Club Journal*, 10 (1992), pp 73-91.

Shine, M., 'Henry Somerville – an unusual Doneraile clergyman' in *Mallow Field Club Journal*, 3 (1985), pp 32-41.

Shine, M., 'The churches of Doneraile' in *Mallow Field Club Journal*, 7 (1989), pp 45-67.

Shine, M., 'The Doneraile yeomanry' in *Mallow Field Club Journal*, 10 (1992), pp 15-7.

Downpatrick, County Down

Magee, J., 'Downpatrick: the Southwell period 1703-1830' in *Lecale Miscellany*, i (1983), pp 47-50.

McRobert, J., '150 years of legal service to the Downpatrick public' in *Lecale Miscellany*, 3 (1985), pp 40-3.

Drogheda, County Louth

Campbell, P.J., 'John Verdon, Clonmore, Co. Louth: parish priest of Drogheda, Bishop of Ferns (1709-1728)' in *Seanchas Ardmhacha*, x, 1 (1980-1), pp 176-92.

Corcoran, M., 'Two Drogheda voter's lists: 1798 and 1802' in *County Louth Archaeological and Historical Society Journal*, xx, 4 (1985), pp 319-33.

Corcoran, M., 'Three eighteenth century Drogheda letters' in *County Louth Archaeological and Historical Society Journal*, xxii, no. 1 (1989), pp 29-35.

Corcoran, M., 'A Drogheda census list of 1798' in *County Louth Archaeological Society Journal*, xvii (1969), pp 91-6.

Fitzgerald, J., 'The Drogheda textile industry, 1780-1820' in *County Louth Archaeological and Historical Society Journal*, xx, 1 (1981), pp 36-58.

Fitzgerald, J., 'Drogheda merchants in the eighteenth century' in *Old Drogheda Society Journal*, 5 (1986), pp 21-36.

Fitzgerald, J., The organisation of the Drogheda economy, 1780-1820, unpublished M.A. thesis, University College Dublin (1972).

Gogarty, T. (ed.), *Council book of the corporation of Drogheda*, vol. i: from the year 1649 to 1734 (Dundalk, 1988).

Grist, B., Drogheda: an urban analysis, unpublished B.A. dissertation, University College Dublin (1970).

Hayden, M., The port of Drogheda, unpublished B.A. dissertation, University College Dublin (1970).

Ireland, A., 'Drogheda and the Fairlough family' in *Old Drogheda Society Journal*, 5 (1986), pp 69-70.

Kiernan, E., 'Drogheda and the British general strike, 1926' in *Saothar*, ii (1986), pp 19-26.

Lynch, A., 'Five documents of Drogheda interest from the registers of the archbishops of Armagh' in *County Louth Archaeological and Historical Society* Journal, xxi, no.4 (1988), pp 407-14.

Malone, M., 'Education in Drogheda through the ages' in *Old Drogheda Society Journal* (1976), pp 29-36.

McHugh, N.,'Drogheda jail during the period of the great famine' in *Old Drogheda Society Journal* (1987), pp 47-58.

Rice, G., 'Four wills of the old English merchants of Drogheda, 1654-1717' in *County Louth Archaeological and Historical Society Journal*, xx, 2 (1982), pp 96-105.

Dublin, County Dublin

Aalen, F.H.A., *The Iveagh Trust: the first hundred years, 1890-1990* (Dublin, 1990).

Aalen, F.H.A., 'Lord Meath, city improvement and social imperialism' in *Planning Perspectives*, iv (1989), pp 127-152.

Aalen, F.H. and Whelan, K. (eds), *Dublin city and county from prehistory to present: studies in honour of J.H.Andrews* (Dublin, 1992).

Aalen, F.H.A., 'Health and housing in Dublin, 1850-1921' in Aalen, F.H. and Whelan, K. (eds), *Dublin city and county from prehistory to present: studies in honour of J.H.Andrews* (Dublin, 1992), pp 279-304.

Andrews, J.H., 'Medium and message in early six-inch Ordnance maps: the case of Dublin city' in *Irish Geography*, vi, 5 (1973), pp 579-93.

Appleby, J., 'The fishing ventures of Nicholas Weston of Dublin: a note on comrnercial contact between Ireland and Newfoundland in the sixteenth century' in *Dublin Historical Record*, xxxix, 4 (1986), pp 150-55.

Appleyard, D., *Green fields gone forever: the story of the Coolock and Artane area* (Coolock, 1985).

Bannon, M.J., 'The making of Irish geography, iii: Patrick Geddes and the emergence of modern town planning in Dublin' in *Irish Geography*, xi (1978), pp 141-8.

Bannon, M., 'The capital of the new state' in Cosgrove, A. (ed.), *Dublin through the ages* (Dublin, 1988), pp 133-50.

Bardon, C. and J., *If ever you go to Dublin town – a historic guide to the city's street names* (Belfast, 1988).

Barnard, T.C., 'Reforming Irish manners: the religious societies in Dublin during the 1690s' in *Historical Journal*, xxxv, 4 (1992), pp 805-38.

Barrow, G.L., 'Justice for Thomas Mooney' in *Dublin Historical Record*, xxiv (1970), pp 173-88.

Beckett, H. J., 'St. Vincent's Hospital, Dublin 1834-1984' in *Dublin Historical Record*, xxxvii, 3/4 (1984), pp 123-36.

Bennet, D., *Encyclopaedia of Dublin* (Dublin, 1991).

Bennett, D., 'Maggie Feathers and Missie Reilly: hawking life in Dublin's city quay' in Curtin, C., Kelly, M., and O'Dowd, L. (eds), *Culture and ideology in Ireland* (Galway, 1985), pp 136-153.

Bhreathnach-Lynch, S., 'A Dublin sculptor: Albert Power R.H.A.' in *Dublin Historical Record*, xiiii, 1 (1990), pp 17-33.

Bolger, W. and Share, B., *Nelson on his pillar, 1808-1966: a retrospective record* (Dublin, 1976).

Booth, L., *History of the Dublin Central Mission, 1893-1993* (Dublin, 1993).

Bowden, T., 'Bloody Sunday-a reappraisal' in *European studies review*, ii (1972), pp 25-42.

Bowman, J. and O'Donoghue, R., *Portraits, Belvedere College 1832-1982* (Dublin, 1982).

Boydell, B., 'Dublin city musicians in the late middle ages and Renaissance to 1660' in *Dublin Historical Record*, xxxiv, 2 (1980), pp 42-53.

Boydell, B., 'Half a century of music in Dublin' in *Dublin Historical Record*, xxxvii, 3/4 (1986), pp 117-21.

Boydell, B. *A Dublin musical calendar 1700-1760* (Blackrock, 1988).

Boydell, M, 'Franz Tieze, 1842-1932: a Bohemian glass engraver in Dublin' in *Dublin Historical Record*, xlv, no. 1 (1992), pp 4-10.

Boydell, B., 'St. Michan's Church, Dublin: the installation of the organ in 1725' in *Dublin Historical Record*, xlvi, 2 (1993), pp 101-20.

Boydell, B., 'Some Dublin glassmakers' in *Dublin Historical Record*, xxvii, 2, pp 42-8.

Boylan, P., *All cultivated people: a history of the United Arts Club Dublin* (Buckinghamshire, 1988).

Bradley, J. (ed.), *Viking Dublin exposed. The Wood Quay saga* (Dublin, 1984).

Brady, C. F., 'Conservative subversives: the community of the Pale and the Dublin administration 1556-86' in Corish, P.J. (ed.), Radicals, rebels and establishments, *Historical Studies xv* (Belfast, 1984), pp 11-32.

Brady, J.E., 'Population change in Dublin 1981-1986' in *Irish Geography*, xxi (1988), pp 41-4.

Brooke-Tyrell, A., 'Michael Jones, governor of Dublin' in *Dublin Historical Record*, xxiv (1970), pp 159-72.

Brooking, C., *The city of Dublin, 1728* (Dublin, 1983 reprint).

Brown, K., 'Larkin and the strikes of 1913: their place in British history' in *Saothar*, ix, 1 (1983), pp 89-99.

Burke, H, *The Royal Hospital, Donnybrook: a heritage of caring, 1743-1993* (Dublin, 1993).

Burke, N., 'An early modern Dublin suburb: the estate of Francis Aungier, Earl of Longford' in *Irish Geography*, vi (1972), pp 365-85.

Burton, N.J., *Letters from Harolds Cross 1850* (Blackrock, 1979).

Butler, B. B., 'Thomas Pleasants and the stone tenter house 1815-1944' in *Dublin Historical Record*, xli, 2 (1988), pp 2-6.

Butler, B. B., 'Thomas Pleasants, 1729-1818' in *Dublin Historical Record*, xli, 2 (1988), pp 172-82.

Butler, K., 'A Sister and her school, Dublin 1830' in *Dublin Historical Record*, xli, 1 (1988), pp 55-69.

Butler, K., 'Dublin's Hallelujah lassies' in *Dublin Historical Record*, xlii, 4 (1989) pp 128-46.

Butler, K., 'Friends in Dublin' in *Dublin Historical Record*, xliv, 1 (1991), pp 34-46.

Butler, K., 'Catherine Cummins and her hospital, 1920-1938' in *Dublin Historical Record*, xlv, no. 2 (1992), pp 81-90.

Butler, K., 'Synagogues of old Dublin' in *Dublin Historical Record*, xxvii, 4, pp 118-30.

Byrne, P.F., 'Fifty years of gaiety: Dublin's Gaiety Theatre 1871-1921' in *Dublin historical record* xxxviii, 1 (1984), pp 37-44.

C.U.S., *Catholic University School, 1867-1967: a centenary record* (Dublin, 1967).

Callan, C., 'The regular operative house painters' trade union: labour relations and working conditions in the Dublin housepainting trade, 1860-1890' in *Saothar*, vii (1981), pp 28-39.

Caprani, V., *A view from the dart* (Dublin, 1986).

Carey, P., 'The Phoenix Park depot' in *An Cosantoir*, xxxii (1972), pp 201-5.

Clancy, M., 'Gaelic League activities in Dublin 1907-15' in *Retrospect*, New Series, 1 (1981), pp 25-30.

Clancy, C., 'Gardiner Street employment exchange' in *Dublin Historical Record*, xliii, 1 (1990), pp 47-51.

Clarke, H., *Georgian Dublin* (Norwich, 1972).

Clarke, H.B. (ed), *Medieval Dublin*, 2 vols. (Dublin, 1990).

Clark, M., 'The Municipal Archives of Dublin' in *Irish Archives Bulletin*, ii (1981), pp 12-7.

Clark, M., 'Free citizens of Dublin: the genealogical significance' in *Familia*, ii, 2 (1986), pp 70-4.

Clark, M., 'List of principal inhabitants of Dublin, 1684' in *The Irish Genealogist*, i, no. 1 (1990), pp 49-57.

Clark, M., 'The Dublin guild of carpenters, 1656' in *Irish Genealogist*, viii, 3 (1992), pp 333-5.

Clark, M. and Refaussé, R., *Directory of historic Dublin guilds* (Dublin, 1993).

Clarke, M., 'Dublin surveyors and their maps' in *Dublin Historical Record*, xxxix, 4 (1986), pp 140-48.

Clarke, P., *Dublin calling: 2RM and the birth of Irish Radio* (Dublin 1986).

Clear, C. and Johnston, M., *Growing up poor: the homeless young in nineteenth century Ireland, Dublin childhoods* (Galway, 1993).

Cocker, W., 'A history of the university chemical laboratory, Trinity College, Dublin' in *Hermathena*, cxxiv (1978), pp 58-76.

Cody, S., 'May day in Dublin 1890 to the present' in *Saothar*, v (1979), pp 73-9.

Cody, S., O'Dowd, J. and Rigney, P., *The parliament of labour: 100 years of the Dublin council of trade unions* (Dublin, 1986).

Colley, M., 'A list of architects, builders, measurers and engineers extracted from Wilson's Dublin directories, 1760-1837' in *Bulletin of the Irish Georgian Society*, xxxiv (1991), pp 3-68.

Comerford, A. (ed.), *The easter rising, Dublin 1916: a collection of contemporary material* (London, 1969).

Condon, K., *The missionary college of All Hallows 1842-1891* (Dublin, 1986).

Condon, K., 'All Hallows College Dublin' in Kiernan, C. (ed.), *Australia and Ireland: bicentennial essays 1788-1988* (Dublin, 1986), pp 227-40.

Conlin, S., *Dublin: one thousand years* (Dublin, 1988).

Cooke, J., 'John Hutton and sons, Summerhill, Dublin: coachbuilders 1779-1925' in *Dublin Historical Record*, xlv, 1 (1992), pp 11-27.

Corrigan, F., 'Dublin workhouses during the great famine' in *Dublin Historical Record*, xx (1976), pp 59-65.

Corry, G., 'The Dublin bar-the obstacle to the improvement of the port of Dublin' in *Dublin Historical Record*, xxiii (1970), pp 137-52.

Cosgrave, D., *North Dublin city and its environs* (Dublin, n.d).

Cosgrove, A. (ed.), *Dublin through the ages* (Dublin, 1988).

Costello, P. and Farmar, T., *The very heart of the city: the story of Denis Guiney & Clery's* (Dublin, 1992).

Cowell, J., *Where they lived in Dublin* (Dublin, 1980).

Coyle, E. A., 'Sir Edward Newenham: the eighteenth century Dublin radical' in *Dublin Historical Record*, xlvi, 1 (1993), pp 15-30

Craig, M., *Charles Brooking: the city of Dublin, 1728* (Dublin, 1983).

Craig, M., 'Academy house and its library' in Ó Raifertaigh, T. (ed.), *The Royal Irish Academy: A bicentennial history 1785-1985* (Dublin), pp 313-27.

Crookes, G., *Dublin's eye and ear: the making of a monument* (Dublin, 1993).

Crowley, M., The social and economic history of Dublin at the end of the nineteenth century, unpublished M.A. thesis, University College Dublin (1971).

Cullen, L.M., *Eason and son – a history* (Dublin, 1989).

Cullen, L. M., 'The growth of Dublin, 1600-1900: character and heritage' in Aalen, F.H. and Whelan, K. (eds), *Dublin city and county from prehistory to present: studies in honour of J.H.Andrews* (Dublin, 1992), pp 252-77.

Cummins, S. 'Extra-parliamentary agitation in Dublin in the 1760s' in Comerford, R.V., Cullen, M., Hill, J. R., Lennon, C. (eds), *Religion, conflict and co-existence in Ireland: essays presented to Monsignor Patrick J.Corish* (Dublin, 1990).

Curran, C.P., *Under the receding wave* (Dublin, 1970).

Curran, C.P., *Dublin decorative plasterwork of the 17th and 18th centuries* (London, 1967).

Curriculum Development Unit, Trinity College Dublin, *Divided city: portrait of Dublin, 1913* (Dublin, 1978).

D'Arcy, F., 'An age of distress and reform: 1800 to 1860' in Cosgrove, A. (ed.), *Dublin through the ages* (Dublin, 1988), pp 93-112.

D'Arcy, F., 'Wages of labourers in the Dublin building industry, 1667-1918' in *Saothar*, xiv (1989), pp 17-32.

D'Arcy, F., 'Wages of skilled labourers in the Dublin building industry, 1667-1918' in *Saothar*, xv (1990), pp 21-38.

D'Arcy, F., 'The Kingstown races' in *Dublin Historical Record*, xlv, 1 (1992), pp 55-64.

D'Arcy, F., 'Unemployment demonstrations in Dublin, 1879-1882' in *Saothar*, xvii (1992), pp 14-26.

D'Arcy, F., 'The artisans of Dublin and Daniel O'Connell, 1830-47: an unquiet liaison' in *Irish Historical Studies*, xvii (1970), pp 22-43.

D'Arcy, F., 'The murder of Thomas Hanlon: a nineteenth century Dublin labour conspiracy' in *Dublin Historical Record*, xxiv (1971), pp 89-100.

Daly, M.E., 'Dublin life' in Kennedy, T. (ed.), *Victorian Dublin* (Dublin, 1980).

Daly, M.E., 'Late nineteenth and early twentieth century Dublin' in Harkness, D. and O'Dowd, M. (eds), *The town in Ireland. Historical Studies xiii* (Belfast, 1981), pp 221-52.

Daly, M.E., 'Social structure of the Dublin working class, 1871-1911' in *Irish Historical Studies*, xxiii, 90 (1982), pp 121-33.

Daly, M. E., *Dublin, the deposed capital: a social and economic history 1860-1914* (Cork, 1984).

Daly, M E., 'Dublin in the nineteenth century' in Butel, P. and Cullen, L.M. (eds), *Cities and merchants: French and Irish perspectives on urban development, 1500-1900* (Dublin, 1986), pp 53-66.

Daly, M. E., 'A tale of two cities; 1860-1920' in Cosgrove, A. (ed.), *Dublin through the ages*, Dublin (1988), pp 113-32.

Daly, G.J., 'Captain William Bligh in Dublin, 1800-1801' in *Dublin Historical Record*, xliv, 1 (1991), pp 20-33.

Davies, G.L., 'The University of Dublin and two pioneers of English geology: William Smith and John Phillips' in *Hermathena*, cix (1969), pp 24-36.

Davis, V., 'Relations between the Abbey of St. Thomas the martyr and the municipality of Dublin 1176-1527' in *Dublin Historical Record*, xl, 2 (1987), pp 57-64.

Dawson, T., 'Between the steps' in *Dublin Historical Record*, xxiv (1971), pp 65-75.

De Bhál, S.A., 'A Dublin voluntary hospital – the Meath' in *Dublin Historical Record*, xxvii, 1, pp 27-37.

De Breffney, B., 'Pupils of Samuel Whyte's school in Dublin listed by him in 1772' in *Irish Ancestor*, xii, 1-2 (1980), pp 36-42.

de Breffney, B., 'Members of two Dublin societies in 1772' in *Irish Ancestor*, xiii, 1 (1981), pp 10-11.

De Burca, S., 'Venereal disease in Dublin' in *Dublin Historical Record*, xli, 2 (1988), pp 23-24.

Delamer, I., 'Freedom boxes' in *Dublin Historical Record*, xxxii, 1 (1978), pp 2-14.

Delaney, R., 'The River Liffey navigation' in *Kildare Archaeological Society Journal*, xvi, 1 (1977-8), pp 36-40.

Dickson, D., 'The place of Dublin in the eighteenth century Irish economy' in Devine, T.M. and Dickson, D. (eds), *Ireland and Scotland, 1600-1850: parallels and contrasts in economic and social development* (Edinburgh, 1983), pp 177-92.

Dickson, D. (ed.), *The gorgeous mask: Dublin 1700-1850* (Dublin, 1987).

Dickson, D. and English, R., 'The La Touche dynasty' in Dickson, D. (ed.), *The gorgeous mask: Dublin 1700-1850* (Dublin, 1987), pp 17-29.

Dickson, D., 'Capital and country: 1600-1800' in Cosgrove, A. (ed.), *Dublin through the ages* (Dublin, 1988), pp 63-76.

Dickson, D., 'The demographic implications of Dublin's growth; 1650-1850' in Lawton, R. and Lee, R. (eds), *Urban population development in western Europe* (Liverpool, 1989), pp 178-89.

Dixon, F.E., 'A Dublin student's diary of 1878' in *Dublin Historical Record*, xxxiv, 1 (1980), pp 28-40.

Donnelly, B., 'Records of the Royal College of Physicians' in *Irish Archives*, i (1989), pp 31-4.

Doorley, B., 'Newgate prison' in Dickson, D. (ed.), *The gorgeous mask: Dublin, 1700-1850* (Dublin, 1987), pp 121-31.

Dower, C.A., 'Dublin and musical culture in the eighteenth century' in *Éire/Ireland*, xxii, 1 (1987), pp 44-58.

Doyle, M., 'The Dublin guilds and journeymen's clubs' in *Saothar*, iii (1977), pp 6-14.

Dungan, T. P., 'John Dungan of Dublin: an Elizabethan gentleman' in *Journal of the Royal Society of Antiquaries of Ireland*, cxviii (1988), pp 101-17.

Dunlop, R., 'Dublin Baptists from 1650 onwards' in *Irish Baptist Society Historical Journal*, xxi (1990), pp 5-16.

Dusek, A., 'Baptisms in St, Brides, Dublin 1633-1710' in *Irish Genealogist*, vi, 6 (1985), pp 711-23.

Dusek, A., 'Baptisms in St. Bride's, Dublin, 1633-1713' in *Irish Genealogist*, vii, 1 (1986), pp 17-30.

Dusek, A., 'Baptisms in St. Bride's, Dublin 1633-1714' in *Irish Genealogist*, vii, 3 (1988), pp 358-77.

Ellis, S.G., 'The destruction of the Liberties' in *Bulletin of Institute of Historical Research*, liv, 130 (1981), pp 150-60.

Empey, C.A., 'The Huguenots and Dublin' in *Proceedings of the Huguenot Society*, xxv, 1 (1989), pp 55-60.

Fagan, P., *The second city: portrait of Dublin 1700-1760* (Dublin, 1986).

Fagan, P., 'The Dublin catholic mob (1700-1750)' in *Eighteenth Century Ireland*, iv (1989), pp 133-42.

Fagan, P., *Dublin's turbulent priest: Cornelius Nary, 1658-1738* (Dublin, 1991).

Fagan, P., 'The population of Dublin in the eighteenth century with particular reference to the proportions of Protestants and Catholics' in *Eighteenth Century Ireland*, vi (1991), pp 121-58.

Farmar, T., *Ordinary lives: three generations of Irish middle class experience, 1907, 1932, 1963* (Dublin, 1991).

Feeney, J.K., *The Coombe Lying-in Hosptial* (Dublin, 1983).

Fenlon, J., 'The painter stainers companies of Dublin and London: craftsmen and artists 1670-1740' in Fenlon, J., Figgis, N. and Marshall, C., *New perspectives: studies in art history: essays presented to Anne Crookshank* (Dublin, 1987).

Ffolliott, R., 'An alphabetical list of the freemen of the city of Dublin, 1774-1824' in *Irish Ancestor*, xv, 1 (1983), pp 21-33.

Finegan, J., *The story of Monto: an account of Dublin's notorious red light district* (Cork, 1978).

Finegan, F., 'The Jesuits in Dublin' in *Repertorium Novum*, iv (1971), pp 43-100.

Flannery, J.W., 'High ideals and the reality of the market place: a financial record of the early Abbey Theatre' in *Studies*, lxxi, 283 (1982), pp 24-69.

Fleetwood, J.F., 'The Dublin bodysnatchers (part 1)' in *Dublin Historical Record*, xli, 2 (1988), pp 32-40.

Fleetwood, J.F., 'The Dublin bodysnatchers (part 2)' in *Dublin Historical Record*, xlii, 2 (1989), pp 42-52.

Fleetwood, J.F., 'Dublin private medical schools in the nineteenth century' in *Dublin Historical Record*, xlvi, 1 (1993), pp 31-45.

Flood, D.T., 'The decay of Georgian Dublin' in *Dublin Historical Record*, xxvii, 3, pp 78-100.

Fredell, T., 'Handel in ascendancy Dublin' in *Eire/Ireland*, xx, 4 (1985), pp 6-14.

Gaiety Theatre, *Dublin, 1871-1971: one hundred years of the Gaiety* (Dublin, 1971).

Gallagher, C., 'Catholic social values in action: the society of St. Vincent de Paul in Dublin, 1920s to 1950s' in *Retrospect* (1988), pp 21-4.

Garrett, A., *Through countless ages: the story of the Church and parish of All Saints*, Raheny (Dublin, 1989).

Garvin, J., 'James Joyce's municipal background' in *Administration*, xxxiii, 4 (1985), pp 551-72.

Geraghty, H. and Rigney, P., 'The engineers' strike in Inchicore railway works, 1902' in *Saothar*, ix (1983), pp 20-31.

Gillespie, R., 'Describing Dublin: Francis Place's visit, 1698-99' in Dalsimer, A. M.(ed.), *Visualising Ireland. National identity and the pictorial tradition* (Boston, 1993), pp 99-118.

Gillespie, E. (ed.), *The Liberties of Dublin* (Dublin, 1973).

Gilligan, H.A., 'Captain William Hutchinson and the early Dublin Bay lifeboats' in *Dublin Historical Record*, xxxiii, 2 (1980), pp 42-55.

Gilligan, H.A., *A history of the Port of Dublin* (Dublin, 1988).

Goodbody, O.C., 'Inventories of five Dublin Quaker merchants in the late seventeenth century' in *Irish Ancestor*, x, 1 (1978), pp 38-48.

Gorham, M., *Dublin from old photographs: with an introduction and commentaries* (London, 1972).

Guinness, D., *Georgian Dublin* (London, 1979).

Hartigan, M., The Catholic laity of Dublin, 1920-1940, unpublished Ph.D. thesis, St. Patrick's College, Maynooth (1992).

Hayes, C., 'Cullen, Newman and the Irish university' in *Recusant history*, xv, 3 (1980), pp 201-12.

Healey, P., 'Skipper's Alley' in *Dublin Historical Record*, xxxi, 1 (1977), pp 33-6.

Healy, E., Moriarty, C. and O'Flaherty, G., *The book of the Liffey: from source to the sea* (Dublin, 1988).

Hearn, M., 'Life for domestic servants in Dublin, 1880-1920' in Luddy, M. and Murphy, C. (eds), *Women surviving: studies in Irish women's history in the 19th and 20th centuries* (Swords, 1989), pp 148-79.

Hearn, M., *Below stairs: domestic service remembered in Dublin and beyond, 1880-1922* (Dublin, 1993).

Hearn, M., Domestic servants in Dublin, 1880-1920, unpublished Ph.D. thesis, Trinity College, Dublin (1984).

Hefferon, M., 'Royal Hospital, Kilmainham' in *An Cosantoir*, xxx (1970), pp 1-4.

Henchy, D., 'Dublin 80 years ago' in *Dublin Historical Record*, xxvi (1972), pp 18-35.

Henry, B., 'Industrial violence, combinations and the law in late eighteenth century Dublin' in *Saothar*, xviii (1993), pp 19-33.

Henry, B., 'Animadversions on the street robberies in Dublin, 1765' in *Irish Jurist*, xxii (1988), pp 347-56.

Henry, B., Crime, law enforcement, and punishment in Dublin, 1780-95, unpublished Ph.D. thesis, University of Dublin (1992).

Hill, J.R., 'Artisans, sectarianism and politics in Dublin, 1829-48' in *Saothar*,vii (1981), pp 12-27.

Hill, J.R., 'The politics of privilege: Dublin Corporation and the Catholic question, 1792-1823' in *Maynooth Review*, vii (1982), pp 17-36.

Hill, J. R., 'Religion, trade and politics in Dublin, 1798-1848' in Butel, P. and Cullen, L.M. (eds), *Cities and merchants: French and Irish perspectives on urban development, 1500-1900* (Dublin, 1986), pp 247-59.

Hill, J.R., 'The politics of Dublin Corporation, 1760-92' in Dickson, D., Keogh, D. and Whelan, K. (eds),

The United Irishmen, republicanism, radicalism and rebellion (Dublin, 1993), pp 88-101.

Hogan, R. and Kilroy, J., *The modern Irish drama: a documentary history, iii, The Abbey Theatre: the years of Synge 1905-1909* (Dublin, 1978).

Holland, C.H. (ed.), *Trinity College, Dublin and the idea of a university* (Dublin, 1991).

Hoppen, K.T., 'The papers of the Dublin philosophical society 1683-1708: introduction and index' in *Analecta Hibernica*, xxx (1982), pp 151-248.

Horner, A.A., 'Change in the urban hinterland – a long-term perspective for Dublin' in *Irish Geography*, xii (1979), pp 82-91.

Horner, A.A., 'Changes in population and in the extent of the built-up area in the Dublin city region 1936-1988' in *Irish Geography*, xxiii, 1 (1990), pp 50-5.

Horner, A.A., 'From city to city-region: Dublin from the 1930s to the 1990s' in Aalen, F.H. and Whelan, K. (eds), *Dublin city and county from prehistory to present: studies in honour of J.H.Andrews* (Dublin, 1992), pp 327-58.

Horton, C.G., 'Working class housing companies in Dublin (1870-1939) and their records' in *Irish Archives Bulletin*, ii (1981), pp 26-32.

Howell, J. B., *A history of the Dublin library society, 1791-1887* (Halifax, Nova Scotia, 1985).

Hunt, H., *The Abbey: Ireland's national theatre 1904-78* (Dublin, 1979).

Hussey, M.O., 'Sandymount and the Herberts' in *Dublin Historical Record*, xxiv (1971), pp 76-84.

Hynes, C., 'A polite struggle: the Dublin seamstresses' campaign, 1869-1872' in *Saothar*, xviii (1993), pp 35-9.

Ireland, J. de Courcy, 'The fight for safety in the approaches to the port of Dublin' in *Mariner's Mirror*, lxxii, 4 (1986), pp 455-64.

Jenkins, R.G. and Simms, G.O., *Pioneers and partners: the story of the parish of All-Saint's, Grangegorman, Dublin* (Dublin), 1985.

Johnson, M., *Around the banks of Pimlico* (Dublin, 1985).

Judge, P.M., *O'Connell school: 150 years 1828-1978* (Dublin, 1978).

Kain, R. (ed.), 'A diary of Easter week one Dubliner's experience' in *Irish University Review*, x, 2 (1980), pp 193-207.

Kane, E., 'John Henry Newman's Catholic university church in Dublin' in *Studies*, lxvi (1977), 262, pp 105-21.

Keane, E., Phair, P.B. and Sadlier, T.U. (eds), *Kings Inns admission papers 1607-1867* (Dublin, 1982).

Kearns, K.C., *Dublin's vanishing craftsmen. In search of the old masters* (Belfast, 1986).

Kelly, D., 'Insolvents in eighteenth century Dublin' in Dickson, D. (ed.), *The gorgeous mask: Dublin 1700-1850* (Dublin,1987), pp 98-120.

Kelly, J. and MacGearailt, U. (eds), *Dublin and Dubliners: essays on the history and literature of Dublin city* (Dublin, 1990).

Kelly, P., 'Drumcondra, Clonliffe and Glasnevin township, 1878-1900' in Kelly, J. and MacGearailt, U. (eds), *Dublin and Dubliners: essays on the history and literature of Dublin city* (Dublin, 1990), pp 36-51.

Kennedy, T. (ed.), *Victorian Dublin* (Dublin, 1980).

Kenny, C., *King's Inns and the kingdom of Ireland: the Irish 'Inn of Court', 1541-1800* (Dublin, 1992).

Keogh, D., 'William Martin Murphy and the origins of the 1913 lock-out' in *Capuchin Annual* (1977), pp 130-57.

Keogh, D., *The rise of the Irish working class: the Dublin trade union movement and labour leadership, 1890-1914* (Belfast, 1982).

Killen, J., 'Transport in Dublin: past, present and future' in Aalen, F.H. and Whelan, K. (eds), *Dublin city and county from prehistory to the present: studies in honour of J.H. Andrews* (Dublin, 1992), pp 305-25.

Kinane, V., 'Printers' apprentices in eighteenth and nineteenth century Dublin' in *Linen Hall Review*, x, 1 (1993), pp 11-4.

Knight of Glin, 'A directory of the Dublin furnishing trade, 1752-1800' in Bernelle, A. (ed.), *Decantations: a tribute to Maurice Craig* (Dublin, 1992), pp 47-59.

Komito, L., 'Dublin politics: symbolic dimensions of clientelism' in Curtin, C. and Wilson, T. M. (eds), *Ireland: social change from above and below local communities* (Galway, 1989), pp 240-59.

Lavelle, R. and Huggard, P., 'The parish poor of St. Mark's' in Dickson, D. (ed.), *The gorgeous mask: Dublin 1700-1850* (Dublin, 1987), pp 86-97.

Lee, J. B., *The evolution of a profession and its dental school in Dublin* (Dublin, 1992).

Lennon, C., *Richard Stanihurst, the Dubliner, 1547-1618* (Dublin, 1981).

Lennon, C., 'Civic life and religion in early eighteenth century Dublin' in *Archivium Hibernicum*, xxxviii (1983), pp 14-25.

Lennon, C., 'The great explosion in Dublin, 1597' in *Dublin Historical Record*, xli, 2 (1988), pp 7-20.

Lennon, M., 'Winston Churchill, Dublin (1662-1668)' in *Dublin Historical Record*, liii, 2 (1990), pp 99-106.

Lennon, C., 'The chantries in the Irish Reformation: the case of St. Anne's Guild, Dublin 1550-1630' in Comerford, R.V., Cullen, M., Hill, J. R., Lennon, C. (eds), *Religion, conflict and co-existence in Ireland. Essays presented to Monsignor Patrick J.Corish* (Dublin).

Lennon, C., 'The bowels of the city's bounty': the municipality of Dublin and the foundation of Trinity College in 1592' in *Long Room*, 37 (1992), pp 10-6.

Lennon, C., 'The beauty and eye of Ireland the sixteenth century' in Cosgrove, A. (ed.), *Dublin through the ages* (Dublin, 1988), pp 46-62.

Levistone Cooney, D.A., A small school in Rathmines' in *Dublin Historical Record*, xlv, 1 (1992), pp 41-54.

Levistone Cooney, D.A., 'A pious Dublin printer' in, *Dublin Historical Record*, xlvi, 2 (1993), pp 74-100.

Lincoln, C., *Dublin as a work of art* (Dublin, 1992).

Lindsay, D., 'The sick and indigent roomkeepers' society' in Dickson, D. (ed.), *The gorgeous mask: Dublin 1700-1850* (Dublin, 1987), pp 132-56.

Loeber, R., 'An unpublished view of Dublin in 1698 by Francis Place' in *Bulletin of Irish Georgian Society*, xxi, 1-2 (1978), pp 7-15.

Loeber, R., 'The rebuilding of Dublin Castle: thirty critical years, 1661-90' in *Studies,* lxix, 273 (1980), pp 45-69.

Luce, J.V., *Trinity College Dublin: the first 400 years* (Dublin, 1992).

Lyons, J.B., *The quality of Mercer's: the story of Mercer's Hospital, 1734-1991* (Dublin, 1991).

Lysaght, M., 'A north city childhood in the early century' in *Dublin Historical Record*, xxxviii, 2 (1985), pp 74-82.

Mac Giolla Phádraig, B., 'Dublin one hundred. years ago' in *Dublin Historical Record*, xxiii (1969), pp 56-71.

MacThomáis, E., 'Seven hills of Dublin' in *Dublin Historical Record*, xxiii (1969), pp 86-94.

MacThomáis, E., *The 'Labour' and the Royal* (Dublin, 1979).

MacLaran, A. *Dublin: the shaping of a capital* (New York, 1993).

MacLoughlin, A., *Guide to historic Dublin* (Dublin, 1979).

Maguire, J.B., 'Dublin Castle: three centuries of development' in *Royal Society of Antiquaries of Ireland Journal*, 115 (1985), pp 13-39.

Maguire, M., 'A socio-economic analysis of the Dublin protestant working class, 1870-1926' in *Irish Economic and Social History*, xx (1993), pp 35-61.

Maguire, M., The Dublin protestant working class 1870-1932: economy, society and politics, unpublished. M.A. thesis, University College Dublin (1991).

Malcolm, E., *Swift's hospital: a history of St. Patrick's Hospital, Dublin, 1746-1989* (Dublin, 1990).

Martin, J.H., 'The social geography of mid-nineteenth century Dublin city' in Smyth, W.J. and Whelan, K. (eds), *Common ground: essays on the historical geography of Ireland* (Cork, 1988), pp 173-88.

Martin, J.H., 'Leeson Street and its environs' in *C.U.S., Catholic University School, 1867-1967: a centenary record* (Dublin, 1967), pp 30-38.

McAsey, C., 'Dubliners and opera' in *Dublin Historical Record*, xxiii (1969), pp 45-55.

McBreirty, V. (ed.), *The Howth peninsula: its history, lore and legend* (Dublin, 1984).

McCaffrey, P., 'Jacob's women workers during the 1913 lock-out' in *Saothar*, xvi (1991), pp 118-29.

McCarthy, C., *All graduates and gentlemen: Marsh's Library* (Dublin, 1980).

McCarthy, D., *Saint Mary's Pro-Cathedral, Dublin* (Dublin, 1988).

McCarthy, L., 'Evolution, present condition and future potential of the Smithfield area of Dublin' in *Irish Geography*, xxiii, 2 (1990), pp 90-106.

McCormack, W.J., *The Dublin paper war of 1786-1788: a bibliographical and critical inquiry, including an account of the origins of Protestant ascendancy and its 'Baptism' in 1792* (Dublin, 1993).

McDowell, R.B. and Webb, D.A., *Trinity College, Dublin, 1592-1952: an academic history* (Cambridge, 1982).

McDowell, R.B., *Land and learning: two Irish clubs* (Dublin, 1993).

McNamara, G., 'Crown versus machinery: the struggle for Dublin 1713' in *Dublin Historical Record*, xxxix, 3 (1986) pp 108-17.

McParland, E., 'Strategy in the planning of Dublin, 1750-1800' in Butel, P. and Cullen, L M., *Cities and merchants: French and Irish perspectives on urban development, 1500-1900* (Dublin,1986), pp 97-109.

McParland, E., 'The wide streets commissioners: their importance for Dublin architecture in the late 18th-early 19th century' in *Irish Georgian Society Journal*, xv (1972), pp 1-332.

Meenan, F.O.C., 'The Catholic university school of medicine, 1880-1909' in Studies, lxx (1981), pp 135-44.

Meenan, F.O.C., *Cecilia Street: the Catholic university school of medicine 1855-1931* (Dublin, 1987).

Meenan, F.O.C., 'The Georgian Squares of Dublin and the professions' in *Studies*, lviii (1969), pp 405-14.

Meenan, J., 'The RD.S., 1731-1981' in Meenan, J. and Clarke, D. (eds), *The Royal Dublin Society, 1731-1981* (Dublin, 1981), pp 1-55.

Meenan, J. and Clarke, D. (eds), *The Royal Dublin Society, 1731-1981* (Dublin, 1981).

Milne, K., *Protestant aid 1836-1986: a history of the association for the relief of distressed. Protestants* (Dublin, 1989).

Molumby, P., 'Lighting Dublin' in *Capuchin Annual* (1973), pp 75-85.

Mooney, T. and White, F., 'The gentry's winter season' in Dickson, D. (ed.), *The gorgeous mask: Dublin 1700-1850* (Dublin, 1987), pp 1-16.

Morrissey, T. J., 'The 1913 lock-out: letters for the archbishop' in *Studies*, lxxv, 297 (1986), pp 86-101.

Murnane, B., 'The recreation of the urban historical landscape: Mountjoy Ward Dublin c. 1901' in Smyth, W.J. and Whelan, K. (eds), *Common ground: essays on the historical geography of Ireland* (Cork, 1988), pp 189-207.

Murphy, F.J., 'Dublin trams 1872-1959' in *Dublin Historical Record*, xxxiii (1979), pp 2-9.

Murphy, F.J., 'Dublin slums in the 1930s' in *Dublin Historical Record*, xxxvii, 3 (1984), pp 104-11.

Murphy, S., 'The Corporation of Dublin, 1660-1760' in *Dublin Historical Record*, xxxviii, 1 (1984), pp 22-35.

Murphy, S., 'Dublin City genealogical sources and Dr. D.A. Chart's list of heads of families from the 1851 Census' in *Familia*, ii, 2 (1986), pp 75-81.

Murphy, S., 'Municipal politics and popular disturbances, 1660-1880' in Cosgrove, A. (ed.), *Dublin through the ages* (Dublin, 1988), pp 77-9.

Murphy, S., 'The Dublin anti-union riot of 3 December 17S9' in O'Brien, G. (ed.), *Parliament, politics and people: essays in eighteenth century Irish history* (Blackrock, 1989), pp 49-68.

Murray, K., 'Transport' in Kennedy, T. (ed.), *Victorian Dublin* (Dublin, 1980), pp 90-7.

Murray, F., 'Public building and colonial policy in Dublin, 1760-1800' in *Architectural History*, 28 (1985), pp 102-23.

Murray, P., 'The First World War and a Dublin distillery workforce: recruiting and redundancy at John Power and Son, 1915-191' in *Saothar*, xv (1990), pp 48-56.

National Council for educational Awards, *Gardiner's Dublin: a history and topography of Mountjoy Square and its environs* (Dublin, 1991).

Neary, B., *A history of Cabra and Phibsborough* (Dublin, 1983).

Nesbitt, R., *At Arnotts of Dublin, 1843-1993* (Dublin, 1993).

Newsinger, J., 'The devil it was who sent Larkin to Ireland': the Liberator, Larkinism and the Dublin lockout of 1913' in *Saothar*, xviii (1993), pp 101-6.

O'Brien, J.V., *'Dear Dirty Dublin': a city in distress 1899-1916* (Berkeley, 1982).

Ó Broin, S., *The book of Finglas* (Dublin, 1980).

Ó Broin, L., *Dublin castle and the 1916 Rising* (Dublin, 1970).

O'Carroll, J., 'Contemporary attitudes towards the homeless poor, 1725-1775' in Dickson, D. (ed.), *The gorgeous mask: Dublin 1700-1850* (Dublin, 1987), pp 64-85.

O'Carroll, M., 'The municipal government of Dublin,1558-1603' in *Retrospect*, New Series, i (1981), pp 7-12.

Ó Cathaoir, E., 'Patrick Lennon 1841-1901: Dublin Fenian leader' in *Dublin Historical Record*, xliv, 2 (1991), pp 38-50.

O'Connor, A., 'John Lewis: a smock-alley scene painter' in *Studies*, lxvi, 261 (1977), pp 51-9.

O'Dea, L., 'North Dublin city from the book by Rev. Augustine Dillon Cosgrave' in *Dublin Historical Record*, xxiii (1969), pp 3-22.

O'Donnell, E.E., *Fr. Browne's Dublin photographs*, 1925-1950 (Dublin, 1993).

O'Donnell, P.D., 'A short history of Portobello Barracks, part 2' in *An Cosantoir*, xxix (1969), pp 37-47.

O'Donnell, P.D., 'Griffith Barracks, Dublin' in *An Cosantoir*, xxxviii, 2 (1978), pp 323-28.

O'Donnell, P.D., 'Dublin's Military Barracks – three centuries' in *An Cosantoir*, xli, 3 (1981), pp 73-7; xli, 4 (1981), pp 102-7.

O'Donoghue, P., 'John Thomas Troy, archbishop of Dublin 1785-1823: a man of his time' in Kelly, J., and MacGearailt, U. (eds), *Dublin and Dubliners: essays on the history and literature of Dublin city* (Dublin, 1990), pp 25-35.

O'Driscoll, F., 'St. Dominic's – the rise and fall of a training college' in *Irish Educational Studies*, iv, 1 (1984), pp 98-114.

O'Driscoll, J., *Cnúcha: a history of Castleknock and district* (Dublin, 1977).

O'Dwyer, P, *Father John Spratt: beloved of Dublin's poor* (Dublin, 1972).

Ó Gráda, C., 'Dublin's demography in the early nineteenth century: evidence from the Rotunda' in *Population Studies*, xlv, 1 (1991), pp 43-54.

Ó Hainle, C., 'Neighbours in 18th century Dublin: Jonathan Swift and Seán Ó Neachtáin' in *Éire/Ireland*, xxi, 4 (1986), pp 106-21.

O'Neill, T.P., 'Discovers and discoveries: the penal laws and Dublin property' in *Dublin Historical Record*, xxxvii, 1 (1983), pp 2-13.

O'Neill, M., 'Dublin women's suffrage association and its successors' in *Dublin Historical Record*, xxxviii, 4 (1985), pp 126-40.

Ó Raifeartaigh, T. (ed.), *The Royal Irish Academy: a bicentennial history 1785-1985* (Dublin, 1985).

Ó Riordáin, B., 'New light on old Dublin' in *Capuchin Annual*, xxxix (1972), pp 53-63.

O'Sullivan, D. (ed.), *Dublin Bay: a century of sailing 1884-1984. A centenary celebration of the Dublin Bay sailing club* (Dublin, 1984).

O'Toole, D., 'The employment crisis of 1826' in Dickson, D. (ed.), *The gorgeous mask: Dublin 1700-1850* (Dublin, 1987), pp 157-71.

Oram, H., *Dublin airport: the history* (Dublin, 1990).

Parkes, S., *Kildare Place: the history of the Church of Ireland training college 1811-1969* (Dublin, 1984).

Parkes, S. and O'Connor, A.V., *Gladly learn and gladly teach: Alexandra college and school 1866-1966* (Tallaght, 1984).

Parkinson, D., *Donnybrook graveyard and interesting historical facts on Donnybrook and its environs* (Dublin, 1993).

Partridge, P., 'Crime in the Dublin metropolitan police district, 1894-1914' in *Retrospect* (New Series) ii (1982), pp 36-43.

Pine, R. and Cane, R., *The Dublin Gate Theatre, 1928-1978* (Cambridge, 1984).

Pollard, M., *Dublin's trade in books, 1550-1800* (Oxford, 1990).

Pollard, M., 'Plain calf for plain people: Dublin bookbinders' price lists of the eighteenth century' in Bernelle, A. (ed.), *Decantations: a tribute to Maurice Craig* (Dublin, 1992), pp 177-86.

Powell, F., 'Dean Swift and the Dublin foundling hospital' in *Studies*, lxx, 228-9 (1981), pp 162-70.

Preston, M. H., 'Lay women and philanthropy in Dublin, 1860-1880' in *Éire/Ireland*, xxviii, 4 (1993), pp 74-85.

Purcell, M. (ed.), 'Dublin diocesan archives: Murray papers (1)' in *Archivium Hibernicum*, xxxvi (1981), pp 51-140.

Purcell, M., 'Dublin diocesan archives: Murray papers (2)' in *Archivium Hibernicum*, xxxvii (1982), pp 29-121.

Purcell, M., 'Dublin diocesan archives: Murray papers (3)' in *Archivium Hibernicum*, xxxvii (1983), pp 43-127.

Purcell, M., 'Dublin diocesan archives: Murray papers (4)' in *Archivium Hibernicum*, xxix (1985), pp 62-87.

Purcell, M., 'Dublin diocesan archives: Murray papers (5)' in *Archivium Hibernicum*, xl (1985), pp 35-114.

Purcell, M. and Sheehy, D., 'Dublin diocesan archives: Murray papers (6)' in *Archivum Hibernicum*, xli (1986), pp 3-71.

Purdon, D.J.D., 'History of the society's shows' in Meenan, J. and Clarke, D. (eds), *The Royal Dublin Society, 1731-1981* (Dublin, 1981), pp 101-17.

Quaney, J., *A penny to Nelson's Pillar* (Waterford, 1971).

Raymond, R.J., 'Pawnbrokers and pawnbroking in Dublin 1830-1870' in *Dublin Historical Record*, xxxii (1978), pp 15-26.

Raymond, R.J., 'Dublin: the great famine 1845-60' in *Dublin Historical Record*, xxxiii, 3 (1980), pp 98-105.

Roberts, R., *The story of the People's College* (Dublin, 1986).

Robins, J., *Custom House people* (Dublin, 1993).

Scoil Mhuire, *Fifty years of Scoil Mhuire, Marino: golden jubilee 1928-78* (Dublin, 1978).

Scully, S., 'Dublin's historic Hollywood' in *Dublin Historical Record*, xliii, 1 (1990), pp 34-43.

Shamráin, A.S. and Purcell, J.C., *The barony of Coolock: a history* (Dublin, 1985).

Shaw, H., *The Dublin pictorial guide and directory of 1850* (Belfast, 1988).

Sheehy, J., *Kingsbridge Station, Ballycotton, County Cork* (1973).

Simms, A., 'Medieval Dublin: a topographcal analysis' in *Irish Geography*, xii (1979), pp

Simms, J.G., 'Dublin in 1776' in *Dublin Historical Record*, xxxi, 1 (1977), pp 2-13.

Simms, J.G., *William Molyneaux of Dublin: a life of the seventeenth-century political writer and scientist* (Dublin, 1982).

Simms, G.O., *Tullow's story: a portrait of a county Dublin parish* (Dublin, 1983).

Smithson, A.M.P., 'Christmas in old Dublin' in *Dublin Historical Record* (1988), pp 146-51.

Smyth, H.P., 'Two hundred. years a-growing: the story of Mackey's Seeds Limited., 1777-1977' in *Dublin Historical Record*, xxxv, 3 (1982), pp 100-15.

Smyth, J., 'Dublin's political underground in the 1790s' in O'Brien, G. (ed.), *Parliament, politics and people: essays in eighteenth century Irish history* (Blackrock, 1989), pp 129-48.

Somerville-Large, P., *Dublin* (London, 1979).

St. Anne's Hospital, *Down through the ages: St. Anne's Hospital 1926-1976* (Dublin, 1979).

Anon., 'Survey of business records in Dublin' in *Irish archives bulletin*, iii, 2 (1973), pp 10-13.

Swan, L. (ed.), *Here lyeth: a record and description of the graveyards of Grange Abbey, Raheny, Coolock, and Kilbarrack and a summary of the history of these parishes* (Dublin, 1986).

Takagami, S., 'The Dublin Fenians after the Rising, 1867-79' in Matsuo, Taro (ed.), *Comparative aspects of Irish and Japanese economic and social history* (Tokyo, 1993), pp 182-237.

Thompson, J., 'Irish Baptist college: list of students from 1892-1963' in *Irish Baptist Historical Society*, xxiii (1991), pp 39-44.

Thompson, J., 'Irish Baptist college: the Dublin years, 1892-1963' in *Irish Baptist Historical Society*, xxiii (1991), pp 26-37.

Toucher, P., *Fear of the collar: Artane Industrial School* (Dublin, 1991).

Travers, P., ' "Our fenian dead" ': Glasnevin cemetery and the genesis of the Republican funeral' in Kelly, J. and MacGearailt, U. (eds), *Dublin and Dubliners: essays on the history and literature of Dublin city* (Dublin, 1990), pp 52-72.

Turpin, J., 'The Royal Dublin Society and its school of art, 1849-1877' in *Dublin Historical Record*, xxxvi, 1 (1982), pp 2-20.

Turpin, J., 'Ireland's progress: the Dublin exhibition of 1907' in *Éire/Ireland*, xv, 1 (1982), pp 31-8.

Turpin, J., 'The school of ornament of the Dublin society in the eighteenth century' in *Journal of the Royal Society of Antiquaries of Ireland*, cxvi (1986), pp 38-50.

Turpin, J., 'The school of figure-drawing of the Dublin society in the eighteenth century' in *Dublin Historical Record*, xl (1987), pp 42-6.

Turpin, J., 'The Dublin society and the beginnings of sculptural education in Ireland, 1750-1850' in *Éire/Ireland*, xxiv, 1 (1989), pp 40-58.

Turpin, J., 'French influence on eighteenth century art education in Dublin' in *Eighteenth Century Ireland*, v (1990), pp 105-16.

Tutty, M. J., 'The 'Dublin Evening Post', 1826' in *Dublin Historical Record*, xxiv (1971), pp 15-24.

Uibh Eachach, V. (ed.), *Féile Zozimus: 18th and 19th century Dublin* (Dublin, 1991).

Wall, R., *Slum conditions in London and Dublin* (Farnborough, Hants, 1974).

Walsh, E., 'Sackville Mall: the first one hundred years' in Dickson, D. (ed.), *The gorgeous mask: Dublin 1700-1850* (Dublin, 1987), pp 30-50.

Walsh, T.J., *Opera in Dublin, 1705-97: the social scene* (Dublin, 1973).

Ward-Perkins, S., 'Bank of Ireland, old parliament house' in *Dublin Historical Record*, xxxvii, 2 (1984), pp 42-53.

Warren, J., 'The Dublin Review (1836-75): its reviewers and a philosophy of knowledge' in *Recusant History*, xxi, 1 (1992), pp 86-98.

Waterman, S., 'Changing residential patterns of the Dublin Jewish community' in *Irish Geography*, xiv (1981), pp 41-50.

Watt, S.M., 'Boucicault and Whitbread: the Dublin stage at the end of the nineteenth century' in *Éire/Ireland*, xviiii, 3 (1983), pp 23-53.

West, A. J., 'The Dublin Zoo' in *Dublin Historical Record*, xxiv (1971), pp 101-11.

Widdes, J.D.H., *The Richmond, Whitworth and Hardwicke hospitals, 1772-1972* (Dublin, 1972).

Widdes, J.D.H., *The Royal College of Surgeons in Ireland and its medical school, 1784-1984* (Dublin, 1983).

Dun Laoghaire, County Dublin

Ffeary-Smyrl, S. C., 'Kingstown congregational church' in *Dun Laoghaire Genealogical Society Journal*, ii, 1 (1993), pp 31-7; 2, pp 70-4.

Fitzsimon, C., 'Dun Laoghaire: Dublin's asylum harbour' in *Irish Welcomes*, xxvi, 1 (1977), pp 18-24.

Gaffney, J., The morphological development of Dun Laoghaire, c.1540-1900, unpublished B.A. dissertation, University College Dublin (1988).

O'Brien, R., The historic building fabric of Dun Laoghaire: a survey, unpublished B.A. dissertation, University College Dublin (1985).

Pearson, P., *Dun Laoghaire/Kingstown* (Dublin, 1981).

Dundalk, County Louth

Allan B., 'The port of Dundalk' in *County Louth Archaeological Society Journal*, xvii (1969), pp 66-78.

Gosling, P., *From Dun Delca to Dundalk: the topography and archaeology of a medieval frontier town*, A.D. c.1187-1700 (Dundalk, 1993).

Malcolmson, A.P.W., 'The struggle for control of Dundalk Borough, 1782-92 in *County Louth Archaeological Society Journal*, xvii (1969), pp 22-36.

Nulty, C., Aspects of the social topography of eighteenth century Dundalk, unpublished B.A. dissertation, University College Dublin (1990).

O'Donnell, P.D., 'Military barracks, Dundalk' in *An Cosantoir*, xxxi (1971), pp 137-40, 276-82.

Ó Dubhtaigh, P. Ua, *The book of Dundalk*, n.d.

Ógra Dún Dealgan, *Dundalk: a tradition in industry* (Dundalk, 1986).

O'Sullivan, H., *Dundalk: a military history* (Dundalk, 1987).

Simms, J.G., 'Schomberg at Dundalk, 1689' in *Irish Sword*, x (1971), pp 14-25.

Wilson, M., 'Dundalk poor-law union workhouse: the first twenty-five years, 1839-1864' in *County Louth Archaeological and Historical Journal*, xx, 3 (1983), pp 190-209.

Wilson, M., Ross, N. and Power, P., *Dundalk, images and impressions* (Dundalk, 1989).

Dungannon, County Tyrone

Hall, R., 'Dungannon: 'a case study in the decline of Ulster capitalism outside Belfast' in *Quest*, xi (1981), pp 14-24.

Dungarvan, County Waterford

Fraher, W., 'The reconstruction of Dungarvan, 1807 – c.1830: a political ploy' in *Decies*, xxv (1984), pp 4-21.

Fraher, W., *Dungarvan. An architectural inventory* (Dungarvan, 1984).

O'Brien, A.F., 'Development and evolution of the medieval port and borough of Dungarvan, county Waterford c. 1200-c. 1530' in *Cork Historical and Archaeological Society Journal*, xcii (1987) pp 85-94.

Ennis, County Clare

Corry, J., Ennis, county Clare, 1850-1900: structural and commercial development, unpublished B.A. dissertation, University College Dublin (1978).

Garner, W., *Ennis: architectural heritage* (Dublin, 1981).

Kelly, T., The history of Ennis in the first half of the nineteenth century, unpublished M.A. thesis, University College Galway (1971).

O'Brien, Sr. Pius, *The Sisters of Mercy of Ennis* (Ennis, 1992).

Ó Dálaigh, B., 'Thomas Moland's survey of Ennis 1703' in *The Other Clare*, xi (1987), pp 12-9.

Enniscorthy, County Wexford

Barnard, T.C., 'An Anglo-Irish industrial enterprise: iron-making at Enniscorthy, Co. Wexford, 1657-92' in *Proceedings of the Royal Irish Academy*, 85, C, 4 (1985), pp 101-4.

Collier, P., *The castle museum, Enniscorthy* (Dublin, 1969).

Anon, 'Dietary of Enniscorthy workhouse, 1842-1847' in *The Past*, 9 (1972), pp 57-9.

Doyle, A., Some aspects of the geography of Enniscorthy, unpublished B.A. dissertation, Univesity College Dublin (1968).

Goff, H.M., 'Education in Enniscorthy, 1800-1900, part 1' in *The Past*, 10, pp 3-18.

Goff, H.M, 'Education in Enniscortby 1800-1900, part 2' in *The Past*, 11 (1975), pp 37-57.

Lennon, S., Enniscorthy – social and urban changes, 1700-1850, unpublished B.A. dissertation, University College Dublin (1991).

Enniskillen, County Fermanagh

Belmore, Earl of, *Parliamentary memoirs: Fermanagh county and borough from 1613 to 1885* (Dublin, 1885).

Dundas, W.H., *Enniskillen – parish and town* (Dundalk and Enniskillen, 1913).

Hunter, R.J., 'Sir William Cole and the plantation of Enniskillen, 1607-41' in *Clogher Record*, lx, 3 (1978), pp 336-50.

Jackson, C. and M., A *history of the Vaughan charity* (Enniskillen, 1985).

Magee, G.J., The rural district and town of Enniskillen, unpublished B.A. dissertation, University College Dublin (1967).

McCullough, C., 'Made in Enniskillen: a brief survey of manufacturing and trading in earlier days' in

Clogher Record, xiii, 1 (1988), pp 26-31.

McCusker, B., 'The county gaol and some past crimes and punishments in County Fermanagh' in *Clogher Record*, xiii, 1 (1988), pp 50-5.

Quinn, J., 'Labouring on the margins: trade union activity in Enniskillen, 1917-1923' in *Saothar*, xv (1990), pp 57-64.

Quinn, M., 'Enniskillen poor law union' in *Clogher Record,* vii (1971), pp 498-513.

Wood, H., *Enniskillen. Images of an inland town* (Belfast, 1990).

Ennistymon, County Clare

Comber, M., A *guide to Ennistymon union, 1839-1850* (1992).

Ó Laoi, P., 'The parish of Ennistymon' in *Ennistymon Parish Magazine* (1986), pp 3-6.

Fermoy, County Cork

Brunicardi, D.N., *Fermoy 1791-1840: a local history* (Fermoy, 1977).

Brunicardi, D.N., *Fermoy 1841-90: a local history* (Fermoy, 1978).

Brunicardi, D.N., *Fermoy, 1891-1940: a local history* (Fermoy, 1979).

Brunicardi, D.N, *John Anderson of Fermoy: the forgotten benefactor* (Fermoy, 1980).

Brunicardi, D.N., *The bridge at Fermoy* (Fermoy, 1985).

Brunicardi, D.N., *John Anderson: entrepreneur* (Clonmel, 1988).

Fethard, County Tipperary

Gallwey, H.D., 'Proprieters of Fethard, Co. Tipperary, 1641-63' in *Irish Genealogist* vi, 1 (1980), pp 5-8.

Luddy, M., 'The lives of the poor in Fethard in 1821' in *Tipperary Historical Journal*, iii (1990), pp 121-27.

Skehan, W.G., 'Extracts from the minutes of the corporation of Fethard, county Tipperary' in *Irish Genealogist*, iv (1969), pp 81-92.

Skehan, W.G., 'Extracts from the minutes of the corporation of Fethard, county Tipperary' in *Irish Genealogist*, iv (1970), pp 183-93.

Skehan, W.G., 'Extracts from the minutes of the corporation of Fethard, County Tipperary' in *Irish Genealogist*, iv (1971), pp 308-22.

Freshford, County Kilkenny

Lanigan, K.M., 'Freshford doorway' in *Old Kilkenny Review*, xxi (1969), pp 5-10.

Galway, County Galway

Coen, M., 'The wardenship of Galway' in Ó Cearbhaill, D. (ed.), *Galway: town and gown 1484-1984* (Dublin, 1984), pp 29-40.

Coen, M., *The wardenship of Galway* (Galway, 1984).

Cooney, D.A.L., *Methodism in Galway* (1978).

Cullen, L.M., 'Galway merchants in the outside world 1650-1800' in Ó Cearbhaill, D. (ed.), *Galway: town and gown 1484-1984* (Dublin, 1984), pp 63-89.

Dolley, M., 'A seventeenth century coin-find from Galway city' in *Journal of the Galway Archaeological and Historical Society*, xxxi (1964-5), pp 5-7.

Fenning, H., 'The library of the Augustinians of Galway in 1731' in *Collectanea Hibernica*, nos. 31 and 32 (1989-90).

Flynn, P., A study of local government in Galway in the early nineteenth century, unpublished M.A. thesis, University College Galway (1981).

Helleiner, J., 'Traveller settlement in Galway city: politics, class and culture' in Curtin, C., Donnan, Hastings and Wilson, T. A. (eds), *Irish urban cultures* (Belfast, 1993), pp 181-202.

MacLochlainn, A. and Regan, T., *Two Galway schools, the Claddagh Piscatory School, the Salthill Industrial School* (Galway, 1993).

Mitchell, J., 'Mayor Lynch of Galway: a review of the tradition' in *Journal of the Galway Archaeological and Historical Society,* xxxii (1965-71), pp 1-72.

Mitchell, J., 'Mayor Lynch of Galway: a review of the tradition' in *Journal of the Galway Archaeological and Historical Society*, xxxviii (1981-2), pp 31-44.

Murray, J.P., 'Health and medicine in Galway' in Ó Cearbhaill, D. (ed.), *Galway: town and gown 1484-1984* (Dublin, 1984), pp 148-64.

O'Bric, B., Landholding by Galway townsmen in Connacht, 1585-1641, unpublished M.A. thesis, National University of Ireland (1974).

Ó Cearbhaill, D. (ed.), *Galway: town and gown 1484-1984* (Dublin, 1984).

O'Dowd, P., *Old and new Galway* (Galway, 1985).

O'hEocha, C., 'The Queens College at Galway – some memories' in Ó Cearbhaill, D. (ed.), *Galway: town and gown 1484-1984* (Dublin, 1984), pp 165-82.

O'Malley, L., 'Patrick Darcy, Galway lawyer and politician, 1598-1668' in Ó Cearbhaill, D. (ed.), *Galway: town and gown 1484-1984* (Dublin, 1984), pp 90-109.

O'Murchadha, M.K., 'Music in Saint Nicholas's collegiate church, Galway, 1480-1912' in *Journal of the Galway Archaeological and Historical Society*, xlv (1993), pp 29-43.

Philbin, E. M., 'Richard Kirwan, a Galway scientist 1733-1812' in Ó Cearbhaill, D. (ed.), *Galway: town and gown 1484-1984* (Dublin, 1984), pp 110-26.

Power, J., 'Archives report Galway diocesan archives' in *Archivium Hibernicum*, xlvi (1992), pp 135-138.

Ryan, M., 'Municipal dignity: a controversy in Galway, 1898' in *Journal of the Galway Archaeogical and Historical Society*, xliii (1991), pp 139-57.

Sanderlin, W. S., 'Galway as a transatlantic port in the nineteenth century' in *Éire/Ireland*, v, 3 (1970), pp 15-31.

Thomson, L., 'Strikes in Galway' in Fitzpatrick, D. (ed.), *Revolution? Ireland 1917-1923* (Dublin, 1990), pp 130-45.

Walsh, P., 'The medieval merchants mark and its survival in Galway' in *Journal of the Galway Archaeological and Historical Society*, xlv, i (1993), p. 28.

Gilford, County Down

Campbell, M.P., 'Gilford and its mills, review' in *Journal of the Craigavon Historical Society*, iv, 3 (1981-2) pp 20-24.

Cohen, M., 'Urbanisation and the factory life: Gilford Dunbarton (1825-1914)' in Curtin, C., Donnan, H. and Wilson, T. A. (eds), *Irish urban cultures* (Belfast, 1993), pp 227-42.

Gort, County Galway

'Tenants of J.P. Smyth at Gort, Co. Galway in 1805' in *Irish Ancestor*, xiv, 1 (1982), pp 20-1.

Granard, County Longford

Burns, J. and Grier, B., *Granard: its history, our heritage* (Granard, 1987).

Kearney, P., 'Granard' in *Teathba*, i (1969), pp 18-23.

Stafford, R.W., *St. Patrick's Church of Ireland, Granard: notes of genealogical and historical interest* (Granard, 1983).

Kanturk, County Cork

Dolley, M., 'A small find of nineteenth century coins from Kanturk' in *Journal of the Cork Historical and Archaeological Society*, lxxvi (1971), pp 150-51.

O'Sullivan, P., 'Land surveys and mapping of eighteenth century Kanturk' in *Journal of the Cork Historical and Archaeological Society*, xcv, 254 (1990), pp 88-106.

Kells, County Meath

Ferguson, P., Kells, a case study, 1865, unpublished B.A. dissertation, University College Dublin (1987).

Kenmare, County Kerry

Eager, I. F., *The nun of Kenmare* (Cork, 1970).

Kildare, County Kildare

Andrews, J.H., *Kildare: Irish historic towns atlas, no. 1: Kildare* (Dublin, 1986).

Boylan, L., 'Kildare Lodge' in *Kildare Archaeological Society Journal*, xvi, 1 (1977-8), pp 26-35.

Costello, C., Kildare, *saints, soldiers and horses* (Naas, 1991).

Hayden, T., 'Kildare town: its ancient roads and streets' in *Kildare Archaeological Society Journal* (1985-6), pp 479-83.

Kilkenny, County Kilkenny

Ainsworth, Sir John, 'Corporation book of the Irish town of Kilkenny 1537-1628' in *Analecta Hibernica*, xxvii (1978), pp 1-78.

Brennan, M.A., 'The Blundens of Kilkenny' in *Old Killkenny Review*, iii, 5 (1988), pp 456-67.

Butler, H., 'The Kilkenny theatre 1801-1819' in *Journal of the Butler Society*, ii, 1 (1981), pp 37-44.

Butler, H., 'Kilkenny Castle' in *Journal of the Butler Society*, 1 (1968), pp 55-60.

Byrne, A., Use of the Civil Survey for the reconstruction of the socio-economic topography of Kilkenny City, unpublished B.A. dissertation, University College Dublin (1985).

Condon, L. and Mullagh, M., 'History of Stephens Barracks' in *Old Kilkenny Review*, iii, 3 (1986), pp 256-66.

Dickson, D., 'Inland city: reflections on eighteenth century Kilkenny' in Nolan, W. and Whelan, K. (eds), *Kilkenny history and society : interdisciplinary essays on the history of an Irish county* (Dublin, 1990), pp 333-44.

Hackett, F., 'The Irish Insurrection, Easter week in Kilkenny, April 1916' in *Old Kilkenny Review*, iii, 1 (1984), pp 17-23.

Hayburn, Fr., 'Edmund Langton, the sale of the Langton mansion on High Street, Kilkenny' in *Old Kilkenny Review*, iii, 1 (1984), pp 75-7.

Jagoe, M. and Oldharn, E., *Records and recollections: a history of the diocesan secondary school for girls 1849-1974* (Kilkenny, 1986).

Kenealy, M., 'Finn's Leinster Journal' in *Old Kilkenny Review*, i (new series), 5 (1978), pp 332-48.

'Kilkenny deeds, 1785-1879' in *Old Kilkenny Review*, ii, 4 (1982), pp 393-400.

Lanigan, K.M., and Tyler, G. (eds), *Kilkenny: its architecture and history* (Dublin, 1977).

Marescaux, G., 'Occupants of Ormeau Houses, Kilkenny, 1641 and twenty years later' in *Journal of the Butler Society*, i, 7 (1977), pp 545-50.

Marescaux, G., 'Occupants of Ormond Houses, Kilkenny, 1641 and twenty years later' in *Journal of the Butler Society*, i, 8 (1978-9), pp 642-45.

McCree, L., The socio-topography of mid-nineteenth century Kilkenny City, unpublished B.A. dissertation, University College Dublin (1990).

McEvoy, F., 'Kilkenny races' in *Old Kilkenny Review*, ii, 3 (1981),

Neely, W.G., *Kilkenny: an urban history, 1391-1843* (Belfast, 1989).

Neely, W.G., A social and economic history of the City of Kilkenny during the Ormond period, 1391-1843, unpublished Ph.D. thesis, Queen's University Belfast (1987).

Ní Chinnéide, S., 'A view of Kilkenny, city and county, in 1790' in *Royal Society of Antiquaries of Ireland Journal*, civ (1974), pp 29-38.

Phelan, M. M., *St. Mary's Cathedral, Kilkenny: notes on its foundation, construction, furnishings* (Kilkenny, 1972).

Woodworth, D., 'St. Canice's Library' in *Old Kilkenny Review*, xxiii (197), pp 15-22.

Wray, K., 'Maudlin Street' in *Old Kilkenny Review*, xxi (1969), pp 11-14.

Killarney, County Kerry

Conlan, P., 'The Franciscan Friary: Killarney 1860-1902' in *Kerry Archaeological and Historical Society Journal*, x (1977), pp 77-110.

Kilrush, County Clare

Ireland, A., 'Kilrush documents' in *North Munster Antiquarian Journal*, xxiii (1981), pp 96-8.

Kinsale, County Cork

Kerrigan, P. M., 'The fortifications of Kinsale, Co. Cork' in *An Cosantoir*, xxxii (1972), pp 239-45.

MacCarthy, C.J.F., 'The American prisoners at Kinsale' in *Journal of the Cork Historical and Archaeological Society*, xciv, 253 (1989), pp 46-51.

Silke, J. J., *Kinsale: the Spanish intervention in Ireland at the end of the Elizabethan Wars* (Liverpool, 1970).

Leixlip, County Kildare

McAuliffe, E.J. and O'Kelly-Lynch, R.J., 'Monumental inscriptions from Leixlip, county Kildare' in *Irish Genealogist*, iv (1969), pp 110-16.

St. Mary's G.A.A. Club, *St. Mary's G.A A. Club, Leixlip: a history* (Leixlip, 1985).

Letterkenny, County Donegal

Bewglass, J.H., 'Letterkenny pastor and parliamentarian: Rev. John Kinnear (1823-1909)' in *Donegal Annual*, x (1972), pp 183-6.

Harrison, G., *Saint Eunan's Cathedral, Letterkenny, county Donegal* (Dublin, 1988).

Johnston, D.C., 'John Storey of Letterkenny (1817-1916' in *Irish Baptist Historical Society Journal*, xx (1987-88), pp 20-25.

Lifford, County Donegal

Gallagher, M. and Barrett, H., 'The Jail in Lifford Diamond' in *Donegal Annual*, 44, pp 88-91.

Limavady, County Londonderry

Black, J.S.P., *Speaking yet: Limavady Presbyterians and Balteragh* (Limavady, 1986).

Limerick, County Limerick

Murphy, C.M., *Limerick City: an architectural guide* (Shannon, 1986).

Bennett, D., 'The silvermakers of Limerick' in *Irish Ancestor*, x, 2 (1978), pp 99-107.

Bradshaw, B., 'Fr.Wolfe's description of Limerick City, 1574' in *North Munster Antiquarian Society Journal*, xvii (1975), pp 47-54.

Cahill, L., *Forgotten revolution: the Limerick Soviet 1919* (Dublin, 1990).

Coonerty, P., 'The Presentation Order and the National School system in Limerick, 1837-1870' in *North Munster Antiquarian Society Journal*, xxx (1988), pp 29-34.

Devane, J., The historical geography of Limerick City, unpublished B.A. dissertation, University College Dublin (1970).

Devereux, E., 'Negotiating community: the case of a Limerick community development group' in Curtin, C., Donnan, H. and Wilson, T. A. (eds), *Irish urban cultures* (Belfast, 1993), pp 63-78.

Egan, B., *Franciscan Limerick* (Limerick, 1971).

Fleming, J., *St. John's Cathedral*, Limerick (Dublin, 1987).

Hill, J., *The building of Limerick* (Cork, 1991).

Kearney, P., 'Toward a University for Limerick, 1934-1972' in *Old Limerick Journal*, 27 (1990), pp 45-56.

Kemmy, J., 'The Limerick Soviet' in *Saothar*, ii (1976), pp 45-52.

Murphy, C., 'Building and related activities in Limerick 1859-99' in *North Munster Antiquarian Society Journal*, xix (1977), pp 51-63.

Murray, K.A., 'Richard Osborne at Limerick' in *Journal of the Irish Railway Record Society*, xiii, 77 (1978), pp 294-300.

O'Flaherty, E., 'Urban politics and municipal reform in Limerick 1723-62' in *Eighteenth Century Ireland*, vi (1991), pp 105-20.

Quane, M., 'Dr Jeremy Hall endowed schools, Limerick' in *North Munster Antiquarian Society Journal*, xi (1968), pp 47-56.

Lisburn, County Antrim

Bass, H.G., *Boyd's of Castle Buildings, Lisburn. A short history of an old family firm* (Lisburn, 1977).

Bayly, H., *A topographical and historical account of Lisburn* (Belfast, 1834).

Bell, S., *Hart of Lisburn, Northern Ireland: the story of Sir Robert Hart* (Lisburn, 1985).

Best, E.J., 'Health and wealth in the Borough of Lisburn' in *Lisburn Historical Society Journal* (1979), pp 34-49.

Clarkson, L.A. and Collins, B., 'Proto-industrialisation in a northern Irish Town: Lisburn 1820-21' in *Proceedings of Economic History Conference*, report 8, Budapest (1982), pp 1-20.

Gillespie, R., 'George Rawdon's Lisburn' in *Lisburn Historical Society Journal*, viii (1991), pp 32-6.

Goodbody, M., 'A Quaker wedding at Lisburn, county Down (sic), in 1867' in *Irish Ancestor*, xiii, 2 (1981), pp 90-2.

Heslip, R., 'Lisburn seventeenth century tokens' in *Lisburn Historical Society Journal*, vi (1986), pp 7-11.

Kineally, C., 'The Lisburn workhouse during the famine' in *Lisburn Historical Society Journal*, viii (1991), pp 26-31.

Lalor, P., 'The Huguenots in Lisburn: an extract from Blaris parish register' in *Ulster Genealogical and Historical Guild Newsletter*, i, 10 (1984), p. 334.

Mackey, B., 'The Market House and Assembly Rooms, Lisburn' in *Lisburn Historical Society Journal*, vi (1986), pp 44-57.

Morgan, V., 'A case study of population change over two centuries: Blaris, Lisburn 1661-1848' in *Irish Economic and Social History*, iii (1976), pp 5-16.

Lismore, County Waterford

Clare, W., 'Lismore cathedral registers, 1838-1869' in *Irish Genealogist*, vi, 2 (1981), pp 247-51.

Longford, County Longford

Hyde, J., 'Entries from the family bible of James Hyde of the town of Longford' in *Irish Ancestor*, ii (1970), pp 23-4.

Lurgan, County Armagh

Blaney, R., 'Blaney of Lurgan, county Armagh' in *Irish Ancestor*, iii (1971), pp 33-9.

Follis, B.A., 'Lurgan free school register, 1786' in *Ulster Genealogical and Historical Guild Newsletter*, i, 10 (1984), pp 335-342.

Gillespie, R., *Wild as colts untamed: Methodism and society in Lurgan 1750-1950* (Lurgan, 1977).

Gillespie, R., *Settlement and survival on an Ulster estate: the Brownlow leasebook 1667-1711* (Belfast, 1988).

McCorry, F.X., 'An historical introduction to the town of Lurgan' in *Seanchas Dhroim Mor* (1990), pp 33-43.

McCorry, F. X., The history of Lurgan, 1610-1963, unpublished Ph.D. thesis, Queen's University, Belfast (1986).

McCorry, F.X., *Lurgan: An Irish provincial town, 1610-1970* (Lurgan, 1993).

Tallon, A., *Memories of old Lurgan* (Lurgan, 1987).

Wilson, I., *John Kelly Ltd, an history* (Lurgan n.d).

Wilson, I., 'Nineteenth century schools in Lurgan, Review' in *Journal of the Craigavon Historical Society*, iv, 3 (1981-2), pp 6-11.

Macroom, County Cork

Cooney, J., *Macroom, people and places: a brief historical sketch* (Macroom, 1977).

Magherafelt, County Londonderry

Larkin, P., 'United Irishmen in Magherafelt' in *South Derry Historical Society Journal*, i, 3 (1982-3), pp 218-20.

Macafee, W. and Morgan, V., 'Mortality in Magherafelt, county Derry, in the early eighteenth century reappraised' in *Irish Historical Studies*, xxiii, 89 (1982), pp 50-60.

Morgan, V., 'Mortality in Magherafelt, Co. Derry, in the early eighteenth century' in *Irish Historical Studies*, xix, 74 (1974), 123-35.

Ó Doibhlin, D. (ed.), *Church of Our Lady of the Assumption, Magherafelt 1882-1982* (Magherafelt, 1982).

Ó Doibhlin, D., 'Magherafelt householders 1766' in *South Derry Historical Society* Journal, ii, 1 (1981-2), pp 130-45.

Mallow, County Cork

Bolster, H.L.F., 'Mallow Methodism' in *Mallow Field Club Journal*, 10 (1992), pp 96-110.

Bolster, E., *A history of Mallow*, Cork (1971).

Cadogan, T., 'Parliamentary politics in Mallow, 1870-74, part 1' in *Mallow Field Club Journal*, 11 (1993), pp 5-21.

Crowley, S., 'The manor of Mallow' in *Mallow Field Club Journal*, 10 (1992), pp 5-16.

Forde, R., 'Aspects of education in Mallow in the nineteenth century' in *Mallow Field Club Journal*, 1 (1983), pp 131-52.

Forde, R., 'Mallow Schools 1824' in *Mallow Field Club Journal*, 7 (1989), pp 115-18.

Leahy, M., 'The Convent National School in Mallow' in *Mallow Field Club Journal*, 8 (1990), pp 111-31.

Lindsay, D., 'A list of the Protestants and Popish inhabitants residing in the town and Liberties of Mallow for 1766' in *Mallow Field Club Journal*, 11 (1993), pp 158-61.

Macra na Feirme, 'History of the Mallow Workhouse' in *Mallow Field Club Journal*, 3 (1985), pp 12-26.

O'Sullivan, M., 'Mallow railway' in *Mallow Field Club Journal*, 1 (1983), pp 63-7.

O'Sullivan, M., 'The river crossing at Mallow' in *Mallow Field Club Journal*, 3 (1985), pp 5-11.

Power, D., 'The Blackwater navigation at Mallow' in *Mallow Field Club Journal*, 4 (1986), pp 17-24.

Roche, C., 'Mallow and the Robinson settlements' in *Mallow Field Club Journal*, 8 (1990), pp 52-9.

Sheehan, D., 'Mallow Church of Ireland parish records' in *Mallow Field Club Journal*, 8 (1989), pp 5-18.

Maynooth, County Kildare

Cullen, M., *Maynooth: A short historical guide* (Maynooth, 1979).

Hamell, P.J., *Maynooth students and ordinations 1895-1984* (Maynooth, 1984).

Newman, J., *Maynooth and Georgian Ireland* (Galway,1979).

O'Connor, R.A., 'The growing demand for Catholic education in the eighteenth century leading to the establishment of St. Patrick's, Maynooth in 1795' in *Irish Education Studies*, i (1981), pp 296-309.

Moate, County Westmeath
Cox, L., *Moate, County Westmeath: A history of the town and district* (Athlone, 1981).

Monaghan, County Monaghan
Dunne, G., *Town of Monaghan Co-op: the first eighty years* (Monaghan, 1983).

Moneymore, County Londonderry
Moneymore and Draperstown: The architecture and planning of the estates of the Draper's Company in Ulster (Belfast, 1979).

Robinson, P.S., 'English houses built at Moneymore, county Londonderry, c.1615' in *Post-Medieval Archaeology*, 17 (1983), pp 47-63.

Mountmellick, County Laois
Houston-Almquist, J., *Mountmellick-work – Irish white embroidery* (Mountrath, 1985).

Mullingar, County Westmeath
Andrews, J.H. and Davies, K M., *Mullingar: Irish Historical Towns Atlas*, no. 5 (Dublin, 1992).

Keaney, M. and O'Brien, G., *Bridging the centuries* (Mullingar, 1991).

Farrell, P., *The book of Mullingar* (Mullingar, 1987).

Naas, County Kildare
Costello, C., 'Two Priests of Naas' in *County Kildare Archaeological Society* Journal xvii (1991), pp 34-48.

Fitzgerald, D., 'A 'Sovereign' Row in Naas' in *County Kildare Archaeological Society Journal*, xv (1971), pp 22-8.

Local History Group, *Nás na Ríogh: from Poorhouse Road to the fairy flax: an illustrated history of Naas* (Naas, 1990).

Navan, County Meath
Connell, P., *Changing forces shaping a nineteenth-century Irish Town: a case study of Navan* (Maynooth, 1978).

Connell, P., 'The changing face of Navan in the nineteenth century' in *Ríocht na Midhe*, vi, 3 (1977), pp 38-59.

French, N. E., *Navan by the Boyne: a history of Navan and surrounding areas* (Navan, n.d.)

Nenagh, County Tipperary
Collins, P., Nenagh: the evolution of an Irish country town, unpublished B.A. dissertation, University College Dublin (1972).

Grace, D., 'The barricading of Nenagh Chapel in 1849' in *Tipperary Historical Journal*, iii (1990), pp 103-8.

New Ross, County Wexford
Benson, C., 'Wild Oats' in New Ross: theatre in an Irish country town, 1789-95' in *Long Room*, xxii-xxiii (1981), pp 13-8.

Newcastle, County Down
Morton, G., *Victorian and Edwardian Newcastle* (Belfast, 1988).

Newcastlewest, County Limerick
Cussen, R., 'Early schools in Newcastle' in *Annual Observer (Newcastle Historical Society)*, i (1979), pp 3-13.

Dore, M., 'The first fifty years of national schools in the Newcastle area and the Christian Brothers interlude' in *Annual Observer (Newcastlewest Historical Society)*, iii (1981), pp 1-12.

Dore, M., 'The Taking of Newcastlewest' in *Annual Observer (Newcastlewest Historical Society)*, (1987), pp 6-14.

O'Connor, P.J., 'An 18th century plan of Newcastle' in *Annual Observer (Newcastlewest Historical Society)* (1981), pp 20-5.

Newry, County Down
Canavan, T., *Frontier town. An illustrated history of Newry* (Belfast, 1989).

Walsh, L., The growth and decline of Newry up to c. 1920, unpublished B.A. dissertation, University College Dublin (1971).

Newtonards, County Down

Ards Historical Society, *Glimpses of old Newtownards* (Newtownards, 1978).

Robinson, P., 'Urban vernacular housing in Newtonards, county Down' in *Ulster Folk Life*, xvii (1979), pp 20-38.

Portadown, County Armagh

Canning, J., 'Fairs and markets in Portadown in the 1850s, review' in *Journal of the Craigavon Historical Society*, vi, 2 (1991), pp 18-23.

Corbett, J.H., 'Pioneering, penetration and progress': being an account of the Baptist Church at Portadown' in *Irish Baptist Historical Society*, xxiii (1991), pp 13-25.

Portaferry, County Down

Blaney, J., 'Portaferry shipping in two centuries' in *Upper Ards Historical Society Journal*, xi (1987), pp 10-5.

Portarlington, County Laois

Doyle, J., The Huguenot Colony at Portarlington, 1694-1817: its impact on the town, unpublished B.A. dissertation, University College Dublin (1987).

Hylton, R. P., The Huguenot settlement at Portarlington, 1692-1771, unpublished M.A. thesis, University College Dublin (1982).

Powell, J. Stokes, *Portarlington: a planted town* (York, 1990).

Portlaoise, County Laois

Midland Health Board, *Tumbling walls: The evolution of a community institution. St. Fintan's Hospital, Portlaoise, 1883-1983* (Portlaoise, 1983).

Portrush, County Antrim

Moulden, J., *A history of Methodism in Portrush – A short history in celebration of the centenary of the dedication of the Clarke Memorial Church, 29th September 1887* (Portrush, 1987).

Portstewart, County Londonderry

Currie, J., *The Portstewart tramway* (Lingfield, 1968).

Rathfriland, County Down

Rankin, J.A., *Historic buildings, groups of buildings, areas of architectural importance in Rathfriland and Hilltown* (Belfast, 1979).

Roscommon, County Roscommon

Cronin, T., 'The town of Roscommon' in *Roscommon Historical and Archaeological Society*, ii (1988), pp 5-9.

Roscrea, County Tipperary

Deegan, T., 'Roscrea poor law union: its administration 150 years ago' in *Tipperary Historical Journal* (1992), pp 96-104.

Rosslare, County Wexford

Anderson, C.B., Historical development of Rosslare Harbour, unpublished B.A. dissertation, University College Dublin (1974).

Kehoe, G., 'Rosslare fort and its people, part 1' in *Old Wexford Society Journal*, iv (1972), pp 43-52.

Maddock, J., *Rosslare harbour: past and present* (Rosslare, n.d.).

Roberts, O.T.P., 'The cots of Rosslare Harbour and of Wexford' in *Mariner's Mirror*, lxxi, 1 (1985), pp 13-34.

Swan, J.B., 'The Manor of Rosslare' in *Old Wexford Society Journal*, iv (1972), pp 80-7.

Turner, J., 'Rosslare: its fort and lifeboat' in *The Past*, 9 (1972), pp 52-6.

Rush, County Dublin

Moloney, F., The evolution of Rush, county Dublin, unpublished B.A. dissertation, University College Dublin (1974).

Skerries, County Dublin
Campion, M., 'Skerries' in *Dublin Historical Record*, xxiii (1969), pp 36-43.

Sligo, County Sligo
McTernan, J. C., *Memory harbour, the port of Sligo; an outline of its growth and decline as an emigration port* (Sligo, 1992).
O'Dowd, M., *Power, politics and land: early modern Sligo, 1568-1688* (Belfast, 1991).

Strabane, County Tyrone
Malcolmson, E.W., 'The politics of 'Natural Right': the Abercor family and Strabane borough, 1692-1800' in Hayes-McCoy, G.A. (ed.), *Historical Studies* x (Galway, 1976), pp 75-86.

Templemore, County Tipperary
Walsh, P., 'The Barracks of Ireland (20): Templemore Military Barracks' in *An Cosantoir*, xxxii (1972), pp 220-4.

Thomastown, County Kilkenny
Gulliver, P.H. and Silverman, M., *In the valley of the Nore: a social history of Thomastown, County Kilkenny, 1840-1893* (Dublin, 1986).
Gulliver, P.H. and Silverman, M., 'Social life and local meaning: 'Thomastown', county Kilkenny' in Nolan, W. and Whelan, K. (eds), *Kilkenny history and society: interdisciplinary essays on the history of an Irish county* (Dublin, 1990), pp 591-616.
Gulliver, P.H. and Silverman, M., 'Hucksters and petty retailers in Thomastown, 1880-1945' in *Old Kilkenny Review*, iv (1993), pp 1094-1100.
Silverman, M., 'The non-agricultural working class in nineteenth century Thomastown' in the *Shadow of the Steeple: Duchas, Tullaherin Heritage Society*, 2 (1990), pp 86-104.

Thurles, County Tipperary
Condon, J., 'Mid-nineteenth century Thurles' in Corbett, W. and Nolan, W. (eds), *Thurles: the cathedral town* (Dublin, 1989), pp 81-92.
Conlan, P., 'The Franciscan House in Thurles' in Corbett, W. and Nolan, W. (eds), *Thurles: the cathedral town* (Dublin, 1989), pp 177-86.
Corbett, W. and Nolan, W. (eds), *Thurles: the cathedral town* (Dublin, 1989).
Lanigan, A., 'The workhouse child in Thurles, 1840-1880' in Corbett, W. and Nolan, W. (eds), *Thurles: the cathedral town* (Dublin, 1989), pp 55-80.
Liguori, Sr., 'Presentation Convent Thurles, 1817-1917' in Corbett, W. and Nolan, W.(eds), *Thurles: the cathedral town* (Dublin, 1989), pp 213-22.
Lillis, M., 'The Ursulines in Thurles' in Corbett, W. and Nolan, W. (eds), *Thurles: the cathedral town* (Dublin, 1989).
Nolan, W., 'Thurles from a distance' in Corbett, W. and Nolan, W. (eds), *Thurles: the cathedral town*, Dublin (1989), pp 1-30.
Ó Drisceoil, P., 'Placenames as politics: Thurles in 1920' in *Tipperary Historical Journal* (1993), pp 59-61.
Ó Dugáin, S.P., 'The Christian Brothers in Thurles' in Corbett, W. and Nolan, W. (eds), *Thurles: the cathedral town* (Dublin, 1989), pp 223-36.
O'Dwyer, C., 'St Patrick's College, 1837-1988' in Corbett, W. and Nolan, W. (eds), *Thurles: the cathedral town* (Dublin, 1989) pp 237-252.
O'Shea, J., 'Thurles savings bank, 1829-71' in Corbett, W. and Nolan, W. (eds), *Thurles: the cathedral town* (Dublin, 1989), pp 93-116.
O'Toole, J., 'The Cathedral of the Assumption' in Corbett, W. and Nolan, W. (eds), *Thurles: the cathedral town* (Dublin, 1989), pp 117-30.
Tierney, M., 'Cashel Diocesan Archives' in Corbett, W. and Nolan, W. (eds), *Thurles: the cathedral town* (Dublin, 1989), pp 267-76.

Tralee, County Kerry
Connaughton, I., Tralee – an urban study, unpublished B.A. dissertation, University College Dublin (1969).
Crean, K., Town plan analysis of Tralee from the Medieval period to 1900, unpublished B.A. dissertation, University College Dublin (1988).

Donoghue, D., The impact of residential expansion on Primary Education: a case study of Tralee, county Kerry, 1936-1986, unpublished B.A. dissertation, University College Dublin (1987).

Feingold, W.L., 'Land League power the Tralee poor-law election of 1881' in Clark, S. and Donnelly, J.S. (eds), *Irish peasants: violence and political unrest, 1780-1914* (Manchester and Winsconsin, 1983), pp 285-310.

Taylor, A., 'Churches and the growth of Tramore in the 19th century' in *Decies*, xxii (1983), pp 33-8.

Trim, County Meath

Walsh, L., 'The Trim Model School' in *Irish Educational Studies*, v, 2 (1985), pp 261-82.

Tullamore, County Offaly

Byrne, M., *A walk through Tullamore* (Tullamore, 1980).

Byrne, M., *Tullamore Catholic parish: an historical survey* (Tullamore, 1987).

Byrne, M., The development of Tullamore, 1700-1921, unpublished M.Litt. thesis, Trinity College Dublin (1980).

Garner, W., *Tullamore: architectural heritage* (Dublin, 1980).

Gray, D.S., 'A gross violation of the public peace': The Tullamore incident 1806' in *Irish Sword*, xii, 49 (1976), pp 298-301.

Tullow, County Carlow

Dickson, D., 'A Census of the parish of Tullow in 1795' in *Carloviana*, ii (1972), pp 25-7.

Waterford, County Waterford

Bennis, E., 'Waterford's Quaker community' in *Decies*, iv (1977), pp 3-6; v (1977), pp 20-1.

Brophy, A. J., 'Waterford Harbour Commissioners' records' in *Decies*, xxviii (1985), pp 25-33.

Burtchaell, J., Society, settlement and culture in nineteenth century Waterford, unpublished B.A. thesis, University College Dublin (1982).

Carroll, J.S., 'Waterford ships and shipping in the nineteenth century' in *Decies*, v (1977), pp 11-6.

Carroll, J.S., 'Waterford of the Ships', 1786' in *Decies*, x (1979), p. 20.

Carroll, J.S., 'Aspects of eighteenth and nineteenth century Waterford city from twenty-three corporation lease maps' in *Decies*, xxvii (1984), pp 13-21.

Carroll, J.S., 'A century of change 1764-1871' in *Decies*, xxxi (1986), pp 17-25.

Cassidy, M.N., 'Veterinary inspection at Waterford port, 1876-1900' in *Decies*, xiii (1980), pp 58-61.

Cowman, D., 'Thomas 'Bullocks' Wyse: a Catholic industrialist during the Penal Laws, part 1' in *Decies*, xxiv (1983), pp 9-14.

Cowman, D., 'Thomas 'Bullocks' Wyse: a Catholic industrialist during the Penal Laws, part 2' in *Decies*, xxv (1984), pp 40-44.

Cowman, D., 'Trade and society in Waterford City, 1800-1840' in Nolan, W., Power, T. P. and Cowman, D. (eds), *Waterford history and society: interdisciplinary essays on the history of an Irish county* (Dublin, 1992), pp 427-58.

Dooley, T. P., 'Politics, bonds and marketing: army recruitment in Waterford city, 914-15' in *Irish Sword*, xviii, 72 (1991), pp 205-19.

Fitzpatrick, R.J., 'The Waterford Church Book, 1805-1914' in *Irish Baptist Historical Society Journal*, v (1972-3), pp 5-17.

Flynn, M., The port and city of Waterford, unpublished B.A. dissertation, University College Dublin (1970).

Friendly Press, *Quakers in Eustace Street* (Waterford, 1985).

Garrett, M., Waterford and the municipalities in late seventeenth century Ireland, unpublished M.A. thesis, University College Dublin (1972).

Hearne, J. M., 'Industry in Waterford City, 1932-1962' in Nolan, W., Power, T. P.and Cowman, D. (eds), *Waterford history and society: interdisciplinary essays on the history of an Irish county* (Dublin, 1992), pp 685-706.

Holt, E., 'A 19th century French traveller's visit to Waterford, pt. 1' in *Decies*, xviii (1981), pp 1-16,

Holt, E.,'A 19th century French traveller's visit to Waterford (ctd)' in *Decies*, xix (1982), pp 61-6.

Ireland, J. de Courcy, 'Sir Thomas Stucley and the maritime importance of Waterford' in *Decies*, xxx (1985), pp 12-7.

Kelly, K., 'Extracts from the Census of the City of Waterford, 1821' in *Irish Genealogist*, iv (1969), pp 122-30.

Kingdon, D.P., 'Charles Hardcastle of Waterford' in *Irish Baptist Historical Society Journal*, ii (1969-70), pp 5-16.

Lahert, R., 'Some charitable institutions of Old Waterford' in *Decies*, xxviii (1985), pp 43-53; xxix (1985), pp 24-31.

Lahert, R., 'A glossary of Old Waterford street names' in *Decies*, xxxiii (1986), pp 21-35.

Mackey, P., *Talk of the town* (Waterford, 1985).

Mannion, J., 'The Waterford merchants and the Irish-Newfoundland provision trade, 1770-1820' in Cullen, L.M. and Butel, P. (eds), *Negoce et industrie en France et en Irlande aux xviii et xix siecles: actes de Colloque Franco-lrlandais d'Histoire, Bordeaux, Mai 1978* (Paris, 1980), pp 27-44.

Mannion, J., 'The Waterford merchants and the Irish-Newfoundland provision trade, 1770-1820' in Akenson, D.H. (ed.), *Canadian papers in rural history*, iii (Ontario, 1982), pp 178-203.

Mannion, J., 'The maritime trade of Waterford in the eighteenth century' in Smyth, W.J. and Whelan, K. (eds), *Common Ground: Essays on The Historical Geography of Ireland* (Cork, 1988), pp 208-233.

Mannion, J., 'Vessels, masters and seafaring: patterns in Waterford voyages, 1766-1771' in Nolan, W., Power, T. P.and Cowman, D. (eds), *Waterford history and society: interdisciplinary essays on the history of an Irish county* (Dublin, 1992), pp 373-402.

Milne, K., 'The Corporation of Waterford in the eighteenth century' in Nolan, W., Power, T. P.and Cowman, D. (eds), *Waterford history and society: interdisciplinary essays on the history of an Irish county* (Dublin, 1992), pp 331-350.

Morris, H.F., 'Extracts from Ramsey's *Waterford Chronicle* 1777' in *Irish Genealogist*, v (1977), pp 471-90.

Morris, H.F., 'Extracts from Ramsey's *Waterford Chronicle* 1777' in *Irish Genealogist*, v, (1978), pp 625-42.

Morris, H.F., '*The Waterford Herald*, 1792: births, marriages and deaths' in *Irish Genealogist*, vi, 2 (1981), pp 154-88.

Morris, H.F., 'The registers of Waterford Cathedral (C. of I.), 1655/6-1706/7' in *Irish Genealogist*, vi, 3 (1982), pp 276-84.

Mulholland, J., 'Tokens issued by Waterford tradesmen' in *Decies*, x (1979), pp 13-6.

Murphy, F.P., 'The Clyde Shipping Company' in *Decies*, xxxviii (1988), pp 28-31.

Nolan, W., Power, T. P.and Cowman, D. (eds), *Waterford history and society: interdisciplinary essays on the history of an Irish county* (Dublin, 1992).

O'Connor, E., 'The Labour movement in Waterford city, 1913-1923' in *Decies*, xviii (1981), pp 17-32.

O'Connor, E., 'Trades councils in Waterford city' in Nolan, W., Power, T. P.and Cowman, D. (eds), *Waterford history and society: interdisciplinary essays on the history of an Irish county* (Dublin, 1992), pp 641-52.

O'Donovan, M., 'The Watership Steamship Company in the 1880s' in *Decies*, xxxvii (1988), pp 30-3.

O'Sullivan, C.R., Waterford: A study of a growth centre, unpublished B.A. dissertation, University College Dublin (1974).

Power, T., 'Ships provisioned in Waterford for Newfoundland, 1765' in *Decies*, xvi (1981), pp 69-71.

Power, C. and O'Sullivan, V.R., 'Rickets in nineteenth century Waterford' in *Archaeology Ireland*, vi, 1 (1992), p. 27.

Power, T.P., 'Electoral politics in Waterford City, 1692-1832' in Nolan, W., Power, T. P.and Cowman, D. (eds), *Waterford history and society: interdisciplinary essays on the history of an Irish county* (Dublin, 1992), pp 227-64.

Rae, E. C., 'The Rice monument in Waterford Cathedral' in *Proceedings of the Royal Irish Academy*, lxix, Sec.C, 1 (1970), pp 1-31.

Solar, P., 'The agricultural trade of the port of Waterford, 1809-1909' in Nolan, W., Power, T. P. and Cowman, D. (eds), *Waterford history and society: interdisciplinary essays on the history of an Irish county* (Dublin, 1992), pp 495-518.

Thornton, A., 'An account of Waterford city's entry into the railway era' in *Decies*, xvi (1981), pp 47-51.

Walton, J.C., 'The freemen of Waterford 1542-1650' in *Irish Genealogist*, v, 5 (1978), pp 560-72.

Walton, J.C., 'The household effects of a Waterford merchant family in 1640' in *Cork Historical and Archaeological Society* Journal, lxxxiii, 238 (1978), pp 99-105.

Walton, J.C., 'The earliest Presbyterian register of Waterford, 1761-1813' in *Irish Ancestor*, xiii, 2 (1981), pp 94-104.

Walton, J.C., 'Wills relating to Waterford' in *Decies*, xxiii (1983), pp 50-4; xxiii (1983), pp 17-22.

Walton, J.C., 'The merchant communities of Waterford in the 16th and 17th centuries' in Butel, P. and Cullen, L.M., *Cities and merchants: French and Irish perspectives on urban development, 1500-1900* (Dublin, 1986), pp 183-94.

Walton, J. C., 'Two descriptions of Waterford in the 1680s' in *Decies*, xxxv (1987), pp 27-32; xxxvi (1987), pp 34-8.

Walton, J.C., 'Waterford city polling lists 1839' in *Irish Genealogist*, viii, 21 (1991), pp 275-89.

Walton J.C., 'Church, crown and corporation in Waterford city 1520-1620' in Nolan W., Power T. P. and Cowman, D. (eds), *Waterford history and society: interdisciplinary essays on the history of an Irish ounty* (Dublin, 1992) pp 177-98.

Westport, County Mayo

Clarke J.D., 'Life in Westport and Castlebar c. 1896' in *Cathair na Mart*, viii, 1 (1988) pp 80-5.

Ireland, A., 'Westport Customs and Excise 1837-1881' in *Galway Archaeological and Historical Society Journal*, xliii (1991), pp 175-6.

Jeffers, B., 'Westport: an early Irish example of town planning, 1734-1950' in *Cathair na Mart* viii, 1 (1988), pp 40-6.

Jeffers, B., 'Westport – an early Irish example of town planning' in *Cathair na Mart*, x, 1 (1989), pp 48-59.

Mulloy, J., 'Some aspects of trade in Clew Bay: part I' in *Cathair na Mart*. xi, 1 (1991), pp 57-64.

Mulloy, J., 'Some aspects of trade in Clew Bay: part II' in *Cathair na Mart*, xii, 1 (1992), pp 55-60.

Ó Flanagain, P., 'George Clendinning born in Westport 1770, died in Westport 1843' in *Cathair na Mart*, vii, 1 (1985), pp 31-7.

Ó Flanagain, P., 'An outline history of the town of Westport: part II, Westport – a new town, 1780-1825' in *Cathair na Mart*, ii, 1 (1982), pp 35-52.

Wexford, County Wexford

Bolger, D. (ed.), *Wexford through its writers* (Dublin, 1992).

Byrne, B., A social topography of 19th century Wicklow Town, unpublished B.A. dissertation, University College Dublin (1988).

Cleary, J., 'Wicklow Harbour' in *Journal of the Wicklow Historical Society*, i, 3 (1990), pp 57-64.

Cullen, B.L., Historical geography of Wicklow town, unpublished B.A. dissertation, University College Dublin (1965).

De Courcy Ireland, J., 'Some notes on Wexford maritime affairs in the middle ages and Renaissance' in *Old Wexford Society Journal*, iii (1970), pp 51-5.

Furlong, N., 'Life in Wexford Port 1600-1800' in Whelan, K. and Nolan, W. (eds), *Wexford history and society: interdisciplinary essays on the history of an Irish county* (Dublin, 1987), pp 150-72.

Furlong, N., *Loch Garman and Wexford* (Wexford, 1984).

Furlong, N., 'The history of land reclamation in Wexford' in *Old Wexford Society Journal*, ii (1969), pp 53-76.

Glynn, J., 'The Catholic Church in Wexford town 1800-1858' in *The Past*, xv (1984), pp 5-54.

Goodall, D., 'John Green and the *Wexford Independent*' in *The Past*, xviii (1992), pp 3-30.

Goodall, D., 'The freemen of Wexford 1776' in *Irish Genealogist*, v (1977), pp 448-63.

Goodbody, O., 'Quakers in Wexford' in *Old Wexford Society Journal*, iii (1970), pp 36-41.

Grogan, 'Wexford Corporation's eighteenth century leases' in *Journal of the County Wexford Historical Society*, xiii (1991), pp 142-48.

Hadden, G., 'The origin and development of Wexford town, Part 4' in *Old Wexford Society Journal*, iii (1970), pp 5-10.

Hannigan, K., 'The national schools in Wicklow town 1832-1919' in *Wicklow Historical Society Journal*, i, 2 (1989), pp 34-49.

Kavanagh, J., 'Early Methodists in Wicklow town and county' in *Wicklow Historical Society Journal*, i, 2 (1989), pp 3-11.

Kavanagh, J., 'The influenza epidemic of 1919 in Wicklow town and district' in *Journal of the Wicklow Historical Society*, i, 3 (1990), pp 36-44.

Kerrigan, P M.A., 'The naval attack on Wexford in June 1798' in *Irish Sword*, xv (1983), pp 198-9.

Moynihan, M., 'The administration of justice in Wexford' in *Old Wexford Society Journal*, xx (1975), pp 5-21.

Murphy, H., 'The Drinagh cement works' in *Old Wexford Society Journal*, vi (1976), pp 38-44.

O'Connor, L., A historical geography of Wexford Harbour and its reclamation programmes, unpublished B.A. dissertation, University College Dublin (1979).

Roche, R., 'The Roches of Wexford' in *Old Wexford Society Journal*, ii (1969), pp 39-48.

Sweetman, W., 'A Wexford Ship-Builder' in *Old Wexford Society Journal*, vii (1978-9), pp 21-30.

Youghal, County Cork

Harbison, P., 'P. Burk(e)'s painting of Youghal: the earliest known signed townscape by an Irish artist' in *Cork Historical and Archaeological Society Journal*, lxxviii (1971) pp 66-79.

McCarthy, C., 'A Youghal Library of 1707' in *Cork Historical and Archaeological Society Journal*, lxxiv (1969), pp 84-7.